A PSYCHOLOGY OF
DIFFERENCE

Otto Rank

A PSYCHOLOGY OF DIFFERENCE

THE AMERICAN LECTURES

*Selected, Edited, and Introduced
by Robert Kramer*

**with a foreword by
Rollo May**

PRINCETON UNIVERSITY PRESS

PRINCETON, NEW JERSEY

LIBRARY OF CONGRESS CATALOGING-IN-PUBLICATION DATA

RANK, OTTO, 1884–1939.

A PSYCHOLOGY OF DIFFERENCE : THE AMERICAN LECTURES / OTTO RANK ;
SELECTED, EDITED, AND INTRODUCED BY ROBERT KRAMER ; WITH A FOREWORD
BY ROLLO MAY.

P. CM.

INCLUDES BIBLIOGRAPHICAL REFERENCES AND INDEX.

ISBN 0-691-04470-8 (ALK. PAPER)

1. RANK, OTTO, 1884–1939. 2. FREUD, SIGMUND, 1856–1939.
3. PSYCHOANALYSIS—HISTORY. I. KRAMER, ROBERT, 1953–

II. TITLE.

BF109.R345A25 1996

150.19′5—DC20   95-43758

THIS BOOK HAS BEEN COMPOSED IN SABON

PRINCETON UNIVERSITY PRESS BOOKS ARE PRINTED
ON ACID-FREE PAPER, AND MEET THE GUIDELINES FOR
PERMANENCE AND DURABILITY OF THE COMMITTEE ON
PRODUCTION GUIDELINES FOR BOOK LONGEVITY
OF THE COUNCIL ON LIBRARY RESOURCES

PRINTED IN THE UNITED STATES OF AMERICA BY
PRINCETON ACADEMIC PRESS

1 3 5 7 9 10 8 6 4 2

In memoriam

Rollo May

(1909–1994)

CONTENTS

TWENTY-TWO

FOREWORD

I HAVE LONG CONSIDERED Otto Rank to be *the* great unacknowledged genius in Freud's circle.

It has been over half a century since we have seen a new book appear by Rank, whose *Beyond Psychology* (1941) lay incomplete at the time of his death in 1939. This collection of Rank's long-forgotten American lectures from 1924 to 1938, edited by Robert Kramer, shows that Rank was astoundingly prescient. Decades ahead of his time, Rank speaks of neurosis as a failure in creativity and the suffering human being as an *artiste manqué*, a failed artist. In these lectures Rank explores in simple English the rich interplay between I and Thou, separation and union, the individual and the collective, will and love, creativity and guilt.

One of Rank's most important learnings, as Robert Kramer notes in his introductory essay, is that "will and guilt are the two complementary sides of *one* and the *same* phenomenon." We have only to look at classical literature, mythology, and primitive religions to discover how universal is this guilt feeling. The ancient Greeks were certainly not a morbid people—indeed, it is often said that they did not know the meaning of our word *sin*—yet the realization of guilt runs centrally through their dramas and gives them profound meaning. The implication is that guilt is inherent in the human situation: men and women are stationed below the gods, said the Greek dramatists, but they are always tending to raise themselves to the divine position.

What is the source of guilt feeling, of the feeling, according to Kafka, that we are *in debt* to something or someone outside ourselves for our existence? Indebtedness seems inseparably connected with freedom, autonomy, and moral responsibility. "Free will," said Rank, whose understanding of creativity and its discontents is unmatched by anyone since Kierkegaard, "belongs to the idea of guilt or sin as inevitably as day to night."

Since human beings possess freedom, they must always be glimpsing new possibilities; and every new possibility brings with it not only a challenge but an element of guilt feeling. In fact, challenge—the movement toward "the new"—and guilt feeling are two aspects of the same thing. Guilt feeling inheres in every state of tension in the person. "We are not our own," said Rank, "no matter whether we perceive the guilt religiously toward God, socially toward the father, or biologically toward the mother."

I believe that guilt feeling, in the deepest sense, is the perception of a "gap," a "hole," or a "void" in the core of the person; in Nietzsche's terms, it is as though human being stands on a mountain over a deep cleft with one foot on this side and one on the other.

Robert Kramer has done us an inestimable service by rediscovering these dazzling American lectures of Otto Rank.

ROLLO MAY
Tiburon, California

CHRONOLOGY OF RANK'S LIFE
(1884–1939)

1884   Born in Vienna, April 22

1905   Sends Freud a manuscript entitled *The Artist*, using the word *artist* in as comprehensive sense as Freud had used the word *sexuality*

1906   Accepts Freud's offer to be secretary of the fledgling Vienna Psychoanalytical Society, the first paid position in the movement; is virtually adopted by Freud as a "foster son"; and is asked by Freud to devote himself to the nonmedical side of psychoanalysis

1907   Publishes *The Artist*, the first psychoanalytic work not written by Freud

1909   Publishes *The Myth of the Birth of the Hero*, with a section on the "family romance" contributed by Freud

1911   Helps Freud edit and revise the third edition of *The Interpretation of Dreams*

1911   Publishes *The Lohengrin Saga*, for which he later receives a Ph.D. from the University of Vienna, the first dissertation ever written on a psychoanalytic theme

1912   Publishes *The Incest Theme in Literature and Legend: Fundamentals of a Psychology of Literary Creation*, a 685-page study of the Oedipus complex throughout world literature

1912   Becomes the youngest ringholder of the secret Committee—Abraham, Ferenczi, Sachs, Jones (and later, Eitingon)—formed by Freud to defend the cause

1912   Co-founds *Imago* and *Internationale Zeitschrift für ärztliche Psychoanalyse*, the two leading journals of the cause

1913   Publishes, with Sachs, *The Significance of Psychoanalysis for the Mental Sciences*

1914   Contributes two chapters, on literature and myth, to the fourth edition of *The Interpretation of Dreams*, his name now appearing (until 1929) below Freud's on the title page

1914   Publishes *The Double*, a study of the core problems of human existence as expressed in cinema and literature: identity, guilt, narcissism, the fear of death, the soul, and the desire for immortality

1916–18   Serves as editor-in-chief of the *Krakauer Zeitung*, the official army newspaper in Poland

1918   Marries Tola Minzer, 23, in Poland

1919   Returns to Vienna to edit *Imago* and *Internationale Zeitschrift* and is asked by Freud to become director of the *Verlag*, the newly created international psychoanalytic publishing house, and vice-president of the Vienna Psychoanalytical Society

1919   Begins full-time practice as a lay analyst and conducts training analyses for visiting Americans

1919   Helene, his only child, is born

1922–23 Drafts with Ferenczi, now his best friend, *The Development of Psychoanalysis*, which advocates the curative effect of emotional experience [*Erlebnis*] over intellectual understanding [*Einsicht*]

1923 Is informed, immediately after diagnosis, of Freud's life-threatening cancer of the jaw

1924 Publishes, with Ferenzci, *The Development of Psychoanalysis*, criticizing the "fanaticism for interpreting" among analysts: "the actual analytic task," they say, "was neglected"

1924 Publishes *The Trauma of Birth*, claiming that the "ambivalent" pre-Oedipal relationship between mother and child is the heart of transference, thereby relegating fear and love of the Oedipal father to a secondary place

1924 Sails for the United States in April and lectures on his pre-Oedipal theory before the American Psychoanalytic Association and other audiences

1924 From the United States, in an August letter, denies Freud's charge that he has "excluded the father; naturally that is not the case and absolutely cannot be, it would be nonsense. I have only attempted to give him the correct place"

1925 Confesses in January to an Oedipal neurosis, "occasioned by the dangerous illness of the Professor," after a soul-baring *Erlebnis* therapy in December 1924 with Freud, who forgives him

1925 At a seminar for the New York Psychoanalytic Society, insists, "The only real new viewpoint in [my] contribution [is] the concept of the pre-Oedipus level"

1926 Recants his Oedipal neurosis, resigns from his editorial and administrative positions, and moves to Paris in April to start a new practice, severing all ties with medical psychoanalysis and the secret Committee

1926 Delivers a series of lectures before the New York School of Social Work, based on Volume 1 of his forthcoming work, *Genetische Psychologie* (1927), whose opening sentence reads: "This book is a direct continuation . . . of my new vision in psychoanalytic theory and therapy"

1926 In his New York lectures, accuses Freud of repressing the role of the castrating pre-Oedipal mother: "The 'bad mother' he has never seen, but only the later displacement of her to the father, who therefore plays such an omnipotent part in his theory. . . . The 'strict mother' thus forms the real nucleus of the super-ego"

1927 Delivers a series of lectures before the University of Pennsylvania School of Social Work, based on Volume 2 of his forthcoming work, *Genetische Psychologie* (1928)

1927 In a lecture at the University of Pennsylvania, announces that he is no longer "going back" to the pre-Oedipal mother: many neurotics belong to the "creative type" but "have failed in the formation and development of their own personality"; they are, in essence, failed artists

1927 In other University of Pennsylvania lectures, defines love in terms of the I-Thou relationship: "The love of the Thou . . . places a value on one's own I. Love abolishes egoism, it merges the self in the other to find it again enriched in one's own I. . . . One can really only love the one who accepts our own self as it is, indeed will not have it otherwise than it is, and whose self we accept as it is"

In the same lecture, defines guilt as a "special emotion," lying on "the boundary line . . . between the severing and uniting feelings; [therefore,] it is also the most important representative of the relation between inner and outer, I and Thou, the Self and the World"

1929–31 Delivers another series of lectures at the University of Pennsylvania based on two books published in English as *Will Therapy* and *Truth and Reality*, claiming that "the real I, or self with its own power, the will, is left out" of psychoanalysis, but stressing repeatedly that "will and guilt are the two complementary sides of one and the same phenomenon"— which he calls the will-guilt problem

1929–31 Reframing Freud's "economic" metaphor of drive, asserts in *Will Therapy* that the neurotic (or *artiste manqué*) "bribes" life itself—for which we all have to "pay" with death: because of extreme guilt and anxiety, the neurotic hurls a Big No at the consciousness of living, refusing the loan, life, in order to escape payment of the debt, death

1930 Publishes *Seelenglaube und Psychologie* (translated, in 1950, as *Psychology and the Soul*), drawing on Bohr's "theory of complementarity" and Heisenberg's "uncertainty principle" to demonstrate that quantum physics has proved that the human being "simply lies beyond lawfulness, and cannot be fully comprehended or explained by the causality either of natural or social science"—or "the cause" of psychoanalysis

1930 In a Washington lecture, attended by a large international audience, says that while he has stopped calling himself a psychoanalyst, "I am no longer trying to prove that Freud was wrong and I am right. . . . It is not a question of whose interpretation is correct—because there is no such thing as *the* interpretation or only *one* psychological truth"

1930 Removed by the American Psychoanalytic Association from its list of honorary members, immediately after the Washington lecture, on a motion by APA President A. A. Brill, seconded by Vice-President Harry Stack Sullivan: reanalysis of his analysands by Freudians is required for them to retain membership in the APA

1932 Publishes *Art and Artist*, showing that only the "human creative impulse" can constructively harmonize "the fundamental dualism" of life and death, a dualism Rank explores along many lines: for example, the wish for—and fear of—separation, the wish for—and fear of—union, the oscillation between life *Angst* and death *Angst*, independence and dependence, I and Thou, and, most importantly, the "will-guilt problem"

1932 Publishes *Modern Education*, concluding that "psychoanalysis is as conservative as it appeared revolutionary; for its founder is a rebellious son who defends paternal authority, a revolutionary who, from fear of his own rebellious son-ego, took refuge in the security of the father role"

1935 Moves from Paris to New York and continues practicing psychotherapy and lecturing in the United States

1936 Meets Carl Rogers and influences him to abandon Freudian technique for "client-centered" and "relationship" therapy

1937–39   Drafts *Beyond Psychology* (published posthumously in 1941), advocating a "psychology of difference" one step *beyond* Freud's "psychology of likeness"

1939   Divorces Tola Rank and marries Estelle Buel, his secretary, in July

1939   Dies in New York from reaction to injection of a sulfa (antibacterial) drug, on October 31—one month after Freud's death in London, from injection of morphine by his personal physician, on September 23

EDITOR'S NOTES TO THE READER

1. Rank delivered his "American lectures" in English. I edited all lectures for readability but retained Rank's gender bias (the generic *man, he, mankind,* etc.), and other usages standard for the time. I also retained spelling of the word *phantasy*, by which Rank meant inner "imagination"—in distinction to outer "reality." (For psychoanalysts influenced by Melanie Klein, the word *fantasy* is now used to designate conscious phenomena, and the word *phantasy* to designate unconscious "mental representation" of biological drives and also unconscious "defenses" against these drives.) The original date and location of each of Rank's lectures appears as a first, unnumbered note to each chapter. For publication information, see the Prior Publication of Lectures section on pp. 277–78.

2. Primary sources located in the Rank Collection, Rare Book and Manuscript Library, Columbia University are referenced throughout the text in italics as *RC*.

3. Bracketed, **boldfaced** numerical in-text references are to the numbered lectures in this book, with lecture number followed, after the hyphen, by page number.

4. In my introduction, bracketed German words corresponding to the English translation of Rank's *The Trauma of Birth* come from his *Das Trauma der Geburt und seine Bedeutuntg für die Psychoanalyse* (Leipzig/Vienna/Zürich: Internationaler Psychoanalytischer Verlag, 1924).

5. In my introduction, bracketed German words corresponding to the English translation of Freud's *Standard Edition* (*S.E.*) come from his *Gesammelte Werke, Chronologisch Geordnet* (Frankfurt am Main: S. Fischer, 1940–68), edited by A. Freud, E. Bibring, W. Hoffer, E. Kris, and O. Isakower, in collaboration with M. Bonaparte, 18 volumes.

6. In my introduction, bracketed German words corresponding to the English translation of the Freud-Fliess letters come from *Sigmund Freud, Briefe an Wilhelm Fliess 1887–1904* (Frankfurt am Main: S. Fischer, 1986), edited by J. M. Masson, with assistance from M. Schröter and G. Fichtner.

7. Original letters to and from Rank, Freud, and Ferenczi are located in *RC*. Most of these letters were published for the first time in German in Wittenberger's *Das "Geheime Komitee" Sigmund Freuds: Institutionalisierungsprozesse in der Psychoanalytischen Bewegung zwischen 1912 und 1927* (Tübingen: edition discord, 1995), pp. 261–337, passim. English translations are my own, and differ slightly from translations previously published in Taft 1958, pp. 78–111, passim and in Lieberman 1985, pp. 204–50, passim. In my introduction and footnotes throughout the text, bracketed German words come from original letters. In typed correspondence, special German characters, such as the umlaut, were not used by Rank.

8. In my footnotes throughout the text, bracketed German words corresponding to the English translation of Rank's *Truth and Reality* come from volume 3

of his *Grundzüge einer Genetischen Psychologie*, published as *Warheit und Wirklichkeit* (Leipzig and Vienna: Franz Deuticke, 1929).

9. In my footnotes throughout the text, bracketed German words corresponding to the English translation of Rank's *Will Therapy* come from volumes 2 and 3 of his *Technik der Psychoanalyse* subtitled, respectively, *Die analytische Reaktion in ihren konstruktiven Elementen* (Leipzig and Vienna: Franz Deuticke, 1929), and *Die Analyse des Analytikers und seiner Rolle in der Gesamtsituation* (Leipzig and Vienna: Franz Deuticke, 1931).

10. In the lectures, bracketed German words come from the original text of Rank's *Grundzüge einer Genetischen Psychologie*, volume 1 (Leipzig and Vienna: Franz Deuticke, 1927) or volume 2, subtitled *Gestaltung und Ausdruck der Persönlichkeit* (Leipzig and Vienna: Franz Deuticke, 1928).

11. Throughout the lectures, I translated the German words *Erlebnis* and *Erfahrung* as "experience." A change in the inner emotional life, *Erlebnis* usually means an intense experience that is lived inwardly, imaginatively, or spiritually. It is considered a stronger word than *Erfahrung*, which usually means an external happening from which practical knowledge, learnings, or discoveries are drawn.

12. Throughout the lectures, I translated the German word *Ich* as "I" wherever Rank was clearly referring to the I-Thou (*Ich-Du*) or I-You relationship; in all other places, *Ich* was translated as "ego." Rank also frequently used the German word *Selbst*, which I always translated as "self."

13. The index was prepared by Leonard Rosenbaum, American Psychological Association, Washington, D.C.

A PSYCHOLOGY OF

DIFFERENCE

INTRODUCTION

INSIGHT AND BLINDNESS:
VISIONS OF RANK

by *Robert Kramer*

A T HEART a poet and writer, Otto Rank took great pleasure in giving literary gifts to his beloved Professor, a past master of the German language. On May 6, 1923, as a gift for Freud's sixty-seventh birthday, Rank presented the father of psychoanalysis with his dreamy new manuscript, completed just days before: *Das Trauma der Geburt*. The manuscript was drawn from a diary in which he had been sketching "impressions from analytic sessions, in aphoristic form," Rank would later reveal. "It was assembled piece by piece, as it were, like a mosaic" (Isakower 1924). Inlaid throughout the poetic work were a number of strange and shocking aphorisms.

"The Mouth of Hell"

In the process of physiological birth, offers Rank, each new arrival on the planet finds its first object, mother, only promptly to lose her again: the primal catastrophe. For the tiny creature, this *trauma* [Greek: "wound"] is a loss beyond words and harbinger of life's incalculable suffering. Even with the kindest of mothers and the least violent of births, the human being is born afraid, a shivering bundle of *Angst* cast adrift in an uncaring world, a small island of pain floating on a vast ocean of indifference. At the moment of birth, feeling neglected and misunderstood, the *infans* [Latin: "not speaking"] is expelled weeping from the paradisal womb, like Adam, leaving behind it an ineffable past. The dividing line between the I, *das Ich*, and the universe is *Angst*, which vanishes only when I and You have become one, as parts of a greater whole. With birth, the feeling of oneness with the whole, *das Ganze*, is lost.

Analogizing to the analytic situation, Rank suggests that the relationship between mother and "*infans*—ultimately the unborn" (Rank 1924, p. 130)—forms a template for the encounter between therapist and patient, who unite in deep sharing, paradoxically, only to learn how to bear the trauma of separation with less pain than before. But there is joy as well as pain in separation. In the healing relationship, therapist and patient merge emotionally into one, like Plato's mythical half-beings "striving [for] reunion" (ibid., p. 173), in order to reemerge in their singular individuality, enriched and spiritually renewed. Only through mutual recognition is healing, or becoming whole, possible. But to find oneself, argues Rank, it may be necessary to lose oneself, if only for a moment: "The I and the You have ceased to exist between us, I am not I, You are not You, also You are not I [*ich bin nicht ich, du bist nicht du, auch bist du nicht ich*]; I am at the same time I and You, You are at the same time You and I" (ibid., p. 177).

With the simultaneous dissolution of their difference into a greater whole, therapist and patient surrender their painful isolation for a moment only to have their individualities returned to them again, recreated and enriched by a brush with the numinous. This mutual identification of therapist and patient is an echo of a lost identity, not merely of "the blessedness of child and mother in union" (ibid., p. 160), but a unity with the universe, the All, which once existed and is now lost. This "cosmic identification" (ibid., p. 65), a unity with the whole, *das Ganze*, has to be surrendered and reasserted throughout every phase of self-development. The longing to restore Oneness, a preobjectual union with a cosmos floating in mystic vapors in which past, present, and future are dissolved, "the *unio mystica*, [or] being at one with the All [*das Einswerden mit dem All*]" (ibid., p. 176), a spiritual union in which space is not a barrier and time and death have vanished, is the primary stimulus for love and art. Affirming difference but paradoxically also releasing from difference, the meeting of I and You, leads, on each side, to a feeling of unity with the other, the cosmos, the All, *das Ganze*, and finally with one's own self.

Taking priority over the Oedipus complex, the tension between surrender and assertion, union and separation, is the spring of life and is re-created anew at all stages of development, from birth and childhood through adolescence, to maturity downward to aging and death. While no panacea for the pain of this world, which is a necessary part of existence, therapy helps the lost soul feel "new born" (ibid., p. 3) spiritually, without suffering too much guilt or *Angst* for separating from the therapist-midwife and simultaneously from outlived or infantile parts of the self. Only by willing to be oneself within a relationship, by accepting one's own difference and having it accepted by another, can the human being discover or recover the creativity to change. A creature born out of a biological mother, constructed from two particles of cosmic dust, the human being is at once creature and creator, or, more accurately, progresses from creature to creator, biology to *psyche*, object to subject, and in the case of the most productive—artist, writer, scientist, or philosopher—chooses himself. To be born twice, in a spiritual sense, is no more miraculous than to be born once, but sadly some lost and vulnerable souls cannot manage even that.

The "primal repression," according to Rank, is failing to accept birth, in other words, "clinging to the mother" (ibid., p. 215)—clinging painfully to the gain of illness, a shadowy precipitate of the lost mother-child relationship. Located somewhere in the labyrinth of psychic space, the "mother-image [*Mutter Imago*]" (ibid., p. 87n.2) is a phantasm of *Angst* and longing, guilt and desire, at once terrifying and thrilling. But seeing the outlines of this invisible ghost is harrowing. "The last thing for which human beings seem to be created is to bear psychoanalytic truth," affirms Rank, and as Freud had often told him, "it was not for everyone to be continuously investigating the dark ravines of the Unconscious with only an occasional glance at the light of day" (ibid., p. 184). With the truth some cannot live. On the title page of his Dreambook, Freud had inscribed a fearless epigraph from Virgil: *Flectere si nequeo superos, Acheronta movebo*: "If I cannot bend the Higher Powers, I will move the Infernal Regions" (*S.E.*, 5:608). Only psychoanalytic truth can bring to light the dark ravines of the Infernal Regions, which flow, says the poet Virgil, into the mythical river *Acheron*, a subterranean whirlpool that leads directly to Hades, an abyss that opens up the terrifying jaws of death—"the mouth of hell" where awaits the devil herself, warns Rank: the "old evil and dangerous primal mother [*Urmutter*]" (Rank 1924, p. 132).

"Nichts zu Sein"

Although biologically based, the trauma of birth is also a symbol of the I's startling discovery of itself and its *Angst*-soaked separation from its first object, mother, now the therapist. The *infans* comes into the world in a caul of *Angst*, long before castration or sexual fears of any kind. The painful awareness of difference, therefore, is "*the first psychical content* of which the human being is conscious" (ibid., p. 50; Rank's italics). At bottom, perhaps *Angst* is nothing but the consciousness of living, in other words, consciousness itself, the dim perception of one's difference as a consequence of becoming conscious of life. I = *Angst*. Recognition of the anatomical difference between the sexes, no matter how important for maturity, comes later. The difference between nonexistence and existence—mere difference—comes first. "And consciousness is the human characteristic *par excellence*" (ibid., p. 216). The trauma of birth, that long malaise, our difference, the consciousness of living, seems to have suffered a greater repression than even infantile sexuality or the anatomical difference between the sexes.

The birth trauma, hints Rank, making "an asymptotic approach" (ibid., p. 7) to the boundary of the metaphysical, the shores of the unthinkable, may even be "derived from the germ plasm [*Keimplasma*]" itself (ibid., p. 188). In the ontological or, better, the preontological sense, this catastrophic *trauma* correlates with a mysterious cleavage in a zygote smaller than the period at the end of this sentence, a fertilized germ cell called "seed [*Kern*] of all things" (ibid., p. 172) by the philosopher Anaxagoras and *der Kern unseres Wesens* by Freud: "the core of our being" (*S.E.*, 5:603). This uncanniest of "wounds" precedes the intrauterine condition as well as the physical passage nine months later through the maternal birth canal. "Whence things originated, thither, according to necessity, they must return and perish," propounds the ancient Greek oracle Anaximander of Miletus, "for they must pay penalty and be judged for their injustices according to the order of time" (Rank 1924, p. 168–69).

But from where, exactly, does the new arrival on the planet originate? The germ plasm? Two specks of cosmic dust or, more precisely, two sets of an infinite number of cosmic unknowns, fuse their nuclei and melt down into nothingness, *Nichts*. Like the Phoenix arising from its ashes to start another life, a human being incomprehensibly emerges nine months later. Is sex the cause of existence? Granted the entire evolutionary process and the most microscopic chemical analysis of cause and effect, still the human being is an inexplicable remainder, germinating from nothing and nowhere, defiantly resisting the deepest probings of the most clever of coxcombs, who, as Nietzsche says sarcastically of Socrates in *The Twilight of the Idols*, insist "that thought, following the clues of causality, reaches even into the deepest abyss of Being, and that thought is able not only to recognize Being but also even to *correct* it" (ibid., p. 181; Rank's italics). But this is the height of folly for a vulnerable and mortal creature, human-all-too-human, a tiny gnat crawling on the planet Earth, as it spins meaninglessly around the awesome and unknowable dark spaces of the universe. Nietzsche savages the *daemon* of Socrates as "a perfect monstrosity *per defectum*" and relentlessly tears down the gigantic intellect of this "great Master of Irony," who influenced his disciples solely by speech, but whose mouth was "a crater full of evil desires" (ibid., pp. 180–81), a hell-hole.

A subject shrouded in darkness, the human being, male or female, is tormented by a question that neither philosophy nor science, for all their great achievements, can ever answer: what does it mean to be conscious, to be alive, during this infinitesimal moment of light, a vacation on earth, between two eternities of darkness? "The very best is quite unattainable for you," broods Nietzsche in a passage from *The Birth of Tragedy* selected by Rank as the epigraph for his manuscript; "it is, not to be born, not to exist, to be Nothing [*nicht geboren zu sein, nicht zu sein, Nichts zu sein*]. But the next best for you is—to die soon" (Rank 1924, epigraph). Everything is profoundly cracked. The longing to get free of the consciousness of living, that long malaise, our difference, is perhaps the strongest emotional force in the individual. Even the boasting, all too-theoretical Socrates seems to have understood this at the end: "*Life—that is to be long ill*," the Master of Irony said before swallowing his hemlock (ibid., p. 197n.1; Rank's italics).

The birth trauma, insists Rank, author of *The Myth of the Birth of the Hero*, is not just physiological. It is also psychological. As shown in all cultural traditions, the myth of the birth of the hero "plainly reveals the desire to enforce his materialization," Rank had written in 1909, "even against the will of the parents." Left to die by exposure, the future hero overcomes "the greatest difficulties by virtue of his birth, for he has victoriously thwarted all attempts to prevent it" (Rank 1909, pp. 64–65). An intruder, uninvited and unwelcomed, the human being is suddenly a "hero" of sorts, offers Rank, "and birth is the real achievement" (Rank 1924, p. 131n.1). According to the Talmudical sages, an Angel of Life tells the *infans* before birth: "Against your Will [*wieder deinen Willen*] have you been formed in your mother's womb, *and against your will shall you be born*, to go out into the world. Immediately," say the Rabbis, "the child *weeps*" (ibid., p. 123n.1; Rank's italics)—for it does not want to leave the blissful paradise, its own asymptotic approach to "the *unio mystica*, the being at one with the All" (ibid., p. 176). Psychotherapy, according to Rank, can help the human being find the courage to affirm, deliberately, the strange existence forced on him by sex—by the unknown and forever unknowable cleavage from which the creature springs forth in *der Kern unseres Wesens*—to choose that which is also absolutely determined: his life. Although we are thrown into the world at birth and thrown out at death, not only do we forget that we are born to die, we also have an astonishing ability to forget that we are living. Life is a loan from "the 'beyond'" (ibid., p. 60) and death the repayment. "We expiate our birth firstly by our life," teaches Schopenhauer, "and secondly by our death" (ibid., p. 169). One cannot refuse the loan, life, in order to escape payment of the debt, death. The unconscious, according to Rank, is beyond sex. Beyond even the germ plasm. The unconscious is a beyond, "the thing-in-itself . . . the only transcendental, and therefore impenetrable, reality" (ibid., p. 178).

The birth of individuation is never complete. "More light," cried Goethe on his deathbed (ibid., p. 197n.3). The trauma of birth ends only with the trauma of death, which is simultaneously the final separation and the final union—the ultimate castration. "At the moment of dying, the body once more severs itself from the mother substitute, 'Dame World,' whose front is comely and beautifully formed," observes Rank, "but whose back is thought to be ugly and horrible" (ibid.). Unconsciously, we worship and fear our mother, an umplumbable navel of life and death. "Everyone born sinks back again into the womb from which he or she once came into the realm of light" (ibid., p. 114).

"A Unique, Gigantic, Hostile Entity"

"One could formulate the hysterical attack," notes Rank aphoristically, "as a cry 'Away from the [mother]!'" (ibid., p. 52). Invariably, the free-floating *Angst* of the *infans* is attached to its mother, its primal object, which, internalized in the psyche, becomes "the nucleus [*Kern*] of every neurotic disturbance" (ibid., p. 46). Only much later is the "fear of her, caused ultimately by the birth trauma" (ibid., p. 90), the wound of unspeakable loss, displaced onto the Oedipal father. Mother is a powerful object, at once tender and monstrous, loving and terrifying, venerated and tabooed. Mother is "a dark threatening power, capable of the deepest sympathy but also of the greatest severity" (ibid., p. 115). In mythological terms, seen from the point of view of a small boy, the mother is "a unique, gigantic, hostile entity, which pursues the hero, identified with the father, and ever challenges him to new battles" (ibid., p. 72). Each new arrival on the planet, hero or heroine, retains an unspeakable revenant of "*primal ambivalence*" (ibid., p. 199; his italics) toward the "lost primal object, the mother [*das verlorene Urobjekt der Mutter*]" (ibid., p. 205).

Separation from the therapist-midwife, "the *essential part* of the analytic work," stresses Rank (ibid., p. 207; his italics), "is accomplished by reproduction of the birth trauma, so that the patient loses his doctor and his suffering at the same time, or, better expressed, must give up his doctor in order to lose his suffering" (ibid.). Exchanging neurotic suffering for "ordinary unhappiness" (ibid., p. 201), according to Freud, is the very best that can be achieved before we shuffle off this mortal coil. But all therapy is "active," on both sides alternately, and "purposes an effect through volitional [*willkürliche*] influence and a change resulting from it" (ibid., p. 203). Change is born from the discovery, merger, and rediscovery of two differences—two wills—endlessly loving, hating, creating, destroying, and re-creating each other, in continuous interaction and counteraction. Relationship takes priority over insight. "Even simple therapeutic action can be arrested by too much knowledge and too much insight" (ibid., p. 202), which may defend against the pain of emotional experience: ordinary unhappiness.

Yearning to return to "Nirvana, the pleasurable Nothing [*Nichts*], the womb" (ibid., p. 119), Schopenhauer was mistaken in decreeing that the essence of artistic achievement is "deliverance" from the painful "Will" (ibid., p. 141n.2). On the contrary, insists Rank, following Nietzsche, who clearly recognized Schopenhauer's repression of will, we can never "celebrate the sabbath" (ibid.) of *not* willing since the will recurs eternally—the same. But will wants separation and union, assertion and deliverance, individuation and merger, at once. Cocooned in the analytic womb, floating in the oceanic feeling, the patient learns to navigate the narrow channel between dread and hope, regress and progress, the urgent will to unite and the even more urgent will to separate. Torn between staying and leaving, the patient must, at long last, accept the "ordinary unhappiness" that is part of existence and affirm the burden of difference: the Godlike but painful consciousness loaned to us, without our asking, as a strange gift from "the 'beyond'" (ibid., p. 60), before which mystery we stand awestruck and in debt. Schopenhauer sought to affirm guilt but deny will, and Nietzsche to affirm will but deny guilt. Both will and guilt, however, belong to each other as inevitably as day to night. Human beings must accept the need to individuate as well as the need to merge, I and Thou, Thou and I, without becoming chained to one at the exclusion of the other. During the agonizing process of learning to accept self and other, the patient cuts the umbilical cord to infantile dreads and longings.

For the patient, each therapeutic hour is a partial living and dying, according to Rank, a microcosmic experience of union and separation. "Every single hour demands from him the repetition in miniature of the fixation and severance, till he is in the position finally to carry it through" (ibid., p. 215). If the individual can accept himself or herself in this fragment of time, without too much *Angst* or guilt, then living and loving more fully outside the allotted hour may also be possible. Remaining chained to the mother *Imago*, or its surrogate, the therapist, is the equivalent of refusing to separate from outworn parts of the I—clinging painfully to fears and desires like a child to a discarded toy. "My analyses," reveals Rank, who has found that the patient's ambivalence about separation and union emerges most starkly during the end phase, "are some of the shortest in duration, lasting from four to eight months at the very longest" (ibid., p. 6). Interminably investigating the unconscious, without being offered a "navel string" to find an "exit from the Labyrinth" (ibid., p. 154), like the navel string Theseus threw down to Ariadne, dooms both therapist and patient to a watery death, entombed forever in the labyrinthine womb of analysis. In collaboration with the patient, short-term therapy sets limits, according to Rank, in order to allow the individual to endure release and separation, first from the authority of parents, and second, from the lived-out parts of the self that these two biological powers represent, which obstruct the person's affirmation of difference—the conscious I or self with its own power, the will, and its lifelong complement, pain and guilt. The freeing of Theseus, by means of a navel string, symbolizes the birth of "the hero, and his detachment from the ancient primal mother [*Urmutter*]" (ibid., p. 155).

"And so we would like to regard our arguments," concludes Rank, "only as a contribution to the Freudian structure of normal psychology, at best as one of its pillars" (ibid., p. 210).

"The Cause"

In 1923, when he presented *The Trauma of Birth* to Freud, Rank was himself a pillar of the cause, and after Freud, "the most important psychoanalytic author" (Lieberman, 1985, p. xxvi). Nothing, of course, was more important to Freud than *die Sache*, the cause of psychoanalysis. "I do everything only for the cause, which, again, is basically my own," Freud confessed to Ferenczi in 1909. "I proceed thoroughly egoistically" (Brabant, Falzeder, and Giampieri-Deutsch 1993, p. 33). For every edition of *The Interpretation of Dreams* since 1911, Rank had helped Freud revise, word by word, every line of his cause célèbre of self-analysis. "I am of intention," Freud confided to Jones in 1911, "to make him a partner in the coming edition of the *Traumdeutung*" (Paskauskas 1993, p. 92). Other than Freud, the first explorer of the Infernal Regions, perhaps no one had plumbed the hidden levels of meaning in Freud's dreams more deeply than "little Rank" (McGuire, 1974, p. 150), who knew the Dreambook virtually by heart.

In 1914 Freud entrusted the thirty-year-old Rank, who published *Der Doppelgänger* [The Double] in the same year, to contribute two full-length chapters, on literature and myth, to his masterwork. Rank's name now appeared just below Freud's on the title page of *The Interpretation of Dreams*. Few could have identified more strongly with Freud than Rank, whose internationally acclaimed essay on the myth of the birth of the hero, written at the remarkable age of 25, contained the following sentence, contributed by the Professor himself: "The detachment of the growing individual from the authority of the parents is one of the most necessary, but also one of the most painful achievements of evolution" (Rank 1909, p. 59).

With his bold new work on the birth trauma, which Rank considered as essential to the future of psychoanalysis as his monumental 685-page study of the Oedipus theme (1912) had been to its past, Rank was constructing a second pillar to support Freud. "Among the strictly scientific applications of analysis to literature," Freud pronounced in 1914, "Rank's exhaustive work on the theme of incest easily takes the first place" (S.E., 14:37). For over fifteen years, Rank had devoted all his creative energies to Freud and *die Sache*, which he knew were one and the same. "He is doing all the work," Freud gushed to Jones in 1919, "performing the possible and the impossible alike, I dare say, you know him for what he is, the truest, most reliable, most charming of helpers, the column, which is bearing the edifice" (Paskauskas 1993, p. 353).

Design of the second column to bear the edifice of Freud started in January 1919, when Rank, just married, with a pregnant wife, began to practice psychotherapy full-time to support his growing family (Lieberman 1985, p. 156). Immersed in the richness of the arts and humanities, Rank had little experience with patients before the Great War, during which he served the fatherland as an army newspaper editor. But Freud had long marveled at Rank's analytical skills and encouraged him, early on, to become the first lay analyst. At 26 Rank published "A Dream That Interprets Itself" (1910), an interpretation so penetrating that Freud could not praise it too highly. "Perhaps the best example of the interpretation of a dream," rejoiced Freud in his *Introductory Lectures*, "is the one reported by Otto Rank consisting of two interrelated dreams dreamt by a young girl, which occupy about two pages of print: but their analysis extends to seventy-six pages. So I should need something like a whole term to conduct you through [it]" (S.E., 15:185).

In March 1919, just weeks after starting his full-time practice, Rank told Jones privately of his growing appreciation that "the essence of life was the relationship between mother and child" (Jones 1957, p. 58). Rank did not keep this new idea, developed mainly from clinical experience but also from personal experience, hidden from his fellow analysts, many of whom he was now responsible for training in therapeutic technique. In 1921, before the Vienna Psychoanalytic Society, Rank dazzled and, in some cases, bewildered his colleagues with a lecture "on the relation between married partners; they, he maintained, always repeated in essence those between mother and child (on both sides alternately)" (ibid.). Each partner projects elements of the mother-child relation on the other and simultaneously identifies with the other's projections, a circuit of continuous exchange, to create anew, through give-and-take, the right balance of will and love first experienced by each within the mother-child relation. The lifelong implications of this mutual projection and identification—seeking at each developmental stage to balance separation and union, differentiation and connectedness, will and love—Rank would work out, systematically, in the coming years and thereby powerfully influence the thinking of a young American named Carl Rogers, just about to start practicing psychotherapy (Kramer 1995).

Everyone in the inner circle knew that Rank occupied "an exceptional place in Freud's life" (Roazen 1976, p. 392), closer emotionally to Freud than even his own natural sons. After the Great War, Rank was the only one of the secretly governing ringholders living in Vienna. He dined Wednesdays with Professor and his family at *Berggasse* 19 before meetings of the Vienna Psychoanalytic Society, over which Rank, now vice-president, presided in Freud's frequent absences (ibid., p. 394). The youngest and freshest of the Committee members, he held a unique position in the nucleus of the secret ring: Freud cosigned Rank's circular letters to the Committee, giving them an imprimatur the others did not enjoy. In 1919 Freud described himself to Jones as "nearly helpless and maimed when Rank is away" (Paskauskas 1993, p. 360). By 1923, at only 39, Rank had become virtually indispensible for Freud, now approaching 70.

In April 1923, when he penned *The Trauma of Birth*, Rank was at the peak of his influence, recognized throughout the tiny psychoanalytic world as vice-president of the Vienna Psychoanalytic Society, director of the *Verlag*, Freud's publishing house, and coeditor of *Imago* and *Zeitschrift*, the two leading analytic journals. Havelock Ellis called him "perhaps the most brilliant and clairvoyant of the young investigators who still stand by the master's side" (Ellis 1923, p. 111). Next to Freud, Rank was the most senior training analyst, "the one-man training institute of Vienna," remembers Franz Alexander (Lieberman 1979, p. 13). His position in the cause was undisputed. Summing up Rank's vital role during these years, Hanns Sachs described him, simply, as Freud's *Doppelgänger*, his shadow: "Lord Everything Else" (Sachs 1944, p. 60).

"The Most Important Progress Since the Discovery of Psychoanalysis"

On first hearing of Rank's revolutionary idea, Freud told Ferenczi, then Rank's best friend: "I don't know whether 66 or 33 percent of it is true, but in any case it is the most important progress since the discovery of psychoanalysis" (Jones 1957, p. 59). But Freud's uneasiness also showed, since he joked, "Anyone else would have used such a discovery to make himself independent" (ibid.). Ferenczi was hailing Rank's manuscript on the birth trauma, which he reviewed in draft, even more enthusiastically than had Freud: "Your presentation of the ideal Greek human being and his detachment from the ancient primal mother [*Ur-mutter*] in art is one of the most brilliant parts of your work," Ferenczi congratulated Rank. "I shall be glad when your book will finally be published, without it I am actually hindered in my own production, since all future work must be based on the trauma point of view" (Ferenczi to Rank, undated letter; *RC*). But whether 100, 66, or 33 percent of it were true, Freud had more—far more—on his mind at this time than the trauma of birth, no matter how important Rank's clairvoyant point of view might be for the progress of *die Sache*.

On April 20, 1923, a few days before receiving Rank's birthday gift, Freud underwent minor surgery to remove "leukoplakia" from the inside of his mouth. It was the first sign of cancer, linked to his lifelong addiction to cigars, an almost sexual craving that he was never willing or able to master. "The role played by [masturbation] in hysteria is enormous," Freud once told Wilhelm Fliess, "and it is perhaps there that my major, still outstanding obstacle is to be found, wholly or in part" (Masson 1985, p. 287). During the first examination of his oral cavity, Freud, who secretly suspected the worst, asked his doctor for help to "disappear from this world with decency" (Clark 1980, p. 438) if he were doomed to die of agonizing pain. Freud then suddenly mentioned his dear mother, Amalia, who at the age of 87 remained vibrant and in excellent health. "It would not be easy to do that to the old lady," he said (ibid.). Inexplicably, there was always an inseparable bond for Freud between the words "my mother" and "my death."

Until he died in 1939, Freud suffered through over thirty operations and was forced to wear a series of painful prosthetic devices, severely limiting his hearing and speech—the very means, ironically, by which psychoanalysis, the talking cure, relieved neurosis. None ever fit properly. "I am constantly tortured by something," Freud complained to Max Eitingon, a member of the secret Committee (Romm 1983, p. 71). For the rest of his life, Freud would call the prosthesis a "monster" (Jones 1957, p. 99), "an uninvited, unwelcome intruder whom one should not mind more than necessary" (Romm 1983, p. 33), "my dear neoplasm" (Clark 1980, p. 439), a "permanent, never-to-be ended misery" (Hyman 1962, p. 298), a murderous, half-tamed *daemon* that had taken up residence in the mouth of hell.

In October and November 1923, Freud underwent two major surgeries to excise cancer from his jaw and palate. By mid-October *The Trauma of Birth* was already printed but not yet published by the *Verlag*. On November 17, while convalescing from the second surgery, Freud requested a voluntary operation on his testicles to ligate the *vas deferens*, a duct that carries sperm to the seminal vesicle. Then in vogue even among reputable physicians, this mysterious procedure, which

Freud surely understood as a kind of castration, was supposed to improve vision, heighten intellectual insight, and halt, or even reverse, cancer (Romm 1983, pp. 73–85). "Do not talk about it—not as long as I am alive," Freud admonished a physician attending him (ibid., p. 84). Known today as a vasectomy, the "ligation allegedly promoted increased activity of the hormone-producing cells of the testes" (ibid., p. 12).

Three days after Freud's vasectomy, on November 20, 1923, Otto Rank paid a visit to Freud in his hospital room at the Sanitorium Auersperg in Vienna. At eleven o'clock that night, after returning home, Rank wrote a letter to Freud about "an interpretation" that had just occurred to him of "the witty dream you told me today." In the dream David Lloyd George, a great English orator, was making a speech on *Das Ich und das Es*, Freud's latest book, just released in April 1923—the same month in which Rank had written *The Trauma of Birth*. As director of the *Verlag*, Rank was responsible for editing and publishing *The Ego and the Id*, which introduced to psychoanalysis a seminal concept: *das Über-Ich*, the "above-I" or super-ego, the shadow of the object that falls, after internalization of the castration threat, on *das Ich*, the "I." Source of *Angst* and guilt-feeling, the *Über-Ich* is the internalized residue of the castrating father—the father *Imago* who is located in the dark and forbidding nucleus of the Oedipus complex. With utmost cruelty the *Über-Ich* rages against the "I," as if it had taken possession of all of one's sadism and hate, a self-destructive expression of the drive toward death (*S.E.*, 19:53)—toward nothingness, *Nichts*.

"Ich-Nichts-Übernichts"

My "interpretation," began Rank, who had been deeply shaken by Freud's life-threatening cancer, "is too apt to be withheld from you, and, I hope, will amuse you":

> It is high time that I [Freud] return to work, the others do not understand me [*verstehen mich ja doch nicht*], do not know how to "translate" me . . . and misuse my psychoanalysis for their personal interests; they understand *nichts* [nothing] or even less than *nichts* [a pun on *Über-Ich* since *übernichts* means "over-nothing" or less than nothing]. It reminds one of the well-known comparisons: *nix-nix aber schon gar-nix*! [nothing, nothing, but absolutely nothing!]. Naturally, this is only one of the actual meanings of the dream, which fulfills your "*Ich*" and relatively your "*Über-Ich*." What *das Es* [the it] has to say to this is probably difficult to find out . . .
>
> But this interpretation may provoke you—I mean "provoke" in both

[*doppelten*] senses—also meaning to provoke you to complete this interpretation, whereby I hope that the deepest strata reveal as decisive a will
for recovery [*Genesungswillen*] as this first one. (Lieberman 1985, pp.
204–5)

Although feeling mortally wounded, Freud savored this letter, a kalei-
doscope of puns, which showed just how profoundly his youthful *Doppelgänger* understood him and the cause of psychoanalysis. An emotional bond had developed between Freud and Rank, tender and loving
foster father and son, who rarely needed to exchange correspondence
since Rank visited *Berggasse* 19 almost daily. On November 26, 1923,
while on his sickbed, still recovering from his cancer operations and
vasectomy, Freud replied to Rank, reaching deeply into the darkest and
narrowest defiles of his unconscious, far down into the labyrinth of the
Infernal Regions:

It has been a long time since you have tried to interpret one of my dreams
in such a powerful analytical way. Since then much has changed. You have
grown enormously and you know so much more about me and the results
are different. Your work gives me the opportunity . . . to examine finally
the interesting problem of the relation of the *Über-Ich* in this dream. I
cannot confirm everything you write . . . but I do not need to contradict
you anywhere. . . . [T]he joke was originally conceived in German: *Ich-
nichts-übernichts* [I-nothing-less-than-nothing]. In the *Tr* [short for *Traum*,
dream; but also a pun on the title of Rank's book, *Trauma*] only the nothing was clear, the over-nothing certainly being an interpolation. Now
comes the question: Against whom is the *Tr* [dream or *Trauma*] directed
[*Gegen wer richtet sich der Tr*]? And the question about the *Über-Ich*? . . .
does it show a brutal will to recovery [*Genesungswillen*]? . . . The *Über-Ich*
merely says to the *Tr* [dream or *Trauma*]: All right, you old jester and
boaster. This is not true at all! [*Da ist ja alles nicht wahr!*] . . .
Attention here, the old one and the young one are interchanged. You
[Freud] are not David [*nicht du bist der David*], you are the boasting giant
whom another one, the young David, will slay. And now everything falls
into place around this point, that you [Rank] are the dreaded David who,
with his *Trauma der Geburt*, will succeed in depreciating my work. After
having changed David back into Goliath, the *Über-Ich* has no further objections . . . and can remain silent. Thus I can continue your interpretation.
I hope to see you soon, I was not operated on again, I am free of pain and
medicines. (Lieberman 1985, pp. 205–6)

In the wake of his bout with cancer, Freud's association to David
murdering Goliath (or perhaps it was the other way around), even if
only in jest, must have startled Rank. Was Rank David or was Rank

Goliath? Was the birth trauma related, in some fantastic way, to Freud's hellish cancer of the mouth? To the speech being severed so terrifyingly from Freud, as a kind of self-imposed castration, perhaps for some obscure and tragic sense of guilt? And who or what, exactly, was responsible for the guilt that seemed to be haunting the "boasting giant," a guilt so dark and unspeakable that it was now threatening, literally, to shut his mouth, forcing the golem to "remain silent"? Could the brutal *Über-Ich* in the deepest strata ever be provoked to show the "will to recovery" solicited by the witty Rank? Even more ominously, did the "dreaded David's" new idea, which emphasized mother at the expense of father, reduce the value of psychoanalysis to *Nichts*—nothing? To *übernichts*—less than nothing?

A few days later, brushing aside any reservations he may have had, Rank personally delivered to Freud one of the first printed copies of *The Trauma of Birth*. On December 1, 1923, although he had not finished reading the book, Freud sent a warm note to Rank, who dedicated his birthday gift "to the Explorer of the Unconscious, Creator of Psychoanalysis." In a tone far different from his earlier letter, Freud was very generous toward Rank's work, and although he accepted the dedication, modestly declined the grandiose title "Explorer of the Unconscious, Creator of Psychoanalysis" but, as if still unsure about the effect of the birth trauma on him, again mentioned death and, oddly, the immortality he expected Rank's clairvoyant idea to bring him: "I gladly accept your dedication with the assurance of my most cordial thanks. If you could put it more modestly, it would be all right with me. Handicapped as I am, I enjoy enormously your admirable productivity. That means for me too: 'Non omnis moriar' ['I shall not wholly die,' from Horace, *Odes* 3.30]" (Taft 1958, p. 85).

"The Germ of Cleavage"

After the publication of *The Trauma of Birth* in December 1923, Theodore Ames, who had been trained in Vienna by Rank and was now president of the New York Psychoanalytic Society, invited Rank to come to the United States to give a series of lectures. In Europe, however, while Rank was preparing to leave for the United States, Karl Abraham and Ernest Jones were raising a storm of protest. The Committee, the secret nucleus of the cause and Freud's collective heir, had developed a crack that was about to split wide open. Abraham, in particular, suspected that Rank's new idea posed a mortal threat to the scientific foundation of psychoanalysis at a time when the Professor was stricken fatally with oral cancer, his surgeon having given him only a short time, at most a few years, to live.

By Christmas 1923, Freud heard from Eitingon about "the 'storm' in Berlin" (Jones 1957, p. 59) emanating mainly from Abraham, who gravely warned Freud that Rank's thesis was "for psychoanalysis a question of life and death" (Chertok and Strengers 1992, p. 87). According to Jones, *The Trauma of Birth* had given Freud a "shock of alarm—lest the whole of his life's work on the etiology of the neuroses be dissolved" (Jones 1957, p. 59). Unaccountably, Rank was redirecting the psychoanalytic floodlight from father to mother, abandoning everything Freud had achieved in a lifetime of struggling scientifically to understand the central role of the Oedipus complex. It followed from Rank's clinical theory, observed Jones with alarm, "that all mental conflicts concerned the relation of the child to its mother, and that what might appear to be conflicts with the father, including the Oedipus complex, were but a mask for the essential ones" (Jones, 1957, p. 58). Was psychoanalytic theory "a mask" hiding something deeper than Oedipus, the nucleus of the neurosis?

In January 1924, Freud wrote a circular letter to the Committee about "a man in our group who sees the germ [*Keim*] of cleavage" (Wittenberger 1995, p. 286) in the work of Ferenczi and Rank, whose recent joint work *The Development of Psychoanalysis*, subtitled *On the Inter-relationship between Theory and Practice*, seemed to share the barely veiled anti-Oedipal thesis of *The Trauma of Birth*. Ferenczi and Rank, Freud's most imaginative disciples, were now convinced that analysis was becoming overly concerned with scientific research to develop a better theoretical understanding of the mind at the expense of therapeutic results. For the sake of learning more about the patient, and thereby advancing Oedipal theory, analysis was becoming interminable. "What we criticized in our joint book," Rank explained to Freud, "is that each and every analyst could, in the name of research, lengthen analyses *without limit*, and let them run dry therapeutically" (Wittenberger 1995, p. 291).

According to Ferenczi and Rank, some analysts were displaying a "fanaticism for interpreting" (Ferenczi and Rank 1924, p. 29), while neglecting the empathic relationship between therapist and patient, the emotional give-and-take between I and Thou, Thou and I, that is at the heart of therapy. Almost always, these "interpretations" concerned the castration complex, now considered to be identical to the Oedipus complex, the primary cause of the patient's suffering. For these analysts, "interpretation"—providing scientific insight, or *Einsicht*, to patients about their father complex—was all. As a result, "in some cases, the actual analytic task was neglected" (ibid., p. 34). This oversight had left a gaping hole in the nucleus of the analysis: "deeper layers of mental life" (ibid., p. 33) were being left unexamined, according to Ferenczi and Rank, completely shrouded in darkness.

Interpreting all the patient's emotional suffering as fear of paternal castration is a mask, suggested Ferenczi and Rank, "a protection against further analysis" (ibid., p. 34). There was more to the castration complex, the nucleus of the neurosis, than had yet been uncovered. It was "much-too 'complex,'" claimed Ferenczi and Rank, "to be treated as elements which could not be further reduced" (ibid., p. 31). Ironically, the "original infantile story," even after exhaustive and interminable analysis of the Oedipus complex, "was never reached" (ibid.). In the case of the small boy, for example, the castration complex cannot always be ascribed simply to the father fixation. The castration complex can also mean "turning away" from the mother in *Angst* and simultaneously "identification with her, from which, according to the fate of the repression of guilt . . . the most pathologic forms can develop" (ibid., p. 17). As an outcome of the castration complex, the small boy's *Angst*-ridden introjection of the powerful mother, at once terrifying and thrilling, may "serve the purpose of avoiding the Oedipus role" (ibid.). For the vulnerable small boy, too-strong identification with the worshiped and dreaded *Urmutter*, for fear perhaps of losing her love, is a retreat from, not an advance toward, the neurotic harbor of his Oedipus complex. "Naturally," concluded Ferenczi and Rank, who had been working intensively on their book since 1922, "this symptom points back to the deeper infantile stages of development"—to the trauma of birth (ibid., p. 17).

Although never explicitly describing their new technique, nor mentioning the birth trauma theory by name, Ferenczi and Rank emphasized that they were not advocating a one-time "stormy abreaction" (ibid., p. 38), "wild activity" (ibid., p. 43), or a manipulation of the transference. On the contrary "almost all of the past . . . expresses itself in actual reactions in relation to the analyst or to the analysis, in other words in the transference to the analytic situation" (ibid., p. 37). The here-and-now relationship takes priority over interpretation, since all interpretation, no matter how carefully timed or earnestly dosed, amounts to suggestion. From the therapeutic point of view, insisted Ferenczi and Rank, fanatically harping on the analyst's *Indifferenz*, or cold and detached neutrality, is a dangerous mistake, that risks dehumanizing the emotional experience of both therapist and patient, since the mother-child relation, at the intersubjective heart of transference, can hardly justify a pose of icy *Indifferenz*.

"An Unnatural Elimination of All Human Factors in the Analysis"

The arid requirement for neutrality during scientific investigation of the patient's unconscious, according to Ferenczi and Rank, had lead to "an unnatural elimination of all human factors in the analysis" (ibid., pp. 40–41) and to "a theorizing of the analytic experience [*Erlebnis*]" (ibid., p. 41): the emotional experience of the I-Thou relationship between patient and therapist. Some analysts now felt an obligation to prove, experimentally, the scientific truth of the Oedipus complex in each and every analysis, as if Freud's own magnificent and already richly validated work were not proof enough. Regrettably, there had developed an inseparable bond between scientific research and the patient's improvement, theory and therapy, Oedipal interpretation and cure. Getting better, insisted the more rigid and less empathetic analysts, universally requires a conscious recall or reliving of repressed Oedipal memories and an emotional acceptance of the intellectual insight offered by the analyst's Oedipal interpretations—in other words, an indoctrination into theory. But the essence of therapy, objected Ferenczi and Rank, "does not consist either in the verification of the 'Oedipus complex,' or in the simple repetition of the Oedipus situation in the relation to the analyst, but rather in the setting free and detachment of the infantile libido from its fixation on its first objects" (ibid., p. 54)—most importantly mother, but obviously also siblings, father, and others. The emotional vicissitudes of relationship, the withering heat of transference and countertransference, come first. Insight into theory, or intellectual understanding of any kind, can come later. Research and therapy should be separated.

Experience, which is scarcely knowable while it is being enacted, is emotional and precedes all intellectual or theoretical insight. Therapy, asserted Ferenczi and Rank, should substitute "affective factors of experience [*Erlebnis*] for intellectual processes" (ibid., p. 62). Scientific research into the Oedipus complex and therapeutic improvement, they argued, do not coincide. By interpreting the human being scientifically, the fanatics were overly intellectualizing *Erlebnis*—living itself—defeating their own ideal, becoming unscientific by denying the most essential aspect of therapy: the emotional experience of the intertwined relationship between patient and analyst, with all its ambivalences—on both sides—about union and separation, attachment and individuation, love and hate. "I have been forced by analytic experiences [*Erfahrungen*] only, and not by mere speculation," Rank explained to Freud, "to understand this *Erlebnis* as a general analytic one, and, hence, as a common human one" (Wittenberger 1995, p. 291).

Erlebnis is emotional surrender to the present, according to Rank, to the here-and-now, where patients' past ways of being alive are readily visible, as well as all their present ways of experiencing (Haynal and Falzeder, 1993a). The patient lives too much in the past, anyway, and to that extent actually does not live—is, in a sense, already dead, a psychological suicide. It is not the infantile past but the living present— the *Erlebnis* of one's own difference, the consciousness of living, with all its painful feeling, thinking, and acting—that the patient denies, forgets, or wishes to escape. For Rank, difference is the *Erlebnis* that the patient has never before been willing to accept, fully and consciously, without feeling overwhelmed by *Angst* or guilt. Still more creature than creator, a helpless object of fate rather than an artist who *makes* fate, the neurotic is not yet willing to affirm his own difference, the strange existence forced on him at birth. Neurosis is a failure in creativity, for Rank, not a failure in sexuality—which, after the cleavage in *der Kern unseres Wesens*, has already successfully produced all that it can ever produce. As Rank had insisted in *The Trauma of Birth*, one should not confuse procreation with creation, biology with *psyche*, the natural with the supernatural—that which is "above" or "beyond" nature: art and culture (Rank 1924, pp. 141–66).

According to Jones and Abraham, however, the purpose of analysis is *erinnern*, to remember, not *agieren*, to act out the past in the transference or, as a reaction-formation, refuse to acknowledge the transference. Repetition is resistance. Short-term therapy and the "activity" now being recommended by Ferenczi and Rank, for both patient and therapist, sacrifices the gold of analysis to the copper of suggestion. *Erlbenis* therapy is "acting out"—resistance to the analyst's insight into the infantile father fixation. Although Freud had spoken enigmatically of repetition as a "way of remembering," (*S.E.*, 12:150), at bottom insight is the only solution. Only insight derived from the analyst's Oedipal interpretations promotes the resolution and dissolution of transference, the termination of mistaken love. Long-term research by the analyst into the archaic past is essential for the patient to work through, to bring to consciousness slowly, ever so slowly, the deeply repressed conflictual emotions of Oedipal infancy and then to be "re-educated" by the analyst to suppress them consciously. "The doctor tries to compel him to fit these emotional impulses into . . . his life-history," Freud had laid down firmly in his papers on technique, "to submit them to intellectual consideration" (*S.E.*, 12:108). Where emotion was, there intellect shall be. In the Vienna of the nineteen twenties, remembers Margaret Mahler, "it was anathema even to speak about analysis with emotion, much less to infuse one's therapeutic work with emotion" (Stepansky 1988, p. 81).

The analyst is neutral and detached, not an active participant. "A good analyst, an 'insider' analyst, could not show *any* emotion under *any* circumstances" (ibid., pp. 81–82; Mahler's italics). The patient knows nothing about the Oedipal source of his or her troubles and continuously resists knowing the truth. This unconscious resistance must be conquered. Therefore, a power imbalance between the two is required. The patient must accept the expert authority of the analyst, who is the final arbiter of whether or not patients' perceptions are real or based on transference, motes in the eye. According to Jones and Abraham, the analyst is a surgical researcher who helps "to fill in gaps in memory," as Freud had never tired of repeating (*S.E.*, 12:148). The hole or blank—the void—in the nucleus of the patient's amnesia is filled by the analyst's interpretations. "I have restored what is missing" (*S.E.*, 7:12), Freud wrote with relief in the case of Dora. Only after Dora fled *Berggasse* 19 did Freud realize that transference can itself be resistance to uncovering the hole in memory: "in such a case 'No' signifies the desired 'Yes'" (*S.E.*, 7:59). The subject of analysis is a failed reminiscence. Where concealment was, implied Freud, there speech shall be. "One must allow the patient time to become more conversant with the resistance that is *unbekannten* [unknown] to him, to *work through* it, to overcome it, by continuing, in defiance of it, the analytic work according to the fundamental rule of analysis" (*S.E.*, 12:155; his italics). The *Indifferenz*, passivity and anonymity of the analyst are necessary to avoid contamination of the transference, as well as for neutral and unbiased investigation of the patient's unconscious. Science demands strict objectivity and neutrality, insisted Jones and Abraham, not blind surrender to *Erlebnis*, or emotional experience, a euphemism for subjectivity. "Transference," said Franz Alexander in a harsh review of the book by Ferenczi and Rank, "*is* experience in analysis" (Alexander 1925, p. 487; his italics).

"The Blinding by One's Own Experiences"

Like the "primal horde" Freud had written about in *Totem and Taboo* (1913b), the Committee was tearing itself apart, and transference had become a battleground. A principal combatant, Ferenczi was deeply concerned that Freud not misunderstand the intent of *The Development of Psychoanalysis*, which scrupulously avoided criticizing anyone by name; on the contrary, it was meant to help other analysts remember that *empathy* or "tact" is of the essence in the therapeutic relationship (Haynal and Falzeder 1993b). "We did not depart by a hair's breath from psychoanalytic terrain," Ferenczi swore to Freud on January 24,

1924, and demanded absolution from the guilt laid at his and Rank's feet by Jones and Abraham (Grubich-Simitis 1986, p. 265). While kindly and forbearing, Freud's response edged one step closer to an unfavorable decision. "I would now judge [your joint book] as not having overcome its birth defect sufficiently," Freud warned Ferenczi on February 4, alluding to the defective birth trauma theory hiding, anonymously, inside the book by Ferenczi and Rank. "'*Erlebnis*' is used like a catchword, its resolution not stressed enough" (ibid., p. 267). Tact was certainly necessary in analysis, but where was *insight*?

Responding to a protest from Abraham, who seemed to have taken the critique of Ferenczi and Rank personally, Freud identified for the Committee the nature of its "cleavage," pointing out precisely where "Rank diverges from me." Refusing to see the preeminent role of the Oedipal father, Rank was claiming that the emotional ambivalence and castration *Angst* so ubiquitous in the patient's *Erlebnis* during the analytic sessions was connected, somehow, to residues of the mother-child relationship: "Basically the attitude toward the [mother] would be ambivalent from the start. *Here is the contradiction*," said Freud. "I find it very hard to decide here, nor do I see [*sehe auch nicht*] how experience [*Erfahrung*] can help us, since in analysis *we always come across the father* as representative of the prohibition. But naturally that is not an argument" (Wittenberger, 1995, pp. 286–88; italics added).

On the verge of handing down a judgment, yet reluctant to inflame either Ferenczi and Rank, his tender enfants terribles of active therapy, or Abraham and Jones, his steely paladins of classical analysis, Freud was in the dark. Although experience cannot help, and always coming across the castrating father in analysis is not an argument, Abraham, unlike Freud, found it easy to decide. On February 26 Abraham complained bitterly to Freud that Rank's birth trauma idea was "regression in the scientific field, the symptoms of which agree in every small detail with those of Jung's secession from psychoanalysis" (Abraham and Freud 1965, p. 350). At first Freud did not agree. "I would like to hear what the threatening danger might be," the Professor, now hearing-impaired from his operations, challenged the inner circle. "I do not see it" (Gay 1988, p. 474). From the beginning Freud had strongly encouraged Ferenczi and Rank to conduct their daredevil experiments with new techniques of therapy to conquer resistance. Virtually "fed up" (Dupont 1994, p. 313) with the frustrations of practicing therapy, Freud had for years fought like a lion, with little or no satisfaction, against his "negroes"[1]—patients who repeatedly refused to accept psychoanalytic insight, defiantly and self-destructively "clinging to the gain from illness" (*S.E.*, 19:49), keeping their dusky unconscious motives shrouded in darkness, using transference as resistance, *Widerstand*, rather than enlightenment.

On February 26 Freud wrote a melancholy note to Rank informing him that the pain in his mouth was getting worse: "In the last two weeks no progress has been made with the prosthesis." Added Freud forebodingly: "the situation gives us many things to consider" (Freud-Rank, February 26, 1924; RC). For fifteen more years, until his death by injection of morphine in 1939, Freud would agonize endlessly over his doctor's inability to construct a prosthesis that would fit, without overwhelming pain, into the increasingly gaping hole in his jaw. In *Civilization and Its Discontents* (1930), he projected his gigantic malaise onto "Man, [who] has, as it were," with the help of modern science and technology, "become a kind of prosthetic God. When he puts on all his auxiliary organs he is truly magnificent; but those organs have not grown on to him," observed Freud poignantly, "and they still give him much trouble at times" (*S.E.*, 21:91–92). Man today "does not feel happy in his Godlike character" (ibid.). "I" = "my prosthesis," Freud confirmed to Abraham, "and my hearing works on one side only" (Abraham and Freud 1965, p. 369).

On March 4, 1924, attempting to soothe a furious Abraham, his long-time *rocher de bronze*, Freud penned a diplomatic letter: "Let us assume the most extreme case, and suppose that Ferenczi and Rank came right out with the view that we were wrong to stop at the Oedipus complex. . . . Then, instead of our sexual etiology of neurosis, we should have an etiology determined by physiological chance. . . . Further, a number of analysts would make certain modifications in technique on the basis of this theory. What further evil consequences," wondered Freud, "would ensue?" (Abraham and Freud 1965, pp. 352–53). Never one to take his own technical prescriptions about maintaining a chilly *Indifferenz*, or "blank screen," too seriously, Freud could not see the evil, and although he emphasized to the Committee that he himself preferred to practice in the old-fashioned "classical" way, he was more than willing to tolerate experimentation with therapy—which all the combatants knew had long ceased to be of much interest for him. Patients "are disgusting," Freud told Ferenczi (Brabant, Falzeder, and Giampieri-Dentsch 1993, p. 85), riffraff, *Gesindel*, useful only for scientific research.

But the keen-eyed Abraham, who had smoked out Jung from his anti-Oedipal lair long before Freud was forced to recognize the malefactor, did see the evil—in the so-called emotional "experience" now being promoted, at the expense of dearly bought psychoanalytic insight, by Ferenczi and Rank. Subverting research into the infantile Oedipal past, *Erlebnis* therapy focused blindly on the here-and-now of the relationship between patient and analyst. But emotional experience is "repetition" and needs to be ruthlessly analyzed, kept firmly subordinate to the intellect, or *Einsicht*, what Freud had always equated with "remembering." To fill the void of memory, it is interpretation and only interpretation that the analyst provides the patient. For Abraham, the analytic relationship was at best a tool of scientific research, at worst a severe resistance to remembering, certainly not an agent of healing. Analysis requires the patient to learn how to divorce her "experiencing," or emotional, self from her "observing," or rational, self, and then, after the analysis is over, marry them again. All emotional experience, however disguised, is a derivative of the sex drive, the *Ur*-cause of neurosis. Unless corrected by the analyst's neutral interpretations, *Erlebnis* disturbs psychic equilibrium, violates Fechner's well-established constancy principle, and interferes with intellectual insight. It is the development of insight that cures the illness, based on the scientific principle that knowledge about the cause of the neurosis has healing power. Knowing is all.

To Ferenczi, then still Rank's best friend, Freud wrote wearily on March 20, 1924: "Last night, I had a long scientific discussion with Rank and confessed that I had made regress rather than progress in the evaluation of your joint book and of his birth trauma. . . . Rank is terribly blunt, he provokes people against him. . . . Now when he is preparing to go to America for half a year—certainly no secret to you—I am afraid that his health will not be up to the strains awaiting him there. . . . I know that what's lost is lost [*verloren ist verloren*]: I have survived the Committee that was supposed to have succeeded me. . . . I only hope that psychoanalysis will survive me" (Wittenberger 1995, p. 296). But even in the midst of this *Sturm und Drang* over the merits of science versus experience, intellectual insight versus emotional relationship, objectivity versus subjectivity, Freud remained deeply attached to Ferenczi and Rank, repeating over and over that he would let neither of them go, as long as they remained on the terrain of psychoanalysis. "My confidence in you and Rank," he reassured Ferenczi, "is unconditional" (ibid.). Yet Freud sensed that Rank, sadly, seemed to be suffering from "the blinding by one's own experiences [*Erfahrungen*]," pointedly resembling the blackguard Jung, with whom he did not want to compare Rank. "Jung was an evil fellow" (ibid.). Tragically, Rank was being blinded by his own clairvoyance. "Now he sees its consequences," added Freud (ibid.).

"He Openly Refuses the Whole"

On March 20, by coincidence, Rank also wrote to Ferenczi, relating the verbatim details of his "penetrating discussion" the night before with the Professor, who confessed that he had finished only half the book and was testing its therapeutic value by giving it to his patients to read: "In direct answer to my question, he openly refuses the whole [das Ganze ablehnt]," complained Rank to the friend already slipping away from him. "He now says that he no longer accepts as true even the few points that had impressed him in the beginning" (ibid, p. 300):

> To my question as to why he does not declare this publicly [to Jones and Abraham], he answers that his judgment should not be so final, he wants to discuss the objections and besides he thinks the applications to cultural adaptation are valuable and good. Asked how this can be brought into harmony with his refusal of the whole [der Ablehnung des Ganzen], his answer was evasive. . . .
>
> [A]lthough he stressed again and again that he will always remain friendly toward both of us, you can judge the resistance we can count on [from Jones and Abraham] if, as is unavoidable, they learn of his position or guess it. Faced with this situation, I am less than ever inclined to make any concessions, personal or scientific. (ibid., p. 301)

In their scientific discussions, Freud was vigorously resisting Rank's point of view that "all the child's *positive* and *negative* feelings [are] originally directed to the *mother*" [8-126] and only afterward are displaced onto siblings, father, or others. Where was Oedipus, the nucleus of the neurosis, in Rank's theory? Where was the powerful castrating *father*?)

By March 26, although retaining his unshakable affection for Rank's person, Freud made clear to Ferenczi that he had turned decisively against Rank's theory which, he now suspected, was an unconscious flight from the Oedipus—the cause of the neurosis: "He says nowhere, expressly I think, that he wants to replace the cause of the Oedipus complex with the trauma of birth but everyone surmises it," Freud confided to Ferenczi. "Here is the strong contradiction" (Wittenberger 1995, p. 312). With the assistance of the ever-vigilant Abraham, Freud had been forced to see, finally, that Rank's theory implicated fear of the mother over fear of the father in the etiology of neurosis—and thus was a blatant denial of the Oedipus complex. Swept away by the *furor sanandi*, the baneful rage to help, Rank had unwittingly left the terrain of the cause. "This need to help is lacking in me," Freud divulged to Ferenczi in 1910, "because I did not lose anyone whom I loved in my early years" (Brabant, Falzeder, and Giampieri-Deutsch 1993, p. 122). Now, in the wake of *The Trauma of Birth*, a misconceived child of Rank's hyperactive imagination, "I cannot absolve Rank from a certain tragic guilt for the reception of his findings" (Wittenberger 1995, p. 312), judged Freud, fed up with the Committee's relentless finger-pointing. "But I am ready, of course, to learn through experience [*Erfahrung*], my own or by others, as in general all my judgments are only provisory" (ibid., p. 313). Terrified at the prospect of losing Freud's love, Ferenczi promptly aborted his own enthusiasm for *The Trauma of Birth* and began to distance himself personally from Rank—whom he shunned during a chance meeting in 1926 at Penn Station in New York. "He was my best friend and he refused to speak to me," Rank said (Taft, 1958, p. xvi).

"An Intellectual Prosthesis"

On April 27, 1924, having just turned 40, Otto Rank sailed for New York harbor to deliver his long-awaited American lectures. Spokesman for Freud, yet recognized internationally as an authority in his own right, Rank had come to the United States to promote psychoanalysis. "We all flocked to him," remembers Abram Kardiner, a pioneer New York analyst. "He had a method to cut down neurosis at the main trunk instead of picking at leaves and twigs . . . the most extraordinary catalytic agent that ever hit the psychoanalytic movement" (Lieberman 1985, pp. 234–35). Addressing large groups of psychiatrists and social workers, Rank modeled his talks after the Clark University lectures that Freud had delivered so masterfully in 1909. "Give my regards to all the squirrels and also feed them peanuts in my name," Freud joked in his first trans-Atlantic letter to Rank, mocking the squirrelly Americans like Kardiner, whose training analyses with him in Vienna he recalled with little satisfaction. "The real zoo to be visited is in the Bronx" (Clark 1980, p. 453).

As Freud had before him, Rank promised a glowing future for psychoanalysis in the United States, if only American therapists were to adopt, after, of course, having tested in practice, "this new point of view, which I introduced into analysis" [2-71]: the trauma of birth. Once he even referred, roguishly, to Freud himself as the "tender and loving foster mother" of psychoanalysis—which Rank characterized, tongue-in-cheek, as an "illegitimate child" [1-51]. Frightened away by the emotional volatility of transference, Dr. Josef Breuer had kept the birth of this child secret, but Freud tenderly "reared the neglected and misunderstood being," joked Rank. "It is now full grown and self-reliant [and] leaves behind it a very interesting past" [1-52]. *An illegitimate child?* What a strange metaphor for psychoanalysis!

Rank was sharply aware, of course, as Jones later revealed, that there was "much reason to suppose that in [Freud's] unconscious his work in psychoanalysis ultimately represented some product of his body, i.e., a child. We were," all the Committee members had vowed secretly in 1913, "trustees for that child" (Jones 1957, p. 44). Sole creator of psychoanalysis, Freud considered himself father and mother to his beloved "problem child, my life's work" (E. Freud 1960, p. 324), as he called the cause in a letter to Ferenczi, one of his *angenommene kinder*, "adopted children" (Grosskurth 1991, p. 52). "I dare say," Freud confided to Jones in 1913, "it would make living and dying easier for me if I knew of such an association existing to watch over my creation" (Paskauskas 1993, p. 148). Like psychoanalysis and all the Committee members, Rank, too, was Freud's adopted child, an especial favorite along with Ferenczi: "If anyone of us is getting rich," Freud often advised Jones, "it will be his duty to provide for [Rank]" (ibid., p. 202).

Naturally, in his 1924 lectures, the now full-grown and self-reliant Rank was also promoting his own "point of view," not just Freud's, whose magnum opus, the Oedipus complex, while a magnificent discovery, needed buttressing by Rank's new birth trauma theory, a contribution to normalizing Freudian psychology, at best one of its pillars. "I would prefer that you listen," he told members of the American Psychoanalytic Association, paraphrasing a famous line from *Hamlet*, "as if a traveler were relating to you his experiences in a yet undiscovered country" [3-78]. The birth trauma went one step "*beyond* the sexual conception of the Oedipus complex" [2-69]; it had undergone "a much stronger repression than even manifestations of infantile sexuality" [3-80]. At once staunch spokesman for Freud and iconoclastic theorist, Rank was Freudian and post-Freudian—a psychoanalytic miscegenation that no doubt perplexed many of his listeners. Perhaps nothing could have been more confusing to an orthodox Freudian in Rank's audience than to hear Rank profess, almost casually, just after taking great pains to laud "the Oedipus complex" as the "kernel" of the cause, "It is, therefore, rather difficult to see what repression tendency should have prevented us from recognizing [the mother-child relationship] immediately in analysis as the deepest root of the phenomenon of transference" [2-70].

One day, out of Rank's mouth suddenly came the most bizarre metaphor of all: psychoanalytic truth is constructed artificially like an "intellectual prosthesis" [4-92]. The first in the inner circle to learn of Freud's terrifying condition, Rank had long anguished over the deadly cancer eating away at the Professor's oral cavity. Yet amazingly, in an aside, Rank praised "psychoanalytic enlightenment" to his American audience as "an artificial support to consciousness—an intellectual prosthesis, so to speak—in the fight against [the neurotic's] too powerful unconscious" [4-92]. *An intellectual prosthesis?* At the precise moment Rank uttered these astonishing words, he knew full well that Freud's "monster" was being removed and refitted, agonizingly, every few days. Covering an open wound that would never heal, the prosthesis was "an uninvited, unwelcome intruder" (Romm 1983, p. 33), a vengeful, half-tamed *daemon* that had come, murderously, to inhabit a mouth of hell in the fight against someone's too-powerful trauma of castration.

"The Ubiquity of the 'Castration Complex'"

Freud, of course, never underestimated the *biological* trauma of birth, an idea he expressed as early as 1908, after a talk by Rank himself at the Vienna Psychoanalytic Society on the myth of the birth of the hero. Summarizing Freud's view in the minutes of this meeting, Rank, who was then secretary of the society, noted laconically, "act of birth as a source of *Angst*" (Numberg and Federn 1967, pp. 71–72). In an obscure footnote added to his Dreambook in 1909, Freud wrote that the "*act of birth is the first Angsterlebnis* [experience of anxiety], *and thus the source and prototype of the affect of anxiety*" (*S.E.*, 5:400–401; his italics). It was this footnote, "an incidental reference of Freud's" [8-116], as Rank later explained to his American audience, that had inspired him to write *The Trauma of Birth* in the first place.

But Freud wanted to confine this trauma to *physiological* anxiety, the potential for "suffocation [that] inevitably brings the infant into mortal peril" (Jones 1957, p. 58). He strongly opposed Rank's new idea that the anxiety of separation at birth is *psychological*—i.e., that *Angst* is psychically anchored (Rank 1924, p. 216) in the *infans* (Sachs 1925). For Freud the *infans* is always "shut off from the stimuli of the external world" (*S.E.*, 12:220) like an unhatched chick floating, blissfully, in the shell of its egg, with no relationship to its mother other than the need for oral or sexual gratification, in a condition of "primary narcissism." Yet even in *Das Ich und das Es*, Freud once again mentioned the birth trauma—*dem ersten großen Angstzustand der Geburt*—"the first great anxiety–state of birth" (*S.E.*, 19:58). What, then, was Rank's heresy?

The problem was the *Über-Ich*. In Rank's view the small boy relates emotionally to his mother virtually from birth not only as the first "good" object but also as the first "bad"—or dangerous—object. For Freud, on the other hand, it is the powerful father who threatens the small boy, and his mother is dangerous only because she is a desired but paternally prohibited sex object. Freud's systematic self-analysis in the late-1890s had produced a brilliant and coherent narrative about the fear of paternal power. "It is hard for us nowadays to imagine how momentous this achievement was," writes Jones of Freud's unprecedented and never-to-be-repeated exploration of the dark continent of his unconscious. "An overpowering need to come at the truth at all costs was probably the deepest and strongest motive force in Freud's personality, one to which everything else—ease, success, happiness—must be sacrificed" (Jones 1953, pp. 319–20). While modest about his ability to relieve the suffering of his unfortunate "negroes," Freud was a brave new Oedipus, wrestling mightily with, and almost conquering, "those half-tamed *daemons* that inhabit the human breast" (*S.E.*, 7:109), the infantile residues of the Oedipus complex. "I am in a co-coon [*Puppenhülle*]," Freud announced to Fliess in 1897, just before giving birth to the Oedipus complex, "and God knows what sort of beast will crawl out" (Masson 1985, p. 254).

In *Totem and Taboo*, Freud held that the Oedipus complex is inherited phylogenetically from the prehistoric time of the murderous "primal horde," perhaps even from the Ice Age (Freud 1987). While writing *Totem and Taboo* in 1911, Freud told Jung, "For some weeks I have been pregnant with a larger synthesis, and hope to be delivered of it this summer" (McGuire 1974, p. 391). At the same time, Freud revealed to Ferenczi, "I am tormented by the secret of tragic guilt, which will certainly not resist [psychoanalysis]" (Brabant, Falzeder and Giampieri-Deutsch 1993, p. 281). But what, exactly, was the nature of the tragic guilt that so tormented Freud while giving birth to *Totem and Taboo* and secretly continued to torment him forever? And in whose "breast" did the half-tamed *daemon* reside?

The first "bad" object to be internalized in the small boy's psyche is, of course, the *Über-Ich*, the superego—the guilt-ridden "heir" to the Oedipus complex. "We are in possession of the truth," Freud rejoiced to Ferenczi in 1913; "I am as sure of that as I was fifteen years ago" (ibid., p. 483), when, during the height of his painful self-analysis, he had discovered the *Kern* of the castrating Oedipal father in the unconscious. In 1918 Freud wrote that the Wolf Man's father was "his first and most primitive object-choice, which, in conformity with a small child's narcissism, had taken place along the path of identification" (*S.E.*, 17:27). Where the small boy's "own experience [*Erleben*] fails him," averred Freud, "he fills in the gaps in individual truth" with phylogenesis, "prehistoric truth," and thereby "replaces occurrences in his own life" (*S.E.*, 17:97). More precisely, said Freud in his *Introductory Lectures*, the small boy "reaches beyond his own experience [*Erleben*] into primaeval experience [*Erleben*] at points where his own experience [*Erleben*] has been too rudimentary" (*S.E.*, 16:371). Transporting himself back into the Ice Age, the small boy can always find the primaeval castrating *Vater*, whether or not his real-life father ever threatens to castrate him. Curiously, at no time did Freud consider the rudimentary mother herself to be a bar, or prohibition, against the incestuous desires of her small boy. The "sexual life of women," according to Freud, is a *"dark continent"* (*S.E.*, 20:212; his italics).

The fear of paternal castration puts an end, Freud believed, to the small boy's incestuous wishes at about age 2 to 5. "The *Über-Ich* arises, as we know, from an identification with the father taken as a model," concluded Freud in *The Ego and the Id* (*S.E.*, 19:54). "The superior being, which turned into the ego ideal, once threatened castration, and this dread of castration is probably the *Kern* round which the subsequent fear of conscience has gathered" (*S.E.*, 19:57). This, then, was the *Kernkomplex* of the neurosis: the castration complex. Every person, said Freud, is an Oedipus "in germ," *im Keime*, "a budding Oedipus" (Masson 1985, p. 272).

In *The Trauma of Birth*, however, Rank explicitly renounced Freud's phylogenetic theory of the "inheritance" of the Oedipus complex (Rank 1924, p. 195) as the bar against incest, the return to the mother. There is no scientific basis, according to Rank, to claim that phylogenesis will "fill in" the *Erlebnis* of "individual truth." Experience contains its own truth. The small boy does not have to reach too far beyond his own *Erlebnis* to discover a unique, gigantic and, at times, hostile entity right in front of his eyes. For the *infans*—boy or girl—the mother represents not only the first "good," loving object, but due to separation from the amniotic "Paradise," she is also experienced as the first "bad" object, a status she confirms repeatedly during breast feeding, weaning, and sphincter training. Fear of the mother, fear attached at birth to the mother's genitals and breasts, perhaps even to her powerful sexuality, takes precedence over fear of the castrating father as the prototype of *Angst*. This anxiety is reproduced, to some extent, whenever the male libido approaches the boundary of the primal state—i.e., the intra-uterine condition. According to Rank, *Angst* is psychically anchored (ibid., p. 216) in the *infans* as a bar to prevent fixation to its mother, which, while offering the illusion of a lifetime free of ambivalence, is, in reality, an idealized but oceanic death—keeping the small boy from ever docking in the neurotic harbor of his Oedipus complex, and taking on the Oedipal role vital for the conduct of mature relationships.

For Rank, the boy's mother is loved and feared, desired and hated, displacing his father to a secondary, but obviously still crucial, position in the intrapsychic world of the *infans*. In short, Rank had recast "the ubiquity of the 'castration complex'" (Rank 1924, p. 20) in terms of the small boy's fearful discovery of, and ambivalence about separating from, the powerful *Urmutter*—not in terms of his fear of the castrating father. The *infans* begins life with a sense of *primal ambivalence* (ibid., p. 199) toward the "lost primal object, the mother" (ibid., p. 205). A main task of therapy, therefore, is to free the adult neurotic, a failed reminiscence, from his unconscious and conflicted attachment—an unspeakable fusion of love, hate, and dread—to the powerful pre-Oedipal mother *Imago*.

"Analytically expressed," Rank emphasized at the end of *The Trauma of Birth*, "this is the phase *before* the development of the Oedipus complex" (ibid., p. 216; his italics). And in his 1924 American lectures, Rank continued to assert that the *Angst* of the neurotic can only be relieved "simultaneously with freeing of the unconscious mother fixation" [2-71]—that is, simultaneously with separation from the shadowy mother *Imago*, a denizen of the dark continent called mind, the painful residue of the weightiest of all attachments, the lost mother-child relationship: *das Trauma der Geburt*.

"Closing the Eyes"

In July 1924 the struggle between Freud, an indefatigable searcher after truth, and Rank came to a head: "I have seen nothing [*nichts gesehen*] in two of my cases that have been completed that confirms your views and generally nothing [*nichts*] that I did not know before," Freud wrote to Rank, still in New York on his successful lecture tour; "I am often much concerned about you. The exclusion of the father in your theory," Freud counseled his young protégé, "seems to reveal too much the result of personal influences in your life, which I think I recognize, and my suspicion grows that you would not have written this book had you gone through an analysis yourself. Therefore I beg of you not to become fixed but to leave open a way back" (Taft 1958, p. 99). If only Rank had been analyzed, his father fixation could have been dissolved through psychoanalytic enlightenment, instead of being deposited in his theory. Psychoanalytic treatment, Freud had insisted from the beginning of his self-analysis, is "founded on truthfulness" [*S.E.*, 12:164], ripping away all veils, facing the darkest truths of the soul, fearlessly and brutally filling in all the gaps of memory. "Turn your eyes inward," he demanded of his patients, "look into your own depths, learn first to know yourself" (*S.E.*, 17:143). Insight is all.

In New York Rank drafted four different responses. What could he say to Freud's ad hominem attack? "I sense the futility of any scientific or personal discussion," he typed in one of the three drafts that he decided *not* to send:

> You strongly resist [*sie haben den staerksten Widerstand*] not only accepting but even merely seeing fundamental facts that will, one day, constitute the analyst's basic A-B-C. You recommend that I leave open a way back,

which is precisely what I cannot comprehend. Do you really want to arrest psychoanalysis, or spiritual development, at a fixed point? . . . You alone determine what sacrifices you are willing to make for the sake of the cause. After my experiences [*Erfahrungen*] with the blessed Committee, I want nothing more [*nicht mehr*] to do with it, since I am convinced that, in the end, no sacrifice is worth cobbling together a lost cause [*verlorene Sache*]. . . . I do not have the slightest ambition to retain any official position in the cause if fate has made it necessary, or even merely desirable, for me to resign. Should this happen, and I am prepared for it, I will go on living peacefully, and without rancor, as a simple private citizen. (Rank 1994, pp. 58–59)

Rank minced no words in the letter he did send, which was even stronger than any of the drafts he rejected. "The fact is," he began carefully, "I have undergone the same experiences as you" (Taft 1958, p. 100). In his intensive analytical work, Rank was finding "day by day and hour by hour nothing [*nichts*] but confirmations and even additions to my point of view" (ibid.) The U.S. therapists whom Freud had analyzed in Vienna [e.g., Kardiner 1977] were reporting privately to him that they had been deeply disappointed by the analysis: "They lost nothing [*nicht*] of their neuroses" (ibid.). Applying the classical technique learned from their training analysis, "they were unable to cure [*nicht heilen*] their own patients" (ibid.) Was Freud suggesting that Rank needed an Oedipal analysis because of his new "point of view"? If so, Rank had seen many analysts in the United States and Europe whose father fixation had been "analyzed" unceasingly, but he was not impressed by their enlightened condition. "After all that I have seen [*gesehen*] of results with analyzed analysts," Rank informed Freud with robust candor, "I can only call it fortunate" (ibid., p. 101). Even self-analysis, hinted Rank in a searing metaphor, may result in "closing the eyes [*Schliessen der Augen*]" to the truth (ibid.). Almost certainly Rank was alluding to a now-famous dream Freud once recorded in *The Interpretation of Dreams*, a book that Rank had helped Freud revise, word by word, for every edition since 1911: "You are requested to close the eyes"—or at least "to close an eye"—Freud dreamed at the time of his father's funeral (*S.E.*, 4:317). Marking "a turning point in Freud's inner life," according to Didier Anzieu, a leading modern scholar of Freud's self-analysis, "[this dream] was responsible for his getting the idea of carrying out a self-analysis and writing a book on dreams" (Anzieu 1986, p. 169).

Minting a phrase that would shortly appear as the title of one of his most important books, Rank now made plain to Freud, the Seer of the Infernal Regions, that nothing less than "truth and reality [*Wahrheit und Wirklichkeit*]" was at stake in their dispute:

When [American] analysts saw [*gesehen*] that they could work more easily with modifications introduced by me and get better results—with their patients as well as their own analyses—they praised me like a savior. I am not so blinded [*Ich bin nicht so verblendet*] as not to subtract a good part from these successes as complex-conditioned, but what remains is a bit of truth and reality that one cannot remove from this world by closing the eyes. I have the strong impression that you will not or cannot see certain things [*dass Sie gewisse Dinge nicht sehen wollen oder sehen koennen*]. Sometimes your objections sound as if you had read or heard absolutely nothing [*haetten Sie gar nicht gelesen oder gehoert*] about what I really said. . . .

Again now you say that I have excluded the father; naturally that is not the case and absolutely cannot be [*kann gar nicht sein*], it would be nonsense. I have only attempted to give him the correct place. . . . I am, for example, strongly convinced that you have no idea how I use psychoanalytic technique. Actually I have taken absolutely nothing [*gar nichts*] from it—I have only added something, which I truly think is very important and which others already consider essential for their understanding of cases. (Taft 1958, pp. 101–2).

The psychoanalytic cause is itself "a fiction," added Rank acidly, "but men who make a movement are no fiction, and for those who are now eager to work at a psychoanalytic movement, I confess, I have no liking" (ibid., p. 103). Rank had taken *nichts* from psychoanalysis. He had only added something. But whatever he took from, or added to, psychoanalysis, *die Sache* was a fiction—a lost cause.

There can be no doubt that this letter was a declaration of independence, pure and simple, but Rank, on the basis of his continuing affection for "dear Professor," ended with a respectful "I was very glad to hear that you are satisfied with your [postoperation] condition." Sending "best regards to your family and cordial greetings to you," he signed it: "Your devoted Rank" (ibid.). Earlier in the letter, however, a bit less devotedly, Rank reminded Freud that "the *Angst* basic" to neurosis is tied originally to the mother and "was transferred to the father only secondarily" (ibid., p. 100).

"The Whole Subject Is Shrouded in Darkness"

Still hoping to return Rank to his senses, Freud sent a letter to New York that crossed in the mail with Rank's August 9 letter: "I know you are not lacking acclaim for your innovation, but consider how few are able to judge and how strong the desire is in most of them to get away from the Oedipus wherever a path seems open" (Taft 1958, p. 105).

When he received Rank's declaration of independence, which arrived the next day, Freud was pained. What had he, Oedipus at Colonus, done to deserve these wild accusations of impaired vision? Pointing out his different view of the matter, Freud nevertheless reiterated his personal attachment to Rank, whom he sincerely did not want to lose:

> My observation has, as yet, not permitted me to make a decision, but up to now has furnished nothing [*nichts*] that would correspond to your interpretation. . . . Your experiences [*Erfahrungen*] are different; do they therefore cancel mine? We both know that experiences [*Erfahrungen*] permit of many explanations, hence we have to wait for further ones. . . . The whole subject [*dem Ganzen Thema*] is shrouded in darkness that I have, as yet, not succeeded in penetrating. Your book has brought it out and has done nothing [*nichts*] to shed light on it. Your treatment of *Angst* seems full of contradictions. . . . Something does not fit here [*Irgend etwas stimmt da nicht*]. . . . But I cannot, as yet, see clearly in this matter [*Aber ich sehe da noch nicht klar*]. . . . An evil *daemon* makes you say that the psychoanalytic movement is a "fiction" and puts in your mouth the very words of the enemy. An abstract cause [*Eine abstrakte Sache*] can be real, too, and is not therefore a "fiction."
>
> Had my [cancer] progressed further it would have saved you a decision [to resign] . . . hardly a comfort that I cannot discover [*nicht entdecken kann*] my own share of the guilt. My feelings toward you have been shaken by nothing [*nichts*]. I cannot, as yet, give up hope that you will return to a better knowledge of yourself. (Taft 1958, pp. 105–8)

Searching his breast, Freud was unable to find the secret of the tragic guilt that was oppressing him. Something did not fit. An evil *daemon* was putting lies, not truth, in Rank's mouth. Harping incessantly on *Erlebnis*—as if emotional experience could ever take the place of insight into the Oedipus complex—Rank now seemed "shattered and offended that I refuse [*ablehnend*] your *Trauma of Birth*" (ibid.). But all this "is still dark and undecided" (ibid.).

Part of the blame for Rank's confused mental condition, Freud felt, was due to the hostility of Ernest Jones and Karl Abraham. "The animosity [Rank] partly had experienced from you and [Abraham] and partly imagined," Freud complained to Jones in September 1924, "had a disturbing effect on his mind, but why his mood should have turned against myself I do not understand" (Paskauskas 1993, p. 553). In self-defense, Jones pointed out that Rank's "manifest neurosis," visible to him as early as 1913, had now "gradually returned in the form of a neurotic character," a "denial of the Oedipus complex" and "a regression of the hostility from the brother (myself) . . . to the father" (ibid., p. 555)—evidently Freud, the father *Imago*. In October 1924, without "a trace of hostility towards Rank," Abraham wrote to Freud diagnosing Rank's neurosis as "an undeniable regression to the anal-sadistic phase" (Abraham and Freud 1965, p. 373).

In November 1924, still wavering on the problem of Rank, Freud received a devastating letter from A. A. Brill that "reported in lurid terms the extraordinary doctrines," according to Jones, "which Rank had been inculcating in New York and the confusion he had thereby created" (Jones 1957, p. 71). By early 1925 Rank was back in the United States, lecturing again on his lurid doctrines. At a January 1925 seminar for the New York Psychoanalytic Society, attended by Brill, Rank insisted, "The only real new viewpoint in [my] contribution [is] the concept of the pre-Oedipus level" (Rank 1925).[2]

In the spring of 1925, while still in New York, Rank began drafting a manuscript called *Grundzüge einer Genetischen Psychologie* (Fundamentals of a Genetic Psychology). By "genetic" Rank meant object-relational and developmental. "However disconcerting it may be that the founder of psychoanalysis, from whom nevertheless my idea grew, has taken such a bitter attitude toward my contribution," explained Rank in the foreword, "it has not disillusioned me or prevented me from continuing my work" (Rank 1927, p. iii).

As reports of Rank's intransigence filtered back to Vienna from the ubiquitous Brill in New York—comparing Rank to the despised Jung, who had also gone to the United States after abandoning Freud—it became clear to Freud that Rank's Oedipus complex was, indeed, not resolvable after all. No matter how genuinely conciliatory and forgiving Freud was, Rank refused to return to a better knowledge of himself, shocking Freud by recanting the "Oedipal" guilt and "brother complex" to which he confessed during an emotionally wrenching "semi-analytic interview" (Jones 1957, p. 73), an *Erlebnis* therapy of sorts, with the Professor in late 1924 and in a transparently artful letter to the Committee "asking for our forgiveness" (ibid., p. 74). "Naturally," reports Jones, with the charity toward enemies that was so characteristic of him, "we all replied reassuring him of our understanding and sympathy" (ibid.). In a confidential letter to Abraham, however, Jones was not so understanding: Rank's confession was mere "*intellectual* insight" (Gay 1988, p. 479; Jones's italics). Validating Jones's suspicions, one historian judges, "It would be sheer blindness to overlook [Rank's] earlier neurotic behavior, and expect the complete restoration of the old Rank" (ibid.). Soon, no one, not even the ever-trusting Freud, would be blinded by Rank's clairvoyance. The "incision" between father and son, as Anna Freud described the Rank affair to Lou Andreas Salomé (Pfeiffer 1985, p. 234), was now permanent, an open wound that would never heal. It was a lost cause: the ship of psychoanalysis was sinking into the ocean—or the oceanic feeling. "It is really a case of the rat," said the Captain of *die Sache*, with his usual mix of confidence and resignation, "leaving the sinking ship" (ibid., p. 143).

"The Theory in Which He Had Deposited His Neurosis"

In the summer of 1905, responding to the brash 21-year old poet and writer who had sent him a forty-eight page manuscript entitled *Der Künstler*, a theory of creativity that used the word *artist* in as comprehensive a sense as psychoanalysis used the word *sexuality*, Freud had written: "If under different circumstances a young writer has sent a manuscript to an older one and the latter has not answered for a while, then a bourgeois tragedy usually develops between the two that usually ends with a discord. Such is probably not the case between myself and Mr. O. Rank" (Freud to Rank, August 25, 1905).[3] An unreconstructed "nemesis of concealment, hypocrisy, [and] the polite evasions of bourgeois society" (Gay 1988, p. xvii), Freud somehow all along had known in his unconscious that "a bourgeois tragedy"—could there be anything more bourgeois than a conflict about who takes priority, mother or father?—was fated to unfold between him and Rank, ending in discord. Even Rank's unconscious may have suspected something. On the title page of *The Artist*, Rank had inscribed a cryptic epigraph (in English) from Shakespeare's *All's Well That Ends Well*: "Is it possible, he should *know* what he is, and *be* that he is?" (Rank 1907, epigraph; italics added).

In April 1926, shortly before Freud's seventieth birthday, Rank paid a farewell call to *Berggasse* 19. Voluntarily affirming his fate, Rank had already resigned in protest from his powerful posts as vice-president of the Vienna Psychoanalytic Society, director of the *Verlag*, and editor of *Imago* and *Zeitschrift*, the two leading analytic journals. From Paris, where Rank was establishing a new practice—with plans later in 1926 to lecture yet again in the United States on his lurid pre-Oedipal theory—he sent another literary gift for Freud's birthday: a 23-volume edition of Nietzsche, bound in expensive white leather (Lieberman 1985, p. 259). The gift pointed to the intellectual debt each owed to Nietzsche, the great precursor of psychoanalysis, whose originality was recognized but never fully acknowledged by Freud. In a harsh letter to Ferenczi, Freud recounted his final interview with the wayward protégé, now almost forty-two: "Two facts were unambiguous: that he was unwilling to renounce any part of *the theory in which he had deposited his neurosis*; and that he did not take the slightest step to approach the [Vienna Psychoanalytic] Society here. I do not belong to those who demand that anyone should be chained and sell themselves forever out of 'gratitude.'. . . So quits! On his final visit I saw no occasion for expressing my special tenderness; I was honest and hard. But he is gone now and we have to bury him. Abraham has proved right" (ibid., p. 260; italics added).

Why should anyone keep Rank "chained" to Freud, the tender and loving foster mother of the cause? "I cannot do it differently [*Ich kann es aber nicht anders*]" (Taft 1958, p. 106), Rank had informed Freud in March 1924. So quits! The day after Rank's final visit, Freud was forced to concede to Eitingon: "I confess I was very deceived in my prognosis of the case—a repetition of fate" (Jones 1957, p. 76). Due to the repetition compulsion, Rank had suffered a breakdown. Rank's mental illness "revealed" itself, according to Jones, "in, among other ways, a turning away from Freud and his doctrines. The seeds of a destructive psychosis, invisible for so long, at last germinated" (ibid., p. 45). The *germ* of cleavage had grown into madness. "Once the most orthodox of Freudians," reports one historian uncomprehendingly, "he became a Rankian" (Gay 1988, p. 471). Against the will of Freud, Rank had chosen to become himself. For this heresy Freud called Rank a *Hochstaplernatur*, an "imposter by nature" (ibid.). "I can't get indignant about Rank," Freud pronounced curtly to Eitingon in June 1926. "Let him err and be original" (Jones 1957, p. 77). Did Rank err? If so, in what way was his error original?

"The Motherland"

From 1926 through 1934, Otto Rank lived and worked in Paris, treating artists such as Anaïs Nin and Henry Miller, and made frequent trips to the United States to lecture and supplement his practice. In late 1926 Rank delivered a series of English lectures in New York, based on his forthcoming work, *Grundzüge einer Genetischen Psychologie*. "This book," Rank wrote in the very first sentence, "is a direct continuation, development, and extension of my new vision in psychoanalytic theory and therapy" (Rank 1927, p. iii). A few paragraphs later, he added "I have now again . . . come up against the [mother] and the object relationship, which just as much presupposes *Angst* as libido" (ibid., p. v).

In his first 1926 lecture, "Foundations of a Genetic Psychology," Rank criticized Freud for being unable to "see" behind the Oedipus situation to the "primal object relationship," for repressing the role of the powerful *castrating mother* in the infant's development, and splitting off his hatred or fear onto women in general: "[Freud] sees in the mother merely the coveted sex object, for the possession of which the child battles with the father. *The 'bad mother' he has never seen, but only the later displacement of her to the father, who therefore plays such an omnipotent part in his theory.* The image of the bad mother, however, is present in Freud's estimation of woman, who is merely a passive and inferior object for him: in other words, 'castrated'" [5-101]. Considering the mother "merely the coveted sex object," implied Rank, was less threatening to Freud than seeing the profound emotional ambivalence—rage, tenderness, desire, love, and hate—on *both* sides of the mother-son relationship. In his 1915 essay on "Instincts and Their Vicissitudes," Freud had concluded that "Hate, as a relation to objects, is older than love. It derives from the narcissistic ego's primordial repudiation of the external world with its outpouring of stimuli" (*S.E.*, 14:139). In *Civilization and Its Discontents* (1930), Freud laid down that aggression "forms the basis of every relation of affection and love among people (with the single exception, perhaps, of the mother's relation to her male child)" (*S.E.*, 21:113). As late as 1933, in his *New Introductory Lectures*, Freud spoke of the outpouring of stimuli from the mother to her son as "altogether the most perfect, the most free from ambivalence of all human relationships" (*S.E.*, 22:133). For some reason the universal law of hostility, the hate that precedes love, was canceled in the single case of the mutual love affair—the inseparable bond—between mother and son. Unaccountably, the narcissistic ego had forgotten "its primordial repudiation of the external world," the motherland.

The neurosis, Freud once told Ferenczi, "is the motherland where we first have to secure our mastery against everything and everyone" (Brabant, Falzeder and Giampieri-Deutsch 1933, p. 247). Yet throughout the *Standard Edition*, the powerful or "bad" mother is Freud's "unthought known" (Bollas 1987), a ghostly phantom, invisible and unthinkable, but ever present between the sheets of his text. "Be it Dora's madly cleaning mother, Little Hans's beautiful seductive mother, or the Rat Man's absentee mother, they all appear as silhouettes against the rich background of other relationships, other entanglements" (Erlich 1977, p. 284). Perhaps the "spectral mother," as Madelon Sprengnether (1990) calls her—and not the "Project for a Scientific Psychology"—is the "invisible ghost" that, James Strachey suggests, "haunts the whole series of Freud's theoretical writings to the very end" (Strachey 1966, p. 290).

Of course, traces of Freud's unconscious are scattered everywhere in the body of his writings, and they leak out, like an open wound, through cracks in his "inhibited, anxious, and symptomatic text, which betrays in its structure the simultaneous fascination and dread that characterizes Freud's most consistent stance in relation to preoedipal issues" (Sprengnether 1990, p. 138). It is a psychoanalytic truism that no mortal writer can keep secrets and, thus, for anyone who "has eyes to see" (*S.E.*, 7:77), betrayal oozes out of Freud's pen in every fractured sentence composed by his unconscious and witty collaborator, "Itzig, the Sunday rider" (Masson 1985, p. 319), Freud's uncanniest *Doppelgänger*, but the mountain of wordy evidence is hidden, like *The Purloined Letter*, right under the reader's nose. "My own approach," says Patrick Mahony, "presumes that Freud's texts, like crystals, have fault lines, and I wonder where they are and how wittingly as well as unwittingly they are covered up" (1989, p. 94). Just before Freud published his Dreambook, for example, Itzig, a Master of Irony, mapped for Fliess's benefit the itinerary for the conquistador's descent into Virgil's Infernal Regions, revealing that "the whole" was far more important than the parts: "The whole thing [*das Ganze*] is planned on the model of an imaginary walk. At the beginning, the dark forest of authors (who do not see [*nicht sehen*] the trees), hopelessly lost on wrong tracks. Then a concealed pass through which I lead the reader—my specimen dream with its peculiarities, details, indiscretions, bad jokes—and then suddenly the high ground and the view and the question: which way do you wish to go now?" (Masson 1985, p. 365). "It is true I am cleverer than all the coxcombs," joked Itzig to Fliess, his friend who was a nose doctor. "I lead my people around by the nose and see that we can know *nicht*" (ibid., p. 329). Said Freud: "I did not start a single paragraph [of the Dreambook] knowing where I would end up" (ibid., p. 319). A concealed pass through the dark forest, best read as a comical performance (Welsh 1994), structured impressively like a language (Lacan 1977), *The Interpretation of Dreams* is at once a maternal return and an open refusal of the whole. Pregnant with metaphors such as "dark woods, narrow defiles, high grounds and deep penetrations," the Dreambook reveals unmistakably in its sexual imagery that "we are exploring a woman's body," according to Stanley Edgar Hyman, "that of Freud's mother" (Hyman 1962, p. 333). Chuckled Itzig in a letter to Fliess: "Most readers will get lost in this thorny thicket and never get to see the Sleeping Beauty behind it" (Masson 1985, p. 362).

"It Becomes Impossible to Shut One's Eyes Any Longer ... "

A regular visitor to *Berggasse* 19 for two decades, Otto Rank had come to meet and know all of Freud's immediate family, including Amalia Freud, the *Urmutter* of the cause. Surprisingly, however, Rank never analyzed the motives for Freud's lifelong amnesia regarding his conflicted attachment to the first "good" and "bad" object—for why "there is no evidence that Freud's systematic self-scrutiny touched on this weightiest of attachments, or that he ever explored, and tried to exorcise, his mother's power over him" (Gay 1988, p. 505). *Systematic?*[4]

During the late 1890s, according to Peter Gay, a faithful servant of historical veracity, Freud "subjected himself to a most thoroughgoing self-scrutiny, an elaborate, penetrating, and unceasing census of his fragmentary memories, his concealed wishes and emotions" (ibid., p. 97). Sifting through this mountainous collection of concealed emotions, Freud persevered in his census every night in order to construct, grain by grain, with painstaking precision, the scientific edifice of human nature. "Freud told me he never ceased to analyze himself, devoting the last half hour of his day to that purpose," exults Jones. "One more example of his flawless integrity" (Jones 1953, p. 327).

Yet Freud's self-scrutiny, systematic or otherwise, was not enough to secure for him a mastery over "the motherland," the dark and unexplored continent of the Seer's most poignant suffering, "umplumbable—a navel, as it were," (*S.E.*, 4:111) of *Angst* and sexual longing, at once terrifying and thrilling. "There is a tangle" of something that "adds nothing to our knowledge of the content of the dream," divulged the Census Taker in his Dreambook. "This is the dream's navel, the spot where it reaches down into the *Unerkannten* [unknown]. . . . It is at some point where this meshwork is particularly close that the dream-wish grows up," adds the priapic Itzig, "like a mushroom out of its mycelium" (*S.E.*, 5:525). Nevertheless, "Ernest Jones's hyperbole has much to commend it" (Gay 1988, p. 98), allows Gay graciously, since the flawless integrity of analysis "is to smoke out a memory, at once terrifying and thrilling, from its lair of repression" (ibid., p. 298). Always committed to unsparing candor, "Freud took considerable pride in being the destroyer of illusions," according to the cheerfully oblivious historiographer, "the faithful servant of scientific veracity" (ibid., p. xvii).

In his American lectures, Otto Rank expressed no interest in smoking out anyone's terrifying and thrilling memory from its lair of repression, or even in filling in the hole in Sigmund Freud's most thoroughgoing self-scrutiny, a gigantic void that remains today precisely as the Destroyer of Illusions left it for all posterity in *The Interpretation of Dreams*: a subject shrouded in darkness. "I probably underestimate the power of this [mother] complex," Freud reported to Ferenczi in 1916, "because of my lack of personal experience of it" (Dupont 1994, p. 307). From his personal and clinical *Erlebnis*, however, Rank did draw one important conclusion about "the germ of cleavage" between himself and Freud, a cleavage that, as Rank told his U.S. audience, "shatters the foundation pillars of his theory" [8-122]. In a 1926 lecture on "The

Genesis of the Guilt Feeling," marking the birth of what is today called "object-relations theory," Rank argued that ambivalence, hatred, and the *Über-Ich* are all pre-Oedipal in origin: "This takes place," he points out simply, "through relation to the *mother object*" [9-131].

In his *Inhibitions, Symptoms and Anxieties* (1926), an uneasy analysis of *The Trauma of Birth*, Freud rehearsed once again all of Rank's most unsavory arguments in order, finally, to refute them: "it becomes impossible to shut one's eyes any longer," Itzig judged with characteristic insight, "to the far-fetched character of such explanations" (*S.E.*, 20:136). The *infans*, "a completely narcissistic creature," according to Freud, "is totally unaware of [mother's] existence as an object" (*S.E.*, 20:130). As to the origin of emotional suffering, notes the Seer drolly, "we are as much in the dark about this problem as we were at the start," after many pregnant years of "psychoanalytic labours" (*S.E.*, 20:149). While crediting Rank for discovering separation *Angst*, Freud circled back in his "inhibited, anxious, and symptomatic text," again and again and again, "like a dog worrying a bone" (Sprengnether 1990, p. 138), to the deeper, much more painful truth of castration *Angst*, which, according to an orthodox Freudian, remains forever the "nuclear anxiety" (Rangell 1982, p. 40), the *Kernkomplex* of the neurosis.

"To make the unconscious conscious, which is the announced aim of psychoanalytic therapy," offers the seriously monocular Gay, "is to threaten the patient with the reemergence of feelings and recollections that he believes are best buried" (Gay 1988, p. 300). With the truth some cannot live. "I have to blind myself artificially in order to focus all the light on one dark spot," Freud once told Lou Andreas-Salomé. "[F]or my eyes, adapted as they are to the dark, probably can't stand strong light or an extensive range of vision" (E. Freud 1960, p. 312). In 1926, after having spent thirty years excavating the dusky secrets of his "negroes," dragging all that is buried and repressed into the full light of day, tirelessly reducing the *daemon* of the unconscious, as he once told Stefan Zweig proudly, to "a comprehensible object of science" (Gay 1985, p. xvii), Itzig now warrants that a certain "*nichts*" that resides in the Infernal Regions still remains hidden and even seems to have been intended as such by him, perversely, perhaps to simplify a certain "*nichts*": "It is almost humiliating that, after working so long, we should still be having difficulty in understanding the most fundamental facts. But we have made up our minds to simplify *nichts* and to hide *nichts*" (*S.E.*, 20:124). In 1926, at the same time that Freud was hiding *nichts*, Rank revealed that "the '*Über-Ich*,' which Freud assumed to be a derivative of the Oedipus complex, ... actually is built up ... through relation to the mother object." The painful "cleavage" in the infant's unconscious is related first to the mother and only later to the father:

"[The infant] brings a definite element of *hatred* into the ambivalent attitude toward the mother, which is of *decisive* importance for all later object relations . . . [9-132]. The 'strict mother' thus forms the real *Kern* of the *Über-Ich* [and] when Freud denied [an] *Über-Ich* (in the masculine sense) to women, he overlooked the fact that the *Kern* even of the masculine *Über-Ich* originates from the mother . . . [9-134]. *The origin of the castration complex is thus really pre-Oedipal"* [9-137]. In his next lecture, entitled "The Genesis of the Object Relation," Rank argued that the small boy "must, so to speak, make his father bad, in order to keep his picture of the good mother clear" [10-142ff]. It was "fundamental facts" such as these that Rank, in August 1924, anticipated "would, one day, constitute the analyst's basic A-B-C." By 1926 Rank had constructed a succinct but comprehensive theory of the genesis of object-relations, a theory that represented, as Itzig presciently said, "the most important progress since the discovery of psychoanalysis." Years later, of course, the alphabet of object-relations theory was expanded and complicated, no doubt overly complicated, by thinkers such as Melanie Klein and Ronald Fairbairn— neither of whom ever credited Rank, whose post-Freudian writings were barely noticed by analysts. "The pre-Oedipal super-ego has since been overemphasized by Melanie Klein," observed Rank as early as 1930, "without any reference to me" (Rank 1930a, p. 26).[5]

Once exorcised, like a bad object, from Freud's inner world, Rank was dead and buried, as far as the analytic community was concerned. So quits! Unwilling to renounce any part of the theory in which he had deposited his neurosis, but not without a measure of empathy for the incalculable suffering of his one-time tender and loving foster mother, Sigmund Freud, tragically "blinded by the castration theory" [8-119], Otto Rank went his own way.

Notes

1. "This strange appellation," which Freud began to use in the early years of his practice, when his consultation hour started at noon, "came from a cartoon in the *Fliegende Blätter* depicting a yawning lion muttering 'Twelve o'clock and no negro'" (Jones 1957, p. 105). After one summer vacation in 1898, Freud worried aloud to Fliess about "whether some negroes will turn up at the right time to still the lion's appetite" (Masson 1985, p. 368). In a 1909 letter to Freud, Jung reported drolly that "the interior of Africa is better known to me than [Jones's] sexuality" (McGuire 1974, p. 208). As late as 1924, according to Jones, Freud was still using the appellation "negro" for an American patient whom he had taken along with him on a vacation on the Semmering (1957, p. 105). Once, in conversation with Rank, Freud compared psychotherapy, his impossible profession, to "the white-washing of a negro" (Rank 1941, p. 272).

Analysis, Freud told Rank in 1924, suits the blackness of Americans like "a white shirt a raven" (Lieberman 1985, p. 228).

2. This is the earliest use by Rank that I have been able to find of the term *pre-Oedipus* or its variant *pre-Oedipal*. It does not appear in either the original German or the English translation of *The Trauma of Birth*, but Rank explicitly speaks of "the phase *before* the development of the Oedipus complex" (Rank 1924, p. 216; his italics). Although Freud had coined the term *pre-genital* in the narrow sexual sense many years before, Rank seems to have been the first to introduce the term *pre-Oedipal* in the modern relational sense into psychoanalysis, at the Bad Hamburg Congress, September 1925, in a speech entitled "The Genesis of Genitality." The original German manuscript of this speech contains the phrase "*präödipalen Entwicklung*" (pre-Oedipal development) as does the published text in volume 1 of *Genetische Psychologie* (Rank 1927, p. 71). In April 1926 Rank's speech was chosen by White and Jelliffe as the lead article in *The Psychoanalytic Review*. In English translation, however, the word *development* was dropped and the phrase appears as "pre-Oedipus situation" (Rank 1926a, p. 130).

It is unlikely that analysts heard much of Rank's speech, since it was read at "Gatling machine gun" speed, according to Smith Ely Jellife. This was the last time Rank was invited to address any psychoanalytic meeting, and by September 1925 almost everyone in Europe had learned that Freud was through with him. "He first excused himself," recounts Jelliffe, "for not discussing the trauma of birth theory which seemed uppermost in the atmosphere of those most centrally interested in psychoanalytic theory, and promised to present his later reflections at a future time" (Lieberman 1985, p. 436n.47). These reflections were presented the next year, in New York, but no one at this congress was interested in hearing Rank by then.

Following a hint by Freud in his *New Introductory Lectures* (*S.E.*, 22:130), Ruth Mack Brunswick is today mistakenly credited with originating the term *pre-Oedipal* in her 1929 article "The Analysis of a Case of Paranoia (Delusion of Jealousy)," *The Journal of Nervous and Mental Disease*, Vol. 70, p. 177. This article was originally published in 1928 in German. Freud himself first used the term in 1931, in his essay on "Female Sexuality," but only in reference to the small girl's relation to the mother, *not* to the small boy's: "Our insight into this early, pre-Oedipus, phase in girls comes to us as a surprise, like the discovery, in another field, of the Minoan-Mycenean civilization behind the civilization of Greece" (*S.E.*, 21:226). Rank studied Freud's essay and, in a letter to a friend, wryly analyzed Freud's omission: "He 'discovers' there the primal significance of the mother as the first object of libido and of inhibition (fear and hate etc.) which I pointed out elaborately in the *Genetic Psychology* [i.e., American lectures], he doesn't mention me, of course, only more recent articles of woman-analysts whom he values now more than his man-pupils" (Lieberman 1979, p. 14). The friend replied: "So far as I can see Ruth B[runswick] took your place" (ibid.). In an earlier letter, Rank observed that the conclusions he drew in the *Genetic Psychology* were "already in the *Trauma* . . . before anybody else dared to conceive of them" (ibid., p. 13).

3. I am indebted to E. James Lieberman for providing me with a transcription of this letter, probably the first ever from Freud to Rank. Anaïs Nin reports Rank's own account of how he met Freud in 1905. Suffering from a lung illness, Rank visited Alfred Adler in his office and, during the examination, "expounded some of his opinions of Dr. Freud's work. He also expressed some dissensions. He was already exploring the possibility of a memory of the body, a visceral memory in the blood, in the muscles, long before consciousness, as a child's first awareness of pain or pleasure, a memory of actual birth. A memory which started with birth itself. The experience of birth. Emotions forming like geological strata, from purely animal experiences. Birth, warmth, cold, pain. Adler was so impressed with Rank that he introduced him to Freud" (Nin 1966, pp. 278–79).

4. Who, exactly, was this powerful and fearsome mother to whose *Imago* Freud seems to have been chained, eternally, in his unconscious? Even today, after an avalanche of books and articles on every aspect of Freud's work and life, almost nothing is known about his mother except for a few scattered reminiscences. The woman to whom *mein goldener Sigmund* [German: "my golden victory-mouth"] made ambivalent pilgrimage every Sunday morning of his adult life, from early manhood into his mid-seventies, until she died in 1930 at 95, was named Amalia Freud (Kobler 1962). "She was charming and smiling when strangers were about, but I," writes Judith Bernays Heller, the maternal granddaughter of Amalia, "at least always felt that with familiars she was a tyrant, and a selfish one. Quite definitely, she had a strong personality and knew what she wanted" (Heller 1973, p. 338). "I really feared" her, says Heller (ibid., p. 335). A "fine-looking" but exceptionally vain woman, Amalia "had a volatile temperament" and was "somewhat shrill and domineering"—the emotional opposite of Jacob Freud, the castrating father of Sigmund, who "remained quiet and imperturbable, not indifferent, but not disturbed, never out of temper and never raising his voice" (ibid., p. 336). Even when ill or recovering from his thirty or so operations for oral cancer, "Professor Freud would always find time [on] a Sunday morning to pay his mother a visit and give her the pleasure of petting and making a fuss over him" (ibid., p. 339).

For an astonishing photograph showing Sigmund and Amalia Freud sitting side by side, arms tightly locked, see the full-page picture in the *Kürzeste Chronik* (Freud 1992, p. 52). Although no date is given for this picture, it seems to have been taken when Freud was in his seventies and his mother in her nineties, perhaps a few years before she died in 1930. Freud declined to attend his mother's funeral, unlike that of his father, Jacob. "I feel only two things," he told Jones after his mother's death: an "increase in personal freedom" and "the satisfaction that she obtained at last the deliverance" that she so richly deserved (Paskauskas 1993, p. 677). He added that he did not share the grief or sorrow "displayed so painfully" by his brother Alexander (ibid.). To Ferenczi, he wrote that he felt "no pain, no grief . . . at the same time a feeling of liberation, of release" (E. Freud, 1960, p. 400). About six months before Amalia's death, Freud told Eitingon: "She bars my way to the longed-for rest, to eternal nothingness" (ibid., p. 392), to *Nichts*.

In the picture Freud's mouth is ajar and the hollow wreckage of his cancerous jaw clearly visible. The extraordinary expression of suffering on his face must be seen to be believed. It is no exaggeration, I think, to describe it as the anguished look of a bewildered and helpless small boy. There is no other photograph of Freud ever published, not even those taken in his youth, that even remotely captures this truly poignant side of his personality. The expression on Amalia's face, although blurred, is clearly one of enormous maternal pride and regal command. According to Thornton Wilder, Freud once told him "that it might some day be shown that cancer is allied to 'the presence of hate'" in the unconscious (Freud 1992, pp. 297–98). No wonder that Lacan would later call for a return to "the truth in Freud's mouth" (Lacan 1977, p. 121). Even Lacan, the least empathetic of analysts, and an avowed foe of object-relations theory, recognized that the truth speaks where there is pain. Although Freud was never able to discover the oceanic feeling in himself, his entire world was "a small island of pain," he once told Princess Marie Bonaparte, "floating on an ocean of *Indifferenz*" (Schur 1972, p. 567n.10).

None of Freud's closest colleagues, many of whom paid courtesy calls on Amalia Freud, ever wondered aloud about Freud's relationship with his mother (Roazen 1993, p. 35). Otto Rank never wrote a single word about it. But in the privacy of his diary, Sándor Ferenczi once hazarded an astounding guess about Freud's feelings toward his mother, linked to a searing critique of the castration complex. In his *Clinical Diary*, written in 1932, the year before his death, Ferenczi speculated on Freud's motive for replacing the seduction theory with the Oedipus complex. Ferenczi knew that Freud had abandoned this theory in 1897, at the emotional height of his self-analysis. By 1932, although never denying the existence of infantile sexuality, Ferenczi was convinced that sexual abuse of children, the "incestuous affection of adults, *which masquerades as affection*" (Ferenczi 1930, p. 121; his italics), was far more common than Freud was willing to admit. Ferenczi wondered about "the ease with which Fr[eud] sacrifices the interests of women in favor of male patients." He hypothesized, without providing any evidence, that Freud "may have a personal aversion to the spontaneous female-oriented sexuality in women: idealization of the mother. He recoils from the task of having a sexually demanding mother, and having to satisfy her. At some point his mother's passionate nature may have presented him with such a task. (The primal scene may have rendered him relatively impotent)." Then, in italics, Ferenczi adds: "*Castration of the father, the potent one, as a reaction to the humiliation he experienced, led to the construction of a theory in which the father castrates the son* and, moreover, is then revered by the son as a god. In his conduct Fr[eud] plays only the role of the castrating god, he wants to ignore the traumatic moment of his own castration in childhood; he is the only one who does not have to be analyzed" (Ferenczi 1988, pp. 187–88). Soon after writing this note, a few days before his last meeting with Freud in August 1932, Ferenczi told A. A. Brill that "he couldn't credit Freud with *any more insight than a small boy*; this," writes Jones, "happened to be the *very phase* that Rank had used in his time—a memory that could but heighten Freud's forebodings" (Jones 1957, p. 172; italics added).

5. To be sure, Rank continued to acknowledge both Oedipal and pre-Oedipal guilt but observed that they are surplus guilt: they come on top of an already-present existential indebtedness: "we are not our own [*nicht unser Eigen sind*]," Rank said in *Will Therapy*, "no matter whether we perceive the guilt religiously toward God, socially toward the father, or biologically toward the mother" (Rank 1929-31, p. 101). Not father or mother or sexuality but *difference*, the strange consciousness of living—the dim awareness that we are alive for a moment on this planet as it spins, meaninglessly, around the cold and infinite galaxy—is the source of our deepest pain. "One might even say," concludes Rank, "that the real etiological factor of the neuroses consists in the fact that we have a psychical life [*daß wir ein Seelenleben haben*]" [8-124]. This is *Angst* for existence itself, according to Rank: "It is simply anxiety in the I and for the I [*Angst im Ich und um das Ich*]" [8-124].

According to Rank, "will and guilt are the two complementary sides of *one* and the *same* phenomenon" (Rank 1929, p. 31; italics added). I = suffering. One can never speak of willing without guilt-feeling, for they are of one piece, a *Doppelgänger*, infusing and shaping each other. It is the never-ending ebb and flow of these emotional currents, for good or evil, that gives music, color, poetry, and drama to human existence, a hymnal of creativity and suffering. Because of the will-guilt problem, as Rank came to call this "great conflict between our biological and our purely human self" [18-234], the I—even with its powerful creative will—is not master in its own house, on either the microcosmic or macrocosmic levels. The trauma of birth, Rank once confided to a friend, "is really a great vision of the idea of separation governing the universe" (Lieberman 1979, p. 18), not just the idea of separation from one's mother or from mental representations of significant others. "And when Freud in his [*Inhibitions, Symptoms and Anxieties*] accepted the idea of separation he did not know what he really was accepting because he *only* thought in terms of individual mother fixation" (ibid.). Difference equals pain.

Guilt, therefore, is not merely a feeling of committing wrong against another, a residue of intrapsychic sexual or aggressive wishes, or a fear of punishment or castration. Like *Angst*, guilt is existential, a given, and is before Oedipus, before pre-Oedipus. As the ancient Greek dramatists knew so well, guilt is double-sided and can never be completely eliminated. In the deepest sense, guilt is what defines us as human beings *as long as we live*, grow and create, or, conversely, as long as we deny and betray ourselves by *failing to live*, refusing to change and develop our potential, unthinkingly remaining embedded in the Other—be it the safety net woven by mother, father, organizations, ideologies, Gods, therapists or lovers. For this reason, said Rank, guilt—the inescapable complement of willing—is an emotional force in the human being as powerful as the biological impulse of sexuality: "Indeed, it is even shown that in many human beings inhibitions manifesting themselves as anxiety and guilt are *stronger* than the drives, that these inhibitions themselves, so to say, operate 'as a driving force' although in a different way from the biological impulses. In a word, we see that the *psychical* has become a force at least equal to the *biological* and that all human conflicts are to be explained just from this fact" [18-229].

Even more profoundly, we must accept and honor this guilt, a necessary and vital part of the fully functioning person (Kramer 1995). In its creative expression, guilt is not to be condemned or analyzed away as a residue of the Oedipus or pre-Oedipus complex. When not too severe, guilt serves as a harmonizing factor between the will to separate and the will to unite, reconnecting I to Thou, part to whole, while allowing the person to retain a powerful sense of difference:

> I think guilt-feeling occupies a special position among the emotions, as a *boundary* phenomenon between the pronounced painful affects that separate and the more pleasurable feelings that unite. It is related to the painful separating affects of anxiety and hate. But in its relation to gratitude and devotion—which may extend to self-sacrifice—it belongs to the strongest uniting feelings we know. As the guilt-feeling occupies the *boundary line* between the painful and pleasurable, between the severing and uniting feelings, it is also the most important representative of the relation between inner and outer, I and Thou, the Self and the World [11-158].

According to Rank, the fully functioning person "must learn to live [*muß leben lernen*], to live with his split, his conflict, his ambivalence, which no therapy can take away, for if it could, it would take with it the actual spring of life" (Rank, 1929-31, p. 206)—a "split" that begins with a catastrophic cleavage in *der Kern unseres Wesens*, the trauma or "wound" of birth.

PART ONE

THE TRAUMA OF BIRTH:

"A MUCH STRONGER REPRESSION THAN EVEN

INFANTILE SEXUALITY"

1

PSYCHOANALYSIS AS GENERAL

PSYCHOLOGY (1924)

LADIES AND GENTLEMEN, I take it for granted that you have already heard of psychoanalysis, and I assume that what you wish to know is whether you are thinking about it in the right way. I can, of course, tell you only what I think about it. To begin with, I do not know how you came to know of it, from what angle each of you has looked at it, or in what sense you have taken it—I mean whether you think of it as a therapy for treatment of nervous suffering, a method of investigation of unconscious life, or a psychological theory.

In any case, my purpose is to present psychoanalysis to you from a general point of view and from its purely practical side. In other words, I want to show you what we today can take from psychoanalytical knowledge, how it is possible to apply this knowledge in various spheres of practical life, and what advantages we can gain thereby.

As far as possible, I will not dwell upon the mere historical development of psychoanalysis and will also try to avoid discussing it as a theoretical system. Both these phases of the subject have been satisfactorily handled in psychoanalytical literature, and I could give you nothing more about them than you can get from that literature. First of all, I want to dispose of a number of obsolete ideas about psychoanalysis that I think are rather in the nature of misunderstandings than actual deficiencies in your knowledge of it. Then I propose showing you how psychoanalysis appears to me today, what in a certain sense it has accomplished, especially what practical contributions to life it has made and has still to make. If we once realize the significance of psychoanalysis for our present social life, we shall at the same time get some idea of the important part it has to play in the near future.

But I must at least give you briefly the most important facts from the past of psychoanalysis, so that you may know whence it comes and what it purposes. Psychoanalysis was born in the year 1881. Its father was the late physician, Dr. Josef Breuer, who for nearly ten years kept secret the birth of this illegitimate child.[1] Dr. Breuer then abandoned the child because it might appear a bastard of scientific medicine, of which he himself was a representative, and of psychotherapy, which is still under suspicion at the present time. It was then that it found a tender and loving foster mother in the person of Sigmund Freud. He reared the neglected and misunderstood being and developed it into what we know today as psychoanalysis. It is now full grown and self-reliant. It leaves behind it a very interesting past and has gone through many adventures that Freud himself has recounted up to the year 1914 in his *History of the Psycho-Analytic Movement* [S.E., 14: 7–66] and since brought up-to-date in some of his later encyclopedia articles ["Two Encyclopedia Articles" (1923a) S.E., 18:235–59].

In order to be able to understand psychoanalysis fully, as it is today, we must—according to a fundamental principle of psychoanalysis itself—grasp the determining phases of its childhood. Breuer's discovery was of a purely practical nature. It had, so to say, been made at the bedside of a patient and was the result of a compelling necessity to give therapeutic help. At that time, it could not be called psychoanalysis. The name *psychoanalysis* was introduced many years later by Freud himself and definitely given to the method of investigation and treatment that he himself had developed. The story of Breuer's first case has already been related so often that it will be enough here to recall just its essential points. It was to this case that he owed his surprising discovery, and also his method of therapeutically influencing the patient. This patient was a young girl who had suffered from a number of hysterical symptoms since she had nursed her father in a severe illness. Breuer, under certain conditions that he later called hypnoid, was able to bring back to her consciousness certain forgotten memories. The content of these memories gave meaning to the symptoms—that is, the symptoms were revealed to be substitutions for the memory of a painful incident that, because it was painful, had been forgotten. The symptoms thus dominated the patient's consciousness in place of the forgotten incident. She called the relief that she obtained in her hypnoid states from remembering forgotten facts the "talking cure" or, jokingly, "chimney sweeping." This related also to the fact that she remembered, so to speak, "repressed" English, which she had not spoken since she was a child and which she now spoke exclusively. This unburdening of soul became the basis of Breuer's cathartic method, and it was this that Freud later developed into psychoanalytic therapy. The surprising fact was that the symptoms apparently disappeared as soon as the forgotten impressions were brought into consciousness or remembered. This problematical state of affairs formed the starting point for a number of investigations that finally led to analytic psychology.

Starting with Breuer's first case, let us disregard the therapeutic factor and follow the development of the psychoanalytic psychology formulated by Freud, which has become the first normal psychology, in spite of the fact that it was developed from pathologic material. For this purpose, we must give a little further consideration to Breuer's catharsis, as the affect-toned remembrance of forgotten impressions was called.

You remember that the symptoms proved to be substitutions for forgotten experiences—that they disappeared as soon as the original impressions had been brought again to the patient's consciousness. Thus the therapeutic task seemed quite easy. It looked as if one had only to consider how to find out those recollections that had expressed themselves so inappropriately as symptoms. This was possible only by bringing the forgotten experiences to the remembrance of the patient, and the easiest way to do this seemed by direct questioning in hypnosis. The patient herself was the stimulus for development of this method. She sometimes fell quite spontaneously into hypnoid states, in which she was able to recall forgotten memories. Breuer tried later to induce this state artificially by hypnosis in other patients who did not produce the same symptom of hypnoid states. As a matter of fact, hypnosis led to practically the same result. And it is to be regretted that Breuer did not make full use of his discovery in this direction, although probably in that case we should have missed the discovery of the real psychoanalysis by Freud.

The story of why Breuer did not continue his investigation, which promised such success, is more than a mere anecdote; it is a specially interesting fragment of the history of the science. We know that he was able to show an undoubted success in the treatment of his first patient; the symptoms disappeared, apparently, with the explanation of their origin.

But something else not noticed and not understood by Breuer appeared in the patient in place of symptoms. This was appreciated by Freud only much later and was the foundation stone of his psychoanalytic therapy as well as of an understanding of neuroses. The story is this. As Breuer one day revisited his patient, at that time almost recovered, he found her again in bed, in a state of excitement accompanied by violent convulsions whose meaning he had not long to look for. His patient cried out to him that she was now bringing forth the child begotten by him. This was enough to horrify any respectable doctor. Consequently he, so to speak, suddenly forgot his cue, took the matter personally, declared the patient insane, and arranged for her to be put into a mental hospital. There, after some time, this acute condition died away of its own accord.

Do not let us reproach Dr. Breuer for not realizing immediately that this curious behavior on the part of his patient was only a newly formed symptom in place of her neurosis, which, like her earlier symptoms, could be made to disappear by bringing into consciousness the real unconscious meaning of her reaction. I think the doctors among you would have treated the case just as he did before Freud recognized in such behavior something typical, which he later, according to his dynamic conception, called by the name of *transference*. So you see Breuer did literally run away from psychoanalysis as from an unwelcome illegitimate child. And perhaps you can understand how even today, in spite of a complete psychological understanding of this phenomenon as transference, psychoanalysis has won a certain sexual notoriety, which has deterred some of Freud's fellow workers since Breuer from further occupation with the subject. But hypnosis, not understanding transference, was the starting point of Freud's own method. He soon found that hypnosis was not appropriate for every patient. Besides, it had in its influence something vague, inexplicable, and mystical, so he finally dropped it. He wanted to know, on the one hand, what occurs in the patient, and, on the other hand—also from practical motives—how one can help the patient without being dependent on the unreliable method of hypnosis. This second question could be answered only by learning more about the processes that go on in the patient, the mechanism of mental life. And so a plan of inquiry was necessary, as also a series of investigations to answer the following questions:

1. How can one bring the forgotten pathological impressions back to the memory of the patient in his normal condition?
2. Why does he remember these impressions with such difficulty?
3. How is it that the symptoms disappear when he has remembered the repressed experiences?

The first question leads directly into the field of general psychology, involving as it does an investigation of the normal psychical state. This is accomplished by the real psychoanalytic method, based on free associations and their interpretation according to a quite determined unconscious aim. The second question—why it is that the patient remembers the impressions with such difficulty—leads from the phenomena of forgetting and remembering to the kernel of dynamic psychology— namely, the concept of *repression*. The third question—how is it that the symptoms disappear when their causation is remembered—leads finally to the doctrine of the *unconscious* and its predominating psychical mechanisms.

The real birth hour of psychoanalysis was that moment, nearly a generation ago, when Freud went beyond questioning the patient in hypnosis and began to investigate psychical mechanisms in the normal state. Then for the first time he got at an understanding of normal unconscious processes, which finally led, through a special method of inquiry and investigation, to psychoanalytic psychology.

Here, first of all, I must explain the manner and character of the psychoanalytic method. There are, properly speaking, two methods, according to their essence quite different, from which Freud, having dropped the hypnotic therapy, built up the psychoanalytic method of investigation: (1) the method of free association, which has as its presupposition the strict determinism[2] of all psychic occurrences; (2) the method of interpretation that has so often been accused of being purely arbitrary. The first method, or free association, is actually a purely scientific principle, which can be experimentally demonstrated by the association test, wherein also the determinism of psychical occurrences is incontestably manifested. With the greatest possible elimination of conscious attention and self-criticism—which generally tests and sifts all ideas—these freely occurring associations betray a more or less conscious relation to a definite complex. The discovery of the unconscious site of the complex was in the beginning very difficult and accompanied by the usual uncertainties. One arrived at the hidden unconscious meaning alluded to in these associations really through a kind of intuitive guesswork, in which one naturally would sometimes go wrong, but in which quite definite rules gradually crystallized into the so-called technique of interpretation. This interpretation appeared subjective and arbitrary[3] only so long as one did not apply to it also the same law of the strict determinism of all psychical life.

By frequent experience we have gradually learned to trace the chain of associations further, link by link, into the preconscious and the unconscious, and so to recognize the psychical meaning of the entire process. This technique of, so to speak, translating was soon formulated into definite rules that for the most part have been since confirmed not only by numerous clinical experiences of many analysts, but in part also by experiment. I think, then, that the interpretations of psychoanalysts have been justified theoretically as subordinate to the law of determinism and have been practically confirmed from various outside sources, such as mythology, folklore, art, and so forth. For instance, symbolism has been demonstrated indisputably to have the same meaning in different spheres of human psychical life. So the whole technique of interpretation, like the method of association, was only a method of investigation used to ascertain the content and meaning of the unconscious psychical life, which you now know under the names of various complexes, as, for instance, the *Oedipus*.

But knowledge of all these unconscious complexes makes it superfluous for the analyst today to take the same difficult route in every individual case. That would be just as if every doctor had to make chemical experiments at the patient's bedside to work out the necessary preparation or medicine, which he can quite easily buy at the druggist's. Today we are in a position to convert directly into practical use the results of a decade's laborious work in analysis. We can apply this knowledge not only to the therapy of neuroses, the field in which psychoanalysis started, but also just as well to various fields of general psychology. Until recently the general psychological knowledge that we owe to the psychoanalytic method of investigation alone was still too limited to serve as a basis for satisfactory therapeutic results. On this account the enormous and as yet incomplete work of investigation was necessary. But now, armed with our enriched knowledge, we can set out in our struggle against neuroses; and not only against disease itself, for we can use our knowledge as a prophylactic by applying it to the betterment of child education and of our social and sexual relations through the psychoanalytic understanding of our own natures and characters. And the development of psychoanalysis has led to this spontaneously, without the drawing up of a program, because in its nature it is practical, real, and humane.

From this it should not surprise you that I have placed psychoanalysis as a general psychology in the foreground and have put into the background its therapeutic function, which yet was the starting point of the entire work and to many appears still to be its essential feature. The disinclination of human beings to recognize the universal nature of the unconscious impulses brought to light by analysis—which it has become impossible any longer to ignore—has led to a conception that unfortunately has marred the image of psychoanalysis. Finally, the objection has been made: "All these immoral, egotistic, sexual tendencies may be found by analysis in the unconscious of neurotics, and may be answerable for their illness. But one ought not to generalize this fact and extend to it the psychology of the normal." Such an objection seems to me like the answer of most children when they learn something of the facts of sexual life. The child usually reacts thus: "That may be all right for so and so's parents or for animals, but for my parents, certainly not!"

Such is the objection to psychoanalysis! But such an objection, while characteristic and intelligible as a defense, is as a matter of fact—one might almost say unfortunately—false, for all the unconscious material brought to light by analysis in treatment of neurotic patients, and recognized in their psychical mechanism, proves on closer inspection to be a common possession of mankind. I said "unfortunately," not because I sympathize with the moral resistances criticized above, but from scientific regret that we have been unable to isolate any specifically pathologic factors, and thus to simplify the problem of therapy. Our experience has been that it is a matter of quantity only; the neurotic becomes ill from the same conflicts that the so-called normal succeeds in mastering.

But we need not regret too much this failure to find something that could be easily understood, easily got at, and so easily cured. Instead, psychoanalysis has found something more valuable—a new understanding of normal psychic life, based upon knowledge of general psychological unconscious contents. These contents had not been recognized before, because no method existed by which one could trace and bring them up into the light of consciousness, which one is obliged to do in psychoanalytical treatment of neurotics, if one really makes an effort to help them. What Freud has formulated in his *Interpretation of Dreams* [*S.E.* 4 and 5], his *The Psychopathology of Everyday Life* [*S.E.*, 6], his sexual theory, his studies of civilization, ethnology, and aesthetics, is nothing but a normal psychology.

The kernel of this psychology is the doctrine of *repression*, which represents a psychical protection and defense mechanism of the ego against something incompatible with it. Let me illustrate the mechanism of repression further by a simple comparison that remains within the range of psychoanalysis. In repression, the ego acts toward a wish impulse arising from within exactly as Dr. Breuer behaved toward the unwelcome message from without, which announced to him a child. The ego wishes to know nothing about it and attempts to turn aside from the idea by depreciating or denying it. If this is not successful, one must at least confine it for a time in the unconscious, as Breuer did with his patient when he put her into an asylum. There in the unconscious the unwelcome wish impulse may be left after a while to its own resources without special supervision. This example illustrates the most favorable aspect of repression. But if by any chance one continually has to use a part of one's psychic energy to restrain or keep guard over this unwelcome impulse or idea, or if the idea is strong enough and permanently rebels, then there is nothing left to do but call for help.

This illustration may give you at the same time an idea of the double consciousness that dominates our inner life and that becomes manifest only in severe cases of neuroses or psychoses. From the fact of repression, the dynamic point of view follows quite naturally to the assumption of something repressed, which strives against the repressive forces of the ego. But this division within the psychic personality need not throughout occur between conscious forces and unconscious repressed forces of the ego; although the simplest case of repression is that in which an unpleasant idea is removed from consciousness into a less approachable level we call the preconscious. Neither need it always be the ego and sexual impulses that strive against each other; although very often the moral ego defends itself by repression of a displaced sexual impulse. On the other hand, repression is neither the only method nor always the most appropriate method of inner psychical defense. There are several other means, as, for example displacement, projection, and still others. But repression, according to experience, often fails, because it mostly opposes the sexual impulses, against whose intensity the defense mechanism of the ego collapses.

Failure with regard to repression at important points in development of the individual has been recognized as one of the important causes of neuroses. But even successful repression—such as the child has to accomplish from the day of its birth, for purposes of adaptation—maintains in the unconscious an underground life. This might be compared to the underworld in the Homeric poems, where dwelt the shades of permanently slain heroes, who could come to life again at any time by drinking blood. Thus, the fundamental law of repression is really the psychological counterpart of the physical law of conservation of all matter. For in the psychical world, also, nothing can disappear without a trace, leaving no memories nor impressions nor affects! Here, also, as in the physical universe, there can be only change, displacement, transformation.

But psychoanalysis has found also a number of normal psychic phenomena in which repressed wishes or thoughts are temporarily and partially fulfilled, and which are recognized and understood in their importance for psychical economy—namely, as necessary outlets. These phenomena are our nightly dreams, in which the repressed wishes of the past, no longer allowed by the developed ego, return in a distorted archaic form of expression, nevertheless subject to quite definite laws. The importance of dreams and their understanding for study of character and human knowledge is now well known, since they grant us wide insight into unconscious life. But just as illuminating are faulty acts or blunders of everyday life, such as slips of the tongue, forgetting, losing things, symptomatic and chance actions. Study of these various blunders leads to a general understanding of normal actions, especially such as are performed impulsively—for instance, writing letters, going for a walk, reading, and the like. But blunders represent the neurotic symptoms of everyday life, and their occurrence in exaggerated form is due to pathological functioning in a process of general importance—namely, to faulty repression, which can be cured only by means of the therapy of "cathartic remembering." The, so to speak, purely private dream life, on the one hand, and slight social errors on the other are keys to understanding everyday psychology, which one can really describe as a psychology of forgetting and remembering, or a psychology of memory. Indeed memory, that human quality par excellence, by maintaining useful or successful repressions of inexpedient experiences, determines our relation to the outside world in the sense of culture-adaptation and culture-formation. Blunders of everyday life and neurotic symptoms incompatible with social life relate to the outer world. The dream of our private life relates directly to the human inner world, and to understanding personality, character formation, and phantasy life, on which are based even the highest accomplishments, such as religion, art, and, to a certain extent, even science.

Deepened understanding of everyday psychology, which explains our relation to the outer and to the inner world, to reality, and to thought, led the psychoanalytic method of investigation to the first real conception of the psychology of the child. Freud recognized that children's inner dreams represent simply wish fulfillments. In other words, the child can represent as real (in the dream) his as yet unrestrained wishes without offending his still-undeveloped ego and higher moral aesthetic claims. Faulty acts of the child have not been investigated, because, as I assume, there are none in the case of a little child, who lacks a firm relation to reality and the social order belonging to it. Indeed, from the point of view of adult adjustment to reality, one could describe the entire child life as a single faulty action, because the child constantly confuses reality and phantasy, forgets that it has to adjust itself, and speaks in such a way that the grown-up person either does not understand it or considers it funny. From the very beginning, the child needs somebody who will always put before it, and explain its relation to, reality; somebody who will draw its attention to material objects, so that the child will not come into conflict with them—in the literal sense of the word, will not knock up against them; somebody who will teach it to differentiate between thought and matter, and who will give it a language intelligible to others also. In other words the child must constantly be reminded of the task of adjustment, which can be successfully accomplished only when the child loves the person who teaches it. For successful adjustment, the child needs to identify itself with the loved person, and to be able to give its interest to the outer world through the medium of this model. Such a person we call an educator where a child is concerned; and a psychoanalyst in the case of an adult in whom complete adjustment has not been successfully effected. The means and ends by which we can attain this end are given us in pedagogy, which yet has much to learn from psychoanalysis, especially in the matter of understanding the relation between child and educator.[4] This relationship rests on love, which we have studied in analysis as transference and which we have also learned to use as a means of education and reeducation.

From study of the phenomena of transference, insight is gained into a wider field of normal psychology—namely, sexual life. This has become the most disputed, as well as the most generally discussed, part of psychoanalysis, which so decisively influenced our social standards with regard to our sexual life. Today it is established that the sexual instinct no more enters into a human being at the time of puberty than the soul enters into the embryo, as was the belief of the church fathers. But we know that this instinct has a genesis, which is revealed in the famous libido theory. If one traces the development of the sexual instinct to its biological source, one finds that, considered from an individual psychological point of view, it is originally nothing else than a regressive libidinal phenomenon. The libido ultimately is nothing else than desire to return to a happy primal condition, which the ego once experienced and which individually can be nothing other than the prenatal state. From my own analytic investigations, in *The Trauma of Birth*, I have developed a concept that this blessed primal state is represented for the individual by the prenatal, intrauterine state, in which the being was perfectly protected and completely gratified.

Through this concept of libido as the tendency to regress to the mother, many problems—for instance, sexuality in the narrow sense—and all neurotic disturbances of sexuality become intelligible. From a dispassionate psychological standpoint, love is the way of satisfying this primal instinct, since one approaches most nearly to primal reality when one comes into closest possible physical contact with the loved being, as one was once with the mother. Only instead of two fully developed egos, a third, just being created, accomplishes the real return to the mother. This temporary, although incomplete, satisfaction of the libido aim in the sexual act simultaneously serves the strongest progressive tendency—namely, creation of children. The human being is enabled to apply the remaining portion of still unsatisfied libido to necessary adjustments to reality and to creation of culture, by using it in the service of sublimation.[5] Even our highest psychical level, involving the thought process, is influenced by our instincts and acts in their service.

This knowledge has great practical importance also and belongs to the principles of psychoanalysis. Breuer's discovery of symptom formation has shown that psychology was wrong in supposing that certain ideas that come into consciousness are rigidly bound to affects that appear at the same time. On the contrary, affects show a great capacity for displacement along certain channels. Affects can be soldered to one idea but just as easily freed again and bound to another. Above all, study of dreams has shown that this is the case not only with pathogenic affects, but nearly all our emotions are, so to say, falsely interpreted by our consciousness or, to express it another way, are "inadequate," because they originally referred and still refer primarily to other objects and situations. Especially is this valid for the human being's two strongest affects, love and anxiety, which regularly are attached to persons in earliest childhood and can only be transferred later to others. A consequence of this analytic concept of the displacement of affect was the recognition that the human being up till now had enormously overestimated his consciousness and especially its highest accomplishment, logical thought. The real driving, determining forces lie in emotional life, which reaches with its roots into the depth of the unconscious.

As compensation for its depreciation of consciousness as the driving force, psychoanalysis has on the other hand increased the power of consciousness as an instrument of knowledge. It does this by extending to an enormous degree the capacity of the human mind for self-observation in a field up till now undiscovered—namely, the unconscious. Consciousness, indeed, cannot govern the unconscious, but it can better recognize it. From this fact Breuer had already started. But it remains one of Freud's merits that he explored this purely therapeutic experience and revealed its general psychological importance. Psychology, which before had dealt only with the intuitive method of self-observation, was placed by Freud on a scientific basis, when he applied the method of objective and exact observation from the self to other people—patients and human beings in general.

The *unconscious*, *repression*, and *libido* are the three fundamental pillars of scientific analytic psychology—the libido as chief motive power; the unconscious as essential content, previously neglected; and repression as the fundamental defense mechanism of psychical life. The latter has to keep the unconscious from the conscious ego and from reality. Dynamically expressed, repression guarantees to the adjusted ego protection from exaggerated claims, both of libido from within and reality from without. All three concepts are derived from a dynamic energetic point of view and make for the first time a psychology that avoids the mystical soul concept of the philosophers and the materialistic conception of physiology. The scientific importance of analytic psychology lies in three fundamental points of view:

1. Psychoanalysis not only maintains that all psychical occurrences are significant but can give proof of this for the first time by taking the unconscious into consideration.
2. Psychoanalysis has thereby shown the strict determinism that rules in psychic life.
3. Psychoanalysis has placed the whole psychic life under the general law of an unconscious aim, popularly called wish fulfillment, more accurately, perhaps, instinct satisfaction.

This is subordinated to general laws of energetics in psychic life, which should be valued as highly as the laws of nature in the physical world. Recognition of the strict determinism of the psychical makes psychology a science. Recognition of the unconscious meaning of everything psychical leads to an unexpected enrichment of the mental sciences. Recognition of the unconscious aim tendency leads to an entirely new orientation of the human being in the world, an intellectual revolution whose final goal is not yet to be seen. Finally, we shall gain an

enormous extension of consciousness through raising instinctive unconscious psychic contents to the level of conscious human thought. This
means an essential stride in development, which may even be considered
comparable to a biologic advance of mankind, an advance that will be
accomplished for the first time under a certain conscious self-control.[6]

Notes

Read before the University of Pennsylvania School of Social Work, June 19,
1924.

1. Frightened by the sexual nature of transference, Breuer delayed publication
of the case of "Anna O.," the *Ur*-patient of psychoanalysis, for ten years. See
my introduction for an exploration of the overdetermined meanings of Rank's
startling metaphor of psychoanalysis as an "illegitimate child" and of Freud as
"tender and loving foster mother." Concerning the latter E. James Lieberman
observes: "Freud has been called many things, but only his foster son called him
a mother! Otto Rank could not have done so unaware of its symbolic meaning"
(Lieberman 1985, p. xvii).
    In this lecture Rank expresses himself unreservedly as an "orthodox" Freud-
ian, giving no hint of the furious debates then raging in the inner circle about
his revolutionary new work on the birth trauma.

2. The question of "strict" determinism would soon become one of the most
important markers separating Rank from psychoanalytic orthodoxy. By 1930,
in his book *Seelenglaube und Psychologie* [Belief in the Soul and Psychology],
translated in 1950 as *Psychology and the Soul*, Rank no longer spoke of "strict"
determinism in the psychological—as opposed to the biological—life of the human being. Drawing on the most recent findings of quantum physics, the last
chapter of *Seelenglaube* argues, along with Einstein, that "contemporary physics
earnestly doubts the practicability of rigid causality" (Rank 1930b, p. 168).
Having independently come to the same conclusion in the psychological realm,
Rank now regretted his own "*too* strict application of determinism" (ibid., p.
171; italics added) in *The Trauma of Birth*. In a 1926 lecture on "The Anxiety
Problem," Rank addresses the views of his critics that "in *The Trauma of Birth*
I reduced psychoanalysis to an absurdity insofar as [I] vainly sought for a specific cause [*Ursache*] of the neuroses [in birth]" [8-123]. While denying that this
was so, Rank later accepted the validity of some of this criticism. As long as
psychoanalysis held fast to the libido theory—as Rank himself did in *The
Trauma of Birth*—it would remain wedded to an outdated Newtonian form of
"strict" determinism.
    Due to Freud's naive faith in the positivistic ideology of nineteenth-century
natural science, writes Rank in *Seelenglaube*, psychoanalysis never recognized
"the individual as such, but [only] as a being whose will is 'causally' explained
by sexual libido" (Rank 1930b, p. 186). In psychoanalytic theory the person,
therefore, is missing in action: "The real I, or self with its own power, the will,
is left out," adds Rank in *Will Therapy* (1929–31, p. 113). Even in recent years,

the word *will* is virtually taboo in psychoanalysis, whether therapists identify themselves as "classical," "object-relational," or "self-psychological" (Mitchell 1988, pp. 239–70). By the time Rank published *Seelenglaube*, four years after having left Freud's inner circle, he is willing to concede that he himself had once entered the cul-de-sac of "strict" determinism, in which psychoanalysts, with rare exceptions, still find themselves trapped today: "I have pursued [in *The Trauma of Birth*] to its ultimate consequences the principle of causality which Freud applied to psychic events in a naive 'physical' way, and have been led inexorably to a point where I simply had to derive mental phenomena from a 'causality of willing' in order to understand them. My conception was not that the principle of causality was 'false,' but that it no longer sufficed for our current level of awareness because its psychological meaning had undermined its heuristic value" (Rank 1930b, p. 171). By "psychological meaning," Rank is referring to human willing, thinking and feeling.

Repeating one of his main arguments in *The Development of Psychoanalysis* (1924), Rank observes that the "therapeutic agent" in psychotherapy is not historical understanding of the past; rather it is "simply *present experience*" (Rank 1930b, p. 176; his italics), what he and Ferenczi called *Erlebnis*, the consciousness of living. In short, the patient must find the courage to *choose* that which is also absolutely *determined*: his or her own life. Compulsion can only be overcome creatively, writes Rank in *Art and Artist*, through the "volitional affirmation of the obligatory" (1932a, p. 64). In the unpublished German manuscript of *Art and Artist* (located in *RC*), this phrase appears as *willensmäßige Bejahung des Gemußten*—i.e., deliberately saying "Yes" to the "Must." We have no choice other than to choose freely that which is *already* given to us: life. In *Will Therapy* Rank adds that the act of human willing "sets in motion a new causal chain" (1929–31, p. 44), a causal chain that does not deny determinism but enriches and deepens the meaning of responsible action. Both determinism and freedom, in short, are valid. Willing expresses itself uniquely for each living being. Will is the subjective experience of living itself, a continuous process of agency that, paradoxically, may elect to deny itself, deny that an actor is even present. Strangely, human beings seen to have been granted the freedom, according to Rank, to "transform will to *not*-willing" (ibid., p. 153; italics added). But it is only in the act of willing, of determined and purposeful choosing, that "we have the unique phenomenon of spontaneity, the establishing of a new primary cause [*einer neuen Ursache*]" (ibid., p. 44). Once Freud's favorite son, an architect of *die Sache*, the psychoanalytic "cause," Rank could not have missed the double entendre embedded in the phrase *einer neuen Ursache*. For Rank, creative willing rather than sexuality was now, as it were, *die Sache*—far more important than "the cause" of psychoanalysis. In other words, will, not libido, is "the cause" of both health and neurosis, which Rank now spoke of as a failure in creativity rather than a failure in sexuality. (See "Neurosis as a Failure in Creativity" [20].) Against the "repetition compulsion" of biological sexuality, Rank would pit the human creative impulse, the even more powerful "drive" for newness and difference, for production not just *re*-production: a lifelong, never-completed process that is balanced precariously on the boundary of nonexistence, *Nichts*, the ultimate and dreaded fate of humankind, biological death.

3. Ostensibly an uncompromising exponent of the scientific *Weltanschauung*, a positivist, Freud nevertheless often spoke of the "art" of interpretation. The question of "arbitrariness" or subjectivity in interpretation, therefore, has long bedeviled psychoanalysis and has not been resolved up to the present (Meissner 1991). Once Rank turned against "strict" determinism, he no longer felt it necessary to leave the impression, as he does in this lecture, that interpretation could somehow be "neutral" or "objective." All interpretation, no matter how delicately timed or phrased, is necessarily a kind of suggestion (see "Active and Passive Therapy" [21]). Never reluctant to confront patients when he felt it was helpful to promote their growth, Rank did not refrain from making challenging interpretations in his therapeutic sessions. But by the late 1920s, he recognized that interpretation, while not necessarily "arbitrary," is always subjective and tentative. Even interpretation of the *present* is scarcely valid or reliable while it is being enacted in the moment of *Erlebnis*. "It is not a question of whose interpretation is correct," says Rank in a 1930 lecture, "because there is no such thing as *the* interpretation or only *one* psychological truth. Psychology does not deal primarily with facts as science does but only with the individual's attitude toward facts. In other words, the objects of psychology are *interpretations*—and there are as many of them as there are individuals and, even more than that, also the individual's different situations, which have to be interpreted *differently* in every single manifestation [17-222].

Well before 1930, even in *The Trauma of Birth*, Rank had already concluded that the *relationship* between patient and therapist was itself therapeutic, not the therapist's "insight" into—or "causal" interpretation of—the patient's infantile past or presenting problem. Relationship takes priority over interpretation. "Not only less theory," says Rank pointedly in *Will Therapy*, "but less 'art of interpretation' is necessary" (1929–31, p. 5). This conclusion was almost certainly a consequence of Rank's stress on short-term therapy. Endless investigation of the labyrinthine infantile past allows both therapist and patient to avoid the emotionally charged *present*: two creative and destructive wills encountering, resisting, trusting, hating, loving, and, if a miracle occurs, healing each other. It is not what the client learns from the therapist's interpretations that is healing. "Knowledge," says Rank, "is certainly not the therapeutic agent" (ibid., p. 167), but "freeing through experience [*Erlebnis*] can bring the insight afterwards, although even this is not essential to the result" (ibid., p. 106). Living, therefore, is simply "emotional surrender to the present" (ibid., p. 27), to the Now. The problem of experience, according to Rank, is not how to understand or speak about shadowy fragments of the past, Oedipal or pre-Oedipal, which have already been interpreted and reinterpreted a thousandfold in memory, but how to *live in the present*: thinking, feeling and willing are always in the present. "Such a new experiencing, and not merely a repetition of the infantile, represents the therapeutic process . . . thus making possible a connection with the reality of the moment" (ibid., pp. 39–40).

4. See "The Prometheus Complex" [15] for Rank's view that education or reeducation—what Freud called *Nacherziehung*—can be perverted in the analytic situation into "indoctrination."

5. By the late 1920s, after abandoning the determinism of libido theory, with the implications of his theory of the creative will fully worked out, Rank would no longer speak of "sublimation" as a "producer" of art or culture. How, he wondered, from a biological drive could there be produced not sexuality but a "sublimated" derivative of sex—the work of art? Who or what is actually doing the *work* of sublimation? Is art a derivative of biology? How does one build a bridge between a biological impulse common to all men and women and the production, say, of Beethoven's *Ode to Joy*, an astonishing and never-to-be repeated masterpiece? Did Michelangelo paint the Sistine Chapel or was the work done, somehow, by a derivative of the sex drive—an impersonal "compromise formation" of biological vectors, intrapsychic forces, and defense mechanisms? "An inexplicable 'remainder' had therefore to be admitted," said Rank in *Art and Artist*, "but this remainder embraced no more and no less than the whole problem of artistic creativity" (1932a, p. 63).

In "Neurosis as a Failure in Creativity" [20], Rank adds that the human creative impulse, "which I also see at the roots of mental (or imaginative) illness, is not sexuality, as psychoanalysis assumed, but rather an *anti-sexual* tendency in man—which we may characterize as voluntary control of the instinctive life. More precisely stated, I conceive of the creative drive as the impulse-life (including sexuality) put at the service of the individual will."

"When psychoanalysis speaks of the sublimation of the sex instinct, by which is meant its diversion from the purely biological function and its direction toward higher goals, the question as to *what* diverts and *what* directs does not seem to be answered by reference to repression—a negative factor that can divert, perhaps, but never direct." [20-253]

6. By 1930 Rank's position on the human value of the "science" of psychoanalysis would take what today might be called a "postmodern" turn. This positivistic "science," concluded Rank,

> has proved to be a complete failure in the field of psychology, i.e., in the betterment of human nature and in the achievement of human happiness. . . . The result of scientific psychology can be summed up today as the recognition that it is necessarily insufficient to explain human nature, far less to make the individual happier. The error lies in the scientific glorification of *consciousness*, of intellectual knowledge, which even psychoanalysis worships as its highest god—although it calls itself a psychology of the *unconscious*. But this means only an attempt to rationalize the unconscious and to intellectualize it scientifically. [17-222]

This repression of the "existential" unconscious, forgetting the mystery of *Dasein*, which remains forever unknown and unknowable, is precisely the criticism later leveled by Lacan against the American form of ego psychology (Taylor 1987).

2

THE THERAPEUTIC APPLICATION OF
PSYCHOANALYSIS (1924)

LADIES AND GENTLEMEN, when Freud was invited by Clark University at Worcester, Massachusetts, some fifteen years ago, to speak of psychoanalysis for the first time to an American audience, his presentation of the subject was essentially from the therapeutic standpoint. This was not only historically logical; it was also natural, from a personal point of view, since Freud himself had started as a neurologist. But he was dissatisfied with the neurology of that time and so had turned his scientific ambition into this new field. In spite of the tremendous progress since made by psychoanalytic investigation, beyond therapeutics, Freud has really never quite given up his original medical point of view and has tolerated penetration of psychoanalysis into wider circles of cultured people with a certain uneasiness. This attitude indeed has some justification, especially when such popularizing of psychoanalysis is possible only in a rough, crude way and by means of striking catchwords. On the other hand, the fierce resistance that Freud's doctrines aroused in his colleagues seemed to indicate that the destined way of psychoanalysis would be through its appeal to the public.

So if I am to speak of psychoanalytic therapy as the original practical side of psychoanalysis, I must announce beforehand that, in view of its present-day position, it would be more correctly spoken of as the application of psychoanalysis to the therapy of neuroses. For, in the last decade, the psychoanalytic doctrine and movement have extended far beyond the bounds of therapeutic interest. Formerly the question was, How can medical analysis be applied to other sciences or to practical life? Today the task is more and more to single out, from the vast psychoanalytic system, those results that can most profitably be used in therapy. Naturally, I do not mean by this to place a final limit on what the psychoanalyst should know of psychoanalysis, but rather to establish a permanent mutual relationship between analytic investigation and practical application of its results to therapy.

In addition to this development within the science itself, which, with the advance in our psychological knowledge, naturally increases our therapeutic abilities, we must also bear in mind the increase in popular knowledge of psychoanalysis and greater willingness on the part of the public to accept its point of view. This may be called a kind of mass therapy, an analytic enlightenment of society in general. Naturally, this cannot have as deep an influence as a methodical individual analysis, yet on that account it has a wider influence. I have already discussed the general social importance of this fact and shall have something to say about its cultural importance in my next lecture, "Psychoanalysis as a Cultural Factor" [4]. Here the question is, What influence has the penetration of psychoanalytic knowledge to the public had on the therapeutic side of psychoanalysis? The fact that psychoanalytic literature is eagerly read by the public, that its problems are discussed extensively in literature and even in the daily press—this fact would be nothing in itself if psychoanalysis as a therapeutic method did not occupy a unique position in medicine. To be sure, other medical problems important for humanity, such as investigation of cancer or the question of tuberculosis, are publicly discussed. But psychoanalysis has two characteristics that make its position unique: first, the general human importance of it keeps the interest of the laity focused on its contents; second, knowledge of the psychoanalytic discoveries itself constitutes a part of therapy, and so far, apparently, the doctor has no advantage over the patient.

This fact must not be neglected, but, on the other hand, its influence must not be overestimated. Breuer made the discovery that neurotic symptoms disappear as soon as the patient remembers the repressed experiences that cause them. As long as the patient himself has to search for these in his own unconscious, he necessarily had to live again these experiences affectively and abreact them in that way. Then Freud later discovered that these experiences, which differ with the individual, had a traumatic influence because they reawakened earlier typical experiences that had been inadequately overcome. Through knowledge of these typical experiences, one could save the patient the trouble of looking for the original traumas; but one had to replace, in some other way, reproduction of the affect, which is essential for the therapeutic result.

This occurs in a way that is quite independent of knowledge of the repressed experiences, because this part of therapy is *not* of an intellectual but an *emotional* nature. In this direction Freud went far beyond Breuer's catharsis. Breuer, as I noted in my lecture on "Psychoanalysis as General Psychology" [1], fled from his work on neuroses when his patient announced to him, and at the same time acted, the delivery of the child allegedly begotten by him. Freud, obviously, was able to free himself to a greater degree from human vanity and so to judge the problem objectively. He soon noticed that other patients adopted the same emotional attitude toward him that would be described in ordinary life as "being in love." But *he* was able to say to himself that this was not on account of any special attraction of his personality but lay in the nature of patients themselves, or in their suffering—belonged, so to speak, to utterances of the neurosis. In this way he made the real psychoanalytic discovery, which he called transference—that is, the fact that human beings in general have a tendency to attach their libido (to a certain extent always free-floating) to a given object. In doing this they gain great satisfaction, which is sufficient to serve as a substitute for the *unconscious gain of illness* that the patient previously got from his suffering. In analysis, in the patiently continued daily occupation with the patient's most intimate unconscious feelings, conditions for such a libido transference are especially favorable. One comes thus into a position to grasp, as it were, the whole libido in its purely concentrated form. The psychical analysis of this libido transference, which was necessary for the healing and freeing of the patient, gave a remarkable result, the practical importance of which went far beyond the therapeutic field of analysis of neuroses and made intelligible a large part of normal psychology. It showed, namely, that the patient's attitude, which one could mistake for love, had throughout nothing new in it, but was to be explained historically as an exact reproduction of earlier relations of the child to parents. It also showed that the patient, not only in analysis but also in life, was constantly compelled to reestablish and repeat this attitude. Thus the analysis of transference led to discovery of the infantile Oedipus complex in mankind. It was so called because the Greek hero, in unconsciously killing his father and marrying his mother, represented the most extreme realization of this libidinal parental relationship.

I should need a good deal of time to show you the importance for development of the individual, as well as society, of the Oedipus complex, which has become the kernel of psychoanalysis. But let me tell you only the most important results. The relation of child to father and mother determines in conclusive ways the love life of the human being, as well as his social behavior. Not only are the love objects of both sexes chosen according to the model of the first infantile love object, but also the child's ideal formation, so important for general social attitude, comes originally from parents. These are later replaced by other persons somehow substituting for them; for example, teachers, public officials, heroes, and so forth. An exact study of the development of the Oedipus complex in the child, which the analytic transference situation allowed us, has made necessary a somewhat complicated formulation of facts with reference especially to the difference of the sexes. As analysis was almost exclusively practiced by men, and the theoretical work of the analytic results was elaborated by men, it was at first easy to assume that transference libido in women as well as men patients contained the infantile relation to the father. This was, namely, in the case of woman the heterosexual component, in the case of man, the homosexual. Naturally, one could not be satisfied with this in the analysis. But often enough the chief task consisted in having to free from repression just the other libido component not manifest in the transference. Thereby, from the purely psychological side, a discovery was made that corresponded to the biological fact of the original bisexual disposition of mankind. This was, namely, that man was capable of a feminine libido attitude in his unconscious, leading up to phantasies of pregnancy and birth; and that woman in her unconscious often had a masculine libido attitude, which expressed itself in extreme form as a phantasy of possessing man's genitals.

Whereas Dr. Breuer was afraid that his patient was personally in love with him and had formed the delusion of having a child by him, Freud was able to explain from his observations that this was no isolated case and nothing special. Every patient is in love in a certain way with his doctor, the difference from real love lying in the fact that this emotional attitude in the transference is quite independent of the personal qualities of the doctor. Thus it rests on a general law, which is intelligible from development of the human libido in the Oedipus complex. It was observed, also, that the actual sex of the analyst, in comparison with that of patient, formed no hindrance to the elementary libido striving. For example, a male analyst can unconsciously represent the mother as libido object, besides, as we already know, personifying the father. From this observation the difference between "being in love" and the transference was made still clearer. Accordingly, a deeper analytic work [i.e., *The Trauma of Birth*] gave a quite specific formulation for transference libido that went *beyond* the sexual conception of the Oedipus complex. The deepest unconscious of the human being knows, namely, only one original libido binding, which is not only first but also the most intensively experienced, and that is the libidinal connection resting on the biological relation to the mother.

It may appear to you curious that so obvious and simple a fact—that all love finally rests on love for the mother—had to be discovered by the complicated method of the analytic situation. If I attempt to show you the reason for this, you must not consider it an irrelevant deviation from our theme. It will, on the contrary, introduce us to the real problems of psychical life and their solving. I do not know if all great discoveries finally concern some simple fact, which had been previously overlooked, as one used to say, for some other cause. But it is certain that all the essential discoveries of psychoanalysis concern very simple things, and that only the way to their revelation was complicated. For example, that the dream is a wish fulfillment is expressed in numerous folk beliefs, proverbs, and poems; that small blunders of everyday life could have meaning was also, before analysis, incidentally known, especially in relation to love affairs. The same psychology relates to the blunders as to quite a number of widespread superstitions. Symbolism also was not only familiar to the ancients but is understood by our contemporaries in wit and in folk songs, as for example, in your American song "Yes, I Have No Bananas." And the fact of infantile sexuality, discovered by analysis, is so obvious that one not only wonders that a discovery was necessary, but one is astonished at the violent resistance encountered by this as by all other analytic perceptions. People's resistances to conscious acceptance of scientific facts that one likes only tacitly to recognize betray, as analysis has taught us, activity of the repression tendency. This repression tendency cannot deny the reality of certain things but attempts to prevent acceptance and recognition of them.

Naturally, here there are again at work strong affective factors, in no way intellectual, which cause and maintain this tendency to repression. The libidinal relation between mother and child has not only not been consciously recognized at all times but has been sung with highest praise as mother-child love. It is, therefore, rather difficult to see what repression tendency should have prevented us from recognizing this immediately in analysis as the deepest root of the phenomenon of transference. It should have been easy to understand that the original libido aim must in the very deepest sense strive for the mother, who even before the beginning of individual life satisfies all the child's needs, those of protection and nourishment especially. From study of neuroses, I could show that for the unconscious this prenatal libido situation is just the ideal prototype of every later libido satisfaction in life. It contains what we might describe as the general desire for blessedness. However, as a complete satisfaction of that kind can never later be obtained, this fact gives to libido the character of insatiability and gives also its capacity for expression, displacement, transference, and sublimation. These characteristics lead to the most primitive acts of adjustment as well as to the highest creations of culture. Of the greatest importance, and in its psychological consequences still not at all appreciated, is the moment of birth, in which the living being is deprived of this blessed primal gratification and so has to put up with various kinds of substitute satisfactions. Through this fact of the loss of an irreplaceable source of pleasure, birth becomes a severe trauma. This trauma of birth establishes on the one hand the primal repression, which has to do with the irretrievable paradise, and on the other hand compels a forward striving that exhausts itself in constantly repeated attempts to gain substitute satisfactions.

I have attempted in *The Trauma of Birth* (1924) to outline in a general way the effects of birth trauma, and I would like here to refer shortly to its importance for psychoanalysis, especially for the doctrine of neurosis. The central problem of the neuroses is anxiety, whose solving occurs simultaneously with freeing of the unconscious mother fixation. In every individual the primary factor is anxiety as it was originally experienced by the child at birth in *physiological* apnea and then became *psychically* anchored to prevent regression. This primary anxiety must always be reproduced, as often as the libido in its regressive tendency approaches this border whose overstepping would signify a renunciation of reality, such as occurs in the psychoses or in suicide. So we recognize in anxiety a biological guard against the libido's regression to the primal state, which state would be equivalent to death. According to the level in the individual at which this anxiety is fixed, it reacts in a definite type of character, and also (when it falls into neuroses) in formation of symptoms. These symptoms I have been able to trace back as being reproductions of the birth trauma or of the intrauterine condition.

I regret that I cannot here illustrate these assertions, which may seem to you bold, with examples from neuroses.[1] I must be content with assuring you that from this discovery, which is based on numerous experiences, not only a practical, useful doctrine of types could be developed, but also a definite psychoanalytic symptomatology. This would supplement clinical symptomatology from the unconscious side. Thus one is able to recognize from symptoms that traumatic primal form to which the ego of the patient has regressed, and is in a position to solve therapeutically the libidinal mother fixation. This is accomplished by rousing anxiety and freeing it in abreactions on the specific border of repression. Thus knowledge of the patient's typical reactions, according to the compulsion of repetition, served as a means of help. We know from experience that the patient's peculiarity is clearly displayed at the beginning of analysis. So, too, the analyst by his training is in a position to recognize at the very beginning the form adopted by the patient when he failed to master his primal trauma.

You must not immediately feel that this new point of view, which I introduced into analysis, is an unexpected and undesirable complication of psychoanalytic theory. Consider it rather, although it leads into the deepest biological layer of the unconscious, as representing an essential simplification of psychoanalytic results. It is in its nature, as in its possibility of application, a purely practical result. This discovery, like every advance in science, makes some earlier theoretical assumptions practically superfluous but does not on that account diminish their scientific importance. There is no contradiction in the statement that psychoanalytic investigation has become ever more complicated in its work of interpreting and formulating theories and ever more simple in its scientific results and practical applications. And at a certain point of knowledge, the way in which that knowledge was discovered does not matter; only the practical use of knowledge is important. Therefore, I need not explain to you here in detail the difficult and complicated process by which the fact of the birth trauma was found; nor need I show you how its importance for development of the whole human race was recognized. Our entire psychoanalytic knowledge, including the complicated technique of interpretation, had to be placed at the service of this investigation, which we now can use for practical application.

In regard to this experience also, it would not be enough to make a simple statement of facts to the patient, as it would have been in Breuer's experiment. Since the tendency to mother regression is the essence of libido, we ought not to expect to alter this biological force by merely explaining it. For the cure itself we need, in addition to this, another analytic point of view, which is derived from dynamic psychology of the ego, to which also belong the therapeutic processes of consciousness and becoming conscious. The freeing of libidinal mother fixation is only the first therapeutic step in analysis, which corresponds to the original physiological separation of the child from the mother—namely, birth. The second part of analytic work consists chiefly in what Freud called re-education, which is similar to education of the child after birth and is mainly an ego formation. As the educator—or parental authorities whom he represents—makes possible to the child an ego formation in the way mentioned in my previous lecture on "Psychoanalysis as General Psychology" [1], so the analyst has to strengthen or weaken the undeveloped or overdeveloped ego of the patient—that is, to bring about appropriate changes in his attitude to the biologically given unconscious and subsequently to reality. Just as the child does this only out of love for his teacher, so the process of re-education of the ego during analysis is carried through by means of the transference. This transference, after the freeing of the mother fixation, must be transformed into an identification with the analyst,[2] as an adjusted representative of the outside world. Finally, this identification has to be analyzed and transformed by the sublimation process of the healing into a new ideal or super-ego created by the patient himself.

For that purpose the analyst also has to deny himself many things, even as he demands and must demand certain renunciations on the part of the patient. He must be able to give up from the first any scientific ambition that may lead him to wish to research something new from his patient's unconscious. He must be prepared with this knowledge. He must further be so sure of his knowledge and its application that he can resist the temptation to prove to his patient this and that, to show why the presuppositions of his theory are right. Of course the patient must grant the degree of authority that he would allow without further ado to any other specialist, and he must accept with a certain amount of confidence any explanation from the analyst. This need not necessarily be an interpretation but a communication, and it must be accepted as an explanation would be from any other medical specialist. Lastly, the analyst, on the strength of his deepest knowledge, must give up all idea of changing the patient's biologically given unconscious, which finally represents the embryonic and cosmic surviving in us all. The analyst can bring the patient only to recognize the unconscious, and to correct his conscious attitude toward it in the sense of re-education. Thus the analyst will be in a position, not only to obtain therapeutic results in a shorter time, but also, with less therapeutic ambition, to bring about in the personality of the patient many intense and lasting changes that will protect him from further regressions and fixations.

This second part—the analytic education, which really lengthens the cure—must bring about, simultaneously with the new ideal formation, freeing of the transference relation to the analyst. The patient has been compelled by transference to loosen this regressive mother fixation bound up in symptoms, so that libido is now available in the analysis and can be forced into a progressive direction to form the new ideal and to achieve re-adjustment. The first part of the task—namely, to get transference of libido to the analyst—is easy; the danger lies in the possibility of the patient's libido remaining fixed in analysis as it was formerly in symptoms. Whether the patient is really in love with the analyst, as is more easily possible with women patients, or whether, as is more the case with men, there is merely an intellectual and social dependency, the effect is the same—namely, failure. In correct analysis, both must be unconditionally avoided, unless one wants to get into the position from which Breuer in his time found no way out. Whether analysis has really accomplished anything for the patient will be shown in the freeing of the transference—that is, if the patient does not again repeat and maintain symptoms that disappeared during the course of analysis. Psychoanalytic therapy does not, by any means, aim at the mere putting on one side of symptoms, which can be attained by other and different methods; it aims at preventing the possibility of their return. And for this knowledge of their origin does not suffice. Results that disappear as soon as the analyst attempts to free the patient's libidinal fixation on him are due only to the success of the transference, as in Breuer's case. Real psychoanalysis, on the other hand, is a radical therapy that starts out by removing the conditions to which symptoms owe their origin. This is not possible by merely communicating analytic knowledge to the patient. An emotional re-experience is necessary. This re-experiencing becomes finally a form of application that the analyst, on the strength of his own knowledge and power, uses for the patient's benefit. If I were to illustrate this by a drastic example, I would say that the analyst acts in the cure as is reported of a doctor in the South, who is said to have announced, "If I don't know what's the matter with the patient, I throw him into a fit, and I'm hell on fits." Thus the analyst can bring about a radical cure only by first rousing the repressed conflicts before setting to work to solve them.

As you will note, a certain amount of *active* intervention is necessary, but this is not especially characteristic of psychoanalysis; it belongs to every therapy. If you will not misunderstand me, I would like to illustrate also the active-affective character of our present-day psychoanalytic technique by an example with which you all must certainly be familiar. Long before analysis, literature made use of this motive, and it has again recently become fashionable in connection with psychoanalysis in the theater and even in movies.[3] In general, the plot is that the hero completely loses his memory, owing to some severe psychic shock; or, as we would put it, a total repression of the content of consciousness takes place in him. The author usually arranges that he shall get his memory back again and at the same time be restored to complete psychic health, by being exposed to another shock of the same kind, where possible in the same situation. This also, I believe, is a common occurrence for everyday life: I think of something I want, which is in another room; I go to fetch it; and when I come to the room, I have forgotten what it is I wanted. I retrace my steps and turn again to go to the other room to exactly the same place at which I was conscious of the desired object. Immediately the memory returns, and this time I succeed in fetching the object. In the same way, only with much finer psychical means and with no help from the outside, we expose the patient in analysis to his primal trauma and allow him to live through the experience again. May I add that this conception—namely, that of curing illness by means of the same germ or shock that caused the suffering—is indeed an ancient one in medicine, and even our modern serology rests on the same principle. As psychoanalysis has recognized that the neurotic is, finally, one who suffers from traumas that most people successfully overcome, so our therapeutic method consists in the re-establishment and reproduction of libidinal mother fixation in reference to the analyst, and in the surgical cutting of this psychological umbilical cord, with which the patient has hitherto always been burdened. Once this has happened, the libido, previously fixed at an infantile level, is transferred almost of its own accord to reality by the process of new ego formation.

The whole process corresponds biologically to bodily separation from the mother and identification with the father, and socially to the task of education, which has to make the child self-reliant and independent of both parents. Therefore, analysis, straight from the beginning, aims to accustom the patient to independence and self-reliance, in the same way as the pedagogue educates the child. The analyst must at all costs be careful not to spoil the patient in any way; because just the fact of being spoiled—namely, the habit of not being able to give up his desires—has made the patient neurotic. He who wishes to educate or to cure a person only by means of love is like a philanthropist who has undertaken to remove all poverty for the world by an everlasting spending of money. Apart from the fact that economically it would be impossible—even though it were undertaken by the richest man in the world—such an event would be harmful, since nobody then would take the trouble to earn for himself. Also, we must not forget what analysis itself has taught us: that neurotic people become ill just from an insatiable libido hunger, which makes them so greedy that the general means of satisfaction—sexual love and socially useful work—do not suffice. They suffer, therefore, as Freud has shown, after all from sexual conflicts, which are reflected simultaneously in unconscious mother fixation and in the transference relation. With analysis of the mother fixation, these sexual conflicts can at the same time be solved, in the sense that the patient can now reconcile himself, even as do his healthy fellow beings, to the possibilities of gratification offered by a normal life. He can overcome his arrest of development in sexual adjustment without entirely giving up mother libido, for sexual love aims at satisfying and continuing the infantile mother-child relation in a grown-up sense, without ever fully satisfying it in the unconscious sense.

I do not know whether my arguments have made quite clear to you what the real essence of psychoanalytic therapy is. But you could hardly expect me to present the specific therapy of neurotic diseases in a general lecture as one would in a medical course. Without detailed representation of the forms of disease and the analytic technique itself, one cannot go deeper into the understanding of therapy. I think, however, that such a presentation would rather bore you, and I assume that the general psychological and cultural importance of psychoanalysis has more claim on your interest. Finally, the chief thing is not whether one cures this or that neurotic. The neuroses have proved themselves to be inevitable symptoms of human civilization and culture, and the much more important question is whether psychoanalysis is in a position to show people the ways and means of fighting this culture disease, so that progress may continue without endangering the individual's possibility of happiness.

But the development of psychoanalysis, from its beginning to its final conclusions, has shown that everything that we believed we had recognized in the neurotic as a specific disease-forming factor is a general human quality, which has led only in this or that case to a neurosis. We all carry the same complexes in our unconscious psychical life, as we all have the necessary life organs in our body. And we all suffer from the same psychical traumas even as we take in all kinds of bacteria, most of us without being permanently ill or suffering any evil consequences at all. So the specific in the neurosis is to be formulated only negatively. The neurotic has failed psychically to master the conflicts and necessary adjustments to reality that the normal person has overcome, with a greater or lesser degree of harm and damage to part of his character and capabilities. Thus psychoanalysis has already gone far beyond the realm of therapy into that of prophylaxis, which is also the ideal of medical science generally, as it is supposed to be the chief task of education to make itself superfluous.

Here, then, in the wide field of prophylaxis, we can make contact with the process of popularizing psychoanalysis, which I characterized in the beginning as a kind of mass therapy. This psychoanalytic enlightenment as to the dangers of the child's sexual development, like social enlightenment on the subject of the venereal diseases, can accomplish good and lasting results only when applied systematically and authoritatively. To accomplish this we need, before everything, a generation of trained social workers, educators, mental-hygiene teachers, and doctors who are familiar with the practical results of psychoanalysis. The growing generation of children must be protected from psychic traumas that psychoanalysis, by laborious investigations of the analyses of neurotic people, has revealed as pathogenic influences. In this way, after the expiration of a time of incubation, everything that we must use today in the service of therapy as a means of curing neuroses, by passing into the general knowledge of human beings as parents, will become a psychical hygiene, which will play the same part in a new society as physical or social hygiene plays in the society of today. We have good grounds for believing that through this analytic work of enlightenment from both sides—therapeutic practice and psychic hygiene—the neuroses in their present form will cease to exist. The sooner psychoanalysis reaches this aim, the sooner will its therapeutic task be terminated, and so much the greater service will be accomplished for the development of mankind.

Notes

Read before the New School for Social Research, New York, May 1924.

1. In *The Trauma of Birth*, Rank gives a number of illustrations. In general, he writes, the neurotic "is not content with the gratification of partially returning to the mother, afforded [for the male] in the sexual act and [for the female]

in the child, but has remained fixedly 'infantile' and even still desires to go *completely* or as a whole back into the mother" (1924, pp. 47–48; his italics).

2. By 1926 Rank had refined his thinking on the value of identification for his patients, especially those whose creativity was inhibited by excessive fear or guilt. In a lecture on "Social Adaptation and Creativity" [14], Rank says:

> One cannot help them by driving them back to old identifications or by offering them new possibilities of identification. One has to help them to get *beyond* the deadlock in their personality and in the process find their *own* self. I think that the so-called inner crises in the human being's life correspond to the stage of his development in which old identifications break down under the burden of his own strengthened ego *before this ego is strong enough to bear the whole burden of the new personality*. Hence these crises occur so frequently when the individual has attained in life a certain success that he justly ascribes to himself, to his own personality, as it is *not* due to identification alone. [14-196]

The germ of this idea may have been planted some years before, by Freud himself. In a 1922 letter to Rank, Freud provides comments on a paper drafted by Rank—"your first pure [i.e., not literary] analytic work" (Taft 1958, p. 75). The paper, on therapeutic approaches for psychological impotency, was being prepared by Rank for presentation at an upcoming International Psychoanalytic Congress. By 1922 Rank had been practicing analysis full-time for over two years and had already experimented extensively with the new "relationship" therapy that he and Ferenczi were then developing. In his letter Freud credits Rank's paper with offering "the new idea regarding the mechanism of healing through identification, one that is very right, but in connection with which you do not dwell upon the limits of desirable identification" (Ibid., p. 76). In his later American lectures, as well as in *Will Therapy* (1929–31, pp. 79–80 and passim), Rank devoted much attention to differentiating the healing value of identification from its limits. (See the lectures in Part Three, "From Projection and Identification to Self-Determination: 'Emotions Are the Center and Real Sphere of Psychology.'").

3. Rank had long been fascinated by movies as an art form since, like literature and mythology, movies powerfully depict the interrelationship of the personal and social, individual and collective, I and Thou. In 1914, at 30, Rank became the first psychoanalytic movie critic, publishing an interpretation of Hans Ewer's popular romantic film *The Student of Prague* in *Der Doppelgänger* [The Double]. "It may perhaps turn out," wrote Rank presciently, "that cinematography, which in numerous ways reminds us of the dream-work, can also express certain psychological facts and relationships—which the writer is often unable to describe with verbal clarity—in such clear and conspicuous imagery that it facilitates our understanding of them" (1914, p. 4).

3

THE TRAUMA OF BIRTH AND ITS
IMPORTANCE FOR PSYCHOANALYTIC
THERAPY (1924)

LADIES AND GENTLEMEN, it gives me great pleasure to join the American Psychoanalytic Association and to meet and get to know personally the representatives of psychoanalysis in the United States, whom I have long ago known from their writings.[1] And I should very much like you also to consider my appearance as a personal introduction. I have in mind to give you only a general impression of what I consider my own contribution to psychoanalysis, as concisely as possible, even at the risk of becoming extreme.

I warn you beforehand that I do not intend to prove anything to you, nor do I wish to convince you. Also, I do not expect you immediately to form any opinion or judgment about what you hear until you have tried to prove it in your own analytic work. I would prefer that you listen as if a traveler were relating to you his experiences in a yet undiscovered country.

I have recently published a book entitled *Das Trauma der Geburt*. I am very sorry that I am not able to start my talk by giving you a definition of what the trauma of birth really is. I could not do this without giving long explanations. For those who want such explanations, I can only refer you to the book itself. What I intend in this lecture is not so much to give a short *résumé*, but to show you the *way* in which I came to the views described in my book, and how I came to use them in psychoanalytic technique.

As I am addressing a gathering of practicing analysts, I can start immediately, *in medias res*. Many years ago Freud stated that there comes a definite stage in the analysis of compulsion neuroses in which, by means of transference, the analysis itself becomes a compulsion for the patient in place of the old neurosis. This analytic compulsion, as Freud explained, is to be freed only by fixing a definite time limit, to which one must strictly keep. Following this Freudian rule in the analyses of a number of compulsion cases, I gradually found quite definite criteria that enabled me to recognize pretty early, without any doubt, the very point at which the patient was ready to receive and accept the notice to quit.[2]

When I became certain of my views, I applied this technique of "active intervention" to all other forms of neuroses. As I expected, this not only definitely shortened the treatment but is quite necessary for a correct conclusion of the analysis, for freeing of the transference, and for final healing of the patient. As an initial side effect, a constant experience resulted, whose eminently practical and theoretical importance soon manifested itself to me. I found that the patient showed quite regularly, under the pressure of this time limit, definite and unmistakable reactions—which led to only one conclusion. These reactions took on a form that could be conceived only as a reproduction of the separation from the first original libido object, namely, the mother. That is, the patient attempts to repeat in a quite obtrusive way the process of birth.[3]

Before you can follow me further in the consideration and judgment of this new experience, I would like to express and remove a criticism that may have immediately come to your mind. You might say that, regardless of the practical importance of a time limit, the reactions roused by it are produced artificially, and their similarity can be explained in that way. But my experiences and observations have convinced me that this is not the case. As a matter of fact, I subsequently remembered former cases of mine that I had treated without setting a definite time limit, and in which the last phase of the analysis occurred in a quite similar, though not so clearly expressed, form. Hitherto, I understood this only incidentally, and not in its general importance.

As I cannot prove this to you by showing you records of these former cases, I must be content to refer you to the well-known *From the History of an Infantile Neurosis* [*S.E.*, 17:7–122], published by Freud in 1918, in which the patient likewise represents and comprehends the end of the cure as a rebirth experience. But I am in the fortunate position of being able to bring a still stronger counter-argument to the objection that these reactions are artificially produced by limiting the time. Namely, when I started new cases with the understanding that the end phase of analysis is actually a reproduction of birth, I soon noticed that patients, indeed of both sexes, *from the very beginning* took the analyst in their deepest unconscious, without any exception, as a *libidinal substitute for the mother*. From the nature of the psychoanalytic situation, it follows that severance from this mother substitute is typified in the form of birth reproduction.

As the final and perhaps strongest counter-argument, I can recommend you personally to notice this fundamental fact in your analyses and thus to be convinced of its bearing and importance. You will then find, as I have found, that in the psychoanalytical situation the primal libidinal binding to the mother shows itself in various attempts to reestablish the intrauterine state. And the first severance of this relation as it occurred in parturition must be re-experienced and fully accomplished in a shortened period of time. From exact reproduction of typical painful birth reactions in the end phase of analysis, I inferred a trauma of birth. This, I suppose, could not have been recognized earlier because it apparently has suffered a much stronger repression than even manifestations of infantile sexuality.

I am not sure how far my short presentation, on the one hand, and your resistances naturally to be expected, on the other hand, have allowed you to follow me up to this point. So I do not know whether I should go on with explanation of the practical and theoretical consequences of this discovery. Be that as it may, I would like in any case to spare you from what I believe are the very important theoretical consequences. But from the practical consequences that may perhaps directly interest you, I can pick out one or two points here and there, chiefly with the purpose of avoiding possible misunderstandings in therapeutic application of this knowledge.

As I have already remarked, the patient has the tendency to reproduce in analysis the birth trauma, and he does this, and did it constantly, whether we understood it or not. In view of this experience, the main therapeutic task took on a new aspect, namely, to prevent the patient from automatically repeating the most important trauma, the trauma of birth, which, as with all other traumas, he is trying to repeat in analysis. In order to prevent the patient from unconsciously reproducing the birth trauma at *the end* of analysis, I proceed in every case, regardless of sex, to reveal straight from the beginning this regular strong manifestation of the mother libido in the transference relation.[4] Naturally, to prevent it entirely is not to be attempted. But reactions occur more gently and enable the patient to accomplish not only an easier but also a complete freeing from the analyst when one analyzes mother fixation from the very beginning.

Besides this great practical advantage, there also results the technical advantage, namely, that instead of unconscious reproduction of the birth trauma one gets at the end the patient's actual conflicts, so to say, pure and unmixed with infantile reactions. These are relatively easy to solve then. Thus the whole analytic procedure for the first time has a definite, sharply outlined content. In other words the analyst knows exactly what he has to do and what he has to expect. I believe that only through this technique will psychoanalytic therapy become a method of healing equal to other medical methods in its certainty and exactness.

That is really everything I want to tell you today. Briefly, it consists in the communication of just one single fact of experience from actual practice. And I request that you try it and prove it in your analyses. I would like to make only one more reference, which I had to isolate in order to make clear, to prevent misunderstanding of my new point of view. I want now to draw your attention to how it links to the sexual etiology of neuroses, known mainly as the Oedipus or castration complex. According to this concept, the neurotic—without exception, as Freud has shown us—withdraws or recoils from the task of normal adjustment to heterosexual life. From my analytic experience that the neuroses are based finally on a pathological regression to, or rather fixation on, the prenatal situation of libido gratification, Freud's concept is extended and biologically supported.

In *The Trauma of Birth* I have attempted to show in detail in what way this refers to the specific forms of neuroses and psychoses, and especially their symptoms, and how my explanation of the symptoms according to the birth trauma supplements the Oedipus theory from a biological point of view. I was able also to make intelligible the castration complex as the psychological representation of the biologic tendency to go back to the mother, which man actually accomplishes to a certain extent in the sexual act and which woman can get only by identification with a man. So the castration complex represents the main conflict in development of the child, namely, the difficult task of transferring libido from the mother to the father, which is much more complicated for woman, whose primal libido object, the mother, has to be changed, whereas man always keeps it.

From here the father relation, which I suppose you are all familiar with as being also reproduced in the attitude of patient toward analyst, takes on a new aspect. Next to the paramount importance of mother fixation, this father relation keeps its significance for analytic technique and therapy, especially insofar as analysis has to be a re-education based on a new ideal formation. This final aim of the psychoanalytic cure is only to be gained through identification of patient with analyst as a father, instead of wanting him to be the mother. But according to my experience, the presupposition for that final aim is solving the libidinal mother fixation. For the patient is compelled by the regressive tendency of his neurosis to reproduce in the analytic transference the primal mother-relation, namely, the *union* and the *separation*.

I would like to sum up the importance of my concept thus: Understanding the birth trauma, practically, signifies a first attempt to form psychoanalytic therapy into a quite definite procedure having but one meaning—namely, freeing from mother fixation and transformation of the libido thus gained into a new well-adjusted *ideal* formation based on father identification. Theoretically, my viewpoint leads to a biological basis for the psychoanalytic doctrine of neuroses. As a general biological factor, the trauma of birth, and especially all attempts to overcome it, prove to be the deepest foundation for an essential part of our whole cultural development. For these wider outlooks I would like to refer you to my book, which is being translated, and which I hope will soon be published in English.[5]

Notes

Read before the American Psychoanalytic Association, Atlantic City, June 3, 1924.

1. On this day Rank was elected an honorary member of the American Psychoanalytic Association (Lieberman 1985, p. 231), which had previously honored only two others, Freud and Ferenczi. In the audience at Atlantic City were such pioneers of American psychoanalysis as Karl Menninger, A. A. Brill, Harry Stack Sullivan, and William Alanson White (ibid.). Jessie Taft, a clinical psychologist at the University of Pennsylvania School of Social Work, also attended. She was analyzed by Rank in 1926 and suggested that he give a series of lectures at the university from October to December 1927. Taft later became a close friend and colleague of Rank's, translated *Will Therapy* and *Truth and Reality* from the German, and wrote the first biography of Rank (Taft 1958).

2. The main "active" technique Rank used was endsetting. Rank did not set endings arbitrarily; sometimes he did not set them at all. He invented a new technique for each patient, as he said in *Will Therapy*, "without trying to carry over this individual solution to the next case" (1929–31, p. 3). All of the patients' inner conflicts, he found, emerged during the process of setting the end— "even when one sets no definite limit" (ibid., p. 13):

> I looked also for criteria in the patient's own expressions of will even if not always obvious, in order to discover when he himself should be ripe for the definite time of termination. It was then evident that the patient, even with his own will directed to ending the analysis, reacted to the fixing of an ending with resistance. . . . [The patient] would demand either the continuation of the analysis with the rationalization that the ending as determined could not possibly allow sufficient time or an immediate breaking off, because in so short a period nothing more was to be accomplished. These demands only mean therefore "No—otherwise!" . . . This automatic reaction, which the therapeutic situation with its apparent disadvantage to the patient regularly produces, governs the entire analytic situation from the beginning. . . . This showed that one was dealing essentially neither with father-resistance, masculine protest, nor yet with mother fixation, but purely with an *inner conflict of will* which manifests itself externally. . . . In the final struggle, this inner conflict becomes evident through the fact that the patient, as we have seen, wants two different things at the same time, both the end and the continuation of the analysis. . . . *On this very conflict, the inability to submit and the inability to put over his will positively, his whole neurosis depends.* . . . What the patient needs is the positive expression of his will without the inhibiting guilt feeling, a goal which is to be attained only by the actual overcoming of the therapist and complete ruling of the analytic moment of experience [*Erlebnismomentes*]. (ibid., pp. 14–17; italics added)

Virginia Robinson, who was analyzed by Rank, "says that as far as she knew in the late twenties and early thirties Rank was not using a *fixed time limit* for

beginning and ending but 'made use of ending with each patient differently'"
(Menaker 1982, p. 106).

Rank agreed with Ferenczi's ultimate view on the "active" technique that
both were experimenting with during the early nineteen twenties: "The analyst,
like an elastic band, must yield to the patient's pull, but without ceasing to pull
in his own direction, so long as one position or the other has not been con-
clusively demonstrated to be untenable. . . . [Finally,] it is the patient himself
who must decide the timing of activity, or at any rate give unmistakable indications that the time is ripe for it" (Ferenzci 1928, pp. 95 and 97).

3. In *The Trauma of Birth*, Rank spoke of *psychological* birth as correlated
with the consciousness of anxiety, the first emotional experience of the newborn
at the moment of *physiological* birth. Birth is *both* a biological and psychological act of separation: "It would seem that the primal anxiety-affect at birth,
right up to the final separation from the outer world . . . at death, is from the
very beginning not merely an expression of the new-born child's physiological
injuries (dyspnoea-constriction-anxiety), but in consequence of the change from
a highly pleasurable situation to an extremely painful one, immediately acquires
a 'psychical' quality of feeling. This *experienced* anxiety [*empfundene Angst*] is
thus the first content of perception, the first psychical act [*der erste psychische
Akt*]. . . ." (1924, p. 187).

See Rank's lecture on "The Anxiety Problem" [8] for his elaboration of the
meaning of the "first psychical act" and the newborn's ambivalent tie to its
mother, "the primal object." It was in this lecture, a response to Freud's publication in 1926 of *Inhibitions, Symptoms and Anxiety* (itself a reaction to *The
Trauma of Birth*), that Rank drew the startling existential conclusion: "*The real
etiological factor of the neurosis consists in the fact that we have a psychical
life.*" In other words, the mystery of being alive, the existence forced on us
inexplicably by fate—more precisely, "the consciousness of living," as Rank
called "the problem of the present" in *Will Therapy* (1929–31, p. 41)—is the
correlative of anxiety. "The tendency to get free of it," Rank wrote of this
ontological *Angst*, "is perhaps the strongest psychic force in the individual"
(ibid.). Nowhere in his writings does Rank refer to Heidegger, whose *Sein und
Zeit* was published in 1927, but Rank would doubtless endorse Heidegger's
main idea. By repressing the trauma—the "hole," "void," or "wound"—of
birth (in the original meaning of the Greek word, *trauma*), we seem to have
forgotten *Dasein*, "a yet undiscovered country."

In his technique Rank used the birth trauma metaphorically not literally, as
he explained in *Will Therapy*: it serves "as a universal symbol of the I's discovery of itself and of its separation from the momentary assistant I, originally the
mother, now the therapist" (1929–31, p. 108).

4. In *The Development of Psychoanalysis*, published in 1924, Ferenczi and
Rank argued, against Freud, that emotional experience (*Erlebnis*) was more important for the therapeutic process than insight into the past, or "remembering." Insight *follows* experience. Therefore, when Rank says he "reveals" the
mother transference "straight from the beginning," he was not "explaining" the
trauma of birth to his patients nor giving patients *The Trauma of Birth* to read
as did Freud. "The Professor," Rank wrote to Ferenczi on March 26, 1924, "is
testing out my point of view in technique, according to his own words [*nach*

seinen eigenen Worten], by giving all his present patients, of whom most have been in analysis for two years, my book to read and asking them to give their impressions. Even as I write this, I still cannot believe [*nicht glauben*] that such a thing is possible but there can be no doubt about it . . ." (Wittenberger 1995, pp. 301–2).

5. The English translation was not published until 1929. Long out of print, it was reissued in 1994 by Dover, in a paperback edition, with an introduction by E. James Lieberman, author of the most comprehensive biography of Rank (Lieberman 1985).

4

PSYCHOANALYSIS AS A CULTURAL
FACTOR (1924)

LADIES AND GENTLEMEN, I tried in "Psychoanalysis as General Psychology" [1] to outline the purely practical side of psychoanalysis and show the possibilities in its application to our daily life and social organization. I did this because in my opinion it would be regrettable if psychoanalysis were considered either as merely a therapeutic method or as pure theory. The truth lies between these two extremes—namely, in its applicability to vigorous life—and that in my view is its chief value. Freud's genius consists in the fact that although he started with the pathological, he did not stop there but made possible a keener perception and a deeper understanding of what is natural and human everywhere. His concept has a closer relation to the content of folk beliefs and popular traditions than to dry doctrine, and so it has never lost its contact with reality.

I do not know whether I shall have your general assent to the assumption that this may be one of the reasons why scientists have been from the very beginning so opposed to psychoanalysis. I believe that they do not want to recognize psychoanalysis as of their kind. In my actual hearing it has often been spoken of as an art and not a science. The scientists are, as it were, embarrassed to show themselves publicly in its company, and then, too, they suspect a little its widespread popularity. And so, in spite of zealous endeavors and certain concessions on the part of psychoanalysts, it is not surprising that psychoanalysis has not succeeded in influencing the natural and mental sciences to an extent commensurate with its scientific importance. All attempts to apply psychoanalysis to the solution of unsolved problems in the various spheres of science have until recently, with few exceptions, been originated by psychoanalysts themselves. A criticism of their often very surprising achievements in throwing new light on various problems was certainly all the easier for the experts because psychoanalysts naturally lacked sufficient knowledge of the particular branch of science involved to satisfy all its claims on their work. The scientists themselves, hitherto critically holding aloof, have resisted the application of psychoanalysis to their various fields. On the other hand, the cultured public accepted the analytic point of view much earlier and more easily and has, to a certain extent, assimilated psychoanalytic thought because of its general human appeal.

Thus, in going beyond its original field of work—the investigation and healing of neuroses—into normal fields where its knowledge could be practically applied, psychoanalysis has influenced the subject matter of the various sciences earlier and more effectively than it has the sciences themselves. Scientists will probably only slowly and gradually adapt themselves to the changed state of affairs. I do not want you to misunderstand me and get the impression that I am reproaching the sciences. The historical character seems the essence of science, in general, which only tells us how things happened. But the sciences seem to show also a disposition that Freud has described as characteristic of the neuroses: they suffer from reminiscences. In other words they show a tendency to remain fixed in some early stage of their development. It may be that this results from the psychology of their representatives, the scientists. Be that as it may, psychoanalysis has encountered resistance in representatives of particular branches of science.

In medicine, to start with the narrower psychoanalytic field, neurologists and psychiatrists, under the spell of materialistic conception, rejected psychoanalysis as unscientific long after it had to its credit such therapeutic successes as had never before been attained in these two branches of medicine. Later, when the fact could no longer be ignored, the convenient formula was evolved: "Everything true in psychoanalysis is old, and everything new is false or is only an exaggeration of well-known facts." But this, as indeed you know, is the usual reception accorded to inconvenient results of a new investigation. It seems to be regrettably true that it is left to the inclination of each individual to accept what he can understand and falsify what he does not understand. Certainly today the literature of psychiatry is permeated by the psychoanalytic point of view. But, in the meantime, the entire medical profession also has begun to recognize psychoanalysis and to take from it whatever is useful and valuable. This seems to have resulted in a tendency toward separation of the clinical unity of neuroses into smaller groups of partial diseases, which can be treated and cured symptomatically by their respected specialists. Certainly the specialists, who hitherto have lacked any psychological medical training, must for this purpose be trained psychoanalytically as they are trained in all other medical branches of knowledge. In the meantime, however, a process of assimilation of psychoanalytic results has begun quite spontaneously in various special branches of medicine. This has led to surprising results, which nevertheless remain isolated from the main body of medical knowledge. We cannot at all foresee what revolutions in the field of medicine will come about when the medical student has to go through a regular course of training in psychoanalysis as he has today to go through a training in, for instance, anatomy and physiology.

Analytic study of hysterical symptoms was the starting point for discovery of the surprising possibilities that lie in the application of psychoanalysis in general medical practice. These symptoms are to be distinguished from those of organic diseases only by a subtle differential diagnosis. From analysis of such symptoms, which lie in the borderland between the physical and the psychical, psychoanalysis has discovered what a large part is played by the psychical in almost all organic sufferings. According to the case, this psychical factor definitely influences the intensity, permanency, outbreak, arrest, indeed often enough the disappearance of the bodily suffering.

A certain degree of psychoanalytic knowledge, therefore, is necessary to all medical practitioners, primarily as an aid in diagnosis and prognosis, but also for therapeutic purposes. Internal medicine especially has need of this knowledge, since the uncertainty of its diagnostic method is often made use of, partly unconsciously and partly consciously, by a certain type of patient to embitter his own or his family's life by illness. Here the doctor should be able to use a psychoanalytically trained insight, and to treat the patient accordingly. But he should do this without taking from the patient the psychical gain of illness by an untimely communication of its psychical motives, and so driving him away from psychical enlightenment to further medical treatment, which is what he desires. Rather, the doctor must set this participation of the unconscious discovered by psychoanalysis into its proper place in the big equation whose factors, in their relation of strength and value to one another, often enough decide for life and death. I am not speaking here of those extreme cases of men suffering from severe psychical conflicts in whom we have discovered a "will to disease" or a "will to die," which is able to diminish their power of resisting germs or aggravate a hitherto harmless suffering into a severe one. We have had opportunity to observe analytically also cases in which death was a welcome escape from apparently unsolvable psychical conflicts, an honorable form of suicide,[1] so to speak, permitted by the patient's own conscience and the judgment of the world. Certain physical sufferings—frequently those of a chronic nature—have for the patient the same unconscious importance, or at least the same secondary gain of illness, as pseudo-organic symptoms have for the hysteric.

But even the surgeon, especially the gynecologist, should not always yield too easily to the wishes of neurotic patients who desire an operation. We know from psychoanalysis that often an operation has for the unconscious a quite definite libidinal significance, which need not be of a purely masochistic nature but is regularly connected with infantile traumas, especially castration and birth. In those cases in which an operation is inevitable, the psychologically trained surgeon must prevent psychical aftereffects of the operation. These sometimes cause the patient new sufferings that can bother him more than the original disease. This is especially true of operations on children, who are far more susceptible to psychic shocks than adults. I would like to mention as an example the tonsil operation, at present so fashionable. It has indeed certain hygienic advantages, but when you realize that this operation, even though performed under an anesthetic, means for the majority of children a psychic shock from which they may suffer all their lives, then in any case you will have to compare, far more carefully than has been done, the physical advantages with the psychical disadvantages of this operation before deciding in its favor. However, American surgeons, as is well known, already consider as much as possible the elimination of psychic trauma.

But if application of psychoanalysis in general medical science belongs to the future, even today psychoanalysis at least gives us the key to an understanding of the psychical process in the origin and progress of organic diseases. And I am sure extensive practical results will be gained from this understanding. But here also—and this point I want to emphasize—psychoanalysis already goes beyond the purely medical field in that it has a distinct contribution to make to general social and psychical hygiene, whose aims are not so much therapeutic as prophylactic.

In the beginning, from the point of view of medical science, psychoanalysis was considered to be not sufficiently materialistic; for the mental sciences, it was not sufficiently spiritualistic. Writers and poets were really the first who took up psychoanalysis and found inspiration in it. To them is due a share of the credit for making it known to a wider public. The interest of this literary circle in psychoanalysis is easily understood. The poets have always represented, as it were, the upper 10 percent, in a psychical sense, of the population, which sees itself mirrored and reflected in their works. And when the first fully related case history was published by Freud under the modest title *Fragment of an Analysis of Hysteria* [*S.E.*, 7:7–122], one said of it quite rightly, "It reads like a thrilling novel." It describes the hysterical illness of a young girl, with a tender solicitude for the most intimate feelings of her psychical life. Poets of all times, but especially modern poets, have striven to do this, but without much success. So poets, working always from the unconscious and creating from it, soon recognized in psychoanalysis an ally, if not a competitor, and tried to get from it as much as was compatible with their artistic purposes. But the possibilities in this direction soon proved limited. The unconscious material discovered by psychoanalysis was no new factor for artistic representation and was only slightly suitable for artistic creation. The hope of poets that analysis would open up to them greater possibilities and capacities for artistic production has remained unfulfilled.

Nevertheless, psychoanalysis has left its imprint on contemporary literature. And, here again, I want to emphasize that it was not until some time later that the science in question—that is, the history of literature or art—recognized that poetic creations of the past were based on unconscious conflicts. Yet psychoanalysis can find corroboration for many of its theories—for example, the Oedipus motive—in poets of the past. And contemporary poets, by their acceptance and use of psychoanalytic material, have spontaneously confirmed that poetic creation in general is based on unconscious motives. Some twenty years ago, in a small study entitled *The Artist* (1907), I contrasted the analytic process by which the unconscious is brought into consciousness with the process by which the artist creates from the unconscious, and tried to show that they are irreconcilable. I do not know how far you will agree with me that developments since this prophecy have proved its truth. I at least— and others with me—have found that the standard for artists who have been influenced by psychoanalysis has not been, as a general rule, raised. We have found, rather, that the initial enrichment of artistic problems and forms due to the psychoanalytic movement has lately suffered a perceptible depreciation with progressive conscious revelation of the unconscious.[2]

In another yet more important social and cultural sphere—that of religion—there has also developed, as so often happens in life, from an original affinity a later opposition. Breuer's catharsis, as the name implies, is akin to Aristotle's doctrine of purification of emotions for Greek tragedy. Aristotle recognized a therapeutic factor in the freeing of repressed affects through a motive of whose make-believe and unreality the audience is ever conscious. But a similar cathartic task is also accomplished by all religious ceremonials, which Freud many years ago showed to be markedly similar to certain ceremonials practiced by compulsion neurotics. Moreover, the original nucleus of the religious ceremonial, the cult of sacrifice, would be intelligible, in its analytic importance and cathartic effect, not only from the compulsory sacrificial actions of certain neurotics, but also from the masochistic tendency to *self-sacrifice* that we find at the bottom of any neurotic suffering, Again, in its technique, in its rule of free, uninhibited speech, analysis resembles one of the chief rites of the Christian church—namely, confession, with which it has often been compared. The essential difference, however, is this. Confession is only a temporary unburdening of the consciousness of guilt, as prayer is expression of a momentary wish fulfillment. Analysis, on the other hand, attempts to remove the need for unattainable wishes, and the seeking for guilt and punishment, by freeing infantile fixations. This naturally enough soon brought upon it the disapprobation of the faithful, who feared that analysis would mean an undermining of religious beliefs, on which indeed a part of the state's authority also rests. Both the church and the state are based upon the parental relation—that is, on the human child's need for protection and help.

In judging these questions, one ought not to forget that psychoanalysis itself must obviously be considered also as a phenomenon of our time and civilization. And from this higher standpoint, it represents man's attempt to replace traditional beliefs and customs necessary for the maintenance of society by more appropriate and efficient conventions. Even before the days of psychoanalysis, the psychology of religion endeavored, although with inadequate means, to understand psychologically the phenomena of religious life; hence, from the standpoint of religious creation, it must be regarded as an attempt at disintegration. It is the privilege of psychoanalysis, however, not only to make possible a deeper understanding of religious phenomena, but at the same time to offer a substitute where religion is no longer sufficient for mastery of individual conflicts. Freud has even said that human beings, of the type that now becomes ill with a neurosis and attempts to withdraw from reality, in the earlier centuries withdrew to the cloister, where a quite definite kind of isolated existence, devoted to God, disguised their neuroses and made them harmless for society.

And what holds good for religion holds good also for ethics, which is intimately connected with and partly represents religion. Naturally I am not speaking here of the ethical standard whose practical achievement involves legislation and administration of justice, whose theoretical foundation in the past was largely the work of speculative philosophers lacking psychological insight. What I mean is individual, everyday conduct. Just here the opponents of psychoanalysis, and the laity who are not yet sufficiently versed in it, fear a harmful influence from psychoanalytic enlightenment. Unfortunately the impression is still widespread that psychoanalysis teaches or furthers freely giving rein to all one's previously suppressed impulses, without consideration for the well-being of one's neighbors or society. What psychoanalysis really strives for is a better, in the sense of a conscious, mastery of the impulses that through repression produce devastating effects. This holds good especially for sexual ethics, whose undermining by analysis the authorities fear. But, as a matter of fact, psychoanalysis is in a position to found and create a real sexual ethics, which will clear away the hypocritical and even harmful repression of our generation. Certainly this reconstruction of ethics by analysis of the social guilt feeling at first, of course, must start with the freeing of the individual. From that, it will be in a position to reform legislation and the administration of justice in light of the new knowledge of the unconscious psychical life.

So the natural sciences and the standards fixed by law have been much more resistant to the influence of psychoanalysis than the material with which they deal. For this reason I have given here less attention to the theoretical importance of psychoanalysis for the sciences than to its practical influence, of which there are certainly already evidences in our individual and social lives. This seems to me to throw an interesting psychological sidelight on scientific work in general and on scientists, who as human beings are naturally dominated by their unconscious emotions like other human beings. Psychoanalysis first made intelligible the effect upon scientific investigation of motives that are not quite conscious. This influence of the unconscious upon the work of scientists may perhaps seem less obvious to you than its influence upon the production of artists. You probably accept without question the revelation of psychoanalysis that the worldviews of former times and periods of culture were definitely created by the unconscious, especially as we can refer to such indisputable material as the mythology of civilized nations or superstitious beliefs of primitive folk. But let us not forget that psychoanalysis has shown also how large an element of superstition there is in the unconscious of all of us. This expressed itself not only in many unpretentious symptomatic and sacrificial actions, but also in the great longing for occultism that at present is spreading over the Western world from the Orient. The same holds true for archaic ideas expressed in mythology, which not only took root in the environment and particular generation that gave them birth, but are rooted also in our own unconscious, as psychoanalytic observation of the insane has proved from the archaic form and content of their phantasies. Both groups of ideas—the superstitious as well as the mythical—go back to the infantile omnipotence of thought. This conception was recognized by psychoanalysis as an overestimation of psychical reality as opposed to objective reality.

But if art, religion, philosophy represent a reflection of the unconscious psychical life of man much more than a reflection of the outside world, one might say of the modern natural sciences that their peculiar value consists in their attainment of an ever clearer knowledge of reality. We must admit to ourselves, however, that we are less completely emancipated from the influence of animism than some of us think or than is perhaps possible. Probably even our scientific worldview is in part a projection of our own unconscious. And a conscious comprehension of this, such as psychoanalysis can give, will help us make very necessary corrections in our deeper self-knowledge, which will place us in the position of recognizing how far we have falsified reality by projection of the unconscious. In this connection I have made an interesting discovery that perhaps may throw new light on the relation of science to the scientist himself and his object, the outer world. I have been able to point out from analytic experiences that a large part of what has become reality for man today—that created by him, his so-called culture—is to a great extent also created by projection.[3] As an illustration of that process of projection we may refer to the biblical creation of man, who was supposed to be created in the image of God. But surely man created God after his own image! This realization, in my opinion, explains also a process enormously important for the whole production of culture—namely, symbol formation. The scientific importance of these facts can perhaps be formulated in an extreme way thus: Every possibility in man of acquiring knowledge, even as every capacity of his psychical apparatus in general, reaches only so far as consciously to recognize—or rather re-recognize—what in the outer world man himself originally unconsciously projected into it. Thus we shall recognize again and again only ourselves in all science, will find always only ourselves in reality. Psychoanalysis has now broken through this vicious circle, at one point, by throwing back this process of recognition, sterile in a certain sense, from the outer to the inner without thereby losing itself in speculation. Psychoanalysis has never lost its hold on reality; rather, it has constantly striven for a better understanding of just this relation between the inner and outer world, with the aim of bringing about in this way a perfect harmony.

So psychoanalysis plays a part in biological development by making possible a better adjustment to the outer world through an immense extension of consciousness in the direction of our own inner psychical life—namely, the unconscious. In the same way, psychoanalytic enlightenment of the neurotic may be considered an artificial support to consciousness—an intellectual prosthesis,[4] so to speak—in the fight against his too powerful unconscious, which prevents him from getting adjusted to reality. The extension of consciousness in general accomplished by psychoanalysis can be understood only in the sense of an advance in culture, as a perfect tool with which to obtain better domination of one's own ego and subsequently the outer world. It is my belief that psychoanalysis may be considered to be as important in the intellectual development of man as the discovery of implements was to his cultural development. And we today can as little foresee the consequences of this advance as primitive man could foresee the development of modern technique from his rude implements.

Yet, at the end of our arguments, let us turn again from the glimpse into a far future back to the present and real life. We have not as yet progressed so far with the analytic process of attaining knowledge as to understand ourselves in relation to the culture that we have created, or even to withdraw ourselves from its pressure, sometimes unbearably. So far we have gained only the first insight in this direction, from which may develop a kind of psychological *theory of relativity*[5] which will teach us to recognize and avoid the subjectively conditioned sources of error in our attitude toward the world. For the time being, the sciences have succeeded in avoiding such sources of error only to a slight degree because they have always remained some way behind irresistibly developing life.

I hope my arguments have done something to convince you that psychoanalysis has enabled us to avoid those drawbacks of the theoretical sciences. If so, I trust that psychoanalytic science itself will be spared the same fate of being subjectively misinterpreted or blocked by resistances in its attempt to throw light on unconscious processes at work even in the sciences, which only then will become really objective.

Notes

Read before the New School for Social Research, New York, May 26, 1924.

1. Rank often spoke of neurosis as a kind of psychical or spiritual suicide, a "will to die"—the obverse of the artist's self-created "ideology" of immortality. In *Will Therapy*, for example, Rank writes that "instead of the more or less naively expressed wish for eternal life, as it appears today in collective ideologies [such as religion, mythology or folklore], we find an apparent desire to die, one might almost say a wish for eternal death" (1929–31, pp. 120–21). See also "The Yale Lecture," in which Rank observes that neurotics are "all suicidal candidates, more or less, whether they say so or not; they want to die, they do not want to live" [19-247].

2. Rank took up this argument again in his posthumously published work, *Beyond Psychology*: "Even modern art in its various 'isms' has not—in spite of all protestations of its theorists—succeeded in expressing the irrational directly. In their extremely conscious effort to reproduce what they call the 'unconscious' modern painters and writers have followed modern psychology in attempting the impossible, namely to rationalize the irrational . . . something which in itself is unknown and undeterminable" (Rank 1941, p. 13). As early as *The Trauma of Birth*, Rank says in a later lecture, he was emphasizing "an unconscious absolutely inaccessible to any *intellectual* grasp" [17-223]. Like Kierkegaard, whose writings Rank studied in his youth (Taft 1958, pp. 37–38), at no time did Rank ever deny or minimize this darkest and most unknowable unconscious, an unconscious that is before Oedipus—before *pre*-Oedipus (Kramer 1995). In Lacan's terms, this unconscious is preontological, corresponding to an unspeakable time before time: "the real." The "real," says Lacan, is a "beyond" (Taylor 1987, p. 92).

3. In *The Trauma of Birth*, Rank explores the creative power of projection in

two chapters, entitled "Symbolic Adaptation" and "Artistic Idealization." He derives symbolism and art, in general, from "(a) the striving for *projection*, decisive for the development of cultural adjustment which has to replace the lost [prenatal] condition in the outer world; and (b) the enigmatic inclination to *identification*, which again aims at setting up the old identity with the mother" (1924, p. 196). In a chapter in *Trauma* entitled "Philosophical Speculation," Rank says in a footnote on p. 167 that "the human being and his inward parts were projected to the heavens (see my *Mikrokosmos und Makrokosmos*, now in preparation)." This note shows that Rank was drafting sections of his greatest work, *Art and Artist* (dated 1930 in the preface but published only in 1932), as early as 1923: "I am reserving the more detailed foundation of this concept in the rich soil of mythological and cosmological material for a book planned [in 1907] under the title *Mikrokosmos und Makrokosmos*" (Rank 1924, p. 73). Chapter 5 of *Art and Artist*, entitled "Microcosm and Microcosm" (1932a, p. 113) deals extensively with the mutual relationship between projection and identification in art and culture. In human relationships, the continuous circuit of exchange between projection and identification—what is today called "projective identification"—was explored in many of Rank's American lectures. For example, in "The Significance of the Love Life," Rank points out:

> I have stated that, in essence, it is *projection* that determines the manner and intensity of our emotional relationship to fellow beings. By the side of this or, more correctly, at the same time, goes on a process that I have designated *identification*: the result of the realization of projection. In the love relationship, as I have already said, these processes of projection and identification proceed and merge into one another from both sides, in the same way and at the same time. In the analytic situation, however, the picture is different. The patient *projects* much more, I would say almost exclusively, at least in the first phase of analysis. In the same phase, also almost exclusively, the analyst has to confine himself to *identification* in order to understand the patient, and, so to say, feel one with him [*ihn einzufühlen*]. As soon as the patient feels this identification emotionally, he begins on his side to identify himself with the analyst. In other words, he can only identify when he feels in the other something kindred, identical [*Identisches fühlt*]—the identification on the part of the analyst necessary for understanding the patient [13-177].

Rank appears to have held this position as early as 1921 (cf. Jones 1957, p. 58), decades before Melanie Klein made "projective identification" central to her theory of object-relations (Rank 1923).

4. The phrase "intellectual prosthesis" is astounding in light of Rank's keen awareness of the wreckage cancer had wrought in Freud's mouth, a "mouth of hell" now covered up by a painful "artificial support." There can be no doubt that Rank's choice of phrase was overdetermined; some of these meanings are explored in my Introduction.

5. See the lectures in Part Four, "Toward a Theory of Relationship and Relativity: 'I Am No Longer Trying to Prove Freud Was Wrong and I Right.'" Einstein published his first treatise on relativity in 1905, the same year in which Rank met Freud. By 1930, in *Seelenglaube und Psychologie* (translated as *Psychology and the Soul*), Rank had fully grasped the psychological meaning of

Einstein's theory of relativity and Bohr's complementarity principle: "Every observer sees and comprehends things from his own individual standpoint, and thus has, as it were, his own 'truth'" (1930b, p. 173n.5c). In a lecture entitled "Beyond Psychoanalysis," Rank observes that, for him, psychology should concern the relationship between I and Thou: "Psychology . . . is purely individualistic, aims at knowledge of the I, of the internal, but also uses in its material data concerning the external—reality, the Thou. Thus it is in essence a science of relations [*Beziehungswissenschaft*] which easily runs into the danger of overestimating either one or the other factor, instead of dealing with the *relationship* between the two" [18-235].

PART TWO

EXPLORING THE DARK CONTINENT OF
MATERNAL POWER: "THE 'BAD MOTHER'
FREUD HAS NEVER SEEN"

5

FOUNDATIONS OF A GENETIC
PSYCHOLOGY (1926)

LADIES AND GENTLEMEN, psychoanalysis, as the name implies, is a method of investigating psychical [*seelischer*] phenomena. But in its results it has hitherto not distinguished among *biological, psychological*, and *social* factors mingled in the complicated phenomena of the ego's relation to the outer world. We will now attempt to make this distinction, insofar as it is at present possible, so that we may be in a position to use the results of the psychoanalytic method of investigation in the development of an effective therapy, the founding of a new sociology, and above all else the formulation of a *genetic* psychology.[1]

It was a great advantage for psychoanalysis that it originated in the field of pathology—indeed, it could have had no other origin. It was not long, however, before Freud found himself dealing with normal psychology, since all analytic discoveries led to a better understanding of the normal without explaining the pathogenic proper. The disadvantage here was that Freud, in his role of investigator, could not help clinging to the medical therapeutic attitude, although he had to deal with phenomena that extended far beyond the narrow medical sphere. His difficulty lay in the fact that, in the psychical sphere, the pathogenic is not as manifest and demonstrable as it is in the organic: it is not a qualitative but a quantitative factor.

Our psychical life [*Seelenleben*] is, so to speak, the *connecting link* between our biological impulses and their social restrictions and so is a means of adjustment, a means of attaining a balance, as it were, between the biological and the social. Pathogenic maladjustments cause disturbances either on the biological, that is sexual, or on the social level. These disturbances actually lie between the biological and the social sphere and hence cannot be pointed out or grasped in any one sphere. The attempt of psychoanalysis to understand them and explain them on a purely psychological basis is unsatisfying for the same reason, the psychical [*das Seelische*] being only the field of battle between the two great hostile powers—the biological and the social—the battlefield on which the never-ceasing conflict rages.

If one considers psychoanalytic problems from this point of view, they fall into two large groups that can be considered separately only to a certain extent, since the phenomena themselves are of a complex nature. These two groups are the sexual, in the biological sense of the word, and the social, in the specifically human sense that distinguishes us from other living creatures with similar group formations. The specific factor in human social organization is just that it rests on psychological presuppositions and has psychological consequences, so that the sexual impulse operates psychologically and socially in forms that we designate as love—which may perhaps be the specifically human characteristic. The love life of the adult represents, so to speak, the biological sex impulse at its social stage of adjustment.[2]

Freud recognized this nuclear human problem in the mythical picture of the Oedipus situation but has not gone *behind* this situation, in which biological, social, and psychological factors are already combined. In analyzing the Oedipus situation, he has not gotten beyond [*nicht weiter gekommen*] the point of seeing [*zu sehen*] in the mother the representative of the sex object, in the father the representative of social restrictions (castration). If, however, one traces the relation to the mother *genetically*, as I have done in *The Trauma of Birth*, from the Oedipus situation, which presents a social picture, back to its biological and psychological origins—the intrauterine situation, birth, and weaning—then one gets an entirely different picture.

Above all, the genetic point of view compels us to consider the object relation from the side of the ego. The construction and development of the ego from the beginning takes place under influence of the object relationship, and, in turn, the ego has an influence upon the object relation. The relationship is mutual. Secondly, this primal object relationship refers *only to the mother* and not, as in the Oedipus situation, to both parents.

For the suckling, the mother is not only an object for gratification of biological needs, but at the same time an object that represents restrictions from the outer world—namely, the "social"—in a primitive sense of the term. If one goes further back into the prenatal genesis of this relationship, one gets the impression that for the child the mother is perceived originally less as an object, in the real sense of the word, than as a part of its own ego, and only gradually, with advancing privations, is the mother accepted as an object of the external world.

Whereas, at the beginning, only *parts* of the mother (for instance her breasts, hands, eyes), insofar as they afford gratifications, are considered as part of the child's ego, later on the mother is accepted as a *whole* person and as a separate object.[3] When, with advancing adjustment to reality, the mother, is, so to speak, pushed out of the ego (projected), the father, as an original object of the outer world, can gradually be received into the ego. In this connection it is important to recognize that disturbing brothers or sisters usually precede him in this role. But, in any case, the relation to the father as an object of the outer world is already decidedly influenced and determined by the earlier established relationship to the mother as an object, which in turn is essentially determined by her own behavior.

This transition phase from the mother to the father object, which is usually prepared for by the relation to later brothers or sisters, I have designated as the *"pre-Oedipal situation"* [*habe ich als "Präödipussituation" zusamengefaßt*].[4] It can be understood only genetically in relation to development of the ego, and it determines all later object relations, the sexual as well as the social. Naturally, the character and behavior of the parents, as well as the family milieu in general, play a decisive role in this developmental process. It is no accident that in most cases of later maladjustment, we find a history of disturbances of a traumatic kind in family life; it may be early death of one of the parents or brothers and sisters, it may be separation of parents, step-parents, and so forth.

Normally, the Oedipus situation is brought about in such a way that the child, in this transition phase, *displaces* the image of the interfering mother onto the father, the mother thereby winning again her original role as libido object, while the father becomes exclusively the representative of the social restrictions of the outer world. Freud, considering the situation only after it has reached the actual Oedipus stage, sees in the mother merely the coveted sex object, for the possession of which the child battles with the father. *The "bad mother" he has never seen,* [*die "schlechte Mutter" hat er nie gesehen*] *but only the later displacement of her to the father, who therefore plays such an omnipotent part in his theory.* The image of the bad mother, however, is present in Freud's estimation of woman, who is merely a passive and inferior object for him: in other words, "castrated." When he recently deprived woman even of a superego,[5] which embraces the higher ethical and social abilities, he quite overlooked the enormous share the mother and the child's relation to her have on the development of the ego and its higher capabilities.

At this point we have already left the purely analytic field and have begun to think *genetically*. Psychoanalysis has considered everything from the standpoint of the libidinal object relation, namely, the Oedipus complex. Even the castration complex, although referring to the ego, has been explained in terms of the social Oedipus stage. The concept of the so-called "pre-genital organization" was formulated from the genital standpoint, that is, from the standpoint of the Oedipus situation— hence sucking must be "sexual" and longing for the mother must be the desire for coitus with her. Hence, too, every time Freud deals with ego psychology, he has had to renounce a part of his libido theory, which was ultimately shaken to its foundation by my revision of the anxiety problem in *The Trauma of Birth*. Adler's earlier attempt to give ego psychology its proper place was certainly meritorious, but it had the disadvantage that he regarded the ego as something static and failed to consider either its genetic origin or its continuous development because he had entirely eliminated the libido as impulse force.

In reality the ego develops along with the libido, and under pressure of its demands, but its development begins long before the Oedipus situation and is independent of it. We must, therefore, understand the Oedipus complex simply for what it is: the relation of the son (child) to the father. The real formation of the ego takes place under the influence of the mother in the pre-Oedipal phase, and what we call psychologically the ego is only a secondary sediment of the original relation to the mother, who in her turn, at the beginning, is taken as a part of the ego. The "ego" with which we work in psychoanalysis is an abstraction. In reality it can manifest itself only in relation (positive or negative) to an object. Only by taking into consideration the mother-child relationship has a genesis of the ego structure from the object relation to the mother become possible.

From this point of view, the Oedipus situation, as I already indicated in *The Trauma of Birth*, appears as a premature interruption of the development of the ego, which rests on the biological mother relationship—an interruption by the father, representing social restrictions. This premature social interruption of the ego's biological development, which normally should last into puberty, is a result of the human being's social family relationship and is brought about through a premature clashing of biological impulses with social demands. On the other hand, the father, as representative of the social element, is for the son the personification not only of all inhibitions, but also of all adult privileges that induce the child to identification with the father. This "identification" is really a competition, whose final aim is complete (not only sexual) possession of the mother, who remains an unattainable ideal. So, later, we are always seeking the primary biological gratification, which the child first experiences [*erfahren*] through the mother, outside in the object—whereas actual gratification, being narcissistic in nature, can be gained only from within, namely, in our own egos. Indeed, we attribute ego gratification to the object, just as we project ego alteration onto the milieu, because both originally came from outside, namely from the mother.

The genetic point of view leads to an understanding of the construction of the ego from its primal object relation. Further, it emphasizes the motives, tendencies, and impulses in the ego, the *reactions* of which in a given situation (or one created by it) it is our aim to estimate.

Freud's analytic method of investigation neglected this consideration and placed the emphasis upon infantile impressions and experiences [*Erlebnisse*] (Oedipus situation), which in later life are assumed to be merely "repeated." In reality, it is the *reactions* of the ego that are "repeated." In other words, these reactions are continually produced anew in similar situations.[6]

When, for instance, a man in later life falls in love with a married woman, it is not simply a repetition of the Oedipus situation. There are present actual compelling motives that force the ego to react at this time in just this way, the same way in which it was forced to react earlier in the infantile (Oedipus) situation. It may be that its pride is wounded, its jealousy aroused, its desire for battle or possession stimulated. Whatever the impulses that determine the reaction, they will have already manifested themselves in childhood, in reactions of the same nature.

Another point Freud overlooks in his concept of the "compulsion to repetition" is that between the original and current experience [*aktuellen Erlebnisses*]—indeed, even *during* the original experience—the ego undergoes a development [*Entwicklung*] that distinguishes the later reaction from the earlier one. When, for example, we interpret a reaction of hatred in later life as "hatred against the brother" (or father), we should realize that we have merely designated genetically the first occasion on which the human being in question expressed jealous and sadistic impulses. And even when we go back to the very earliest expressions of life, in birth, as I attempted to do in the genetic sense, we should conceive of them only as the first occasions, the first opportunities, for manifestation of affect-reactions that will emerge again later from the ego on similar occasions.

The chief fault of the whole psychoanalytic point of view lay in its overestimation of infantile life and its neglect of later life, in which the ego reacts as it has already reacted in its first experiences [*die ersten Erlebnisse*]. It cannot be denied that the past, what has already been experienced [*das Erlebte*], forms the human being, but this process is unintelligible if one considers only the experience and not the ego [*nur das Erlebnis und nicht das Ich*]—which partly forms the experiences and reacts to them. The neglect of this point of view in psychoanalysis is a source of error in that the actual [*das Aktuelle*] not only remains unconsidered but is even denied [*verleugnet*]. Thus we have situations and affect-reactions from the actual analytic situation projected into the past. Insofar as the insights [*Einsichten*] thus gained can be confirmed from direct observation of the child, they are useful in the construction of a genetic psychology. But they add nothing to our understanding of the construction of the ego, and therapeutically they are of no effect.

Notes

Read before the New York School of Social Work, fall 1926.

1. The word *seelischer* has no English equivalent. By *seelischer*, usually translated as "psychical," Rank means four interrelated psychical, or, what we now call psychological phenomena: consciousness, emotional experience, feeling, and willing. See also notes 1 and 2 of "Beyond Psychoanalysis" [18]. By *genetic*, Rank means object-relational and developmental.

2. In "Beyond Psychoanalysis" [18], Rank says that "sexuality is biological I-expansion, love is emotional or psychical I-expansion." Rank believed that the individual's creative will—except in mutual love— is always in conflict with the procreative species drive, represented by the biological force of sexuality. The human (individual) struggles eternally with the biological (species).

From the reproductive "point of view" of the species, i.e., nature, the individual is nothing but a germ cell. Even while constructing his object-relations theory, therefore, Rank never abandoned Freud's notion that sexuality (*der Kern unseres Wesens*) is the *central* human problem, the starting point for understanding conflicts in the human being. However, unlike Freud, he did not view object-relations as a derivative of drive gratification.

Why does sexuality, then, become a problem? In *Beyond Psychology*, Rank explained, "The individual's inner resistance to the biological sex urge, insofar as it does not serve the aim of purely personal pleasure, must be taken as one of the most fundamental facts of human life and as the starting-point of any investigation of social behavior" (1941, p. 213).

He added:

> In this sense, all the tabus and restrictions which modern man finds so inhibiting in his sexual life were originally willful expressions of his ego in subjugating the sexual instincts. . . . The only way, evidently, in which the individual is able to accept the [species] coercion of sex is by yielding it willfully to one, the beloved person. . . . This connection explains, in the last analysis, the individual's innate resistance to sex; for with the acceptance of it as a dominating force of his nature he simultaneously accepts death as the natural twin-brother of sex (in Greek tradition *Eros* and *Thanatos* were always pictured as inseparable). This is also the meaning of the Biblical Paradise-story, where the discovery of sex brings death into the world. For the personality is ultimately destroyed by and through sex, regardless of whether he accepts or denies it. In the latter case, however, this destruction is self-willed and set against the ever-threatening destruction which nature in any case has in store for the ephemeral ego. (ibid., pp. 233–34)

3. In the mid-thirties, Melanie Klein maintained that the infant oscillates throughout the first year of life between experiencing the mother as a "part object" and "whole object." An integration into "wholeness"—of self or object—is never complete, according to Klein, and the human being oscillates between these two "positions" throughout life (Hinshelwood 1991).

In *Will Therapy*, Rank also focused—in existential terms—on the "part-whole problem" (1929–31, p. 134) and said that this problem needed continuous solution and re-solution throughout all phases of life, during the "development of the individual from birth, via childhood and puberty to maturity and from there downward through old age to death" (ibid.). However, Rank did not subscribe to the death instinct nor would he have agreed with Klein that the infant under six months suffers from "persecutory anxiety" that is projected "into" the mother's breast and then later re-introjected. On the other hand, Rank did have a profound appreciation for what Klein called projective identification and saw this as a form of *creative* molding of the object. (See "Social Adaptation and Creativity." [14])

In *Will Therapy* Rank said:

> The trauma of birth [is] the beginning of a developmental process which goes through various phases and ends only with the trauma of death. If there is a symbol for the condition of wholeness, of totality, it is doubtless the embryonic state, in which the individual feels himself an indivisible whole and yet is bound up inseparably with a greater whole. With birth, not only is this oneness with the mother violently dissolved but the child experiences [*erfährt*] a second trauma, the partialization to which it is forced through adaptation to the outer world. In the first developmental stages after birth, the child has lost not only the feeling of connection with the mother, but also the feeling of wholeness in himself. In relation to the outer world, he becomes successively mouth, eye, ear, legs, and so forth and for a long time, in a certain sense all of his life, remains related to the world partially until he can establish again in his ego feeling [*Ichgefühl*] something similar to the original totality. (1929–31, pp. 134–35)

"Puberty," continued Rank, "with its new demands and difficulties of [sexual] adjustment, seems to bring the individual once more face-to-face with the part-whole problem which it has already had to solve once in childhood. Perhaps every critical level of development makes necessary a renewed settlement of this economic life principle" (ibid., p. 139).

"Life demands continuous partialization, and the well adjusted man must always be ready to live by a continuous partial paying off, without wanting to preserve or give out his whole ego [*ganzes Ich*] undivided in every experience [*Erlebnis*]" (ibid., p. 135).

Thus, in considering the "narcissism" (ibid., p. 141) of the modern neurotic, Rank said that "it seems as if this concentration on [one's] own ego were only a defense mechanism against the partial giving up of the self, cement as it were, that holds the parts of the ego together so firmly that they cannot be given out separately. . . . *All neurotic symptomatology is just such an unfortunate part for whole solution*" (ibid., italics added).

4. The quotation marks around the term imply that Rank believed he was *coining* a word, *pre-Oedipal*. Rank introduced the term *pre-Oedipal* into psychoanalysis at the Ninth Congress of the International Psychoanalytic Association, Bad Hamburg, September 1925, in a lecture entitled "The Genesis of Genitality" (Rank 1926a). See also note 3 of my Introduction.

5. In his 1925 essay, "Some Psychical Consequences of the Anatomical Distinction between the Sexes," Freud wrote: "For women the level of what is ethically normal is different from what it is in men. Their super-ego is never so

inexorable, so impersonal, so independent of its emotional origins as we require it to be in men" (S.E., 19:257).

6. Over fifty years later, Hans Loewald used virtually the same words as Rank: "Psychoanalysis has always maintained that the life of the individual is determined by . . . early experiences . . . ; but everything depends on how these early experiences are repeated in the course of life, to what extent they are repeated passively—suffered again even if 'arranged' by the individual that undergoes them . . . and to what extent they can be taken over in the ego's organizing activity and made over into something new—a re-creation of something old as against a duplication in it" (quoted in Wallwork 1991, p. 91n. 23).

6

DEVELOPMENT OF THE EGO

(1926)

LADIES AND GENTLEMEN, one can fully understand ego problems and conflicts only when one connects the *genetic* mode of thought with a second dynamic point of view, necessarily arising from it: the *evolutionary*. *Evolution* here is not meant sociologically in the sense of "progress," but in the sense of "biological development and psychical [*psychischen*] change." From this point of view, new perspectives open before us, giving us an understanding of normal development as well as of pathological maladjustment. We recognize then that fixation is not traumatic but natural; what is really traumatic is *development*.

Phylogenetically, development probably represents changes in milieu and the progressive adjustment that they necessitate; ontogenetically, development means growth and continual change in one's own ego. The tendency of the libido to remain fixed comes into conflict at this point with the tendency of the ego to develop. This explains why the normal biological processes of development—such as birth, weaning, puberty, or the climacteric—may, under certain conditions, operate traumatically to effect disturbances in ego development. In the sexual stage of development, the fight between individual and species (generation) certainly becomes decisive,[1] while earlier traumas, such as, for example, birth or weaning, are purely individual and concern only the ego. In the other case, it is a question of conflict between narcissistic libido gratification through the object—which creates guilt-feeling—and gratification of the object itself, by loving it.

The evolutionary position is the only one that can explain becoming ill and being healed. What happens, then, to make man psychically ill? Energies have become unfavorably displaced; a protection mechanism has failed; a means of help has, through one's own further development or changed reality, become a burden; a substitute has become disturbing, superfluous, or useless. From this point of view, one sees that an experience [*Erlebnis*] that apparently is traumatic in itself was not so from the beginning but became traumatic only in progressive development of the ego beyond this experience [*Erlebnis*].

The experience [*Erlebnis*], far from being traumatic per se, is very often originally a healthy attempt to free oneself from an ego conflict, an attempt in which the experience [*des Erlebnisses*] is used only as a temporary aid to progress in ego development. During this progress the experience [*Erlebnis*], dragged along with one, often becomes traumatic in its aftereffects, especially if the ego feels guilty because of having used the experience only as a means. Analysis, as an experience [*Erlebnis*] of the most intense kind, should make this progress in ego development possible with better results, but certainly it brings with it the same danger of traumatic aftereffects. There is, therefore, little sense in explaining the traumatic effect of an experience [*eines Erlebnisses*] as the "compulsion to repetition" (for example, of the Oedipus situation) without bearing in mind the ego development. Sometimes this very experience [*Erleben*], as I indicated, is the result of an ego conflict projected onto the object. In this sense, also, there are no infantile "fixations" (or repressions) that are preserved through our whole life. The idea—recently given up by Freud[2]—that the Oedipus complex, for example, is preserved in a kind of Pompeii-like burial, could result only from a misunderstanding of the analytic situation and its projection back into the individual's historical past.

The patient is not "fixed" at the Oedipus stage; he only reacts to the analytic situation with the same impulse (jealously, etc.) with which he reacted in earlier situations. The same is valid in a later period for experiences [*Erlebnisse*] of another kind, experiences that the patient only seems to "reproduce" in the analysis, while really he is reacting to the analytic situation. Why he does this, in indirect ways, by living again through earlier experiences [*Erlebnisse*] is a problem of great theoretical and practical importance, to which we will return later in speaking of the "denial" mechanism.[3] Here we need only mention that it is a kind of "artistic"[4] disguise in a historical form of an actually painful experience [*eines aktuellen peinlichen Erlebnisses*].

The "compulsion to repetition," as Freud himself admits, is deduced from phenomenon of the transference and really signifies an admission of therapeutic impotence. In reality this "compulsion to repetition" consists of the fact that the patient reacts in the analytic situation as in earlier situations. But insofar as the concept of "transference" rests on the presupposition of an exact repetition, it is false, for there is no such thing as an exact repetition; everything comes and goes and can be again, but never exactly the same. There is no real repetition because there are no two situations alike.

There is, indeed, as Nietzsche says, a wish for "the everlasting return of the same," but this can never be fulfilled, because of changes in us. So the desire for repetition proves to be a reaction against our continual development and change, which continually demands new orientations and new adjustments. Perhaps our development and the experience [*Erleben*] following from it would not be traumatic if we could live it again unchanged, if we could say, as Goethe says to the moment, "Remain! You are so beautiful!" But this would mean giving up life itself.

The evolutionary point of view has an important methodological consequence, which in its complete significance we can only estimate later, when we shall attempt to formulate the place of psychology within science. Here it is advisable, in forming the foundation of a genetic psychology, to preface my remarks by a fundamental point that may serve as a sign in the still twisted paths we must first follow in regard to psychoanalytic investigation.

My point concerns the "compulsion to repetition" and the principle of development operating against it. If we want to establish and investigate laws of whatever kind, it can only be a matter of finding those factors that repeat themselves and can therefore be predicted. Obviously, the psychological meaning of this urge to investigate "natural laws" is to avoid anxiety and gain certainty. However, this is only possible by neglecting the evolutionary principle, which is characterized just by the interplay of unforeseen factors.

In other words, every theory formation is a *post festum*, with the tendency to predetermine the genesis and future lines of development from knowledge of the past. Because theory formulates laws and fixes their termination, it is and remains always purely descriptive and static, whereas the phenomena themselves are dynamic and can be understood only from the principle of development.

This point is valid in a quite particular degree for the psyche. In the description and explanation of psychological functions, we must of necessity be "un-psychological"—in that we attempt to represent the dynamic and evolutionary, which is truly individual, and which is scarcely to be comprehended. Methodologically, this is an unavoidable disadvantage of psychology, the significance of which I must be clear about even in relation to my genetic presentation. For the present, I see only one possibility of limiting the dangers of such ways of presentation in psychology. This is by means of a clear elaboration of the *purely* psychological viewpoint, with the greatest possible avoidance of its being mixed with other—especially biological and social—factors.

It was the chief attribute of the psychoanalytic viewpoint that Freud, coming from the medical profession, discovered the psychical in illness and attempted to give a scientific foundation to it in "psychology" while introducing with sex a first-class biological factor. But the development of psychoanalysis shows, just as surely, that this very soon led to a biologizing—not to say sexualizing—of psychology, from which Freud finally had to seek a way out into real psychology, namely in ego phenomena.

With the genetic viewpoint, which I worked out from consistent application and perfection of the psychoanalytic method of investigation, I would like to attempt to reestablish psychology—enriched by all the experiences [*Erfahrungen*] and viewpoints of psychoanalysis—as knowledge of the psyche [*als Lehre vom Seelischen*]⁵ purified from the dross of foreign admixtures, which entered because of the beginnings of psychoanalysis in the pathological and its interest in the biological.

Notes

Read before the New York School of Social Work, fall 1926.

1. Rank developed this point at length in *Art and Artist* and often spoke of it as *the* basic human conflict: the dualism between mortality and immortality, individual and species, creation and procreation, freedom and fate, artist and creature. "Now, more than ever before, my feeling is that artistic creativity, and indeed the human creative impulse generally, originate solely in the *constructive harmonizing* of this fundamental dualism of all life" (1932a, p. xxii; italics added). In his theory of sublimation, Freud made artistic creation itself a derivation of sex: art is nothing but the transubstantiation of libido—the same force that leads to neurotic suffering. Rank disagreed: sex can lead only to sex, reproduction or procreation, not to art—production or creation. "We fail to see," he said, "how the sex urge, which is designed primarily to preserve the race, [can produce art] . . . unless we build the bridge of the individual will, which converts the propagation of the species into a perpetuation of the ego (ibid., pp. 84–85).

"The will, conscious or unconscious," continued Rank, "will always be the expression of the individual, the indivisible single being, while sexuality represents something shared, something generic, which is harmonious with the individually willed only in the human love-experience and is otherwise in perpetual conflict with it" (ibid., pp. 85–86). This "fundamental dualism" is also what Rank called "*the great conflict between our biological and our purely human self*" in his lecture entitled "Beyond Psychoanalysis" [18-234].

2. Rank is referring to Freud's 1924 essay, "The Dissolution of the Oedipus Complex" (*S.E.*, 19:173–79), the *first* written by Freud after the publication of *The Trauma of Birth*. In German the title was *Der Untergang des Ödipuscomplexes. Untergang* means "destruction" or "annihilation"—a much stronger connotation than Strachey's "dissolution" (Loewald 1959, p. 752).

With his title Freud was expressing a fear that Rank's theory of the birth trauma had "destroyed" the preeminence of the Oedipus complex, by subordinating father to mother. "You may be right," Freud wrote to Ferenczi on March 26, 1924, "that *the affectively stressed title points to an impulse in me that has to do with the Trauma of Birth*" (Wittenberger 1995, p. 312; Freud's italics).

In a self-analysis of his writings composed in 1930, Rank describes the contents of four *unpublished* pages at the end of Freud's essay. In them "Freud discusses birth anxiety as a possible explanation of castration-anxiety and comes to the conclusion that the boy and the girl seem to react differently to the birth trauma which they have in common. My explanation presupposes that the child has some vague idea of parturition. From his own experience he can support the assumption that the child has general impressions from its pre-natal existence, but any assumption beyond that has to be proved" (1930a, p. 23). Rank does not speculate here about why Freud declined to publish these pages.

In a March 20, 1924 letter, Rank told Ferenczi that Freud "will leave it for me to decide if and when this work should be published as he thinks it would be considered by the analysts 'as opposition to me' mitigated only by our personal relationship. . . . It is entitled '*Der Untergang des Ödipuscomplexes*' (the ambivalence already appears in the double meaning [*Doppelsinnigkeit*] of the title) and shows that the Oedipus complex is not repressed in development but destroyed [*zerstört*] and indeed by the castration complex, which I tried to replace by the trauma of birth, where he could not follow me [*worin er mir nicht folgen könne*]" (Wittenberger 1995, p. 300).

3. See "Love, Guilt and the Denial of Feelings" [11].

4. See "Neurosis as a Failure in Creativity" [20].

5. Rank here is approaching the point he makes explicit in "The Anxiety Problem": "the real etiological factor of the neurosis consists in the fact that we have a psychical life" [8-124]. We may thus "get a first glimpse," Rank said in his lecture on "Neurosis as a Failure in Creativity" [20] into "the human significance of *neurosis as a general resistance to coercion*. . . . The neurotic's whole attitude toward life betrays a tendency to control external coercion inflicted upon him not only by his fellow men but by Nature herself. All *neurotic reactions can thus be reduced to one Big No that men hurl at life*" [20-258]. Neither the neurotic nor the artist is able to accept death, the inevitable fate of life. However, the artist, said Rank in his lecture on "Modern Psychology and Social Change" [22], can find "a way to objectify his self-creation in the work of art, whereas the neurotic remains fixed on his own ego. . . . This *refusal* of himself, on the part of the neurotic, renders him incapable of either giving positive expression to his individuality, or of finding constructive mediums upon which it can externalize itself. Moreover, this rigid self-denial forces the individual creative capacities into negative symptoms" [22-268–69]. In *Will Therapy*, Rank understood how radically different his idea was from the psychoanalytic disparagement of neurosis as a failure in sexuality: "[My] evaluation of illness as an expression of the individual creative force leads to a wholly different conception of the neurotic . . . [who] unites in himself potentially the possibilities of destructiveness as well as of creativeness" (1929–31, p. 160).

7

THE PROBLEM OF THE ETIOLOGY OF
THE NEUROSIS (1926)

LADIES AND GENTLEMEN, the crucial problem of psycho-analysis, as a whole, concerns formulation of a theory of neu-rosis in general, and an explanation of the choice of neurosis [*Neurosenwahl*] in particular. While development of psychoanalytic investigation and theory formation has often been described in this connection, nevertheless this most important point has not yet been cleared up—as is evident from the fact that one is continually trying to find the etiological [*ätiologische*] roots of neuroses in any new discovery or new approach.

At first the roots appeared to be in the real traumas of childhood until they were revealed in part as phantasies. Moreover, those infantile traumas are so common among human beings who turn out to be non-neurotic that one cannot regard them as of etiological significance. Later, the root was ascribed to the "complexes," so-called by Jung, until Jung himself, from his investigation of *dementia praecox*, became convinced that the neurotic (and psychotic) suffer from the same complexes that the healthy go through without obvious harm. Then there appeared to be a hierarchy among the complexes themselves, and, for a long time, the Oedipus complex was considered the nuclear complex of the neuroses [*Kernkomplex der Neurosen*], but this was possible only through an overweighting of the concept. Finally, it was replaced by the castration complex, which today, in its extended form, figures as a first-class etiological factor.

Freud, under the influence of my criticism of the castration complex, now begins to comprehend it as partial symptom of the great anxiety problem—which after all is common to humans, not especially neurotic. In *The Trauma of Birth* I have, therefore, resisted the temptation to find in the act of birth a specific etiological factor [*Moment*] in the formation of neuroses, although both Freud and I see it as the primal source of anxiety. I explicitly state [*ausdrüklich erklärte*] there that while it would be very alluring to find the factor in the trauma of birth, birth belongs to *normal* psychology. Therefore, I came to the conclusion that the psychological problem of the neuroses is partly a quantitative one and partly a problem of form. Doubtless, there is a general human necessity to find a simple and tangible cause [*Ursache*] for everything that happens, especially when it might lead to a cure of illness. However, in the case of neuroses, I think a special factor is added that is responsible for the failure of this purpose. The search for a specific cause [*Ursache*] of the neuroses arises from the purely medical attitude that neuroses are diseases of the "nerves."

Psychoanalysis has taught us that they are not diseases in the medical sense but in the social sense. They correspond to maladjustments, and hence the analytic treatment can be no causal [*kausale*] therapy in the medical sense. Instead, as Freud himself always emphasized, it is rather an education, or *reeducation* [*Nacherziehung*]. A causal therapy of the neuroses would mean a radical reform of our society and cultural life that is not only socially impossible but also psychologically impossible—because we ourselves have created this social milieu. Just this realization is one of the chief merits of psychoanalytic investigation, which, according to its very nature, can never give us a specific etiology for the social maladjustments that we still describe by the old medical term *neuroses*. Hence, our therapeutic endeavor, by means of the technique of analytic investigation, cannot start out to heal men of a disease that is not purely internal but exists in the impossibility of adjusting themselves to the social and cultural demands that they themselves have created.

The patient's re-education for better adjustment to his milieu consists then not so much in raising him to a desired level but in showing him the general nature of his problem and his suffering, in order to reconcile him to his milieu. He becomes partially free from the guilt-feeling resulting from false ideal-formation in seeing that other men wrestle with the same problems. They are no better than he, and so he can content himself with an adjustment that is neither better nor worse than others, instead of always striving after an ideal in which he sees only the unattainable, which creates in him a feeling of inferiority.

Therefore, we do better not to use the medical concept "normality" in analysis but speak rather of "the average" and of "average adjustment." While this unavoidably brings in a valuation, it seems to me less presumptuous than the medical ideal of "normality," which at best signifies an adjustment laboriously maintained, involving sacrifices. From these considerations, it is clear that, above all, we must give up the concept of "the neurosis," a neurological relic that has no further justification on psychoanalytic grounds. Whether the occasionally proposed terms (for example Stekel's *parapathie*) are more suitable seems to me less important than realizing that, in essence, it is matter of difficulty in adjustment to a given or imposed social and cultural milieu.

This point of view leads me beyond the narrower problem of choice of neurosis to the real theme of my work: *construction of a genetic psychology that embraces the relation [Verhältnis] of the ego to its milieu in its biological, psychological, and social relations [Beziehungen]*. This fundamental problem of the relation of ego to object we meet first in the narrower problem of the choice of neurosis and the individual reaction of the ego in trying to adjust itself to a given milieu. The specific choice of neurosis, however, seems analytically to be as insoluble as the etiology of neurosis in general.

In *The Trauma of Birth* I have already expressed a doubt as to the theory of specific pathogenic fixation-points to which the individual regresses according to the specific form of his neurosis. The gradual development of libido in different stages was a useful explanation for a first orientation but was finally given up by Freud himself in that he distinguishes between two great impulse groups: the life instinct and the death instinct. But if this libido organization is given up—as Freud admits in *Inhibitions, Symptoms and Anxiety*—then the etiology of the fixation-point also falls.[1] The compulsion neurotic, for example, no longer regresses to the "sadistic stage," which was mere description, but the *whole* individual is somehow built up on this sadistic level. This explanation ultimately falls back on the assumption of a strong, constitutional, sadistic disposition with equally strong inhibitions and becomes again only a problem of quantity. As there is no specific etiology, so there is no longer a specific symptomatology, but there are mechanisms, which for want of a better expression, one could call compulsive (reaction-formation), hysterical (conversion), paranoid (projection), but which in normal psychical life are expressed as inhibitions, affects, perceptions and are only exaggerated in the corresponding pathological disturbances.

Out of this approach to neuroses as maladjustments, there emerges the problem for practical psychology of the *relation* between phantasy and reality, inner and outer, ego and world. If reality had been overestimated in the original childhood trauma-theory, the next and most essential phase of analytic development clearly represents an overestimation of phantasy life—characterized by the concept of "psychical reality." Without underestimating the great merit of this line of development, it must be said that it became a little too easy and finally led analysis to take refuge in phylogenesis to an unjustifiable degree. So Freud came ultimately to the "primal-phantasies" with which analysis still operates as if they were primal realities [*Urrealitäten*]—a phylogenetic past.[2]

One very important contribution of the *The Trauma of Birth* lay in the fact that it endeavored to replace the so-called primal phantasies by real, individual experiences [*reale individuelle Erlebnisse*]. For example,

I traced the womb-phantasy back to the physiological intrauterine existence, the never-experienced [*nie erlebte*] death or castration anxiety
back to the certainly experienced birth anxiety, the rebirth phantasy
back to one's own birth. In a word I attempted to give to the purely
psychological state of affairs that analysis had revealed in the psychical
life [*Seelenleben*] (phantasy) an actually experienced [*real erlebtes*] biological correlation, instead of contenting myself with projecting psychical realities back into the historical or prehistorical past.

Notes

Read before the New York School of Social Work, fall 1926.

1. In this work Freud wrote: "We began by tracing the organization of the
libido through its successive stages—from the oral through the sadistic-anal to
the genital—and in doing so placed all the components of the sexual instinct on
the same footing. Later it appeared that sadism was the representative of another instinct, which was opposed to Eros. This new view, that the instincts fall
into two groups, seems to explode the earlier construction of the successive
stages of libidinal organization" (*S.E.*, 20:124–25). Two sentences later, however, Freud backtracked: "What we are concerned with are scarcely ever pure
instinctual impulses but mixtures in various proportions of the two groups of
instincts. If this is so, there is no need to revise our view of the organizations of
the libido" (ibid.).

2. Although he was deeply influenced by Darwin, Freud also remained attached to the views of Lamarck. In *Totem and Taboo* Freud speculated that the
incest bar of the Oedipus complex was a phylogenetic inheritance in the unconscious of each infant from the prehistoric time of the murder of the Father by
the primal horde of brothers. Rank believed that the phylogenetic theory ob-
scured the powerful role of the mother, both good and bad, in infant development. By pointing to archaic heritage as the ultimate source of guilt, Freud
(1987) bypassed the emotional dynamics of the actual ambivalent relationship
between mother and child, displacing at least some of the etiological factors in
neurosis from early development to the mythical past.

"Rank deviates from me," Freud wrote to the Committee in January 1924.
"He refuses [*Er weigert sich*] to discuss phylogenesis. . . . Basically the attitude
toward the [mother] would be ambivalent from the start. This is the contradiction [*Dies der Widerspruch*]" (Wittenberger 1995, p. 288).

8

THE ANXIETY PROBLEM
(1926)

LADIES AND GENTLEMEN, closely connected with the problem of neurosis, indeed almost identical with it, is the problem of anxiety—which might be designated as the nuclear problem [Kernproblem] of the neurosis. Freud's attempt to solve the neurosis as a libido problem must be considered unsatisfactory. While Freud interpreted neurotic anxiety in the so-called "actual neuroses" as a result of libido repression, and from that developed his "castration theory," I later attempted in The Trauma of Birth, using an incidental reference of Freud's, to deduce the anxiety affect genetically from the birth experience [Geburtserlebnis].[1]

My decisive step beyond Freud was linking physiological birth anxiety, which was all that Freud had in mind, to separation from the mother as a trauma of great *psychological* importance.[2] I would now like to show how this conception may be introduced historically, as well as systematically, into the development of psychoanalysis and at the same time I shall prepare the way for the genetic psychology that follows from my new orientation in The Trauma of Birth and develop it further. Finally, I would like to discuss Freud's position in relation to my anxiety theory.

In a projected (but unpublished) monograph on the anxiety problem, I began with the Freudian supposition "that, under certain conditions, anxiety takes the place of libido; indeed, in place of every repressed affect, anxiety may appear." It is obvious then that the most important task is to recognize and explain how it takes place and what happens therewith. At that time I ventured the guess that libido is not converted into anxiety, but that libido (gratification) covers up anxiety and when libido is repressed (denied), anxiety again appears. But even during, or along with, libido-gratification, anxiety never quite disappears for those in whom it was not properly mastered by the ego, but was only "concealed." In such cases this shows that libido gratification itself may be accompanied or followed by anxiety; for example, neurasthenic anxiety about the consequences of masturbation or "actual-neurotic" anxiety regarding infection, pregnancy, or adultery that creates moral conflicts during intercourse. We now know that while anxiety may appear under the above-mentioned conditions, it does not originate there primarily and is only attached to them secondarily. This shows the inappropriateness of such a neurotic "covering up" of anxiety by libido instead of working its way through [*Aufarbeitung*] the ego.

In *Inhibitions, Symptoms and Anxiety* [*S.E.*, 20], Freud gives up his theory of the conversion of libido into anxiety, since he is now compelled to admit that anxiety is not, as previously supposed, "newly created in repression; it is reproduced as an affective state in accordance with an already existing mnemic image" [*S.E.*, 20:93]. He goes back to his earlier statement that in man this is the process of birth [*S.E.*, 20:133]. What he will not accept is my own contribution—namely, the association of this reproduction of affect with *separation from the mother*—although in one place he recognizes "the discovery of this extensive concatenation" as of "undoubted merit" [*S.E.*, 20:151].

Freud's contradictory presentation may be explained from the fact that it is very difficult for him to give up his concept of anxiety as castration anxiety or to bring it into harmony with the theory of birth anxiety. He admits that castration anxiety is not "the sole motive force of the defensive processes which lead to neurosis" [*S.E.*, 20:143] and he limits its pathogenic significance to the phobias [*S.E.*, 20:122]. Whereas in hysteria it is loss of the love object that conditions anxiety, in the obsessional neurosis it is fear of the super-ego [*S.E.*, 20:143]. On the other hand, his critical discussion of his own cases of phobias of animals ("Little Hans" and "Wolf Man") leads to the result that in them "genital excitations" (tenderness and fear) are expressed in "the language belonging to the superseded transitional phase between the oral and sadistic organizations of the libido" [*S.E.*, 20:105]. Freud tries here to save the castration theory by comprehending these sadistic oral expressions as "substitutes by distortion for the idea of being castrated by their father" [*S.E.*, 20:108]. He does not state a justification, but his purpose of saving the castration theory is just as unmistakable as it is unsuccessful, since he makes a shallow "interpretation."

If Freud, while writing his work in the summer of 1925, could have used my *genetic* theory, then he would have understood not only the primary relation of the sadistic-oral "language" to the *mother object*, but he would also have been able to put castration anxiety, which relates only to the later (genital) Oedipus stage, in its proper place. In neglecting the genetic relation between the (oral) mother level, and the (genital) father level, Freud "interprets" the one as a "substitute distortion" for the other and, at the same time, has to give up his new concept of anxiety as a *reproduction* and so looks for an actual cause [*aktuellen Ursache*] for castration anxiety at the genital level.

In tracing "realistic fear" back to "a fear of a danger which was actually impending or was judged to be . . . real" [*S.E.*, 20:108], doubt is again present as to whether anxiety cannot be newly produced from economic conditions of the situation and not merely reproduced from the birth situation as an affective signal of danger. Thus the great question still remains whether anxiety-affect (or affect in general) is *newly produced* or only *reproduced*. Freud attempts to solve this problem by assuming "a transition from the automatic and involuntary fresh appearance of anxiety to the intentional reproduction of anxiety as signal of danger" [*S.E.*, 20:138]. This "transition," however, is not very clear because in a certain sense all affects are reproductions, and this fact—as Freud himself once hinted—determines their real nature and explains, I think, their intensity and painfulness.

As I see it, every affect is a "reminiscence" that is renewed—newly produced—by an actual experience [*actuellen Erlebnisses*].³ But this "reminiscence" finally goes back to the first anxiety-affect experienced at birth, as Freud himself indicates in his discussion of real anxiety: "since the danger is so often one of castration," anxiety "appears to us a reaction to a loss, a separation" [*S.E.*, 20:130]. Hence, corresponding to my concept in *The Trauma of Birth*, birth would be the first anxiety experience and *separation from the mother would be the prototype of castration anxiety*. But since Freud will not give up the castration theory as the pillar of the sexual etiology of neuroses, he must deny the traumatic character of separation from the mother in parturition, again destroying [*zerreißt*] "the extensive concatenation" discovered by me in his assumption that "birth is not experienced subjectively as a separation from the mother, since the foetus, being a completely narcissistic creature, is totally unaware [*unbekannt*] of her existence as an object" [*S.E.*, 20:130].

I would now like to point out the difficulties of such a position. Freud rightly emphasizes the fact that we know too little about the newborn and its sensations to be able to draw compelling conclusions about it [*S.E.*, 20:135]. But the same would be true—in spite of isolated observations of children and even child analyses—to a great extent for the *child* itself, in whom hitherto much too much "adultism" [*viel zu viel Erwachsenes*], especially adult sexuality, was projected.

Freud's caution in relation to sensations of the suckling remains but is also valid for his assumption that the mother does not represent an object for the newborn. I mean we do not know [*wissen wir nicht*] this absolutely, or rather it amounts to the same thing as a quibble over words. For it is certain that the newborn loses something [*etwas verliert*] as soon as it is born, indeed even as soon as birth begins, something that we can express in our language in no other way than loss of an object, or if one wants to be more precise, as loss of milieu. It is just the characteristic quality of the birth act, that it is a transitional phenomenon par excellence, and perhaps just this determines its traumatic character. *In parturition, one might say, the ego finds its first object only to lose it again immediately—and this may possibly explain many peculiarities of our psychical life [Seelenlebens].*

Without such an assumption, or one similar to it, one will not understand correctly, as Freud himself admits [*S.E.*, 20:136], the *later* anxiety of the child. For only from *reproduction* of the severance in birth does it become intelligible why the child—when it misses the mother—reacts with anxiety instead of simply longing for the lost object like the adult. Just as little will one be able to understand longing for the womb— which is, doubtless, biological (and not merely a search or flight, which it can also be)—if one does not conceive it in the same sense as an attempt to reestablish an early existing "object relation."

Freud's attempt to sexualize this simple biological state of affairs, in the meaning of his castration theory, does not become more plausible in referring to Ferenczi's genital theory. To conclude "that for a man who is impotent (that is, who is inhibited by the threat of castration) the substitute for copulation is a phantasy of returning into his mother's womb" [*S.E.*, 20:139] may perhaps be occasionally valid in the case of patients in the analytic situation; but, as a general psychological explanation of the universal longing for the womb, also found in the potent, it is unjustifiable—logically, psychologically, and biologically.

That the penis is an instrument for completely taking possession of the mother at the genital stage, I have myself maintained, just as corresponding to it, castration signifies separation from the mother in the meaning of birth. That longing for the womb, however, should be as Freud supposes a substitute for coitus, contradicts even Ferenczi's concept, which goes biologically deeper than Jung's and, in linking to my concept, maintains just the reverse—namely, that coitus is a (genital) substitute for biological longing for the womb.

I must call attention to the fact that in my presentation of the Freudian concept I considered birth anxiety as a physiological reaction and estimated it as a reaction to a danger. When Freud, blinded by the castration theory, emphasizes this moment, he overlooks the fact that the first danger situation in birth is a risk of life (death-anxiety, birth-anxiety)[4] and does not signify loss of the penis. I meant only that this *physiological* anxiety (independent of the loss of object) in parturition, which is of a highly complex nature, experiences a *"psychical anchoring"* [Rank 1924, p. 216] in relation to the mother and the tendency to return to her. In Freud's presentation there is no mention of this emotional anchoring of anxiety (or of a similar assumption), so I really cannot see how he comes from *physiological* birth anxiety to a *psychical* problem of anxiety at all. For he draws the conclusion "that the earliest phobias of infancy cannot be directly traced back to impressions of the act of birth and that so far they have not been explained" [*S.E.*, 20:136].

Freud indeed admits that later anxiety at the loss of an object is "psychical," but that is no more than saying that physiological birth anxiety affect somehow becomes psychical in relation to the object. I posit this *psychical* anxiety in the birth act itself, of which even according to Freud's opinion the newborn is capable, and not first of all in early childhood where it clearly arises at the loss of the mother, thus goes back to the first separation from her. Freud gives no conclusive reason why anxiety at the loss of an object (*psychical* anxiety) could not just as well have its origin in parturition as later in the small child, where this connection is obvious. It is clear, however, why he does not want to admit the mother in parturition as an object: because—on account of my birth anxiety theory—he has given up his theory of anxiety from libido privation, he also denies the presence of a libido object in parturition.

In doing so, he overlooks the fact that my presupposition was not at all that anxiety in birth proceeds from the loss of a libido object. (The reaction could only be a longing—a longing for the womb.) I say rather that anxiety arises from physiological (life) danger and only "incidentally" is connected with loss of an object, a connection that is certainly characterized and significant for all of human development, especially for our emotional life. Hence my supposition was that the ego is the place of anxiety. The proposition that libido changes to anxiety I had already de facto given up in *The Trauma of Birth*—where I deduced anxiety not from suppressed libido but from (physiological) birth anxiety.

Analytic observations and experiences have brought me to the insight [*Erfahrungen zur Einsicht gebracht*] that, in analysis of patients, libido (wish excitations) as it were, covers up anxiety, i.e., that anxiety temporarily disappears because libido is gratified, but not because a conversion takes place. Freud, on the other hand, from acceptance of birth anxiety as the source of anxiety in general, draws the logical conclusion that the assumption of such a conversion is no longer necessary. Freud now posits my sundering [*Zerreißung*] of the connection between libido and anxiety (originated by him) in parturition, by saying that anxiety even in parturition was not produced from libido—whereas I maintain that anxiety is not produced from libido at all but is linked with loss of object; as I said, is "psychically anchored."

Since Freud, perhaps for the first time, does not speak in this book from his own analytic experiences [*Erfahrungen*], but uses my experiences [*Erfahrungen*] deductively and critically, he comes to no positive result apart from the one in relation to anxiety. Even before analytic work it was concluded that anxiety was reproduced as a reaction to a danger situation, as it were, a signal of danger. Freud has to admit that the first danger—and so the prototype of every anxiety affect—is birth; on the other hand, he cannot deny that the neurotic anxiety that most interests us is "anxiety about an unknown danger [*Angst vor einer Ge-fahr ist, die wir nicht kennen*]. Neurotic danger is thus a danger that has still to be discovered. Analysis has shown that it is an instinctual danger. By bringing this danger which is not known to the ego into consciousness, the analyst makes neurotic anxiety no different from realistic anxiety, so that it can be dealt with in the same way" [*S.E.*, 20:165]. On the other hand, he asserts in another place that "an instinctual demand is, after all, not dangerous in itself; it only becomes so inasmuch as it entails a real external danger, the danger of castration" [*S.E.*, 20:126]—which again is only partially right, for where neuroses arise in our culture, castration is no external danger at all [*nichts weniger als eine äußere Gefahr*].

Faced with this dilemma, Freud finally says, "This anxiety differs in no respect from the realistic anxiety which the ego normally feels in situations of danger, except that its content remains unconscious and only becomes conscious in the form of a distortion" [ibid.]. I believe that this distinction is enough to sharply differentiate real anxiety from neurotic anxiety. Besides this, we have to explain why it remains unconscious, just as we need to explain where and how it becomes distorted. For this purpose one has perhaps to understand the anxiety dream, the earlier Freudian explanation of which has fallen to pieces with the giving up of the theory of conversion of libido into anxiety. In his whole presentation, Freud does not mention the anxiety dream. In the anxiety dream, it is certainly not a matter of an external danger and yet anxiety is quantitatively greater than is usually the case in reality.

This leads to the weighty problem of quantity, and to the "therapeutic" idea of abreaction bound up with it. In general estimation of my concept [*S.E.*, 20:150–56), Freud does not accept [*nicht anerkennen*] the quantitative moment (intensity of birth trauma) emphasized by me; yet in another place, he finds it "highly probable that the immediate precipitating causes of primal repressions are quantitative factors [*Momente*] such as an excessive degree of excitation and the breaking through of the protective shield against stimuli" [*S.E.*, 20:94]. After a thorough discussion of all problems concerned, however, he comes to the conclusion that "*quantitative* relations—relations which are not directly observable but which can only be inferred—are what determine whether or not old situations of danger shall be preserved, repressions on the part of the ego maintained and childhood neuroses find a continuation" [*S.E.*, 20:154]. Everywhere he comes to the incomprehensible quantity-moment as the final conclusion!

Freud will not admit the intensity as conclusive only with regard to the trauma that stands at the beginning—namely, the birth of the individual—or, if it is so, it should at least be measurable and demonstrated. The same apparent contradiction of me exists in relation to abreaction of the trauma, with regard to which Freud expresses doubt [S.E., 20:151]. In further discussion of the problem, where he traces the anxiety reaction back to the danger situation, he comes finally to the conclusion that "anxiety is therefore on the one hand an expectation of trauma, and on the other a repetition of it in a mitigated form" [S.E., 20:166]. This implies the idea of abreaction in the reproduction, by which children seek "to master their experiences psychically" [S.E., 20:167]. He adds, "If this is what is meant by 'abreacting a trauma' we can no longer have anything to urge against the phrase" [S.E., 20:167].

Freud's book is full of contradictions [voll von Widersprüchen] that mainly go back to resistance [Widerstände] to drawing the consequences from the problem raised by me. This problem shatters the foundation pillars of his theory. Above all, the chief support of his libido theory falls, namely, the enigmatic conversion of libido into anxiety. And, with it, the most important mechanism of his ego psychology—namely, repression—experiences a marked limitation, since it no longer, as he formerly assumed, causes [verursacht] anxiety, but vice versa, is a consequence of anxiety [S.E., 20:109]. Hence Freud at present makes valid the mechanism of repression only in connection with the genital organization of libido [S.E., 20:125, 163], while for other phases and processes that he formerly categorized under repression, he now reinstates "the old concept of 'defense'" [S.E., 20:163].

But this mechanism of defense is again too general a concept and, as a matter of fact, Freud is compelled in discussion of this theme to refer to special mechanisms—in particular, to a "procedure, that may be called magical, of 'undoing' what has been done" [S.E., 20:164], by which he carefully avoids using the more appropriate terms proposed before by others. (For a long time I have used the term denial [Verleugnung]).

If Freud finds it "almost humiliating that, after working so long, we should still be having difficulty in understanding the most fundamental facts" [S.E., 20:124], then his resistance [Widerstand] against accepting any ideas originating from others is partly to be blamed. If, however, he is finally compelled to consider their value, then he again attempts to refer back to one of his earlier viewpoints and hold fast to that. This attitude explains to a great extent the difficulties that he still finds in the anxiety problem. For example, he will admit only that my merit is to have called attention to his concept of anxiety as a result of the birth process. "Rank's contention—which was originally my own—that the affect of anxiety is a consequence of the event of birth and a repetition of the situation then experienced, obliged me to review the problem of anxiety once more" [S.E., 20:161]. My own contribution—*linking this birth anxiety with separation from the mother*—he cannot accept in spite of the fact that he acknowledges its importance and that it materially influences his conception.

Freud's remark about the birth anxiety affect being the prototype of later anxiety lay buried for twenty years in a footnote, in the second edition of *Interpretation of Dreams*, and would have led to no further revision of the anxiety problem and, with it, the whole psychoanalytic theory, had I not attempted with my concept of the mother relation in *The Trauma of Birth* to *bridge* the gulf between the biological and psychological.

When Freud compares my own attempt to solve the neurosis problem as an anxiety problem with Adler's attempt [S.E., 20:150], he neglects the most decisive mark of distinction. In his theory of inferiority, Adler does not place anxiety, as I do, at the center, but places the organic, thus a quality, at the center. Also, I see a quantitative moment as the decisive etiological factor. And that is finally also the conclusion to which Freud comes in admitting that "*quantitative* relations" [S.E., 20:154] are decisive, the effect of which I say begins at birth, whereas Freud explains that they "are not directly observable but . . . can only be inferred" [ibid.]. So Freud, in his recent book, comes to the same conclusion that I had already drawn in *The Trauma of Birth*: psychoanalysis can give us no specific cause [Ateologie] for the neuroses [S.E., 20:152–53]. In my book I brought "experimental" proof for this to a certain degree. If one has claimed that such general human experiences [Erfahrungen] as the Oedipus complex—that is, the relation to the parents—are the cause [Ursache] of neuroses, why not equally admit birth, this universal experience [Erlebnis], to be a cause? In this sense a critic would be able to maintain that in *The Trauma of Birth* I reduced psychoanalysis to an absurdity [ad absurdum] insofar as it vainly sought for a specific cause [Ursache] of neuroses.

When Freud states as one advantage of the birth trauma over other causal [verursachenden] factors that it is accessible to direct observation, even to statistics, he is right only to a certain extent. I believe, however, we can spare ourselves from the beginning the work and trouble of such an investigation. For we know, beforehand, that a number of people are born who do *not* later fall into neurosis. It is just as certain, however, that extreme cases of birth have a decisive influence in the later formation of neurosis. Between these two extremes, there are innumerable transition stages corresponding to the quantitative character of this factor, which are just as little measurable as other etiological factors (Oedipus complex, etc.).

What Freud in his discussion of my theory has not valued enough is the second essential part. I have, indeed, shown mainly that it is not merely the intensity of anxiety experienced at birth—rather, it is the *psychical anchoring of this affect to the mother* and loss of this irreplaceable libido-object so important for the ego. In *The Trauma of Birth*, I conceived this anxiety anchored in the mother-object, so to say, as the primal-psychical [*Urpsychische*]. One might even say, therefore, that the real etiological factor of the neuroses consists in the fact that we have a psychical life [*daß wir ein Seelenleben haben*] and just in that—as in the production of the neuroses—we differ from the animal, which is likewise capable of physiological anxiety.

This is now the point to limit another of Freud's too far-reaching conclusions. If Freud's earlier anxiety theory was too psychical (repressed libido), then his present concept of anxiety goes to the other extreme and is too biological; for the appearance of anxiety affect as a signal of danger is perhaps one of the most primitive reactions of the living being but certainly provides no viewpoint that can help us further in understanding the neuroses.

If we want to understand these to some extent, then we must keep to the psychical representations of anxiety—one of which, I have stated in *The Trauma of Birth* (and even much earlier), is guilt-feeling, formerly derived from repressed libido, with which it is certainly later connected. This connection of anxiety with libido, which Freud now wants to deny entirely—because he can no longer hold to the theory of conversion— actually exists, if one follows my genetic development from primary birth anxiety to the guilt-feeling.[5] The only point to which Freud still holds in linking libido and anxiety is the castration complex, but this appears to me only a last attempt to save his earlier libido theory. For the castration theory still implies that anxiety arises from suppressed (forbidden) libido, a mechanism that Freud at the same time has already given up!

On the other hand, with the recognition of birth anxiety as source of anxiety, an important part of the castration theory has fallen. Castration anxiety can be traced back neither to a real danger situation nor is it, in the Freudian sense, anxiety at loss of an object. It is simply anxiety in the I and for the I [*Angst im Ich und um das Ich*].

Indeed, Freud now has to admit [*S.E.*, 20:123] that the anxiety theory of castration for women has no value—which quite depreciates the castration complex as the etiological factor in the formation of neuroses. For men, also, the castration complex has only the significance of a "narcissistic" threat to the ego. The anxiety operative in neurotic sexual disturbances in men is—corresponding to the connection in women—an anxiety of the (feminine) genitals. This is anxiety not because they seem to be "castrated," which may sometimes be the motivation, but is simply anxiety—such as neurotic women have of the masculine genitals. That is, it is simply anxiety that becomes *attached* to the sexual organs. I have only attempted to trace this anxiety of the feminine genitals—which is no castration anxiety—back to birth anxiety experienced at the female genitals.

Whether we know how this happens or not, or even whether this attempt to explain is right or wrong, seems to me for the moment unimportant. It relates, however, to a fact that one may observe in analysis and that also becomes theoretically intelligible through the assumption of primal anxiety at birth: there is an anxiety of the female genitals that is no castration anxiety, but that I have explained from the biological tendency to go back to the womb along with its inhibition through the anxiety reaction experienced at parturition.

If *The Trauma of Birth* has a fault, it is certainly not that which was ascribed to the book in analytic circles, namely, that it is too radical in wanting to put new concepts in place of old. Freud's presentation implicitly contains the reproach that I have not been radical enough because he is not afraid to draw further consequences from my insights [*meine Einsichten*]. When Freud states [*S.E.*, 20:150] that my book stands on analytic, that is, Freudian ground, he is right insofar as I still try to bring my own experiences [*meine eigenen Erfahrungen*] into harmony with his libido theory. But I am less embarrassed by this attempt to save the libido theory—since, according to the criticism of conservative analysts, I have not succeeded in doing so. Moreover, Freud, by his final change, now wants to place my concept on psychoanalytic ground, which he himself, in consequence of further pursuit of my views, has already left. Freud has rightly found the weak point in my presentation, the desire to save the libido theory, but this criticism has at the same time compelled him to give up his libido theory—a step that I did not trust myself to make completely in *The Trauma of Birth*, although Freud himself and others sensed it.

A second place where Freud, in criticizing my concept, was compelled to give up his own idea is the theory of repression. Freud reproaches me: in tracing the child's anxiety back to the birth trauma, "Rank dwells, as suits him best, now on the child's recollection of its happy intrauterine existence, now on its recollections of the traumatic disturbance which interrupted that existence—which leaves the door wide open for arbitrary interpretation" [*S.E.*, 20:136]. Yet he seems to overlook the fact that he thus denies not only the justification of "interpretation" in general but also the doctrine of repression on which the entire principle of interpretation rests. For, according to Freud's formulation, the essence of repression makes up the affect-conversion so frequently manifesting itself in the presentation of the opposite—which we cancel through "interpretation." If, as Freud thinks, my interpretation of the child's anxiety is methodologically unjustifiable, then the doctrine of repression and the technique of interpretation based on it fall together. In the first work written directly under the influence of my birth trauma concept, which has the ominous title "*Der Untergang des Ödipuscomplexes*,"[6] Freud has actually put forward the assumption that the old wish excitations, which had played such a great role in the wish-fulfillment theory, do not continue to live on in the unconscious but are annihilated [*vernichtet*] [see Freud's footnote, S.E., 20:142].

This leads to a third, still more important point, which is of decisive significance for the whole libido theory and the therapy of neuroses. This point Freud scarcely touches in his presentation yet, in discussion with me, he brought it up as an objection. I considered all the child's *positive* and *negative* feelings as originally directed to the *mother* and assumed that they are only later displaced to brothers and sisters and father (or other persons). In criticizing this concept, Freud again goes back to his earlier assumption ("On Narcissism," 1914) that all libidinal object cathexes are sent out newly from the ego and are again also taken back into the ego. If this is right—and I think it is to a further degree than Freud assumes, because it concerns all affect excitations—then also the doctrine of the transference falls, which I have already intimated in my technical works by emphasizing the "analytic situation."[7] I have there linked transference with the more general problem that large parts of psychoanalytic theory are simply projections from the analytic situation back into a historical (eventually, even prehistorical) past.

In his recent *Autobiography* (1925a) Freud says that seduction phantasies—which patients so frequently report from their childhood and which he, in the beginning, thought really had occurred—were only expressions and representations of the Oedipus complex.[8] He obviously does not yet see [*Er sieht aber nicht*] that they arise in the analytic situation, related definitely to himself, thus were newly produced by the ego of the patient placed again back into an infantile situation and were not "transferred."

In *The Trauma of Birth*, I tried to avoid this source of error by starting the reverse way—from the analytic situation—and said that in it definite birth anxiety reactions occur, from which one must first investigate how far they can be taken historically (as reproductions), and how far they are produced by the analytic situation itself.

Some have attempted to depreciate the theoretical and therapeutical importance of the birth trauma and womb regression by considering it to be valid only as a flight tendency. Apart from the fact that I myself emphasize the regressive character of longing for the womb and set up prevention or weakening of the birth reproduction as the therapeutic aim, this objection could be raised against all material coming up in analysis. Indeed, I might say—and I will follow it up elsewhere[9]—that the whole analytic situation and analysis can and must be conceived as phenomena of regression. Is not the "Oedipus complex" a flight from real sexual adjustment, and castration anxiety a flight from the Oedipus complex? Even the birth situation, which one has already fortunately overcome in the sense of the consoling mechanism, as I brought out in *The Trauma of Birth*, can be a flight from "castration"—indeed from every adjustment (in Jung's sense)—and the intrauterine situation, finally, a flight from the painful danger of birth!

One might consider the whole [*das Ganze*] from another viewpoint— namely, the *genetic*—by which fruitful insights [*fruchtbare Einsichten*] are given into therapy. Although the concepts of libido and anxiety, of object and ego, mingle at the psycho-physiological juncture of birth, we still want to guard ourselves against the desire to solve all these problems in this place of origin. Not only for lack of statistical investigation of the newborn, but also from theoretical and practical grounds, we must go back to analysis of adults in order to understand more about our impulses and mental life. Children have long been observed without the "Oedipus complex," or even without clear expression of their sexuality. This is valid all the more for the less clear expressions of infant or newborn. *Long years spent in the most careful observations of the newborn could not help us decide the question when the mother is first valued as an "object."* And even if we should find clues for this, they would help us little in understanding the adult's normal object choice or the neurotic's difficulties in adjustment.

On the other hand, I hope to show how a genetic study of the adult's object choice throws light on the very beginning of object relations in the newborn, and that we must work *genetically* to understand the object relation, in general—which primarily is simply a problem of the ego and its first relation to the mother. This problem of the relation of ego to object and reality represents the essential theme of my genetic psychology, which I am now constructing on results of the analytic method of investigation.

Notes

Read before the New York School of Social Work, fall 1926.

1. In a footnote added to the second (1909) edition of *The Interpretation of Dreams*, Freud wrote that "*the act of birth is the first experience of anxiety*

[*Angsterlebnis*], *and thus the source and prototype of the affect of anxiety*" (*S.E.*, 4:400–401).

2. Rank wrote in *The Trauma of Birth*: "Thus, with the birth trauma and the fetal condition preceding it, we have at last made tangible the much disputed border of the psychophysical, and from this we understand not only anxiety, that primal symptom of mankind, but also conversion, as well as the entire life of the affects and impulses, which take root in the psychophysical" (1924, p. 190).

3. Rank here is offering a twist on Freud's principle, enunciated in the Wolf Man case, of *Nachträglichkeit*—"deferred action" (*S.E.*, 17:47). By the time he wrote *Will Therapy*, however, Rank concluded that living fully in the present cannot be a reminiscence. "The neurotic," he said, "lives too much in the past anyway, that is, to that extent he *actually does not live*. He suffers, as Freud himself has said, from reminiscence, not because through his libidinal id he is fixated on the past but because he clings to it, *wants* to cling to it in order to *protect* himself from experience [*Erlebnis*], the emotional surrender to the present" (1929–31, p. 27; italics added). "This, then, is the New, which the patient has *never experienced* before" (ibid., p. 65; italics added).

4. As the epigram to the published German version of this lecture, Rank quoted Thomas Hobbes (in English): "I and fear are born twins." Rank believed that primal anxiety is an existential given, which is "brought" into the world at birth: "The discovery [*Die Erfahrung*] that the freeing or satisfaction of sexuality does not necessarily do away with fear but often increases it," he said in *Will Therapy*, "and the observation that the infant experiences fear at a time when there can be no question of outer threats of any kind, have made the sexual origin [*Ursprung*] of fear, and its derivation from the outside, untenable" (1929–31, p. 122).

In "The Claims of Psycho-analysis to Scientific Interest," Freud had written that "a child who produces instinctual repressions spontaneously is thus merely repeating a part of the history of civilization. What is to-day an act of internal restraint was once an external one, imposed, perhaps, by the necessities of the moment" (*S.E.*, 13:188–89). In a similar vein, he asserted in "Thoughts for the Times on War and Death": "In the last resort it may be assumed that every internal compulsion which makes itself felt in the development of human beings was originally—that is, in the *history of mankind*—only an external one" (*S.E.*, 14:282; his italics).

Rank maintained that anxiety and repression cannot be derived from the outside—either from the mother or the father, ontogenetically or phylogenetically. *Angst*, he wrote in *Will Therapy*, is at once a fear of life and a fear of death: "The inner fear, which the child experiences [*erlebt*] in the birth process (or perhaps even brings with it?) has in it already both elements, fear of life and fear of death, since birth on the one hand means the end of life (former life), on the other carries also the fear of the new life [*die Angst vor dem neuen Leben mit sich bringt*]. The stronger emphasis on the one or other of these two fear components in the birth act itself still seems to me to contain the empirical meaning of the birth trauma for the later fate of the individual" (1929–31, p. 122).

"Birth fear," continued Rank, "remains always more universal, cosmic [*kosmisch*] as it were, loss of connection with a greater whole, in the last analysis with the 'all' [*dem All*], while the castration fear is symbolic of the loss of an important part of the ego, which however is less than the whole [*das Ganze*], that is, is *partial*" (ibid., p. 124; italics added).

5. See "The Genesis of the Guilt-Feeling" [10].

6. See "Development of the Ego" [6:110n.2].

7. The analyst, in Rank's view, is fully implicated on a moment-by-moment basis in the analytic situation. While Rank appears to be dismissing transference, what he really was rejecting was the idea of transference by "spontaneous combustion," a doctrine current in the mid-twenties among orthodox analysts. According to this doctrine, transference arises solely due to the infantile "intrapsychic" condition of the analysand: the presence of the observing analyst is unrelated to the emergence of transference. This is a one-person psychology, which denies the inescapable conflict of wills between analyst and analysand, I and Thou, Thou and I. For Rank, analysts cannot be passive observers of analysands, without disturbing what they are looking at, just as quantum physicists are not observers of electrons but part of the experiment: *participant* observers. The physicist is inextricably entangled with the object of observation.

By 1930, in *Psychology and the Soul*, Rank was already drawing on Bohr's theory of complementarity, first published in 1928, to support his idea of a two-person "relationship therapy" rather than a one-person "interpretive therapy" (Rank 1930b, pp. 173–74). It is an emotional experience in the "here and now" (Rank 1929–31, p. 39) relationship with an empathic therapist that is more important for healing than interpretations that claim to uncover the repressed "truth" about infancy, make the unconscious conscious, or provide insight into "intrapsychic" conflicts.

In the mid-fifties, Anna Freud cautiously offered what she called, "technically subversive thoughts" about the real relationship:

> With due respect for the necessary strictest handling and interpretation of the transference, I still feel that somewhere we should leave room for the realization that analyst and patient are also two people, of equal adult status, in a real relationship to each other. I wonder whether our—*at times complete*—neglect of this side of the matter is not responsible for some of the hostile reactions which we get from our patients, and which we are apt to ascribe to true transference only. But these are technically subversive thoughts and ought to be handled with care. (A. Freud, 1954, p. 373; italics added)

8. In this work Freud wrote: "When, however, I was at last obliged to recognize that these scenes of seduction had never taken place, and that they were only phantasies which my patients had made up or which I myself had perhaps forced on them, I was for some time completely at a loss. . . . I had in fact stumbled for the first time upon the *Oedipus complex*, which was later to assume such an overwhelming importance, but which I did not recognize as yet in its disguise of phantasy" (*S.E.*, 20:34; his italics).

9. "It is paradoxical," said Rank in *Will Therapy*, "that the analytic therapy

which is finally to free the individual from the fixation on the past, in its whole method and theory should strive for the opposite, namely in every single psychic act [*seelischen Akt*] and in the entire experience [*Gesamterleben*] not only to bind the individual to the past but, as it were, to *make him past*, by interpreting him on the historical level of the infantile Oedipus complex" (1929–31, p. 35; italics added).

9

THE GENESIS OF THE GUILT-FEELING

(1926)

L ADIES AND GENTLEMEN, adopting the same point of view as in
my previous lecture, I will not begin with the Oedipus situation
and trace back analytically the guilt-feeling localized there—but
will try to present its development *genetically* from the mother-infant relationship. In doing so, I will be obliged to relinquish the Freudian explanation of guilt-feeling as arising in the "castration complex," which itself is
only a symptom of guilt-feeling. I shall also shed new light on the Freudian
"super-ego"—which Freud assumed to be a derivative of the Oedipus
complex but which actually is built up genetically from inhibited sadism
long before the Oedipus complex is formed. This takes place through
relation to the *mother object*, to whom the inhibited (sadistic) child
learns to adjust itself by subjugating its ego (masochistically).

The first real privations imposed by the mother—apart from the great
biological privation, the trauma of birth—have to do with nourishment
at the breast. The child apparently accepts temporary interruption of
this nourishment placidly, so long as the physiological need for nourishment stands alone in the foreground and so long as its satisfaction
brings also complete libidinal gratification. But soon the need for ob-
taining oral pleasure appears independent of hunger or the feeling of
satiation and manifests itself in the compulsion to suck the finger.

This shows that the child has clearly recognized the mother's breast
as an organ for gaining pleasure and that it misses the breast libidinally
in the intervals, constantly increasing, during which the breast is with-
drawn. For the child at this stage, withdrawal of the mother's breast
seems to take on the character of a "privation." As a reaction to this,
the child's *ambivalent* attitude toward the mother—already preformed,
in my opinion, by the birth trauma—clearly appears for the first time.
Felt as unpleasant, privation is accepted only under protest, such as
crying, weeping, struggling reactions in which unsatisfied oral-sadistic
libido is partially abreacted as rage, anger, hatred toward the mother.
The other part of oral-sadistic libido is dammed up in the ego and there
leads to construction and elaboration of inhibitions or, in other words,
inner privations.

Even in *The Artist* (1907), my first analytic work, I assumed that this
inner self-inhibition of an impulse is the most essential mechanism for

the building up of character and the moral ego, whereas Freud assumed them to be products of *external* impulse-inhibition (privation) only. Lately, in his concept of the super-ego, Freud has accepted this mechanism of inner inhibition, but *only* in the case of the later *father* identification—in the sense that the paternal threat of castration is incorporated in the ego.[1]

The child, from the beginning, is able to accept the maternal privations only by looking for and finding substitute-gratifications on its own body (finger, toes, lobe of the ear), the most suitable of which it soon discovers in the biologically preformed genital zone. Thus, another part of sadism, having become libidinally ungratifiable at the mother's breast, is directed against the mother herself, insofar as she is already felt as an object. It is important to bear in mind that the mother—as I have already indicated—is recognized and accepted as an object when she imposes privations and thus behaves like the rest of the hostile external world.[2]

A process similar to that of weaning takes place in the child at the next stage of privation: that is, at the first effort to train him in habits of cleanliness (sphincter control), which is made, according to the character of the mother and child, either early or late, in milder or in stricter form. The child accepts these privations in the free expression of the pleasure of excretion more or less willingly. He will obey the mother partly out of love for her, partly out of fear, at the same time protesting against her with acts of rebellion. Finally, the child adapts itself, under more or less silent protest, by suppressing, either from love or fear, its aggressive rage against the mother and expressing it in compromise symptoms of stubbornness toward her. I have already indicated how the oral sadism dammed up in the ego strengthens this obstinacy and brings a definite element of *hatred* into the ambivalent attitude toward the mother, which is of *decisive* importance for all later object relations.

After having shown the child's reactions to privations imposed by the mother at the purely biological stage, namely, weaning, we will now follow its reactions at the "social" stage of training in cleanliness. In this process two given factors work together, the constitutional equipment of the child and the mother's influence over it, which represent the hereditary and fortuitous elements in the situation. Doubtless a premature or brusque action on the mother's part will strengthen the child's reaction; or the father's share in this early infantile training will essentially influence the picture. But if we consider the whole process from the standpoint of the child's ego, the education of which consists in fitting into a definite milieu, then, from analytic experiences [*Erfahrungen*] with pathological material, we see built up genetically the following *average* picture.

As a result of the economic division of the oral-sadistic libido in the ego, part of which is dammed up as inhibition, the privation-causing mother—irrespective of whether she is *really* strict or not—is comprehended as a punishing object by the auto-sadistically [*auto-sadistisch*] charged ego. It is this mechanism that, at a later stage, we might describe as "identification" with the (punishing) mother. To understand the mechanism of identification, we must turn back from analysis of the object and object-relation to analysis of the ego. That means, in terms of our problem, that the child's ego is even at this stage, in consequence of partial weaning, so far invested auto-sadistically—i.e., inhibited— that it recognizes the mother as an external inhibiting force. The result is that it saves itself inner efforts but at the same time has to subjugate itself masochistically. So long as one does not postulate this psychological ego mechanism, one will always have to assume a "borrowed guilt-feeling" (Freud) resting on identification. In this sense every consciousness of guilt may be regarded as borrowed, but this point of view seems to me both clinically and genetically untenable: clinically because the patient's guilt consciousness is always justified objectively; genetically because in its kernel [*im Kern*] it proves to be a sediment of ego-formation built up as a result of privations that are not only socially but also biologically necessary. Even the "social" element does not come first from the father but is prepared for at the early transition stage from the purely biological relationship to the mother.

In essence it comes to this: the child cannot, because of love, and dare not, because of fear, react with (oral) sadism against the depriving and punishing mother but has to inhibit this impulse and so, even at this stage, reacts sadistically and punitively against its *own* ego. Here is to be sought the origin of what we find later in the ego as "need of punishment," which genetically represents a reestablishing in the ego of the mother—not the father—relation.

Thus, from inhibited sadism—the object of which has become one's own ego—an image of the strict (punitive) mother is formed as a result of privations experienced at the hands of the mother. In this image the ego finds relief from its own inhibitions, a relief that we find later on magnified in masochistic gratifications. One can understand neither the pleasure of perverse masochists nor the need for punishment of the child, neurotic, and the criminal, unless one takes into consideration this *inner unloading tendency*—which finds extensive gratification in reestablishment through punishment from without of a part of the mother-child relation. Insofar as sadism cannot unburden itself in revenge and the infliction of pain on the object—the depriving mother— the sadistic impulse is dammed up in a kind of self-inhibition. This again represents the depriving mother, whose withdrawal of libido gratification is experienced as punishment. If the mother *really* punishes, then the ego is unburdened at least temporarily of these tense, often unbearable *self-punishing* inhibitions. Identification with the strict mother, therefore, affords simultaneous outlet and gratification of the child's sadistic tendencies.

The "strict mother" thus forms the real nucleus of the super-ego. [*So bildet die "strenge Mutter" den eigentlichen Kern des Über-Ich.*] We may put it in another way and say that early super-ego formation based upon inhibitions set up as a result of maternal privations is objectified in the image of the strict, punitive mother, which later on is sought in masochistic gratification. When Freud denied a super-ego (in the masculine sense) to women,[3] he overlooked the fact that the nucleus [*Kern*] even of the masculine super-ego originates from the mother and can be described, in a psychoanalytic sense, as the result of struggle with the depriving mother. This *genetic* concept throws a clear light not only on the psychological development of the child, but also on a number of the human being's pathological expressions and reactions, as well as on the possibility of influencing them by therapy.

It is remarkable that we often find a very strongly pronounced guilt-feeling in individuals (especially women) whose mothers have *not* been strict in the usual sense of the word. This confirms our theory that the strength of *inner* self-inhibitions increases in the absence of adequate *external* inhibitions, inasmuch as such external inhibitions afford an opportunity for a corresponding abreaction of aggressive sadistic impulses, which then do not so strongly inhibit the ego. Anal, urethral, and sexual "naughtiness" or symptom-formation (in child or adult) may be understood as an attempt to unburden the ego, which tries to provoke punishment (from the mother) in order to get rid of inner inhibitions and at the same time to make sure of the mother's love. What appears as a "masochistic" punishment tendency or as a "protest" against the strict mother may be understood as an attempt to unburden oneself of inner inhibitions and to set up again the primitive code of punishment.

In the therapy of such cases, one must avoid everything that could possibly oppose the patient's tendency to unburden himself and so secure gratification of his masochistic guilt-feeling. One must rather, by a passive attitude (not by interpretation), allow him to build up a correctly functioning super-ego, instead of gratifying libidinally the primitive one. Strict education, necessary on the whole, spares the child a superfluity of inner inhibitions that would cause it to react neurotically. In cases where the child has not later developed a social super-ego, analysis has to further the inner erection of these inhibitions by not allowing the patient to gratify the punishment tendency. This brings him—through love and not through fear—to accept the ethical demands of his milieu and adjust to the social "love-code."

When the analyst forbids, scolds, and punishes, then—aside from sat-isfying his own sadism—he only gratifies the masochism of the patient, enabling him to give up temporarily symptoms of his self-punishment tendency (guilt-feeling), but not to succeed in setting up a socially func-tioning super-ego. Other symptoms, those from which the patient is getting a masochistic pleasure because they are socially condemned—as, for example, drunkenness or certain perversions—can never be re-moved by active intervention however hard the patient may try to move the analyst to give prohibiting commands, against which he would only protest. Here, also, by patiently showing up these tendencies for what they are, one must bring the patient himself to renounce them for love of the analyst (mother), instead of using them as touchstones of the analyst's love for him.[4]

In tracing further the genetic development of these inhibiting tendencies at the genital stage, it will be best to treat male and female development separately. So far the two have shown more similarities than differ-ences; certainly the inhibitions that manifest themselves as anxiety and guilt-feeling in both sexes originally relate to the mother and only later are reconnected according to the sex role. This new orientation occurs in the Oedipus situation, which, in a certain sense, signifies for both sexes a decisive change in attitude.

The girl changes the libido object, making it quite clear that the guilt-feeling toward the mother does not arise from the Oedipus situation; rather it represents, almost without exception, a hindrance to the attain-ment of this normal object stage. The mother is not the source of hatred and guilt-feeling *merely* as a rival with the father; she was already that by reason of her earlier restrictions of the ego and its narcissistic grati-fication tendencies.

But the mother has played the same role in the boy's infantile devel-opment, so this factor alone is a strong inhibition against the captiva-tion of the mother as a sex object—even in the absence of the father as an external hindrance. Indeed, in such cases we frequently find the boy later becoming homosexual, not because of father fixation but because there was no father; thus the boy strengthens his primary inhibitions against the mother in complete flight from her, in order to counter-balance the lack of restrictions from the father. Normally, the boy's inhibition against the strict, depriving mother, which is operative at the sexual stage also, is overcome through sadistic mastery of the woman in the sex act, a sadism that plays an essential part in the pleasure grati-fication. The sexual possession of woman is in no way made difficult for man by the Oedipus complex but rather is *facilitated*, in that it enables him to objectify a part of his own inner inhibitions *in the father* and through this to remove them *in himself*. We see here a second step in the formation of the super-ego, deduced by Freud from the "father-identification." The boy projects, as it were, his primitive *maternal* super-ego onto the father, while—at the same time—identifying himself with the father in possession of the mother. Here is the first appearance of the specifically inhibiting role of the father, which, to distinguish it from the primary (biological) restriction of the ego in the pre-Oedipal phase, I have called the formation of the "social" super-ego, included by Freud under the term *castration complex*.

So both sexes have to undergo a change of viewpoint: Woman *changes* the libido object and keeps in the mother-identification the primary super-ego; man *keeps* the libido object and changes the super-ego, or builds up the paternal social super-ego over the primary maternal. Guilt-feeling toward the father no more arises from the Oedipus situation in the case of the boy than the guilt-feeling toward the mother in the case of the girl. Both are only to be understood genetically in terms of ego psychology.

Thus the boy's guilt-feeling is not so much a reaction to desire for the mother; rather, it is objectively justified, inasmuch as the boy has created for himself an "evil father" by projecting the mother's strictness and his own inhibitions onto the father. Castration anxiety at the social (father) stage thus has the same psychological significance as biological privation at the mother stage, since both result from inhibition of a sadistic-aggressive impulse against the mother, which arose first at the oral then the genital stage. At the genital stage, however, sadistic aggression—inhibited this time by the father—produces anxiety, guilt-feeling, and the self-punishment tendency that manifests itself in sado-masochistic phantasies. This is what Freud has described as the castration complex. Only thus can be explained the typical form of castration phantasy, which does not go back to an external threat made by the father but arises in an inner defense of sadistic tendencies, the instrument of which at this stage is the genitals. The threat of castration is not the cause [*bewirtkt nicht*] of libido inhibition, but sadism—already inhibited within—is the cause of the masochistic castration anxiety. The sadistic counterpart of this is, however, never lacking and often appears in the impulse to castrate the father, that is, the rival.

The case of woman is different, normally just the reverse. Simple observation shows that woman, in general, has less anxiety than man, indeed one might almost say a *different* kind of anxiety. Her super-ego consists much more of inhibitions and guilt-feeling, whereas anxiety dominates in the male super-ego. At first sight, this seems to confirm the castration theory, and it is certainly connected not merely with the anatomic sex differentiation but also with the biological sexual role—which itself seems to determine in conclusive ways the varying sadistic elements in man and woman. In any case it is sadism that determines the kind and degree of anxiety and with it also the sadomasochistic castration phantasies.

We shall be able to trace these relations further when we follow the relation of the sexes beyond the purely biological sex function into the so-called love-life.[5] Here it is enough to mention that it is less anxiety in woman than its positive counterpart—narcissistic pride of the ego—that makes her shrink from accepting her passive sexual role. On the other hand, one sees clearly how guilt-feeling enables woman to give herself, surrender, to man—a yielding against which her ego strives. Hence a too-extensive submission frequently occurs as masochistic bondage which, however, is only a pathological exaggeration of normal biological submission, and which manifests itself psychologically in the form of being in love. Woman's sexual anxiety is anxiety of the ego at the dependence and submission demanded of her by her biological role. So the anxiety of woman, who has no "castration complex," is a sexual anxiety in the narrow sense, whereas the anxiety of man is a social anxiety in the broad sense, involving suppression of sadism. With regard to the anxiety problem of woman, it seems to me also no matter of indifference that a woman in parturition at least partially re-experiences [*wieder erlebt*] the anxiety affect originally experienced at her own birth and thus abreacts it, whereas man reproduces it only at other levels.

The origin of the castration complex is thus really pre-Oedipal [*vor-ödipal*]. It is not first brought into being in the Oedipus situation but is conditioned by the anatomic differentiation of the sexes and obtains its pathogenic significance only at the Oedipus stage. Before that stage, there was the significant anal relationship to the strict, punishing mother, by reason of which the child learned to feel that genitals are "dirty" and later on that sexuality is objectionable. The Oedipus complex serves the purpose of partly overcoming this early phase in that the boy attempts genitally to return to the mother, on the genital level. He is, however, continually prevented by prohibitions imposed by the mother. For in the return to the mother at the genital stage, the boy comes into conflict not only with the disturbing father, but just as much with the depriving (punishing) mother whom, in this role, we have considered hitherto *only* in relation to the *girl's* Oedipus complex. The boy's disappointment in the unattainable—because depriving—mother is just as great and momentous as the girl's disappointment in the father. So, after a short and intensive period of biological genital development (Oedipus situation), the child is thrown back again upon its own ego, as once before by the first maternal privations. The difference is that now—in the Oedipus-situation—the parent of the other sex is, for psychobiological reasons, made responsible for the privation, a change of attitude that manifests itself particularly in the boy in the father complex: in castration anxiety.

If we want to understand this second retreat of the child to his narcissism, we must keep in mind the relation established in the meantime toward the punishing (depriving) mother, which also forms the nucleus of the guilt-feeling. Bearing in mind the genesis of this guilt-feeling, we might consider it as a kind of "negative narcissism." For narcissism also (or what we find as a symptom of it) has proved itself analytically a sediment of the relation between mother and child, as a result of which the ego loves and admires itself as once it was loved by the *good mother*—or as it desired to be loved by the ideal mother. On the other hand, identification with the *bad mother*, with emphasis placed on the inhibiting and punishing tendencies, is expressed in the ego as guilt-feeling. The attitude of the individual toward these two primal mother types—which Jung worked out mythologically as good and evil mother—determines not only the construction of one's ego and with it one's whole type of character, but also one's relation to fellow men, in general, as well as to the love object, in particular.

Notes

Read before the New York School of Social Work, fall 1926.

1. "In contradistinction to this viewpoint," said Rank in *Will Therapy*, "I assumed even in my first book [*The Artist*] a capacity for inhibition inherent in instinctual life [*Triebleben*] itself, almost an inhibition instinct [*Hemmungstrieb*] which I was not able to distinguish as will [*Willen*] until later after I had recognized its positive side as the organ of integration of the impulsive self [*Trieb-Ich*] and its constructive capacity for ruling, developing and changing, not only the surrounding world but the self" (1929–31, pp. 152–53). Inhibition or guilt does not arise from identification with the castrating father but is a byproduct of the separation-individuation process, a precipitate of the infant's struggle against the mother. The development of "will," according to Rank, always takes place at the expense of an *other*.

Rank suggests that the first trace of ego development is readily visible as "counter-will" in the infant's earliest resistance to its mother's ministrations. At the time of this lecture, 1926, Rank was formulating what he would later call "creative will," initially seen in the form of self-inhibition of biological sadism by the infant. Esther Menaker offers an excellent interpretation of what Rank meant by this lecture:

> These inhibitions are motivated by the libidinal attachment to and the consequent fear of separation from the mother who is experienced as all-powerful, both giving and depriving. Since Rank understands that the inevitable frustrations and deprivations the child must experience very early in his relationship to the mother are essen-

tial for ego formation and psychological growth, the self-inhibition of destructive, sadistic impulses must occur out of fear that were the child to act on them, he would lose the mother on whom he is dependent and to whom he is libidinally attached. The unavoidable deprivations of child-rearing by bringing about inhibition of impulse provide the groundwork for the child's perception and acknowledgement of his mother as separate and different. The cleavage between inner and outer world is thereby created. (Menaker 1982, pp. 52–53)

"Guilt," according to Menaker, "arises not through identification with a forbidding father but as a precipitate of ego formation through separation from the mother. . . . The child incorporates the strict mother image as a part of his own ego which demands punishment out of guilt for his sadistic impulses. This internalization and the taking of the guilt upon oneself perpetuates the relationship to the mother and stands in the way of separation from her" (ibid. p. 53).

Rank began to use the term "creative will," perhaps for the first time, in a lecture on "Social Adaptation and Creativity" [14-190]. His discovery of mature or healthy "will" evidently came from experiences of creative resistance patients showed him in the analytic situation, particularly during the endsetting. But resistance is not necessarily a form of acting out and in its *creative* form— that is, in the will to separate from the analyst, internalized *Imagos*, and the analytic situation—must be distinguished from unhealthy resistance to uncovering unconscious wishes. See "Neurosis as a Failure in Creativity" [20] for a discussion of Rank's mature view of "will."

2. Rank ignores, or has changed his mind on, a point he made in the prior lecture on "The Anxiety Problem" [8]: "*Long years spent in the most careful observations of the newborn could not help us decide the question when the mother is first valued as an 'object'*" [8-127].

3. See Freud's 1925 essay "Some Psychical Consequences of the Anatomical Distinction between the Sexes": "[Women's] super-ego is never so inexorable, so impersonal, so independent of its emotional origins as we require in men" (*S.E.*, 19:257).

4. At this point Rank began a dense discussion of a variety of maternal privations at the sadistic pregenital oral and anal stages. He reviews this material more clearly later in the lecture, so it has been omitted here.

5. See "The Significance of the Love Life" [13].

10

THE GENESIS OF THE OBJECT RELATION

(1926)

LADIES AND GENTLEMEN, we have attempted to show how the mother (that is, her breast) is originally regarded by the suckling as belonging to its own ego or self. And we have shown how the child, as it gradually learns to accept its mother as an object of the external world that can be denied it, tries to find an independent and permanent substitute for her on its own body—its finger or genitals. This process of narcissistic cathexis might be described as the first real psychological manifestation of the ego [*die eigentliche psychologische Entdeckung des Ich*]. We have also learned that the mechanism of every object relation is a kind of "maternalization." By this I mean that, in the relation of object to ego, the object is invested with libido originally transferred from the ego to the mother and later taken back into the ego. This mechanism explains not only the "libidinal cathexis" of the outer world (Jung's "interest"), and the loss of this cathexis in the psychotic's idea of the end of the world; but, more important still, it explains the relation of the ego to other human beings in love and social life.

The withdrawal of the object leads, as we have seen, to the search for a substitute in one's own ego, but, on the other hand, every object ca-thexis definitely contains ego elements [*Ich-Elemente*]. By this I mean that the ego tries to find itself or part of its beloved self [*seines geliebten Selbst*] in the object. Moreover, the relation of ego to object is twofold: in the sense just described and, secondly, because of the child's original conception of its mother as both a good (protecting) and a bad (depriv-ing) object. We have shown how a substitute for the good mother—the mother as the source of pleasure gratification—is sought on one's own body by sucking or masturbation or, later on, psychically in one's own ego [*seelisch im eigenen Ich gesucht*]. At the same time, the depriving mother is set up in the child's ego, through identification with maternal inhibitions, as a feared and punishing element, which manifests itself as anxiety or guilt-feeling.

A boy on the way to social adjustment in the biologically conditioned Oedipus situation learns gradually to identify the bad, depriving, feared mother with his father. In the Oedipus situation, he learns to recognize his father as the real possessor of his mother. While progressing from pre-Oedipal rivalry with brothers and sisters at the biological mother stage to social rivalry with his father, a boy reestablishes his original picture of the good, protecting his mother—a prerequisite for establishing mature love and sex relations with a woman. By contrast, the girl on the way to her Oedipus situation again finds the interfering, denying mother, and she gradually has to learn to find in her father a substitute for the pleasure-giving mother or breast. This comes about through equation of breast and penis, which presupposes a displacement from above downward and with it a reestablishment in the vagina of the original, oral sucking activity. The biological Oedipus relation can thus be completely established only if the positive and negative attitudes toward the mother, which manifest themselves in the ego as narcissism and guilt feelings, have become simultaneously projected again in an object relation.

This new object relation at the Oedipus stage differs from the primary object relation to the mother in that the two mother roles, the good and the bad, are now divided up between father and mother, the role assigned to each depending on the sex of the child. The success of this division determines the kind and intensity of the child's later sexual and social relations. This is why the Oedipus complex has such an important bearing upon the later fate of the human being's object relations. But that should not blind us to the fact that the Oedipus complex is only a transient phase of development, and that its success or failure has been decisively determined beforehand by the original relation to the mother.

The Oedipus situation compels the child to project onto both sexes the ambivalent attitude that originally referred to the mother *only*. The child has already built up this ambivalence in its ego as narcissism and guilt-feeling. The child's projection of its infantile ego in the Oedipus situation is an unburdening, enabling the ego to find again in objects gratifications and inhibitions that maternal deprivations had forced within the ego. The Oedipus situation and the love relations corresponding to it psychologically at a later stage enable the individual partially and temporarily to cancel earlier ego developments that involved a psychical expenditure [*einen psychischen Aufwand*]. One can, so to speak, unburden oneself in the love relation because one *objectifies* parts of one's own ego in the partner. This explains the definite, clear "object hunger"—Ferenczi's phrase—that we see manifested to a marked degree in the analytic transference situation. But the aim of this unburdening is not merely reestablishment of the Oedipus situation as such, or even reestablishment of the original libido relation to the mother, as analysis of the neurosis undoubtedly teaches us. It also serves to relieve the ego of anxiety and guilt-feeling. This tendency of the ego to seize every available opportunity to unload itself of inner tensions through the object relation shows us that the ego is, as it were, built up against its own will [*widerwillig*], by necessity, as a result of deprivations. And it shows us, too, that the ego is always ready to un-ravel its structure in object relations as soon as it finds suitable objects and situations.

There are certain dangers in this unburdening tendency, which appear in various social and sexual maladjustments. Certainly this tendency is the psychological prerequisite to the establishment and maintenance of all human relationships. But if it goes too far in any one direction, as, for example, the pathological forms of being in love or in paranoiac projections, then it leads to partial dissolution of the ego structure, which disturbs its social adjustments inasmuch as absorption in one object relation, or pathological restriction to a definite kind of object relation, makes social relations to other objects impossible. Another danger, that of narcissistic limitation, threatens the ego when it strives too much *against* the tendency to form object relations, that is, when it will not submit to any form of dependency on any kind of object.

To understand all the possibilities of outlet in normal and patholog-ical ways, we must not only consider the psychic mechanisms that are constructed on the biological mother relationship. We must also take into account influences and disturbances of the given milieu, which are also important for a therapeutic understanding of the individual. In analysis we regularly find the picture of the strict, bad mother, quite irrespective of the parents' real attitude or character type and educa-tional influence on the child. From that time on, the image [*die Imago*] of the father and mother is *created* in the Oedipus situation. This image, as I have said, does not always represent the real character, but it plays a great part in analytic and educational situations. Thus the trans-ference proves to be not so much a repetition of the real Oedipus situa-tion as a projection of one's own inner parent image [*der eigenen in-neren Elternimagines*], which is often contrary to the actual facts. This conception of the transference is consistent with the fact that *it is a state of "being in love" and thus represents an attempt to solve one's ego problems on, or by means of, an object*. One must, therefore, in the analysis not only interpret all expressions of the transference as repeti-tions of infantile reactions, referring in the analytic situation to the an-alyst, but must also make them intelligible to the patient as expressions of *ego* tendencies.

The following picture of the genetic development of the object rela-tion is average. Both sexes will form and model an image of the parents from their own attitudes toward the good and bad mother, and in ac-cordance with their need of it for later object cathexis and ego unbur-dening. In general the boy, as we have said, has to find at the Oedipus situation the bad mother *in* father, irrespective of whether or not his father is strict. The boy must, so to speak, make his father bad, in order to keep his picture of the good mother clear. This enables him later on to develop a proper love relation to a woman. This process is complicated not only by the child's actual relation to the parents and their real characters but also by the fact that the original mother relation has left behind it a sediment in the ego and thus determines the ego's relation to other libidinal objects. We have already noted how the original use of the two mother images in the ego decides the formation of either a narcissistic or a more neurotic type. In the boy, for instance, an especially intense disappointment in his mother will have as its consequence an inability to make an adequate displacement of the image of the bad mother onto his father. In life, too, he will continually have to look for and find the bad mother, which may lead to being repelled by women and attracted to men. Playing the part of the good mother himself, he will either love himself solely and narcissistically or look for the good mother in other men. The same is true for the girl, who, as a result of holding on too tightly to the depriving mother, comes to play the ideal mother toward other girls—in whom she loves herself. Individual character types and behavior can thus be explained according to whether an individual plays in life the good mother or looks for her in the object. This point of view also throws light on those forms of behavior that one might designate "negative object relations," that is, those in which hatred, anxiety, and especially guilt-feeling predominate. Guilt-feeling betrays the important role played by the ego in object relations: some guilt-feeling is present in all love relations.

All these negative emotional relations, which play such a large part in the love life, are intelligible only as attempts to solve conflicts in the ego, which seeks to free itself from inner tensions and inhibitions. At the same time, such attempts at freeing bring a new, secondary guilt-feeling with them, since the moral ego [moralische Ich] cannot bear the idea of making use of "the other" (in the Kantian sense) as a means to an end. In many human beings, sensual gratification seems to bring about the same reaction, because they cannot bear to use the other (or the other sex) as a means for narcissistic gratification. It is, therefore, no wonder that guilt-feeling is typically attached to orgasm, which represents the climax of sexual gratification and hence something forbidden. This prohibition can regularly be traced back to the earliest maternal deprivations of narcissistic pleasure gratifications on the individual's own body and reaches its climax in the masturbation conflict. This conflict proves to be a conflict in one's own ego, which is now independent of outside deprivations and prohibitions and is intelligible in genetic terms only in connection with early biological privations imposed by the mother. The projection of these ego conflicts also explains why in crises through which the ego passes, the love object is frequently made the representative or, as it were, scapegoat of one's own inner inhibitions and conscience. We find the same attempt to solve an ego conflict on, or by means of, the object in the relation of patient to analyst. This explains the strong guilt-feeling that necessarily develops from the analytic situation. Getting rid of this guilt-feeling involves many great difficulties.

Again we learn that every relation to an object consists of parts of one's own ego and ego conflicts, rather than a mere repetition of a biological situation. Certainly this ego that is projected into the object relation was originally built up and developed on the basis of an object relation—mainly on its biological relation to the mother, the development of which we have already sketched as far as the Oedipus situation. The primary deprivations imposed by the mother compel the child to go back again to its own ego and so create narcissism, which, in later object relations, is again split up into its original components. The degree of narcissism is a decisive factor in these later object relations, since it determines whether the original *object* is sought and found or whether one's own *ego* is objectified. This not only leads in extreme cases to homosexuality but also determines whether the heterosexual relation represents a reestablishment of the original object relation or an attempt to find one's own ego again.

I have stated elsewhere[1] that in every object choice and love relation the two components, object and ego, are operative side by side. I should only like to add that the greatest difficulties in the real love choice are to be explained by these two tendencies working *against* each other and also that most love conflicts arise when development of the ego disturbs a previously gratifying object relation. Postponing discussion of the circuitous and mutual influence of ego development on the object relation,[2] let me turn back to the simpler situation of the original object relation to the mother. I shall try first to work out certain typical consequences of this relation as manifested in character types.

One masculine type retains the negative attitude to his mother and, side by side with this *maternal* super-ego, develops later an inadequate *paternal* super-ego. Either he is narcissistic in the positive sense of wanting to be loved and thus playing the child who looks outside for the good, ideal mother but never finds her, or he himself plays the good, ideal mother to other human beings, whom he helps, whom he must save: the "savior phantasy." His sex life is a protest against the strict mother rather than reestablishment of the libidinal relation to the protecting mother and, accordingly, suffers from the restricting influence of guilt-feeling. The other masculine type builds up paternal inhibitions *over* maternal prohibitions and so identifies himself with his father, not his mother, but, at the same time, projects everything negative onto his father. He is more manly, active, and heterosexual than the first type, who often enough projects his negative attitude toward his father back again on his mother and in this way arrives at homosexuality or impotence. In such cases it is the task of therapy to bring the patient to recognize this primal image of the bad mother, whom he tries to deny by himself playing the part of the ideal, good mother. This succeeds only if he can work off his suppressed revenge toward the strict mother in the analytic situation, instead of in a real relation to the woman—we see here the threads tying the Don Juan syndrome to impotency and homosexuality.

Disappointment in the mother is also an essential factor in the boy's later negative attitude to the father and in the girl's to the man. It rests on the deprivations experienced from birth, weaning, and cleanliness training up to the Oedipus situation and is aggravated through the advent of brothers or sisters, who interfere with the relation to the mother. In this pre-Oedipal phase, other children and *not* the father interfere with exclusive possession of the mother. Mother is made responsible, as it were, for the additional children, as well as for all the deprivations suffered at her hands. At the stage of cleanliness training, this often comes to light in the infantile theory of the "anal child." From analysis one gets the impression that the whole "anal-birth theory" belongs to this pre-Oedipal stage, in which the father as procreator plays no part, the forbidden deed being perpetrated by the mother alone. The idea of the anal child often has the added implication that the child can be thrown away, a worthless waste product and so no longer disturbs anyone.

The later disappointment of the boy on finding that his mother has no penis is neither his first nor his most important disappointment in her. Indeed, it is possible only because of the earlier disappointments. She is, first, a narcissistic disappointment, because the boy, who for a long time accepted her as a part of his own ego (by means of identification) now finds her to be *unlike* his ego [*als ichfremd empfindet*], that is, unsuitable for identification and the narcissistic ideal formation based on it. Again, as we have already noted, it is not only fear of his father that holds the boy back from his mother but also his *own* fear of ego difference (lack of penis), which he gradually has to accept as he has all previous disappointments. This kind of disappointment he learns to recognize at the genital stage as a consequence of the anatomical difference in sexes. At the same time, the father is recognized as owner of the penis, and his part in the procreation of children is imagined or learned from experience [*oder erfahren wird*]. Then the mother's "lack of penis" can be felt as an advantage in a double sense. On the one hand, it absolves her from sole responsibility for the advent of other children; on the other hand, the recognition of her feminine sex role frees her from the boy's ego (and identification), so she can become a real object in the sense that she can be possessed sexually. This is the progressive side of the Oedipus situation, although, to be sure, the powerful father is still recognized as possessor of the mother.

At this stage the boy completes his real biological adjustment, because he definitely gives up his mother as an ego object (part of his ego) and accepts a real, libidinal object in harmony with his later sexual role. He has to effect his change and adjustment independently of his father, while his father, in playing the inhibiting part, helps the process by making it possible for the boy to project a great part of his disappointment in his mother, as well as his own inner difficulties, onto his father. In other words the boy makes his father responsible for all these disappointments and frustrations. It is no longer the strict, punitive mother who keeps him from herself and sex, but his father who represents all external and internal hindrances. This makes it possible for the boy to desire his mother again instead of fearing her.

But even at the biological stage of the sexual-object relation, the woman cannot be taken purely as an object. This new object relation is made possible only through establishment of a new *ego* relation, which we recognize in the complicated psychic process of *being in love*. This being in love is an ego problem, pure and simple, and seems to have the function of bringing the demands of the biological sex role into harmony with the ego. This becomes particularly clear in an analytic study of so-called "homosexuality," in which psychoanalysis long ago recognized a narcissistic ego problem. But here again psychoanalysis stopped with the libidinal explanation, characterizing the homosexual object choice as narcissistic; that is, one loves oneself in the same sex, as one's mother loved (or should have loved) one. However, this is only one form of narcissistic object choice: the *ego* phenomena lying at its base is just as active as in the heterosexual object relation. In order to understand this, one must go *beyond* the libidinal explanation and take up my genetic, evolutionary point of view. It then becomes evident not only that one always looks for, or hopes to find, the ideal mother or the ideal ego in the love object, which is always chosen naricissistically, but that object relations in general are a kind of dumping ground for outworn phases of one's own ego development. Depending on the experiences [*Erlebnissen*] that come into play, at one time it may be a matter of wanting to find again the "original" object or one's own ego, at another time of wanting the "idealized" object or ego or even the "depreciated" object or ego.[3] This last case, that of seeking the "despised" object or ego, which is so important for an understanding of pathogenic development, makes it clear that all object relations represent attempts to solve ego conflicts.

The object relation, in every sense, serves as a dumping ground for some former phase of the ego, which has to be given up, which one wants to keep in the object or in the relation to the object, and from which, on the other hand, one tries to free oneself by "objectifying" it. This explains most of the conflicts connected with object relations, which become more complicated and destructive as this process of ego deposit continues during the whole course of the object relation, so that the real depreciation and the final renunciation of this part of one's *ego* development is accomplished only through a depreciation and renunciation of the *object* itself.

This mechanism of ego deposit is clear in homosexuality, which involves a second self [*Doppelgänger*] who represents sexually, as well as in other ways, one's own ego or higher or lower self [*Über-Ich oder Unter-Ich*]. In the heterosexual object choice, the same mechanism is operative but is complicated by the factor of sex differentiation, which disturbs the ego tendencies. Psychoanalysis has attempted to account for this by means of the "castration complex" but without taking into consideration the important mechanism of the ego psychology involved.

For the girl, in accordance with her infantile adjustments to her biological sex role, the man has the importance of an ideal ego [*idealen Ich*] that she wants for herself—so-called "penis envy"—and with which she can identify herself in a positive sense if she is able to "deposit" her ego ideal in the man. But if she is, or wants to become, this ideal—that is, cannot sufficiently project this part of her wish-ego [*ihres Wunsch-Ich*]—then all the conflicts and difficulties that psychoanalysis has included under the concept of "masculinity complex" will follow. As for the boy, we have already seen how he learns to give up his mother as an ego object and accept her as a sexual object if he is able to renounce narcissistic identification with her and accept a love object that is obviously different—"castrated"—from his own bodily self.

The psychological problem is, How can human beings, with their narcissistic disposition and development, love another sex different from their own, that is, from themselves? The answer would be very simple if its practical application did not encounter all the difficulties that we find in love conflicts of humankind. The answer would be, namely, that individuals arrive at a sexual object relation because of their biological sexual role and the natural attraction of the sexes for each other. This would be the case if individuals did not have to make such interminably complicated detours, and build up such elaborate justifications to adjust themselves psychologically for their natural part without conflict. It is their ego and its development that oppose the demands of their biological sex role and that need the complicated apparatus of love to justify sensuousness, to compensate for sadism by tenderness, and finally to admit, in the unavoidable guilt feeling, that sex and love are a highly egoistic affair, which is resisted by one's moral ego [*moralisches Ich*].

For man, as a condition and result of his acceptance of woman as a love object, two possibilities are open, similar to those that we have already described for woman. For her, the more favorable possibility generally results: she accepts man as her ideal ego. By contrast man seems more inclined or compelled to "objectify" woman as a kind of lower self [*Unter-Ich*], as previously described. This has its foundation not only in the idea of "castration," which causes man to identify woman with the anxiety-charged part of his own ego and to see in her, as it were, his own feared fate. But his disappointment, that is, discovering woman's lack of penis, is, as we have noted, only the last in a series of earlier disappointments that go to form the picture of the bad, destructive mother. Woman's object choice, by contrast, represents an idealization, a finding of the desired ego ideal in the other sex. This is only partly the case for man, since, although he also desires the ideal mother, he can no longer find her because of his ambivalent attitude toward her. To the girl, on the other hand, her father appears irreproachable, although this ideal attitude, too, can be interfered with through the "penis envy" aroused by her brothers.

In this whole process of ego finding, ego projection, and ego depositing, two possibilities offer themselves, each in turn involving three possible outlets. From the mother-child or "object-ego" relationship, in conjunction with one's "narcissistic" ego cathexis, one may project and objectify either more of one's own *ego* or more of the original mother *object*. In either case one may project as "true" an image as possible, an "idealized" image, or a "depreciated" image. In both men and women, the various types of object choice and relations of ego to object depend upon which of these possibilities eventuate. But the development of this ego relation to the object also determines the character of the individual, whose object choice is only a symptom of one's ego development.

Thus from the beginning and at every later stage of development, object relations, in every form, are attendant phenomena and sediments of the developing ego. This explains not only changes in object relations, but also the difficulties involved in making such changes. In the most favorable cases, the ego grows and develops in biological harmony with and for one's children, in whom one deposits large parts of one's past (depreciated) and future (ideal) ego development. At the same time parents enable children, through identification, to develop their own egos and to build up their own ego structure. Every object relation nevertheless holds destructive elements within it, since the deposit of overcome and renounced ego phases always involves a breaking up and reorganization of the ego structure, which we know and fear as the destructive side of love.

Notes

Read before the University of Pennsylvania School of Social Work, fall 1926.

1. In the chapter entitled *Idealbildung und Liebewahl* [Ideal-formation and Love-choice], published in Rank's 1926 book *Sexualität und Schuldgefühl* [Sexuality and Guilt-feeling], pp. 141–54, the last book to be released by Rank under the imprint of his own psychoanalytic *Verlag*. It has never been translated into English. According to E. James Lieberman, this book anticipates the fundamental dualism that runs through all of Rank's later writings on will, neurosis, and art: "the inevitable conflict between individuality and conformity, psychology and biology, likeness and difference" (Lieberman 1985, p. 262). As Rank observes later in this lecture, and repeatedly throughout his American lectures, the same dualism is played out in the relationship between "ego" and "object," I and Thou.

2. See "The Significance of the Love Life" [13].

3. By constantly juxtaposing the word *ego* with the word *object*, Rank is saying that "I" (ego) am *always* in relationship, internally in my psyche or externally in the world, with "Thou" (object). Here Rank anticipates by over two decades the object-relations theory of Ronald Fairbairn, who describes the psychic world of human beings as composed of "internalized objects" with which "ego-parts" (such as the "libidinal" ego, "antilibidinal" ego, or "central" ego) have relationships. According to Fairbairn, the mother is an internalized "bad" object, split into an "exciting" and "rejecting" part, (Hinshelwood 1991, p. 306). Against Freud, both Rank and Fairbairn insist that "ego" is engaged in an ambivalent interpersonal *and* intrapsychic relationship with the mother from the beginning of life.

It is virtually inconceivable that Fairbairn, now credited by many as the inventor in the 1940s of modern object relations theory (Grotstein and Rinsley 1994), could have known of Rank's object-relations theory. By 1926 Rank was persona non grata in the official psychoanalytic world. There is little reason to believe, moreover, that any of the other writers credited with helping to invent object-relations theory (Melanie Klein or Donald Winnicott, for example) ever read the German text of this lecture, published as *"Zur Genese der Object-beziehung"* (Toward the Genesis of Object-Relations) in volume 1 of Rank's *Genetische Psychologie* (1927, pp. 110–22). However, in 1928, the young Heinz Hartmann, co-founder with Anna Freud of modern ego psychology, published a short abstract of volume 1 of *Genetische Psychologie* in *Allgemeine Zeitschrift für Psychotherapie*, 1:720.

In a 1930 self-analysis of his own writings, Rank observes that "the pre-Oedipal super-ego has since been overemphasized by Melanie Klein, without any reference to me" (Rank 1930a, p. 26). According to Phyllis Grosskurth, author of the definitive biography of Klein, it would have been impossible for Klein to quote from Rank after 1925, even if she had read him, for fear that she might suffer the same fate that befell him: personal and intellectual excommunication (Grosskurth 1986, p. 127). Rank refers favorably to Klein's pioneering work in child analysis in a number of places, including *The Trauma of Birth* (1924, p. 21) and *Modern Education* (1932b, p. 208). Five years after Rank's death, in 1944, at the height of the "Controversial Discussions" raging over Melanie Klein in the British Psychoanalytic Society, Edward Glover observed that "Mrs. Klein's theories, although differing in content from those of Rank [in *The Trauma of Birth*], constitute a deviation from psycho-analysis of the same order. The implications are identical. . . . The resemblance between the two deviations is indeed remarkable" (Grosskurth 1986, p. 345).

PART THREE

FROM PROJECTION AND IDENTIFICATION TO

SELF-DETERMINATION: "EMOTIONS ARE

THE CENTER AND REAL SPHERE

OF PSYCHOLOGY"

11

LOVE, GUILT, AND THE DENIAL

OF FEELINGS (1927)

LADIES AND GENTLEMEN, in the genetic part of my lectures, I
have studied the ego's development from the object relationship.
Now I want to consider the force that keeps these processes going:
the *emotions*. The human emotional life [*Gefühlsleben*] is thus basically
the center and real sphere of psychology. One could designate the emotional life as "Thou-Psychology" [*Du-Psychologie*]—because it determines
our relation to fellow men and, at the same time, to reality in general.

Perhaps we know least of all concerning this part of psychology, our
own emotional life. Even psychoanalysis has contributed relatively little
to understanding the emotional life. This is shown in the mystical concept of the unconscious, in which all things possible are brewed or
mixed together as in a witch's cauldron. One has even got into the habit
of speaking of "unconscious feelings." This is less a linguistic than a
psychological impossibility. By it is expressed a lack in understanding of
the emotions, in consequence of which everything emotional is comprehended *in* an "unconscious."[1]

I say the term "unconscious" feeling is not so much a linguistic impossibility—by which I refer to the interesting fact that the word *feeling*
[*Gefühl*] signifies for us something vague, indefinite, indefinable. In the
psychoanalytic literature it is scarcely used, although in essence our
whole emotional life rests on feelings and is directed by feelings. The
concept *affect* [*Affekt*], which was used in the early psychoanalytic literature, seems to imply something other than the concept *feeling*.

What I describe as "affect" is a pathologically intensified feeling that
energetically demands an outlet. (*Pathologically* is used here in the original sense of the word *pathos*.) Thus anxiety, jealousy, hatred I call
affects. Love, yearning, hope I call feelings. It appears as if the affects
were the painful, pain-releasing, thus "pathological" feelings, whereas
what I designate as *feeling* in the real meaning of the word is of a more
pleasurable nature.

But this differentiation, although correct in a certain sense, is perhaps
not fundamental enough: as an example, we speak of the "guilt-feeling"—which is anything but pleasant. Therefore one might say that the
guilt-feeling is an affect. I think, however, that there is yet another crite-

rion: namely, "feelings" are *uniting* or binding, "affects" are *separating* or isolating. Or still better, the affect is a *reaction* to the feeling [*Gefühl*] of separation, isolation.

This definition best characterizes the value of feelings in the human emotional life and in psychology. They are forces that bind us to our fellow beings and the world. We see this clearly in the *love feeling*—which unites our I with the other, with the Thou [*dem Du*], with men, with the world and so does away with all fear. What is unique in love is that—beyond the fact of uniting—it rebounds on the I. Not only, I love the other as my I, as part of my I, but the other also makes my I worthy of love. The love of the Thou [*die Liebe des Du*] thus places a value on one's own I. *Love abolishes egoism, it merges the self in the other to find it again enriched in one's own I.*[2] This unique projection and introjection of feeling rests on the fact that one can really only love the one who accepts our own self [*unser eigenes Selbst*] as it is, indeed will not have it otherwise than it is [*ja es garnicht anders will*], and whose self we accept as it is. At the same time, however, we do not hold firmly onto this self. We develop it by means of identification and form ourselves according to the ideal of the Thou. This conforming to the love ideal of the Thou does not occur, however, through conscious work of adjustment, indeed is not to be attained at all by this means but occurs emotionally through identification.

Analysis of the love feeling shows us that, in essence, it rests on identification. Perhaps love feeling even creates the ability to identify; it certainly increases it. In this sense love feeling would be the gate to the world of reality. It begins in the child's feeling toward its mother. In all its manifestations, it proves to be decisive for our relationship to the outer world. However, study of the love feeling teaches us that this feeling is something that rests absolutely on reciprocity, i.e., has identification not merely for its presupposition but also has the setting up of an identity as its aim.

Let me now add to my earlier definition that the feeling is something uniting. It is easily understood that all tender feelings—and particularly the emotion of love—aim at reciprocity. As a rule, they are gratified as well as increased and permanently maintained when the other fosters or expresses the same feelings. It becomes a purely inner problem when the other does not have the same feelings, or at least we seem to miss them in the other. Then in our emotional life, by means of our feelings, we establish what is lacking: namely, the *identity* that in reality does not exist or does not satisfy us. In having to admit this—or, in other words, when the function of feeling for uniting and identifying has failed—there results the "pathological" expression of feelings that I call affect. It may be that there is no real feeling of reciprocity, or it may also be that we cannot establish it by means of inner substitution. In either case disappointment follows the perception that the feeling is not returned. The reaction to this perception of being "disunited" is the feeling of isolation or separation—which manifests itself as the affects of anxiety or hatred.

Before going further in discussion of the emotional life, I would like to propose the following definitions. The reciprocal feelings, especially in the sphere of the love life, which may also lead to a mutual *physical* expression, I would like to designate as *sensations*. These sensations are especially contrasted to the purely inner feelings that I designate as *emotions*.[3] The term *affect* I want to reserve for expression of the feeling of separation. With such separating affects as anxiety, hate, anger, or annoyance goes admission that the uniting force is not present or has failed. But, at the same time, the affect tries to deny even the tendency, the attempt, to unite—indeed, as it were, tries to deny the object itself. In other words I distinguish among three kinds of manifestations of feeling: two external and one purely internal. The *external* ones are either uniting, pleasurable "sensations" or separating, painful "affects"; the *internal* one is what I call emotional.

The emotional life, the expression of feeling, and the affect reactions seem to reflect in a purely psychical sphere a process that I once described as "adjustment to reality by means of denial." Let me now follow up more closely the connection of the emotional life with denial.

In doing this, I start first from the sphere of purely inner feeling, establishing emotionally an identity that in reality does not exist or does not satisfy. The feeling or emotion in this inner sense amounts to a denial of the lack of identity. The feeling says, This identity between me and the other exists because it exists in me. Often enough, a very strong feeling can release in the other exactly the same feeling, the corresponding emotional reaction. This then leads to a pleasurable sensation because it objectifies a merely inner identity. The recognition of the nonexistence of this identity leads to a painful feeling the expression of which I designate *affect*, and which signifies the acknowledgement of a nonidentity, of a *difference*. The inner feeling that lies between the gratifying sensation and the ungratifying affect is more pleasurable—for example, longing, hope—but yet is not quite free from painful elements. These obviously correspond to the occasional and partial perception of the process of denial. With perception of the real difference appears the painful affect of *separation*.

Denial itself begins at the primitive level as an attempt to designate everything different from the ego, everything non-ego [*Nicht-Ich*], everything painful as at the same time nonexistent—obviously in order to avoid or admit pain. I have already shown that this result is not attained because the process of denial is in itself painful or secondarily causes pain. Denial is a first attempt to disavow that which is unattainable for the ego and to say No to [*verneinen*] or refuse that which is painful. Only when this attempt fails is the ego compelled to another kind of defense against pain, the most important of which is that of identification. But denial is a much more primitive mechanism than identification. Denial says, What causes me pain does not exist [*nicht existiert*]. Identification eliminates this source of pain by assimilating it in one's own ego. The process can go so far as to internalize this source of pain into one's own ego and so transform it into a source of pleasure, by means of "masochism."

When we understand emotion as a denial of the difference [*als Verleugnung der Differenz*]—that is, as an attempt to establish *within* an identity that does not exist or does not satisfy *externally*—then we understand at once one of the most remarkable characteristics of the emotional life. In the analytic situation, and the emotional life in general, we find that the individual is inclined to nothing so much as to hide even from himself, or to deny, his feelings. In other words, not to admit to himself—nor to others—that he cherishes this or that feeling. This is one of the most conspicuous characteristics of the emotional life, particularly of neurotics, and hitherto according to my knowledge has found no explanation.

As the feeling is an attempt to establish within oneself an externally lacking identity with another, then we can understand why one is so much ashamed of one's feelings and therefore wants to hide them not only from the other but even from oneself.[4] This seems to me to explain the feeling of shame, in general, or why so many neurotics feel ashamed when there is no apparent reason for it, shame being an emotional reaction to recognition and admission of feelings that are one-sided. In other words, one is ashamed of having feelings at all if they are not reciprocated, the unpleasant feeling of shame again being an emotional reaction to *realization of difference*, of separation.

This denial of one's own feelings manifests itself in different forms and in different spheres. The most important seems to me to be the sexual sphere, not only because it plays a large part in the love life [*Liebesleben*], but also because in the psychoanalytic doctrine it has been misunderstood. In psychoanalysis so much is said of "impulses" where it would be better to say emotions; thus, an important relation between the emotional life and the sexual life has been overlooked. Certainly sexuality is a sphere in which feelings find their emotional outlet; this occurs in the form of pleasurable, physical sensations. But just as frequently the sexual life is a means of saving emotional expenditure [*Gefühlsaufwand*], of *hiding* feelings, or of attaining the end on a primitive physical level *instead* of an emotional one.

We can best study this in the analytic situation. We see there, because the situation is one-sided, all these processes being enacted in clear form. Above all, we see the function of the feeling as a uniting factor aiming at the establishment of identity. The patient has such strong emotional feelings not only because they are roused and then inhibited but also because, on that account, he *himself* supplies the feelings of the partner in his *own* emotional life. This we do generally in our phantasies—about which, moreover, the human being is just as much ashamed as of his feelings. Hence we see the patient resisting the verbalization of his feelings and wanting to admit them in emotional reactions. But the realization of his desires in the analytic situation would be destructive because it might prevent him from an inner emotional solution of his conflicts.

The emotional solution of his conflicts consists in *canceling the denial* of his whole emotional life. That is, in the analytic situation, he has to admit that he has feelings and, moreover, admit this not only emotionally but also verbally. In doing so, at the same time, he cancels the blocking of his emotions, which he learns to express at least verbally. The therapeutic significance of this emotional release lies in the fact that the patient learns to express feelings without having them reciprocated, just as a means of self-expression. He learns to renounce the establishment of identity, and this enables him to accept the different one, the other, as an object.

So the patient in the analytic situation learns through acceptance of his own emotional self to accept the other, learns to adjust to the external world foreign to him *without* reacting to it by affectively denying it or by emotionally identifying with it. He learns to accept the fact that not everything is the ego [*nicht alles Ich ist*], that there is also a Thou or other egos whom he has to accept without wanting to destroy or devour them.

In a prior lecture, I have also discussed the question raised by Freud as to whether or not all affects are perhaps reproductions, and there I pointed out that this would explain their painfulness.[5] I meant that an intense affect might not only be reaction to the present stimulus, but at the same time might be a reaction to a similar, earlier situation. In this connection one could go still further and say that the affect itself is a memory, a reminiscence of an earlier experienced trauma [*erlebtes Trauma*].

In this sense, all feeling would be painful, the emotional life itself painful, apart from what particular emotions are concerned. This seems to be proved by experience [*Erfahrung*]. For even the not predominantly painful emotions of love, yearning, and hope have also their painful side. The pleasurable element comes only secondarily into the emotional life, namely insofar as one succeeds in realizing in another reciprocity of feeling and in expressing it emotionally. In this, however, the pleasure is less of a positive quality than a result of the freeing from an inner tension, thus again an unburdening of the ego. The real pleasure in it is purely an ego satisfaction in that it expresses the pleasing perception that we succeeded in arousing the identical feeling in the other.

The affect thus originally seems to be the painful reaction to a trauma [ein Trauma], a privation. Or, generally speaking, it is the painful reaction to the inner perception that the object is *different* from our ego, is a non-ego [Nicht-Ich]— or reality—and hence is painful. The most primitive affect of this kind is anxiety or fear, which represents the most general reaction to everything foreign to the ego. The feeling tries to remove this isolating result, in that it establishes an *inner* identity that was missing *externally*.

There is one particular feeling that seems to have the special ability for doing this: *guilt-feeling*. This explains the great importance that both theoretically and practically is attached to guilt-feelings. I think guilt-feeling occupies a special position among the emotions, as a *boundary* phenomenon between the pronounced painful affects that separate and the more pleasurable feelings that unite. It is related to the painful separating affects of anxiety and hate. But in its relation to gratitude and devotion—which may extend to self-sacrifice—it belongs to the strongest uniting feelings we know. As the guilt-feeling occupies the *boundary line* between the painful and pleasurable, between the severing and uniting feelings, it is also the most important representative of the relation between inner and outer, I and Thou, the Self and the World [von Innen und Außen, Ich und Du, dem Selbst und der Welt].

This ambivalent or, better, this ambiguous character of guilt-feeling is most clearly expressed in the part it plays in the love life. Guilt-feeling certainly disturbs the harmony in love, prevents emotional identification or identity, which separates the lovers. Yet, in this same sphere, we also see clearly its uniting, binding power. Guilt-feeling often enough not only makes real separation impossible but it has positive uniting qualities: it compels one to devote oneself to the object, to surrender to the object. In the light of our doctrine of the emotions, one might say that the guilt-feeling is a phenomenon of confession—but not in the concrete sense that one admits a definite guilt or obligation as such. It is, rather, an admission of love, of feeling in general. In other words, guilt corresponds to an abolishing of the denial of feeling [Gefühlsverleugnung]. For many, especially neurotics, guilt-feeling is the only way of expressing feelings at all; in other words, the only form in which they can express their feelings—thus admit them at all—is in the feeling of guilt or shame.

This consideration leads to another problem, namely, the relation of the emotional life to the character type. In taking the emotional life into consideration, we must also estimate its relation to the mechanisms of *projection* and *identification*. We have not actually said it but it is clear that what is projected is the feeling, and also what one identifies with is the feeling; further, it is clear that identification occurs by means of the feelings. The same must naturally hold good for projection, the only difference being that identification rests on the perception of *identity* in feeling, whereas projection has for its presupposition the perception of *difference* in feeling. In other words, the identity that the ego tries to establish in the other by means of projection is an identity of feeling, and identification is the pleasurable affirmation of this perception of emotional identity. If one likes, it is an introjection. I have hitherto avoided Ferenczi's term *introjection*, because it means something only with regard to the emotional life. For that which can be "introjected," taken into the ego, as it were, from without—is obviously only feeling.

If we now consider the relation of the emotional life to the character type, then we come up against a new problem. This problem is the intensity or *quantity* of feeling as distinct from the *quality*, the kind, of feeling. If we consider the "projection" or "introjection" type from an emotional viewpoint, we can do so only in terms of quantity or intensity. We must say that the projection type apparently has not different kinds of feelings, but only stronger feelings of the same kind as the identification type. And by means of projection, he wants to establish in the other, not so much the same feeling as the same *intensity* of feeling—which also necessitates the same expression of feeling in the other.

Here new questions arise. First, what determines the greater intensity of the emotional life, or is it really only a greater intensity, and if not, what besides compels the one type to project, the other to introject feelings? Are there two such fundamentally different types at all, or are there not rather different ways of reaction, the predominance of which determines the one or other type?

Naturally I can aspire to no solution of these fundamental problems of psychology within the border of the arguments just roughly outlined. I only want to refer to some observations. It seems quite certain that there are individuals with stronger and richer emotional life than others, and just as certain that the intensity of the emotional life is somehow connected with the strength of the impulse life [*Trieblebens*]. However, this is no real psychological problem as long as the impulse life and emotional life correspond to one another. The psychological problem begins with the question, What does the individual of originally stronger impulse disposition do with his rich emotional life? Does he accept and express it freely? Does he deny it or project it?

Experience [*Die Erfahrung*] seems to show the following paradoxical relation. The richer—that is, the more varied and complete—the individual's emotional life, the less is he driven to projection, and the more will he incline to identification. His outlet and satisfaction comes in identifying himself with the emotions of the other. On the other hand, the narrower and more restricted the individual's emotional life, the more intense will be his fewer emotions, the less will he be inclined to, and capable of, identification—the lack of which he has to compensate for by projection. Projection thus proves to be a compensatory mechanism that adjusts for an inner lack. Identification, on the other hand, is an expression of abundance, of the desire for union, for alliance, for sharing.

The projection type is thus, to a certain degree, poor in emotion, but the few feelings he has are as a consequence stronger because the impulse energy is, so to say, undivided—in other words, more concentrated. The identification type has a richer emotional life, which is less intense not so much in itself as in its expressions. The intensity of expression seems less in the identifying type because it is a matter of mutual giving and taking in relation to the other. The projection type seems to give more, but this giving is no real gift: it is the gift of a poor man who pretends to be wealthy, who, so to say, only gives in order to be able to take back again. The identification type gives more just because he does not take, as he himself is rich enough.

One might now think that these two types would exactly complement one another emotionally. But often experience [*Erfahrung*] shows this is not the case. Also in the social sphere, riches cannot always give what the poor man needs; still less can the poor man always take what riches can give. The same holds good to a greater degree in the emotional life. And here we come back to the earlier problem of *quality* and *quantity* of emotion. What the projection type, relatively poor in emotion, looks for and needs is apparently not the tender and rich emotional scale of the identification type, but his own limited intensity of feeling. On the other hand, what the identification type looks for and needs is the variety and tenderness in feeling corresponding to his own emotional counterpart in the other, and only biologically and characterologically is compelled to the complementary type.

Here we find again the same paradox that seems to be characteristic of human psychology. The projection type who expresses his feelings, indeed exhibits them, seems characteristically to be the one who gives but psychologically is the one who receives, takes back again. The identification type who hides his feeling more but shares it in silence with the other, is really the one who gives, who not only does not take but gives in addition. What he adds is, however, the same feeling, thus *quality*, whereas the projection type looks for the same *quantity*, intensity.

Thus we see in the sphere of the emotional life that the giving and taking types correspond emotionally to the mechanisms of projection or identification, *between which* the guilt-feeling operates.

This leads me to the connection between the emotional life and the real self [*wirklichen Selbst*]. It seems that our true self [*wahres Selbst*] is the emotional self that is not expressed but rather is hidden. This true emotional self [*Gefühls-Selbst*] again seems to be closely connected with the biological I [*biologischen Ich*]. Speaking quite generally, man represents the projection, taking type, and woman the identification, giving type. Accordingly, again speaking generally, man has the poorer, woman the richer, feeling and as a rule woman is the one who gives emotionally, man the one who takes. At the physiological level, it is reversed, as seen in the sex act and procreation: man is the giver, woman the receiver. In the characterological sphere, finally, man seems to be the one who gives, woman the one who receives. In other words, when we compare the three spheres being considered, namely the biological, the emotional, and the characterological, the following pattern for man and woman results. Man seems to be biologically and characterologically the one who gives, but in the real emotional sphere, namely in feeling, he proves to be the one who takes, the projection type. Woman, on the other hand, biologically and characterologically appears to be the one who receives but emotionally proves to be the one who gives, the identification type.

In these conflicts of the emotional life manifested in the individual himself, as well as in his relation to the sex partner—or in the corresponding type in general—we see guilt-feeling operating as a *balancing* mechanism. However, it does not always function successfully, because the types are too mixed and the conditions in general too complicated. Guilt-feeling enables woman to receive what she wants to give and forces man to give where he wants to take. This may be the case in either the biological, characterological, or emotional spheres.

What has been said of the sexes is valid for the human types corresponding in general to them. Guilt-feeling unites not only the biological I with the biological Thou, i.e., helps the ego to accept the sex role even though it is not in harmony with the emotional or characterological type. Guilt-feeling is a still more important factor in one's own emotional life: it there unites the contradictory tendencies of giving and taking, of domination and submission—indeed, makes it possible for these tendencies to exist side by side. In other words, guilt-feeling represents an essentially *harmonizing* factor in the ego, in that it there unites emotionally the biological I with the (often enough) contradictory characterological I, and this role of uniting or combining only continues further in relation to the object.

The production of guilt-feeling is thus a necessary process of fermentation in our character development from the biological I to the emotional expression of personality. This balancing function of guilt-feeling fails where it is too strong, thus, again as a rule, in the projection type with its intense emotions—apart from whether this type is a man or woman. And it fails because there, where it is too strong, it exercises its separating function instead of operating to unite [verbinden zu wirken], in the meaning of inner feeling.

Thus guilt-feeling seems to have the function of balancing the inner conflict between wanting to take and having to give, between wanting to dominate and having to submit; in a word, between the biological and the characterological I. In my terminology one could also say that guilt-feeling grows out of the conflict between the tendency to project and the necessity to identify. From the analytic situation, as from the love relation, we have learned that when projection oversteps its mark it creates [schafft] guilt-feeling. Identification, on the other hand, does away with guilt-feeling, abolishes it. Projection leads inevitably to guilt-feeling since it makes use of the other, i.e., compels or at least does not consider [Nichtberücksichtigen] the other. Identification removes guilt-feeling because it signifies an understanding of the other, a love for, a sharing with, the other. Projection creates [schafft] guilt because it is based on denial of the other self [verleugnung des andern Selbst]; identification liberates from guilt because it is a recognition of the other [Anerkennung des andern ist].

The relation of these two fundamental mechanisms to the emotions can be formulated in the following way. What is projected, as I have stated, is without doubt the feeling; in the same way identification occurs emotionally and by means of feelings. Both mechanisms of projection and identification aim at establishing a purely emotional identity, which is only realized in one situation, the mutual [gegenseitigen] love emotion.[6] And this realization in the sensations and feelings of the love life gives pleasure. All other realizations of emotion unloaded as affects are of a separating nature and cause pain. Therefore, the sexual sphere—in which feelings are experienced pleasurably—is by far the most important. What psychoanalysis has called libido seems to be nothing else [scheint nichts anderes] than this pleasurable way of experiencing emotional sensations. The unloading of affects, on the other hand, is more of an ego reaction.

The pleasurable feeling is most frequently realized in the sexual sphere (to which Freud wants to restrict it), but it is possible also in other spheres (as Jung has maintained). The experience of pleasurable feeling is not only bound to positive conditions, but just as much to the lack of a negative factor, namely, guilt-feeling—or, more correctly, one might say, to lack of the "plus" in guilt-feeling that goes beyond the amount necessary for balancing inner conflicts.

Pleasurable emotion can be experienced [*erfahren*] only when projection and identification, giving and taking, domination and submission, the discharge of emotion and affect, are operative from *both* sides together, and in one another, to the same degree and at the same time. Then no "plus" of guilt-feeling can arise—but this does not mean that no guilt-feeling is present, for without it such a mutual harmonization would be impossible. Under the most favorable conditions, pleasurable feelings arise in the uninhibited emotional expression of the true self [*des Wahren Selbst*]—which is just as spontaneously returned by the other and, hence, makes possible acceptance of the purely egoistic emotions of pleasure, without being disturbed by guilt-feeling. In other words, it is not the lack of guilt-feeling that makes it possible to accept pleasure; rather, it is the *use* of the inevitable guilt-feeling to balance inner conflicts, chiefly for the purpose of attaining the love identification [*Liebesidentifiezierung*] with the other.

In all these emotional processes, besides the problem of quality and quantity, there is added yet another factor that plays an important role: the time factor. It is easily seen and confirmed by daily experience [*tägliche Erfahrung*] that in the emotional life, a "too-early" or "too-late" is just as important as a "too-much" or "too-little." This experience [*Erfahrung*] again only confirms that feeling rests absolutely on reciprocity or, psychologically expressed, strives for the establishment of an inner identity. The feeling of the other should be the same in quality and quantity as well as temporally. But, beyond this, the whole problem of time, in general, seems to me to be an emotional problem, a thought that I can here only mention without going further into detail.[7] I refer to the daily experience of how our feeling of time changes with our general emotional attitude or, as we say, our "moods." I also refer to the well-known fact that all disturbances in the emotional life—which have been described as neuroses—show the essential characteristic of a disturbance in the sense of time.

Neurotic patients mostly complain that they think too much in the past and worry about the future, instead of living in the present [*der Gegenwart zu leben*]. Another type, the impulsive, on the other hand, lives exclusively in the moment and bothers too little about the future consequence of his actions. However, in every case it is clear that the kind and degree of our emotions determine our relation to time and to times—namely, the present, past, and future; in other words, feelings determine our whole attitude to life and experience [*die Gefühle unsere gesamte Einstellung zum Leben und Erleben bestimmen*].

Notes

Read before the University of Pennsylvania School of Social Work, fall 1927.

1. Far from denying the mystery of "the" unconscious, Rank wants only to explode the conventional reification of it as a container of past emotions that can be opened, repackaged, and closed by analysis. Abandoning Freud's archaeological metaphor, Rank said in *Will Therapy*:

> [There is no] "unconscious in the topical [i.e., topographical] sense of the word. The undischarged, unreleased, or traumatic experiences are not repressed *into* the unconscious and there preserved, but rather are continued permanently in *actual living* [*aktuellen Erleben*], resisted, carried through to an ending or worked over into entirely new experiences [*Erlebnissen*]. Here, in actual experience [*wirklichen Erleben*], as in the therapeutic process, is contained not only the *whole present* but also the *whole past*, and only here in the present are psychological understanding and therapeutic effect to be attained. (1929–31, p. 28: italics added)

2. In *Art and Artist*, Rank compared the artist's "giving" and the enjoyer's "finding" of art with the dissolution and rediscovery of the self in mutual love:

> For this very essence of a man, his soul, which the artist puts into his work and which is represented by it, is found again in the work by the enjoyer, just as the believer finds his soul in religion or in God, with whom he feels himself to be one. . . . But both of them, in the simultaneous dissolution of their individuality in a greater whole, enjoy, as a high pleasure, the personal enrichment of that individuality through this feeling of oneness. They have yielded up their mortal ego for a moment, fearlessly and even joyfully, to receive it back in the next, the richer for this universal feeling. (1932a, pp. 109–10)

Rank took the experience he calls "dissolution of . . . individuality in a greater whole" to yet another level: there is a "cosmic" (or existential) form of identification as well as an ordinary "human" form. Thus, aesthetic pleasure

> produces a satisfaction which suggests that it is more than a matter of the passing identification of two individuals, that it is the potential *restoration* of a union with the Cosmos, which once existed and was then lost. The individual psychological root of this sense of unity I discovered (at the time of writing *The Trauma of Birth*, 1924) in the prenatal condition, which the individual in his yearning for immortality strives to restore. Already, in that earliest stage of individualization, the child is not only factually one with the mother but beyond all that, one with the world, with a Cosmos floating in mystic vapours in which present, past, and future are dissolved. The individual urge to restore this lost unity is (as I have formerly pointed out) an essential factor in the production of human cultural values. (1932a, p. 113; Rank's italics)

3. From this point on, Rank uses the word *emotion* to describe the uniting, binding feelings—principally love but also guilt-feeling. In its relation to gratitude, devotion, and self-sacrifice, guilt is one of the strongest uniting feelings, a necessary harmonizing factor between the self and the world, I and Thou. In the

epigraph to the German version of this lecture, Rank quotes Goethe: *"Gefühl ist alles* [Feeling is all]" (Rank 1927, p. 75).

4. "One could characterize the neurosis as secretiveness with regard to the self," said Rank in *Will Therapy*, "and the necessary modification of this attitude in the therapeutic relationship would explain in part the therapeutic effect. On the other hand, the therapeutic process with all honesty still offers rich opportunity for hide and seek, since the secret self [*das geheime Selbst*] projects itself upon the therapist and must be read off from there" (1929–31, pp. 205–6).

5. See "The Anxiety Problem" [8].

6. See "The Significance of the Love Life" [13].

7. Rank took up the problem of time in "Happiness and Redemption," the last chapter of *Truth and Reality*:

> With all so-called psychic mechanisms, we have to do ultimately with the shortening or prolonging of psychic states; to shorten to the point of nothingness [*Nichts*] as, for example, denial does, or to prolong to infinity as in the belief in immortality. . . . For pleasure is a certain brevity of consciousness, pain a lengthening of consciousness, at least on the level of neurotic self-consciousness, where consciousness disturbs experience [*Erleben*] in the form of self-consciousness and guilt consciousness, and accordingly the individual wants to be saved from it. Therefore from the standpoint of the psychology of the emotions, consciousness shows itself as a time problem. (1929, pp. 88–89)

12

EMOTIONAL SUFFERING AND

THERAPY (1927)

LADIES AND GENTLEMEN, it is the merit of psychoanalysis to have recognized the neuroses as disturbances of the emotional life. But if the painful emotions that we designate as affects (in the pathological meaning of the word) are the cause [*Ursache*] of suffering, then it is easy to see where the healing process must start and in what it consists. The excess of painful emotions that we call suffering comes from the failure of the emotional life in its task as a uniting factor. As a consequence the emotion of separation, of isolation, becomes conscious to us as pain or even agony. Its essential symptoms are anxiety, an excess of guilt-feeling, or the feeling of inferiority—but in every case a feeling of being different [*Gefühl von Differenz*], of isolation, from the other.[1]

Hence the therapeutic formula seems easy to prescribe: the emotional life must again function in a uniting instead of in a disuniting way. In place of the feeling of isolation must appear the feeling of union. In place of the emotional perception of difference must be identity. This should take place gradually: first of all, with one individual, then with others, the cosmos, and finally with the world of reality.[2] As one can easily see, the establishment or reestablishment of this uniting element occurs in love. But this formula is neither so banal as it seems, nor yet so easy in its application, if one only remembers how complicated is the emotion of love. There are in it elements of tenderness, devotion, submission, gratitude, to which are contrasted the impulsive ego-strivings such as cruelty, domination, jealousy, and the desire for possession.

The emotion of love is in itself an absorbing, uniting feeling that paralyzes mere ego-strivings. Consequently, it may easily overdo it. Then it leads to compensatory manifestations, which we then see in such characteristics as bondage, masochistic submission, and self-sacrifice. Here already we discover an important fundamental principle for psychotherapy. Just as in the dynamics of the emotions it is always a question of a "too-much" or "too-little," there are at least two pronounced types of patients—each of which needs a little different means of help. The patient has either too much ego or too little, too many inhibitions or too few, too much or too little projection or identification, too much or too little guilt-feeling. But what in every case is lacking is the *real* love emotion—an emotion that makes for harmony within, with oneself, and at the same time externally unites one in harmony with the other, the Thou.

In a well-balanced love emotion, the other, the Thou, is without doubt necessary, because the Thou justifies [*rechtfertigt*] the I. The Thou belongs just as much biologically as characterologically—i.e., ethically—to the I. Therapy, which has to establish the Thou emotion [*Du-Gefühl*], can be applied in each of these spheres. Therapy is most effective when it accomplishes this in all spheres at the same time. But therapy should not be restricted to the sexual sphere; it should also take into account the other spheres. For the ethical conflict[3] is inseparable from the sexual conflict and the conflicts can just as well be approached from the ethical as from the sexual side. The question as to how in psychoanalysis an overestimation of the sexual factors arose leads to connections of fundamental importance for the therapeutic problem. In essence, it is the medical viewpoint that is responsible for this attitude. In most neuroses the most noticeable symptom is disturbance of the patient's sex and love life; the patient's own complaints are also mostly related to this.

Reminding ourselves of the meaning of the love life,[4] and bearing in mind the part in it played by the sexual function, we can then easily understand what sexual conflict signifies. It is nothing other than that the individual in the disturbances of his emotional life—in what we call the crises of his ego-development—has resorted to sexuality as an outlet and means of cure. It is the same mechanism that we see in the analytic situation, where the patient always tries to avoid the *emotional* solution of his conflict. In life it is exactly the same.

In crises that emotionally isolate the ego, it seems to be the easiest means of cure to seek a lost union [*verlorengegangene Verbindung*] with the other, with the world, in the love emotion. But since these individuals are not capable of the love emotion—otherwise they could not have got into the ego crises—they seek the uniting element in the *physical* instead of in the emotional sphere. Naturally, this not only does not solve the emotional problem—but, in consequence of the resulting guilt-feeling, only increases it. When patients come for help, as a rule they present the sexual conflict and the guilt problem. The sexual conflict, however, may already be considered as a failure in the patient's attempt to recover from an ego crisis and the manifest guilt-feeling is a proof of the failure. At the same time, it is proof that the sex conflict is an ethical conflict in the ego.

Naturally, the physician to whom such a state of affairs is represented sees only the disturbances of the sexual life. Even when he recognizes the ethical part in the conflict, he does not know how to deal with it, for ethics is no part of medical study and so is not his affair. On the other hand, the sexual function is something physical about which the doctor has learned, although the last decades have shown how much medical study has neglected the human side of the sexual life in favor of the biological and anatomical sides.

Also, Freud began with a purely medical treatment of the sexual life, for he ordered patients to stop certain sexual practices that he had recognized as harmful. In many cases this proved to be effective, a good therapeutic idea. But in many cases it remained ineffective or in its application was not at all adequate. Along the path Freud has taken, far from this medical point of departure—leading even to the creation of a psychoanalytic worldview—he has never yet completely overcome the medical viewpoint.

In its development from the idea of sexual trauma to the discovery of guilt-feeling, psychoanalysis has shown that the so-called neuroses are not a medical problem but a human problem, which cannot be conceived from a purely medical point of view. In other words, neurosis is no disease in the medical meaning of the word, but an emotional suffering—primarily no disturbance of the sexual function, but of the ego function. Indeed, the symptoms of the neuroses, especially those of a sexual nature, might be considered attempts to *heal* these ego crises, as Freud maintained for many processes of the psychoses. Just as Freud designated the dream as a "guardian of sleep," which only sometimes fails, so generally speaking one might consider neurotic reactions or symptoms as "guardians of health," or as manifestations of self-preservation. They warn the individual that something is wrong in his emotional life just as a slight physical pain may indicate the beginning of a severe illness.

But as little as the dream succeeds in preserving sleep, so just as little does the symptom warn the individual and save his health. For the symptom is not only a warning but also a sign that some kind of destructive process has already begun. Here, then, is where therapy comes in. While medical therapy, in general, aims at preventing the destructive process by removing its cause [Ursache], psychotherapy on the other hand is somewhat different. Certainly we therapists also endeavor to alleviate suffering, but emotional suffering is *different* from physical suffering with regard to its cause and effect. First of all, *we cannot entirely remove the cause of emotional suffering*—even when we find it—because suffering is in the nature of human emotional life. The emotional life itself is full of suffering and pain, and therefore it can be only a question of the more or less. To want to prevent emotional suffering would be to uproot the emotional life, as the Indian doctrine of healing attempts in practice, the Christian doctrine in certain of its dogmas, and the psychotic in his deadened emotions.

All this, and still more, proves to be the individual's own therapeutic attempt to remove by the root the foundation of all human suffering: namely, the life of the emotions and feelings. If one may compare these attempts to a surgical operation, then there are other ways of spontaneous therapy of self-help that are of a more calming and liberating nature. These forms of help do not pretend to uproot the cause of the evil—the emotional life—but they accept it, affirm it, and attempt to give it liberating possibilities of expression. In a word, they are cathartic. However, they unburden only temporarily and have to be applied again and again.

To this form of therapy belongs, first of all, love—moreover, the enjoyment and production of art, as production in general, no matter in what sphere. To it also belong pleasure in knowledge in the intellectual sphere, religious ecstasy in the emotional sphere; indeed, all ecstatic states from the love emotion to drunkenness have only one purpose: to deaden pain. We see here clearly how these two therapeutic tendencies, the destructive and the liberating, correspond to the two fundamental sides of our emotional life: the *uniting* and the *separating*.

Surgical therapy is uprooting and isolates the individual emotionally, as it tries to *deny* the emotional life. Cathartically liberating therapy is uniting, seeks and finds the same emotions in the Thou, in one's fellow beings, and thus share with them both suffering and joy. The one therapy attempts relief from within, the other looks for relief from without. As we see, these two kinds of spontaneous psychotherapy correspond to the two types we have described as the "projection" and "identification" types. Although these types in reality are not so sharply distinguished—the mechanisms lying at their foundation simultaneously working with and against one another—consciously applied therapy still has to take them into consideration. The kind of therapy the patient needs will depend on the predominance of one or the other tendency: in a word, on the type.

In the sphere of physical suffering, according to the kind and severity of the illness, not only different means of help but also different kinds of therapy are used. With regard to emotional suffering, however, the view that everything "can be cured from one point" seems to predominate. This similarity may occur with regard to the desired result, namely, alleviation of emotional suffering. But the way in which this is attained is different, depending on the type of individual. The one who projects too much has to learn to affirm, the one who is too much inhibited has to learn to express, the emotions. This learning, however, results in a most remarkable way, psychologically. Above all, it does not occur intellectually but emotionally, by means of *identification*.

The necessary understanding is also not gained purely intellectually, but by means of *projection*—which teaches us to recognize our true self [*wahres Selbst*] in the mirror of the other. The essential factor of this healing process, namely the learning, as a whole results emotionally; that is, again through suffering. In a word, psychotherapy, as attempted artificially by psychoanalysis, does not remove emotional suffering but only teaches patients how to bear the inevitable suffering. Indeed, in regard to the primal source of suffering—the emotional life—psychotherapy [*die seelische Therapie*] often enough is more painful than the original suffering itself. Recognition and acceptance of the emotional life is itself painful and this pain originally led to the destructive tendency to uproot it. The patient perhaps suffers less after the therapeutic experience [*therapeutischen Erlebnis*], but it is certain that now he has learned to bear suffering more easily: it may be in recognizing it as inevitable or it may be that it seems less compared with what he has been through.

This is also only one side of the problem. The patient learns not only to suffer—or rather to bear suffering—he also learns to love, to endure his emotional life and express it. Psychotherapy again gives both—namely pleasure and pain—without doing away with conflict, without making pleasure undesirable, without making pain avoidable. But it can and should do something else. I said previously that the aim of medical therapy is the removal of the cause [*Ursache*] of suffering. In this sense, therapy as such is negative. Psychoanalysis teaches us that psychotherapy cannot aspire to such a claim, for the evil is suffering and its cause is our emotional life [*seine Ursache ist unser Gefühlsleben*] which we cannot remove—indeed, can scarcely influence. Hence in the emotional sphere, it would be better not to speak of therapy at all but simply of "psychology"—I mean psychologically guiding, a kind of pedagogic guidance that rests on emotional identification and becomes effective through love and suffering. What this guidance can and should have as its aim is not removal of the cause of suffering [*der Ursache des Leidens*], the emotional life, but to make means of expression accessible to the emotional life, or to provide them. In a word, a psychical cure can be effective only insofar as it is *constructive*.

In the sphere of the emotional life, there can be no destructive surgical therapy. The inhibited tendencies that are liberated seek means of expression, which have to be directed so that they do not operate destructively. For in the *emotional* life there is a compensatory tendency that nowhere else dominates so strongly, and that expresses itself dynamically, as soon as the inhibitions are liberated or reduced. Indeed, also in the biological sphere there is a similar compensatory tendency for healing in the sphere of *physical* suffering, the use of which has been proposed by Wilhelm Ostwald. It is possible that a physical cure can result without compensation. In the emotional sphere, however, I believe it is not possible. This is another reason why psychotherapy can only be constructive—and then it has little in common with therapy as understood medically.

The need for ecstatic, cathartic therapies shows clearly that the surgical means of uprooting fails in the emotional sphere. Indeed we see both tendencies—the defensive, destructive, and the affirming, ecstatic—simultaneously effective. In the lover as in the artist, the mystic as the psychotic, the neurotic as the average—they all simultaneously try the pain-deadening means of help, the uprooting and denial, just as much as the affirmation and gratification of the emotional life. Again we see these two contradictory tendencies conditioning one another. Denial of emotional suffering does not remove it but produces new suffering—which has to be numbed by ecstasy. Ecstasy again leads to catharsis and this again establishes a state of painful tension after a temporary alleviation.

Before I speak about the really constructive elements of psychology, I want to point out where real therapy operates. It is on the *borderline* between the physical and the psychical, or better, at the connection between physical and emotional suffering. In the study of human illnesses, we learn that nearly all physical suffering is evoked and becomes acute through an emotional conflict. The mechanism of this experience [*Erfahrung*], proved beyond doubt, is easy to understand in light of our doctrine of the emotions. Denial of emotional suffering, especially when produced in us by another, leads to displacement of suffering from the psychical to the physical sphere, by which the pain is justified, to a certain extent, is objectified.

This "conversion" of the painful emotion appears clearly only in hysterical symptoms, where no organic change is to be found. But it also lies at the base of physical phenomena of suffering. From numerous experiences [*zahlreichen Erfahrungen*] in psychoanalysis, I have found that real organic diseases also appear to be precipitated through converted psychical pain. In all these cases, the conversion concerns a painful affect displaced from the emotional to the physical sphere—instead of its being able to express itself. A simple symptom of this kind is the headache, which appears instead of weeping that has been suppressed and which, as is well known, alleviates pain—*if* the ego will permit this painful admission. This typical example enables me to illustrate most clearly the process of affect-conversion. It is a turning of the emotion *within* that leads to isolation, to a kind of stubborn withdrawal from the other. Instead of looking for help and alleviation in the sympathy of the other, the proud ego denies this human inclination and its cause [*Ursache*]—namely, the painful emotion. It cannot, however, be removed but only goes within—into one's own body—instead of without, as an expression of affect concerning the other.

In this sense the patient's appeal for help already is the beginning of the process of healing. The admission that he needs help, that he suffers, is not only the symbol of a good prognosis but in the emotional sphere signifies the cure itself. Do not wonder that patients only seek help when in desperation; they must be desperate in order to compel themselves to admit they need help. Often enough a physical symptom has to assist in overcoming the last resistance. Therapeutically, as often in the purely organic sphere, one has to let the process run its course and in so doing to a great extent trust to nature. What can be done therapeutically, in essence, is chiefly one thing: to enable the patient free expression of his emotions at least in speech and so to give *externally* a certain discharge of affect.

If one notes the similarity to confession in this cathartic verbalization, then let me emphasize again the positive constructive character of this process. It is at least just as much, if not more, an accusation against the other who has caused the suffering as it is a self-accusation or confession. Indeed, it seems almost that admission of one's own guilt is only the balancing weight to the violent accusations against the other brought by the patient in analysis. It seems also that accusations against the other are more painful than self-accusations (which the neurotic produces so liberally), because they contain the painful admission that the pain was arranged by another. However that may be, in every case this seems to me to be the difference between the Christian cure of souls and pedagogic guidance of souls. In one, the individual is exhorted to self-accusation; in the other, he should be led to self-expression. This self-expression, in essence, consists of accusing the other who has pained the ego. This is so liberating because such an admission corresponds to a *removal* of denial.

Two dangers lying in the nature of the analytic situation seem to threaten final success. The first is that the patient soon projects these accusations against the *analyst*, sometimes directly, but always indirectly or silently, as a resistance—which then threatens the analytic situation. The handling of this resistance is indeed a technical problem. Difficulties in it, however, also concern the patient's whole situation: he must do something with these accusations. If he turns them against himself, then unbearable guilt-feeling is the result; if he turns them against people in his environment, then he can no longer live with them; if he turns them against the analyst, then the final result of the treatment is threatened. The second danger is that the patient will continue outside the analysis, after its termination, the uninhibited expression of emotions that he was permitted inside the analysis, indeed, was commanded to express. This is, however, not always possible. On the other hand, the patient has learned to express his feelings instead of suppressing them. The difficulty lies in the fact that he has to find a middle course—which, formerly, he could not find without falling from one extreme into the other.

This is the most difficult problem of psychotherapy. The analytic part has shown us how the individual can become neurotic. The "constructive" part, as I call it, shows the individual how he himself might be if he accepts his true self [*wahres Selbst*]. When the patient in the so-called transference wants to hold fast so strongly to the old mechanisms of projection and identification (parental image), he is right in this resistance—insofar as he fears to express his own feelings freely and in an uninhibited manner as his own responsibility.

In the so-called "training analysis," it may be practicable to discharge the analytic candidate at the stage of identification with his analyst—as, indeed, the admitted aim is that he *ought* to become like his analyst. Unfortunately, however, most *therapeutic* analyses end in this way—because the analyst himself, as a rule, has not come beyond the stage of identification with his own training analyst. It even seems as if the analyst's own "training analysis" could do harm in his practice of analysis, either when he is not able to bring his patient beyond the stage of identification or when—as a reaction to identification with his training analyst—he now projects his own repressed self [*sein eigentliches verdrängtes Selbst*] onto patients. It is, of course, otherwise when the analyst can develop and express his own individuality and personality so that he has no need to do this in the analytic situation. Only then will he be able to avoid projecting his own self [*sein Selbst*] onto the patient, and so compel [*zwingen*] him to an identification.[5]

As one sees, in the analysis it is fundamentally a matter of personality development, and indeed on *both sides*: first on the analyst's and then on the patient's. Technically this might be described in the following way. In every correctly handled analysis of the emotions, there is a moment on which the success of the whole work depends. At this moment, one has to *free* patients from the analytic pressure. The form in which this results, I have described as *the setting of the time limit*.[6] But in it, as I have stated, one must take care that the termination is not fixed arbitrarily but that definite criteria for it are to be found in the patient's reactions.

The criteria are different according to the type of patient, but all emerge at a definite place in the analysis and may be reduced to the following common denominator. It is in those real phases of resistance that appear when the patient has overcome the first difficulties in establishing the transference and has got to the point where he wants to end the analysis—because, otherwise, he is in danger of getting too deeply into it. This is the point at which the resistance takes on *constructive* significance, which the analyst must not overlook if the analysis is to succeed.[7] When the patient makes progress in a constructive sense, that is, the more independent and self-reliant he becomes, the more must he react with resistance against the analytic situation—*which keeps him dependent and not self-reliant*. When the analyst does not recognize at the right time the constructive side of this resistance and does not use it for setting the time limit, this leads to a complete failure of his task: namely, letting the patient begin to free himself emotionally when the first urge to freedom appears.

For this purpose the analyst *himself* must be free—free from anxiety, free from vanity. This is necessary because the patient cannot directly express his desire for freedom, as he feels bound to the analyst by love and guilt. The patient's direct admissions of the transference are, often enough, the first compensatory expressions of his guilt-feeling, which appear as a reaction to his desire for freedom. When one then makes conscious the patient's wish to escape from the pressure of the analytic situation, and yields to it, then one gets new reactions of resistance—which are raised against this offense. Whether or not he himself wants it, he still feels that he is sent away and this wounds his pride. At the same time, with this resistance he excuses himself from the responsibility of having wanted to end the analysis and then as a rule willingly resigns the final setting of the time limit to the analyst. In the time between the first appearance of the patient's desire for freedom—when the time limit is set—and the real end of the analysis, one must make *constructive* use of the patient's tendency to free himself. This is done, first of all, by removing the guilt feeling toward the analyst in the analytic situation itself.

Briefly the analysis should and must lead the patient *beyond* the stages of projection and identification to the development of personality, the first and most important accomplishment of which is the *creation of his own analysis*. The patient himself carries out the analytic task, corresponding in each case to his own type. That is, he does the analysis in his own manner and way. He forms and uses the analytic situation according to his needs and desires. The analyst must have so much insight [*soviel Einsicht*] and stand so far above the situation that he not only does not hinder the patient in this—his striving for personality—but supports it. The analysis can and should be made a personal *creation* of the patient's [*persönlichen Schöpfung des Patienten*], which he then accepts without guilt feeling and without extreme reactions, as his own accomplishment—indeed as an expression of his own *newly created* personality.

We do not deceive ourselves with the belief that this is an ideal picture. Not all individuals, no matter what their conflicts, have creative abilities, and still less can most individuals endure the independence, self-reliance, and responsibility bound up with it. The average human being needs to be dependent and to identify in order to be able to adjust himself, just as the child also is unable to stand alone. To such people, the analytic experience [*Erlebnis*] sometimes gives only a taste of how dangerous—but also how impossible—the free development they apparently want so much would be for them. In these cases it can be called a success if the analyst convinces [*überzeugt*] the patient that he had better remain as he is.

To the different character types and methods of cure correspond different therapeutic aims and results. That we cannot always attain the ideal is clear. But we have to bear in mind that we should not even strive for it always in the same way. What would be an ideal solution for one individual might be destructive for another. And so really *every case has its own technique, its own analysis, and its own solution*. This adjusts itself to the patient's personality and to the situation and ought not to be molded according to theoretical presuppositions and ideals.

Notes

Read before the University of Pennsylvania School of Social Work, fall 1927.

1. "The mere fact of difference," of individuality, said Rank in *Will Therapy*, "in other words, the existence of our own will as opposite, unlike, is the basis for the [self] condemnation which manifests itself as inferiority or guilt feeling" (1929–31, p. 56). I = pain. Difference = suffering.

2. Rank described the "cosmic" or existential dimension of identification in *Art and Artist*:

> At the highest level of human personality we have a process which psychoanalysis calls (without explaining its deeper biological and human aspects) identification. This identification is the echo of an original identity, not merely of child and mother, but of everything living—witness the reverence of the primitive for animals. In man, identification aims at reestablishing a lost identity: not an identity which was lost once and for all, phylogenetically through the differentiation of the sexes, or ontologically in birth, but an identity with the cosmic process, which has to be continually surrendered and continually reestablished in the course of self-development. (1932a, p. 376)

This "identity with the cosmic process" is pre-objectual, *before* object-relations, *before* even the amniotic experience of the infant in its mother's womb: it is, Rank says, "not merely" an echo of the relationship between "child and mother."

3. Rank uses the term *ethical conflict* to refer to the relation of I to Thou, self to other, one will to another, one "difference" to another "difference." He places guilt-feeling in the space between these two differences, a space that expands in hate and contracts in love. A synonym for *ethical conflict* is the *will-guilt problem*—a problem to which Rank devoted much of *Will Therapy*. The will that Rank speaks of is not the nineteenth-century "faculty" of will. Nor is it the evil will of Schopenhauer or the glorified will-to-power of Nietzsche. For Rank, will means nothing other than "difference," and "difference" always brings guilt in its wake. "In a word," he said in *Truth and Reality*, "will and guilt are the two complementary sides of one and the same phenomenon" (1929, p. 31). Unlike Kant, Rank never spoke of the will as a "purely" autonomous agent. Will = guilt.

4. See "The Significance of the Love Life" [13].

5. There can be little doubt that Rank is suggesting that Freud unconsciously projected his "own repressed self" onto patients, "compelling" them to identify unconsciously with his projections. See "The Significance of the Love Life" [13], for more on the dynamics of projection and identification in the analytic situation.

6. See "The Trauma of Birth and Its Importance for Psychoanalytic Therapy" [3].

7. See "Neurosis as a Failure in Creativity" [20] for Rank's differentiation of resistance along three lines: in the initial, middle, and end phase of analysis.

13

THE SIGNIFICANCE OF THE

LOVE LIFE (1927)

LADIES AND GENTLEMEN, man's true self [*das wahre Wesen des Menschen*]—that which differs from character—expresses itself only in one sphere: namely, the love life. There it is manifested quite spontaneously and in real love is just as spontaneously accepted and reciprocated. We are able to study this emotional relationship, and with it also the true self manifested in it, only in the analytic situation. The phenomenon that Freud called transference reveals itself only in a deeper analysis, beyond the sexual level, as a phenomenon related to love. In the analysis, however, it remains one-sided. It is not reciprocated in the same spontaneous way. As a consequence there follows a somewhat distorted picture of the emotion, but at the same time we can now pursue the development of its different phases.

I have stated that, in essence, it is *projection* that determines the manner and intensity of our emotional relationship to fellow beings. By the side of this or, more correctly, at the same time, goes on a process that I have designated *identification*: the result of the realization of projection. In the love relationship, as I have already said, these processes of projection and identification proceed and merge into one another from both sides, in the same way and at the same time. In the analytic situation, however, the picture is different. The patient *projects* much more, I would say almost exclusively, at least in the first phase of analysis. In the same phase, also almost exclusively, the analyst has to confine himself to *identification* in order to understand the patient, and, so to say, feel one with him [*ihn einzufühlen*]. As soon as the patient feels this identification emotionally, he begins on his side to identify himself with the analyst. In other words, he can only identify when he feels in the other something kindred, identical [*Identisches fühlt*]—the identification on the part of the analyst necessary for understanding the patient.

In the phase of projection, as in all later projections, the patient *reveals* his real self [*wirkliches Selbst*]. In identification he seeks it in the other; i.e., tries to *disguise* it. This is the state of affairs described as resistance, especially as "transference-resistance"; as one can see, it is given in the nature of the analytic situation and is unavoidable. Technically, the analyst not only has to decrease it by pointing it out, but also to paralyze it, by avoiding a spontaneous counterreaction. The analyst has to further the kind of projection that leads to self-reflection and self-revelation and has to *decrease* identification, which serves the purpose of self-disguise. If the analyst's narcissism leads to misunderstanding or, more correctly, misinterpreting the situation, then emerges the so-called "counter-transference." This consists in the analyst going *beyond* the identification necessary for understanding the patient. The analyst, in his turn, now projects onto the patient, who identifies with this projected part of the analyst's ego, leading to the form of emotional relationship [*Gefühlsbeziehung*] we call infatuation.

A correct technique allows the analyst to trace this phenomenon of infatuation in the patient. I will review how this proceeds. The patient projects his true self [*wahres Selbst*] onto the analyst, who is not intimately known to him. He finds in the analyst not only the willing, *passive* object for this projection but also soon feels the analyst's *active* identification necessary to understand the patient. The analyst's identification makes possible for the patient, on his side, an identification based on projection, which manifests itself in the forms of infatuation.

Thus what we can study in the patient, in the ways to be described still more in detail, is not the love relationship [*Liebesbeziehung*] itself but the *first* stage of it, namely, infatuation, which in essence rests on projection and which can finally develop into love only with *complete* reciprocity. We have defined identification as the perception [*Wahrnehmung*] of projection; likewise, we can designate love as the perception of an accomplished infatuation. In other words, having described infatuation as the first stage of love, we see that love is the completion of infatuation: that is, the actual [*die wirklich*], not only psychologically perceived, identification.

Infatuation—such as ecstasy or adoration from a distance—does not necessarily include physical union, the bodily identification, but rests more on emotional identification, the mechanism of which we have described as projection. It is normally a pronounced phenomenon of adolescence and describes, exactly as in the analytic situation, the first step in our emotional relationship [*seelischen Gefühlsbeziehung*] to fellow-beings. Infatuation is a *transitional* phenomenon preparing us for the more lasting state of love which, with all its physical expressions, is, so to say, much more concrete and real. Love also goes back to the sensuous, physical gratifications really experienced [*wirklich erlebten*] by the individual from the mother in childhood.

In love there is, if one likes, more repetition of gratifying situations already experienced [*vergangener*], whereas infatuation is much more of a new and imaginative *creation* of one's own individuality, of one's self [*des Selbst*]. Therefore, we find infatuation later on in life every time the individual's ego goes through a new phase of development, manifesting itself as a crisis, like puberty. Hence we may call infatuation a symptom of a crisis in the ego [*Ich-Krise*]. I mean that the ego creates [*schafft*] this new love relationship by projecting one part of the self onto the object and so can easily adjust to it.

If we study more closely this process of infatuation in the analytic situation, we come up against two of its chief symptoms, the analysis of which compels us to a finer definition of projection. It is not quite correct to say that the patient always projects his true self [*wahres Selbst*] onto the analyst, if we understand by the true self the impulsive ego [*das impulsive Ich*]. For just as often, but certainly in definite phases of the analysis—as at the beginning—the patient projects onto the analyst his inhibitions [*Hemmungen*], what we call character. In reality, it is a matter of a continuous change, often a simultaneity, in the projection of these two sides of the personality, respectively.

The two extremes of this projection constitute the chief symptoms of the conditions of infatuation: *bondage* and *jealousy*. We are able to study their mechanisms in the pathological extremes described as "masochism" and "delusion of jealousy." Masochism is the result of a too-far-reaching projection of one's own *inhibitions* onto another; the delusion of jealousy is the result of a too-far projection of one's own *impulses* (temptations).

In masochism one projects one's own inhibitions onto another, whom the ego raises to the position of lord and master, i.e., bearer and executor of its inhibitions, which have to restrict and, at the same time, gratify the remaining impulses. The idealization of the master going along with it is a result of projection and, in the overestimation of the super-ego [*Über-Ich*], compensates for humiliation to the impulse-ego [*Trieb-Ich*]. In jealousy, in contrast to this, the impulse-ego in the form of sexual temptation is projected onto the other, and what remains is the super-ego. This manifests itself as pathological guilt-feeling and inhibits all impulses, which one ascribes to the other.

If the bondage of the masochist leads to submission to another ego, then the pronounced tendency of the jealous one leads to domination of the other ego, i.e., forbidding him temptations that one cannot inhibit in oneself. Whereas in the jealous one the impulse to possess is definitely marked, so the masochist shows a tendency to give up, to sacrifice. In other words, in neither of those extreme manifestations is there the reciprocity characteristic of *real* love, where a desire to possess as well as the ability to give up is equally strong in both, and *mutual*. In love there is a simultaneous and mutual intermingling of projection and identification on both sides, which paralyses the *exaggerated* manifestations of a too-far-reaching projection or identification, respectively, leading to neurotic reactions.

Study of pathological masochism thus helps us understand normal bondage as an accompaniment of infatuation, just as delusion of jealousy explains the proverbial jealousy of the infatuated. These are necessary accompaniments of the process of infatuation. Projection of one's own inhibitions onto the beloved gives free rein to the demands of the impulse-ego; projection of one's own impulses onto the other justifies their uninhibited expression, since we find them again in the other. Thus there takes place already in the first stage of infatuation an enormous *unburdening* of the ego from inhibitions and a freeing of impulses; and accompanying them we find bondage and jealousy. If projection—whether of inhibitions or impulses—goes too far, then the pathological symptoms I have just described will follow: namely, masochism on the one side and delusion of jealousy on the other. In the analysis of both these symptoms, we also come up against *guilt-feeling*, which I now want to explain in this connection.

The bondage of the lover corresponds more to an emotional dependency, as if, so to say, one needed the other *only* for projection. Real masochism carries dependency onto a more concrete physical level; as in love, it goes back to infantile situations (such as being beaten, etc.). Guilt is added later, at the ethical stage, and tends to justify dependency, submission, and humiliation. It is as if the individual would say, "I will not lower myself to my impulse-ego, but I deserve this humiliation (as punishment)." Naturally, the humiliation itself again increases guilt-feeling, and so is formed the cycle of projection, impulse gratification, and guilt-feeling. In masochism, as mentioned, it is a matter of a projection of all higher inhibitions of character onto the other. With guilt-feeling and desire for punishment, the ego falls back again to the primitive and lower stage of morality. Physical punishment, which was originally imposed on the ego, becomes ethically motivated through guilt-feeling from impulse gratification. From the primitive formula— the uninhibited impulse gratification deserves punishment—comes the higher ethical formula: "I want punishment because I deserve it."

As the analysis of bondage has led us to masochism, and finally to guilt-feeling, so we come from jealousy to sadism and narcissism, which both strive against submission. Sadism strives against it in the physical sphere by inflicting pain (beating), jealousy at the emotional level, and narcissism at a third level by placing one's own ego above the other ego in an antiethical way.

Until now I have spoken of love and infatuation without mentioning *biological* sexuality. This was not on purpose, but only because the phenomena with which I have dealt lie beyond the biological sex problem and are rooted in the ego. Analytic infatuation—"transference"—and actual infatuation, with or without physical expression, is possible, as is well known, just as much between persons of the same sex and, indeed, with accompanying phenomena such as bondage and jealousy. Attempting to explain even the pathological manifestations of these symptoms from the sexual role alone is unsatisfactory. Without doubt the biological sex role of the male is active, that of the female, passive. But in psychology we do not get further with this simple formula, not even if we consider biological bisexuality. Man can be just as masochistic as woman; indeed it is a well-known fact that pathological masochists are recruited from men who want to be dominated by a strong woman. But this is not so much a change of biological sex role as a psychological activity and passivity, which either harmonizes or comes into conflict with the biological. In any case it is the *psychological* activity-passivity problem with which we have to deal. It manifests itself in a person's character and can be therapeutically influenced, whereas *biologically* given activity or passivity, i.e., masculinity or femininity, is unalterable. But activity and passivity in the psychological sphere are no longer strange to us, for we can easily recognize in them the two sides of our personality I have described as "impulse-ego" and "inhibition-ego" [*Hemmungs-Ich*]. The impulse-ego is active, the inhibition-ego is passive, for *both* man and woman.

Sex differentiation—i.e., the biological sex role—becomes important insofar as woman's biological passivity strengthens the inhibiting character and so leads to a more passive inhibited type. But if this goes too far, as frequently happens, the consequence is that woman becomes incapable of real love. She is, so to say, so passive that she cannot accept love or devotion. As a consequence of her inhibited activity, she is unable to give love in return, since give-and-take is the presupposition of love. In extreme cases this inability to accept love manifests itself pathologically as guilt-feeling and leads to frigidity.

On the other hand, in man the biological sex role as a rule strengthens the impulses and decreases the force of inner inhibitions. But in their place man has more external inhibitions, which we may summarize as "social" anxiety. If, in the case of man, the strengthening of the impulse-ego by biological activity goes too far, then follows the uninhibited "impulse-character" ["*triebhafte Charakter*"]. In pathological cases, we see the necessary reestablishing of inner inhibitions taking the form of complete incapability of action, manifesting itself as depression. But normally we see the wholesome constructive effect of this mutual influence of biological and characterological activity and passivity.

Man, with a stronger biological activity, will perhaps strengthen his "inhibition-character" as a self-protection, or for the purpose of adjustment. Woman, with a stronger biological passivity or femininity, will strengthen her "impulse-character" in order not to be too passive or, in other words, to be capable of love. It is apparent that with all these complicated and subtle mechanisms, the borders can easily be crossed in either one or the other direction. Then the individual is either too little or too strongly inhibited. This can manifest itself equally in the sexual as in the social sphere.

In the conflict between the biological ego [*biologischen Ich*] and the characterological ego [*charakterologischen Ich*], which we try to harmonize and to balance in our personality, the love partner plays a part that we might designate as assistant-ego [*Hilfs-Ich*]. By means of projection and identification, we are able, at least temporarily, to establish a better equilibrium. A "plus" or "minus" in characterological activity or passivity, which disturbs our equilibrium, we can throw onto the other by means of projection or find in him by means of identification. And when the emotional need of the other corresponds with our own, the two "assistant-egos" complement one another and form a complete, harmonious self [*harmonischen Ich*]. This constitutes the happy state of love or, rather, the process of mutual intuition, projection, and identification leading to love, the first stage of which we have described as infatuation.

In the course of development, we can differentiate the following three phases of the ego's attitude to the love object. In *childhood*, identification with parents predominates in the meaning of education and adjustment. *Adolescence* signifies the great effort to free oneself from parents, namely in the first real infatuation, which has no prototype in relation to parents but is the first strong expression toward the development of personality, in the form of projection. The first creative self-expression of the personality, at the same time, corresponds to a freeing from the yoke of parental identification. Finally, in *maturity*, we see a phase that tries to unite harmoniously and lastingly the two extremes of a predominant identification in childhood and an exaggerated projection in adolescence. This is the lasting relationship to a person, a relationship we might designate as marriage, apart from whether or not it leads to a legal state of matrimony.

With the further development of the ego, new adjustments are necessary, which, in the case of matrimony, lead not easily to the change of object but to a lasting and increased effort of adjustment to the same object. But this is possible only in the simultaneous, parallel development of the partners, which does not always take place spontaneously. Indeed, as a rule, one finds in the partner at first resistance to any change, a resistance that may be given up only gradually. As in every lasting love relationship, also in marriage, the partner, at first a protection against temptations, now becomes the representative of one's own inner inhibitions, and eventually an external hindrance, a fetter. This is felt especially strongly in the case of matrimony. Analysis also shows that emotional bondage in cases of free unions or alliances is much stronger than in marriage, because everything rests on the feeling of inner responsibility, a burden which in the case of matrimony is borne by the law and so signifies a stronger emotional unburdening.

So much for the constructive side of the love life, for infatuation, so to say, as a therapeutic means for the healing of ego-conflicts. Like all means of cure, this also has its dangers. A too-strong dose of it creates again new symptoms that can no longer be healed by the same medicine. Although it is attempted again and again, the fact of its becoming habitual leads to a kind of paralysis, which finally makes it ineffective. We cannot, therefore, be surprised that, where it fails, the results— namely emotional conflicts—prove to be just as much if not more complicated than the infatuation that led to them.

I cannot here follow in detail the different conflicts and symptoms in which the new dissension of the ego manifests itself after it has once been exposed to the love therapy [*Liebes-therapie*]. In any case, the conflicts are, as a rule, more difficult afterwards than they were before, because they have become complicated by the addition of a new element. If, formerly, they were purely internal, now during the infatuation they do not cease to exist; they were only projected externally and paralyzed by this distribution. When, however, the balance is disturbed, difficulties increase because the real conflicts now react against the internal ones.

The common mechanism that intervenes in the mutual relationship between the internal and the external is self-protection. Regardless of whether the love partner is a representative of our impulses or our inhibitions, in either case, projection onto the love partner is a protective measure against a complete abandonment of the self. I mean that, by this method of projection, we unburden ourselves of some of our impulses or inhibitions that otherwise would be unbearable in ourselves or would lead to pathological expressions. This protective role of the partner designated by the term *assistant-ego* can very easily pass over into the role of hindrance, especially if the equilibrium was established by the "assistant-ego" and if we think we no longer need it. In this case the partner—from being a representative of our ego—becomes a real hindrance to it, against which the impulse-ego defends itself with all its power, as earlier it defended itself against its own inner inhibitions.

In such situations one generally calls up a new or second "assistant-ego" in order to protect oneself against the first and, if possible, exchange it for the first. These are the well-known triangular situations, which not only exist between man and woman, but also between the same sexes, indeed do not even presuppose a sexual relationship at all. Tracing back such triangular situations to the Oedipus situation signifies not much more than that the child has already been accustomed to work with such "assistant-egos."

Inasmuch as the first "assistant-ego" changes from a protection into hindrance, the second "assistant-ego" becomes a protection against the first, and at the same time, a representative of the temptations of the impulse-ego. In other words, the desire for a new love object seems to be impeded though the hindrance of the earlier one but is, in reality, determined just through the fact that the earlier one has become a "hindrance." Such triangular situations are an indication that inner transformations and displacements are taking place. These also necessitate a new external distribution, that is, a new projection. Thus they correspond to a transitional stage, are a new stage in ego development, and a means to this end.

This explains why they are always accompanied by guilt-feeling, which is the more intense the more the other individual is used in the part of "assistant-ego." At the biological level, this state of affairs is designated by the term "sexual-object," which signifies that the other is a mere object for gratification of the sex drive. But even at this level we must apparently justify the sex drive, in that we interpret it as a means for the propagation of the species, for begetting children. At the psychological level, in relation to the love object, the justification seems to be given in the development of one's own personality in the creation of one's own ego, instead of in the creation of children [*im Schaffen am Ich, anstatt in der Schöpfung des Kindes*].

As one sees in the emotional life, sexuality receives various symbolic meanings and finally is even interpreted psychologically. So, for example, masculine and feminine are connected not only with active and passive, strong and weak, superior or inferior but, as mentioned, are also interpreted psychologically. In this an important role is played by the idea that the intellectual is "masculine," the emotional "feminine." We find, at this stage, in place of the biological relation of impulse and inhibition, the psychological relation of emotion and intellect. The inhibitions are no longer directed against the impulses, but against their psychical representatives, the emotions. The impulses, however, become still more carefully suppressed and concealed because their uninhibited expression leads rather to disappointment and causes much stronger inner pain as a reaction.

Impulse gratification on the physical level is more mutual than on the emotional level, where it can be one-sided. But even dissatisfaction at the physical level is never so painful as a disappointment on the emotional level. This explains most of the difficulties and conflicts in the human being's sexual life. The sexual impulse is no longer purely biological but serves much more the purpose of the ego strivings than it does in the case of animals. Hence, perhaps, also the important difference between the animal and the human sex impulses. In the animal it is definitely restricted to periods in the so-called rutting-season. The human sexual need, on the other hand, is determined more by emotional factors, which are rooted in the ego.

It is well known that many human beings, out of a disappointment in the ego, take refuge in masturbation as consolation and substitute. The same often enough holds good of sexual acts with another person, and, for example, can plainly be seen in homosexuality, especially in men. But such a use of sexuality, exclusively or predominantly in the service of the ego, is for the most part unsatisfactory, both for the ego and the sexual impulse itself: for the ego, because sexuality in this case operates only as a temporary sedative; for the sex impulse, because there is lacking the essential factor in sexual gratification, namely emotional reciprocity and devotion [*Hingabe*] to the object.

The chief symptom in which this dissatisfaction manifests itself is guilt-feeling, which produces secondarily the most varied symptoms, earlier described as "neurasthenic." Thus it is not, as Freud first thought, the repression of the sexual impulse that causes guilt-feeling and anxiety but is the ego's *false* use of, if one likes, the misuse of, sex. Here also, as everywhere, guilt-feeling proves to be an ethical index for the *degree of egoism that has gone too far*. At the biological stage, it is fear or anxiety that corresponds to guilt-feeling, likewise being an index of the danger into which the ego enters or finds itself.

If we consider these general, biological, psychological, and ethical reactions of the human being separately for each sex, then we can make the following rough distinctions—which, naturally, may not always appear clearly in every case. For this purpose we have to go back to the difference between biological activity and passivity and character, formerly described as "impulse-ego" and "inhibition-ego."

In woman the conflict between these two parts of the self will generally be greater than in man, and therefore more difficult to harmonize one with the other. The reason for this is that in woman the activity of the impulse-ego is inhibited or paralyzed by the passivity of the biological sex role. Normally, in the relationship with an active male partner, woman finds her complement. But this is gradually becoming more and more difficult in our cultural milieu, because increasing social claims and demands on man inhibit him more and more, characterologically. As a result of this, we eventually see man and woman meeting as two passive egos [*zwei passive Iche*], who inhibit rather than complement one another.

In other words we see that in the human being, the "biological ego" is overtaken by the "characterological ego" and is so dominated by it that the simple biological sex role is no longer gratifying. Something else has to be added in order to make the sex life acceptable to the characterological and ethical self. And this necessary addition is *love*, which, so to say, harmonizes the biological and characterological demands emotionally and justifies them ethically. If this fails, we see anxiety and guilt appearing at the biological or ethical level respectively.

In simple words, conflict arises from the fact that man and woman have grown more alike with regard to their ego psychology, with regard to general character traits, emotions, and ethical ideas. This only emphasizes the biological *differences*. To the extent that the emotional and the characterological in the human life have become more important than the biological, to that extent man and woman are becoming more and more alike. This characterological similarity makes it more difficult to harmonize the two individualities biologically at the sex level. Hence, conflicts in the sexual and social relationships between man and woman are increasing.

This explains, in my opinion, the whole movement of feminism—the so-called endeavors of woman to become masculine—so much discussed and fought over in the present day. The slogan is, Woman wants to be like man, to be a man. It seems to me that both sides are neither right nor wrong, because they entirely overlook the real problem. I think that woman has already actually become like man in the sense I just mentioned. Therefore, I think that the masculinity tendencies are only expressions or, rather, symbols of an already-existing psychological similarity. The whole problem takes on a different aspect and meaning if one sees in feminism the establishment of a fact instead of a claim to it. In other words, it is not that we *want* to be like man, but we *are* like him and, therefore, we claim the same rights. But these "rights" are actually psychical [*seelische*], not social: woman has the same rights because her emotions [*Gefühlsleben*] are governed by the same psychological laws.

This concept, psychologically well-founded, has its support in another phenomenon of our times, which is as conspicuous as feminism but not so much discussed. I refer to the fact that so many men nowadays are definitely becoming feminine and ape women no less than women are aping men. With effeminate men, where there is no possibility of rationalizing this impulse socially with regard to privileges, it becomes obvious that this striving for equality is an expression of the existing similarity of which we have spoken.

This throws a new light not only on the social side of the relation of the sexes to one another, but also on certain manifestations today in the sexual sphere. By this I mean the noticeable increase in so-called homosexuality. Of course, I am not using *homosexuality* as a psychiatrical term denoting pathological aberration. I mean two persons of the same sex living together in a union with all the characteristics of a marital relationship. I think we can understand this undeniable tendency in the sex life of our times in the following way: Man and woman have become psychologically too much alike, so that they no longer complement but rather inhibit one another biologically. Whereas, before, biological difference formed a strong complementary attraction, now it is felt as a hindrance to a complete equality on the biological level, and so this complete equality is sought and found in the same sex. Such relationships, therefore, are sometimes much more satisfactory from an emotional as well as from an ethical viewpoint than are the heterosexual ones. But they are far from being free from conflict, which here arises from biological dissatisfaction, whereas conflicts in heterosexual relationships are more apt to be caused by emotional frustration.

In my discussion of love and its problems, I can scarcely avoid introducing historical viewpoints in referring to some phenomena in our modern sex life. This historical aspect becomes necessary because love, as I understand it psychologically, proves to be a rather late development in human life, quite in contrast to sexuality, which belongs to the biological fundamentals of our existence. I cannot be concerned here in pointing out when and how love originated.[1] Certainly there was a long period covering most of ancient times, when love as we understand it was practically unknown. From what I have said about the mechanism of infatuation, it seems that it is the same development toward individuality and personality leading to psychological similarity that compels the individual to this modern "romantic" emotional expression. As I have said before, the essential mechanism of infatuation is projection.

Projection, however, is nothing but a desire to find one's own self in the other, to create it even if it does not exist there [*das eigene Selbst im Andern finden zu wollen, auch wenn es nicht dort existiert*]. If we succeed in this, the result is the maximum of happiness. The other is now allowed to complement the ego biologically because the partner has been made part of the ego. If projection misfires [*mißlingt die Projektion*], however, there result all the severe disturbances in the emotional equilibrium that manifest themselves as maladjustments in sexual or social spheres of our life.

Notes

Read before the University of Pennsylvania School of Social Work, fall 1927.

1. Rank traced the historical and literary development of *Eros* and *Agape* in "Two Kinds of Love," a chapter in *Beyond Psychology. Eros*, or biological

desire, "was used to make sex acceptable, that is, 'good,' instead of making man good in the meaning of *Agape* [i.e., the theological idea of being loved by God]" (1941, pp. 196–97). But, paradoxically, erotic sex, according to Rank, is also the human symbol of death, dissolution into Nothingness, *Nichts*: "No attempt to overcome neurotic fear of death by sex can ever be successful. . . . *Agape*, on the other hand, can overcome the fear of death, for it is the most positive expression of [death]. In the yielding love-emotion, the individual *voluntarily* accepts the dissolution of the Self by freely submitting to something bigger than the ego and *also* bigger than the other person, the Thou. Thereby the individual conquers death, and with it sex, in a *willing* surrender to the bigness of nature" (ibid.; italics added)—in other words, to the All: *das Ganze*.

In *Will Therapy* Rank analogized the state of "being in love" to religious emotion without disdaining carnal sexuality or accepting the literal reality of "God." The lover attempts to project his or her own will into the beloved in order to unburden—momentarily—from ontological guilt for existing; i.e., so as to transform one's painful *difference*, at least for a brief time, into *likeness*: "'Being in love' is the continuation of the unreal will justification in God, through the earthly deification of a real person whose will must be as like ours as possible and [yet] always remain different" (1929–31, p. 60).

> Thus sexuality is the most universal symbol for *fulfillment* of will as well as for the *submission* of will and accordingly leads to happiness and release. The will expression relates to the powerful *overcoming of difference* and enjoys a brief happiness with a subsequent reaction to the renewed perception of difference, of the strange will, while the subjection of [one's] own will to the other emphasizes the similarity, particularly in the *emotional* sphere which binds and identifies. The first is more physical, the second is more lasting, more psychic, and leads to *release* from difference, to the feeling of *unity* with the self, with the other, with the cosmos (ibid., p. 58; italics added) . . . and finally with the ALL. (ibid., p. 155)

Like Freud, however, Rank recognized the dark underside of romantic love, especially as expressed in the analytic relationship: "That this 'thou' then so easily becomes the 'all' of the patient . . . constitutes the most difficult aspect of the treatment of the neurotic type, which is formed on the all or none [*nichts*] psychology so that either aspect has for him a death meaning, that is, tends to unleash *Angst*" (ibid.).

14

SOCIAL ADAPTATION AND CREATIVITY

(1927)

LADIES AND GENTLEMEN, in my lecture on "Foundations of a Genetic Psychology" [5], I attempted to show how the ego develops genetically from its relation to the object. This has finally led me to a synthesis in the doctrine of character, which I consider the borderline between genetic and constructive psychology. Character as originally formed from identifications is a product, the result, of ego development.

In my lecture on "The Significance of the Love Life" [13], I made a first attempt to show how the finished character of the human being, the fully developed personality, behaves toward an object in the external world, in the love relationship. Therefore I no longer went back, as I did in my genetic lectures, to the mother. I took into consideration only the characterological sediment of the mother in the ego. To justify this, I would like to bring to your notice two factors. First, the fully developed character of the personality includes in it much more than, and something else besides, the sediment of the maternal relationship: above all, the development of one's *own* self from the ideal formation. Second, the sediment of the maternal relationship in the ego is preserved not purely as such but is diluted, displaced, and elaborated.

But in emphasizing the share that our own self has in development, I emphasize at the same time the "constructive" side, if one likes, the creative side in ourselves. For the relation of I to Thou is no longer a mere repetition of the child-mother relationship but is a *new creation* of this relationship.[1] The individual's character itself was formed first of all on the basis of this relationship in childhood but works creatively in the love relationship. One could designate this side of the individual best of all as the *creative* side because it newly molds the Thou according to the I—that is, tries to make it like the I or ego. The love life, in which I tried to show this creative function in its different phases, is not only my best example, but also the only one that relates to reality, whereas otherwise the creative function of the ego is restricted to the phantasy life, to art.

In this sense one could designate the love life as the sphere in which the ego's creative impulse normally attains its end, whereas art is a related but not generally accessible outlet for the creative impetus of the ego. To both expressions is common the creative element, which psychologically I define as the tendency to transform the object, or the world, into an expression of our ego [*das Objekt, die Welt zu einem Ausdruck unseres Ich*]. In artistic creation this impetus can spend itself uninhibitedly, because the object and the material scarcely restrict the personality's artistic endeavor to imprint the complete stamp of its ego on everything. In the love relationship it is more complicated, since the object represents just such a personality as one's own ego and has the same creative endeavors as one's own self. Under favorable conditions, however, there remains enough scope for gratification of the creative needs of the ego. On the other hand, here it is much more difficult to change the love object if it does not subject itself to the creative will [*dem schöpferischen Willen*].[2]

In art and love, the ego creatively imprints the stamp of its own personality in a pronounced way on the object; in one case on the *material* object, in the other the *living* object. In both situations adjustment or the will to adjust is lacking. It is completely lacking in art, where we find the so-called free play of creative phantasy. It is lacking in the love relationship where, similar to the artist, we have the choice of a suitable object and in case this is not sufficient, we have the possibility of another choice, of a change. In both cases, however, it is a matter of changing reality, the external world, in the meaning of our ego and the service of our personality. The underlying tendency is to make the object or the world a part of our ego, similar to and like it.

It is quite otherwise if we go from art, as an exceptional sphere, and love, as an exceptional state, back to the so-called normal relation of the individual to others and the world of reality in general. Here we have before us just the opposite process. In this process our own ego is forced into the role of an "assistant-ego" with regard to reality. In the world of reality there are persons, objects, or situations that we can neither choose nor change as we would like. Indeed, as a rule, they are stronger than our ego, in any case not subjected to or influenced by it. Often enough they even try to influence our ego, to alter and restrict it. I refer to factors such as milieu in general, and strong personalities in particular, who want to imprint on us their stamp, but in any case to compel us to adjustment.

As one can easily see, everything that falls into the category of education in particular, and of the school of life in general, belongs here; everything beginning from the first maternal privations and weaning up to life's mature experiences and destinies; likewise everything that we shall describe later as helpful for adjustment. But in order to understand the psychological and constructive important of this social adjustment, we must first of all study its mechanisms in a situation where it is manifested one-sidedly and is distorted, but on that account quite clearly

visible. This is the love relationship. According to its nature, love as-
pires to a minimum of adjustment, but as I mentioned, is not so successful as in art, because in love it is a matter of a second personality, who
demands a particular kind of adjustment.

The simplest case is the purely biological relation of the sexes. Here
adjustment is nothing other than pursuance of the sex role for the one,
and acceptance of the sex role for the other. But as soon as we leave the
purely biological sphere—and that we have to do in the human being's
love life—this relationship becomes complicated, as I described in my
lecture on the love life. Although in my consideration of the love life I
emphasized the creative side, now I want to stress the other side. This I
designate as "adjustment" and will now follow in its effects on the ego
and from there in its reactions on the object. In this I will show also
how the union of these two elements, the creative and the adjusting,
leads to that which I designate as the *relation* between the ego and the
external world, thus, to the foundation of our social life and our attitude to the world in general.

The establishment of the relationship between ego and object determines success or failure in adjustment, in extreme cases illness or health
and not least of all happiness or unhappiness. What kind of relationship
is this, and how is it established? To answer this question, we must go
back to the two fundamental facts of our emotional life: *projection* and
identification. With reference to the relationship between ego and object, one might say that these two mechanisms are themselves representatives, indeed exact manifestations, of this dualism between ego and
object. Projection is a pronounced ego-mechanism [*Ich-Mechanismus*],
identification a pronounced object-mechanism [*Objekt-Mechanismus*].[3]

Under primitive conditions this state of affairs is simple. With the
development of human individuality and intellect, these processes become more and more complicated. As is well known, primitive man
projects his ego or part of his ego into the world of gods, spirits, and
heroes, as a reality worthy of belief. This does not in the least disturb
his adjustment to reality; on the contrary, it seems to facilitate it. We
have not only the same need for projection, but with the development
of personality has grown the need to imprint things with the stamp of
our ego. On the other hand, our intellectual development blocks the
way to a naive projection onto the heavens. And so nothing else remains for us but art in the form of a fictitious world, in the reality of
which we do not believe. Besides this, there is another less pleasant way
that leads us back to the problem of success or failure in adjustment.

This solution, or rather this detour, is the following. On one side
there is the modern individual's increased need for projection, and on
the other a blocking of the primitive's outlet into a fictitious reality.

This forces us to new ways of expression. With the exception of art, we now project our ego into the *actual* world of reality. But there the conjunction with realities foreign to our ego creates conflicts that demand new solutions. This throws a light, by the way, on the significance of technology as a means of subjugating opposing reality to our will. Here I leave this interesting theme to the side and want only to refer to the fact that man in his technical discoveries and organizations to an incredible degree projects his own ego physically and emotionally.

What I want to follow further is the projection of the ego onto one's fellow being in general and the love object in particular. Apparently this took place in human history when the idealization of the ego in gods and heroes became impossible through intellectual disillusionment. The need, however, still existed and was then projected onto fellow human beings, in whom one wanted to find one's ideal. This led to the love relationship. The Greek humanizing of the god-ideal, as seen in the Homeric description of heroes, was the beginning of the twilight of the gods. This culminated only centuries later in the Christian Man-God. In a similar way the last human projection, namely love, may eventually be unmasked by the new psychology likewise as an illusion.[4]

For the present the love problem itself is in a state of "twilight," that is, we have to deal with all the difficulties and conflicts in adjusting to the love object and hence to reality in general. In order to understand these, we turn back to the fundamental patterns of projection and identification. If we look at the mutual effect of these two mechanisms—the factors representing inner and outer—for the attainment of adjustment, we see two things: the ideal aim of projection is to make the *object* absolutely like the ego and so dispense with superfluous adjustment. The aspiration of identification is to make one's own *ego* like the object and in this way to establish the desired *identity*, which at the same time also requires a minimum of adjustment. But naturally neither of these two ways is ever completely successful. In both tendencies we can again clearly recognize the two types already described; projection corresponds to the active impulsive masculine, sadistic type; identification to the passive inhibited feminine, masochistic type. This differentiation explains at the same time in what cases projection or identification fails and leads to maladjustment.

Both mechanisms have the tendency to smooth down the difference between the two individuals and to establish an identity. But in both cases there is already a certain degree of equality or similarity in the other, the presupposition for projection or identification. This presupposition is clearer in identification which, according to Freud's first definition, rests on something really common existing between the two. But on the "more" or "less" of what is really common to both depends the manner, degree, and success of the identification. The ego may become absorbed in a too complete identification. If too little is in common, then what is missing will be supplemented by projection. But this is an uncertain factor, as the love life clearly shows. For with an alteration or development of the ego, the projection also changes and with it totters identification resting on it. Hence, in the mechanism of projection, a "plus" or "minus" is more dangerous than in identification. In other words, if the relation rests only on identification, the need for projection remains unsatisfied and seeks other, often pathological, outlets. On the other hand, if there is nothing in common and something first has to be created, then this leads to pure illusion and soon to complete disillusion.

If now after this description of the constructive and destructive effects of these mechanisms, we follow their genetic development, we get the following picture. In the child with its weakly developed ego, there is scarcely any projection but very much identification. In other words, the child has potentially every possibility in itself to develop the powers and capabilities it sees in the adult. And it accomplishes this by means of imitation or identification. The child's adjustment is thus, in my meaning, a passive receptive one, resting on identification. It is the weaker one's way of adjustment and might be called masochistic because it does not strive for mastery of the object but for subjection to the object. In other words, the *ego* is made similar to or like the object.

Adolescence, with its symptoms of storm and stress, is the individual's first attempt to free himself from the yoke of the identification mechanism, the symbol of which is the parental *Imago*. Hence the revolt accompanying adolescence in the social and sexual spheres. Hence also the first infatuation or falling in love, which is by no means a seeking and finding of the parental *Imago*, but a seeking and finding of one's own rebellious self in another ego of the same age or, better, of the same youthfulness, frequently enough even of the same sex. In the adult, finally, with complete development of the personality and its striving for expression, we find a compromise in the love relationship that unites the *old* parental patterns of identification with the *new* creative individualistic urge toward expression, chiefly in projection.

At this stage of the mature, fully developed love life, we find, however, the projection and identification mechanisms operating in a new constructive way. Identification is no longer—or at least should no longer be—a copy of the infantile submissiveness to the object. In other words, it should no longer be a dependent or forced identification sanctioned by the ego through projection. Projection is also different from that occurring at puberty. Whereas at that time there was *too much* projection—as in childhood *too much* identification—now, at the mature level, projection is based on a real identification just as identification is sanctioned by projection.

The *constructive* development of projection and identification, as representatives of ego and object, toward a mutual love relationship manifests itself also at different stages of the emotional life, as well as in other human relationships. In a word, we can describe this process of development as progress from the "identification character" to the formation of personality, or from *adjustment* to *creation*. If earlier the unconscious aim of pure projection was the establishment of an identity, now in its relation to others the result is adjustment. Instead of wanting to transform the other—in our meaning, to make the other like us—we are now able to *accept the other as he is*, that is, to adjust ourselves by means of identification. The result of this endeavor is the establishment of the "relationship." The means to it at this conscious level is understanding that rests on *empathy* [*Einfühlung*] and corresponds to unconscious identification. This acceptance of the other is only possible when we first of all are able to accept ourselves—that is, our true self [*wahres Selbst*]—rather than throwing it out of ourselves, projecting it onto the other.

Instead, we can choose at this stage the real object so that it corresponds to our inner need without demanding too much expenditure of projection or identification. Then there result three possibilities. Either the object complements our ego in the sense of *impulse* or *inhibition*, or it is a copy of our *whole* personality, impulse as well as inhibition. It seems that the relationship to the complementary ego yields more possibilities of friction and conflict and hence, on the whole, operates constructively and leads to a permanent adjustment. This may also be the case because adjustment to the complementary ego fits into adjustment to the complementary *biological* self. Relation to an identical ego is more primitive, perhaps more pleasurable, and demands less adjustment but may easily operate destructively. In particular cases, however, where there is a lack of external inhibition but instead—through development of one's own personality—an adjustment by inner self-criticism, such a relationship can also work out creatively.

Here we touch the problem of the relation of character-type and love-choice to work, in other words not only to adjustment but to social accomplishment, which under certain conditions can become creative. If we start with creative work, which is more easily accessible to our investigation, we find that this relationship is not so constant as one would expect. Perhaps this comes from the fact that the creative type in general is much more dynamic and hence in its relations, whether to man or work, is less constant. In creative work, as in the love relationship, it is a matter either of a compensatory projection of a *part* of the ego or of projection of the *whole* personality. Presumably this differentiates the two creative types that I have distinguished as the artist who creates from inner need and the artist who creates from a superabundance. The first is a "romantic" type who must *complete* himself in work; the other, a "classical" type who *expresses* himself in work. These types correspond, of course, to the projection type and identification type.

In reality, however, these types are not sharply defined. As in every type, it is a question of the "more" or "less." In any case there is a clear correlation between life and work. So, for example, a creative type with a love object not merely complementary but contrary can be "classical" in form with "romantic" content. In other words, his work betrays the disunion hidden in his personality, because the love object is neither identical nor complementary and so he projects his whole personality into work. The other type would be disunited in personality, strongly projective in his love life, who finds his complement in work and expresses it in "classical" form. In other words, he finds in work the union that is lacking in his personality, whereas in his love life he seeks not the complement but the identity that he does not find in work.

One might describe the state of affairs thus: the romantic type *seeks* his ego ideal in work and his ego in love life: the classical type *gives* his ego ideal to work and his ego to love life. Hence the love life of the classical type is more banal and bourgeois, his work on the other hand is romantically glorified. The romantic appreciates his work as little as his ego but on that account glorifies the love object.

If we pass from this consideration of the extreme creative types to the *average* social accomplishment, then all the characteristics just mentioned disappear or became indistinct. We should not know how the so-called social adjustment of the average human being occurs if we could not study his disturbances in cases of maladjustment. Such study shows that the fundamental mechanisms are the same in all cases. In the simple merchant as in the intellectual worker, the occupation is as much an expression of the striving of personality as it is in the creative artist. Also the relation between love life and occupation is dynamically determined in the same way. The creative type, however, generally inclines more to *contrasts* or compensations between his social and love lives; whereas the average person inclines to *parallels*. This difference corresponds to a predominance of *projection* in the *artist* and *identification* in the *average person*.

In other words, the occupation and love life of the average human being is on the whole formed on *identification*. The son often enough actually carries on his father's occupation, continues as it were his work and family life. Still more clearly does the daughter carry on her mother's life. Such persons never get *beyond* identification but as a consequence are better adjusted to reality. If their adjustment becomes unbalanced, however, it is almost impossible to help them, because they have not the possibilities of a personality within themselves and they can hardly develop one. In most favorable cases, one can give them a *new* identification—which, however, even if it works at all is not very productive. Many so-called "nervous breakdowns" are actually break-downs of *old* identifications that could not be replaced by formation of a personality of one's own.

But just as many of the so-called neurotics belong to the other, cre-ative, type—no matter what occupation they may practice. They have failed in the formation and development of their own personality.[5] However, one cannot help them by driving them back to old identifica-tions or by offering them new possibilities of identification. One has to help them to get *beyond* the deadlock in their personality and in the process find their *own* self. I think that the so-called inner crises in the human being's life correspond to the stage of his development in which old identifications break down under the burden of his own strength-ened ego *before this ego is strong enough to bear the whole burden of the new personality.* Hence these crises occur so frequently when the individual has attained in life a certain success that he justly ascribes to himself, to his own personality, as it is *not* due to identification alone.

However this may be, in these common emotional crises we see also the relationship to the love object weaken, and the individual looking for new solutions. Here it is sufficient for my purpose if I again only single out typical situations and estimate them in their relation to my theme. A human being's choice of object can occur in three ways: the love object is either a mother substitute [*Mutter-Ersatz*] or an ego sub-stitute [*Ich-Ersatz*], or finally an ego complement [*Ich-Ergänzung*].

The mother substitute and the ego complement are related insofar as they represent two opposite types that stand at the beginning and end of an individual's development. In the middle is the ego substitute, charac-terologically a negative ego complement. The mother substitute, a posi-tive ego complement, corresponds to an adjustment in the primitive in-fantile sense of subordination to the object, of identification with the object. The ego complement corresponds to an adjustment in the con-structive sense, in that by means of mutual projection and identification a real wholeness is attained. Between these two possibilities of adjust-ment lies the object-choice in the sense of a complete ego substitute [*kompletten Ich-Ersatzes*] that requires no kind of adjustment at all.

Normally the ego develops historically from the need of a mother substitute conforming to childhood, by way of the ego substitute con-forming to puberty, to the ego complement conforming to the mature personality. Naturally, in reality, it is a matter of transition and mixed forms, and the crises in the development from ego to personality are characterized just through the fact that either one cannot become free in one's own inner being from the earlier type, or difficulties of new adjustment lie in the object.

To this threefold possibility in the emotional relation to the love object corresponds a threefold possibility in man's general social relationship. The mutual relationship between these two, namely the social and love life, can be either parallel or contrary. Here we want to consider the social side alone. We then see, as already mentioned, that the average type rests more on identification, the creative type more on development and objectifying of one's own self or ego-ideal. In the purely social sphere, we find the creative type as *leader*. This type is represented in mythology in idealized form as hero. Here we will consider the leader only as a psychological type apart from whether he exhibits himself in the political sphere or in any other kind of sphere.

The leader is a creative projecting type, what I would call a man of will or man of action, one who wants not only to preserve his ego and his personality but also wants to impose it on others. For the average human being, the significance of the leader in this sense is, so to say, a compromise in that the leader *spares* the average person the formation of personality, that is, makes it possible through identification. If the leader were not driven by his inner need toward development and expression of his personality, I could almost say that the average person orders the leader to accomplish this difficult and painful task, for example, as expressed in Christ suffering for all mankind. But the genuine social leader, whether politician or general or employer, or any kind of "master," as a rule is well paid for this position through which the others profit by means of identification. In other words, he uses the others and their labor to strengthen and further his *own* ego. In the social sphere it is obviously those who work for the leader who play the part of "assistant-ego" [*Hilfs-Iche*]. The whole class war bears witness to this fact. But the whole class war is as hopeless as vain, because it takes into consideration only the physical and mechanical labor on the one hand and the leader's material profit on the other hand.

Our study of other human relations—for example, the love relationship—teaches us to recognize the emotional side also in the leader problem. In love or friendship, we let the other work for us emotionally and our development benefits from it. When we can supply a similar service for the other, then this relationship is ideal. But often enough it is as one-sided as that of leader and led, or master and slave. However, even in the relationship to the leader it is not so much one-sided as it seems to us. The leader himself needs adherents or supporters not only for physical or emotional work, but first of all for justification of his creative need on the one hand, and as material for his creative need, on the other hand. *Just as the sculptor needs clay or the painter canvas and color, so the leader needs living material.* For the average person who subordinates himself to a leader, the physical or emotional effort represents the price he pays in order to buy identification with the leader's personality and so save himself the painful effort toward development and creation.

My discussion of the leader problem in its social and emotional relation leads me back to the psychoanalytic situation and from there to the problem of education. If formerly the analyst was compared on the one hand with the partner in the love relationship, on the other with the parental educator, recently he has been compared with the leader. I think this comparison is as one-sided as were the previous ones. The analyst does or at least should represent a union of all this, and at the same time something else *beyond*, which does not correspond to a combination alone of these different roles. In the analytic situation, we can study the psychology of the love relationship and the leader relationship as well as the relationship to the educator. From this we can deduce new constructive viewpoints for the emotional side of the educational relationship.

Notes

Read before the University of Pennsylvania School of Social Work, fall 1927.

1. Esther Menaker observes that "when the wish to return to the mother as a way of mastering anxiety is expressed creatively, either as a merging of oneself with some higher ideal or in the projection of a part of the self into a product that will outlive the self—a point at which the wish for oneness with the mother and the wish for immortality meet—we are confronted with a new theory of creativity" (Menaker 1982, p. 75).

2. This is probably the first time Rank used the term *creative will* in his American lectures. In his later writings, he often dropped the adjective *creative*, perhaps because it was redundant, and referred simply to *will*. In *Truth and Reality* Rank recognized that this will—a matter of "the first rank"—would be resisted by analysts who reduced all creativity to a derivative, however disguised, of the sex drive: "My reintroduction of the will concept into psychology solves a succession of problems in such a simple and satisfying way that it may seem to some a *deus ex machina*. . . . Only after a struggle against prejudices of every kind did the acceptance of will as a psychological factor of the first rank seem unavoidable but soon also became a matter of course, so much a matter of course that I had to say to myself that only a tremendous resistance could have hindered the complete recognition and evaluation of will as a great psychic power" (1929, p. 13).

Jessie Taft, who attended many of Rank's lectures, writes that it was not until 1930 that "*will* as the central force in the therapeutic relationship [was] made the focus of [Rank's] teaching . . . [although] the implications of a new recognition of the critical value of the will psychology for therapy had already been thought through by him both technically and philosophically" (Taft 1958, p. 144).

Rank saw no need to define will for the patient in the analytic situation. "Most patients," he told a seminar of clinicians in 1930, "don't ask for a definition [of 'will'] because each has his own and therefore does not feel it necessary to ask. It is well to let the patient use his own terms for 'will' provided the analyst understands what he means. There is no need to force terminology on a patient, because when the dynamic aspect of any situation is considered, the content does not matter" (Rank 1930c, p. 18).

3. In a 1926 New York lecture on "Identification and Ego Construction," not included in this book but published as "*Identifizierung und Ichaufbau*," a chapter in Volume 1 of *Genetische Psychologie*, Rank gave a dense, highly technical definition of these two mechanisms:

> Projection is the mechanism by means of which the ego unburdens itself of the narcissistic mother-child relation, it determines later object-relations, their various forms and deviations depending on what elements in the mother-child relation are projected and to what degree they are projected. Identification, on the other hand, is the underlying mechanism not, like projection, of object choice, but of the construction of the ego [*Ichaufbau*]. It leads ... to a further development of the strict mother within oneself, the discovery of the father as an object and finally to establishment of the paternal super-ego ("father-identification"). This super-ego is based upon the original maternal inhibition in one's own ego. So identification must be understood genetically as a biologically founded mechanism for re-establishment of the prenatal mother-child relation. ...
>
> Identification is really always a secondary process; it is, so to speak, a re-identification with a part of one's ego that was originally or has become a part of the mother.... Every object relation is ultimately narcissistic and maternal; and the various combinations of these two elements, the relative degrees of intensity of the one or the other, determine the various forms and deviations of the human love life (Rank 1927, pp. 134–35).

4. In *Truth and Reality*, Rank said that he saw "the first intimation" of the love problem in the biblical story of Adam and the creation of Eve from man:

> Here the woman is a product of the creative man, who ascribes to himself this divine creative power and divine knowledge—like the Greek Prometheus. We recognize therein the first faint beginnings of that magnificent process of rivaling the Gods which we have understood psychologically as the gradual acknowledgement of the conscious individual will in the human being. It appears in a glorious fashion in Greek culture with the heroes rebelling against the Gods, and reaches the peak of development in Christianity with the humanizing of God and the deifying of man. If man had first to manifest his own creative will in the formation of God, but at the same time had to justify it, so in the heroic period, at the other extreme, he fell into the deification of himself, of his own individual will in order finally to deify and worship in the individual love experience the other individual who represents the creation and redemption of his own individual will. (1929, pp. 70–71)

5. This became one of the central themes in Rank's therapy: the neurotic as *artiste manqué*, a person who has failed to accept the burden of his or her difference. (See "Neurosis as a Failure in Creativity" [20]) The burden of self-responsibility, however, is always *thrown back* on the individual in the feeling of guilt for "*unused* life, the unlived in us" (Rank 1929–31, p. 149; italics added).

15

THE PROMETHEUS COMPLEX

(1927)

LADIES AND GENTLEMEN, if we approach the problem of education in light of the analytic situation, we see in it first of all an emotional relation of educator to *child*. The analytic situation represents chiefly an educational problem, with the only difference that it is an adult who needs reeducation and guidance. The role of the analyst has been designated as that of a *leader* in an emotional sense, in other words as a *parent*.

In the pedagogic situation, we see the problem of the leader in its purest form, and its prototype is also the parental relationship. In it, the leader from the very beginning is the natural lord and master of the situation. Those led are, from the beginning, in the natural role of the weak in need of help and learning. This is the state of affairs in the psychological relation of parent and child, before the child in the Oedipus situation attempts the first revolt against the lasting establishment of this primal state decreed from the beginning. Even in situations where it is not a matter of premature physical labor, or direct cruel actions on the part of parents, the child is in every case an emotionally exploited object [*ein seelisch ausgebeutetes Objekt*].[1] Yet education itself, in the narrow as well as broader meaning, is nothing else than an attempt of the educator to enforce his personality and his views on the child's ego. Parents want to extend the biological *procreation* of the child in the creation and development of its character.

Hence if we want to understand the pedagogic situation fully, we must introduce a new concept—referring to parents—in order to complete the picture. To the Oedipus complex—which, as I said, represents the first revolt by the child against subjection of his ego by parents—we must contrast the *parental complex*, which we could designate, best of all, as the *Prometheus complex*.[2] In our own emotional life, this Prometheus complex is as important as the Oedipus complex, if not more important.

Whereas the Oedipus complex is founded on identification, indeed— at least in the meaning of psychoanalysis—symbolizes identification, the Prometheus complex is not only the symbol of the need or desire to create but also arises in the individual creatively, that is, spontaneously, at a crucial point, and *not* in identification with parents. Its first appearance is indeed just as crucial as the Oedipus complex, but unlike this complex is not condemned to failure and disappointment. Emerging in puberty, it is the expression of the first period of storm and stress and—just like the Oedipus complex—is overcome by only few human beings. The *overcoming* of it occurs in the creative man, who, under Promethian pressure, wants to form men in his own image. He attains this in (and for) himself by *developing and unfolding his own personality*.

In introducing the concept of the Prometheus complex, let me elaborate on its different meanings. In Greek mythology Prometheus symbolizes a threefold role. Firstly, he assumes that he can create men just as well as the gods; thus he himself is a god—or better, a Man-God, a hero. But his identification with the creating god is nothing else than the canceling of the earlier projection by means of which the gods themselves had been created. Thus Prometheus symbolizes the *dethroning of the gods created by men*, and in place of the gods, man now installs himself with his fully developed personality and his need to create.

Secondly, Prometheus creates men after his *own* image—just as earlier, men had created the gods. In relation to the creation of men, this again is a mechanism of projection but is different from the early creation of gods. It is a matter of creating *real* men, who after their creation by Prometheus, live their own lives—to which he himself has to adjust by means of identification.

Thirdly, Prometheus creates not only men after his own image, but also the *love object*; in the Prometheus saga, Pandora is created as a wish fulfillment. This stage corresponds to the creative tendency of the personality in love life: namely, the creation of the love object by projection, in the sense of the wishes of our self. But, at the same time, Pandora (as also the other creatures) is a *child* on whom the creator wants to imprint his own characteristics, and we understand this also to be the case for the pedagogic situation, in which the same imprinting occurs.

Here lies the justification for the *punishment* of Prometheus, whose chaining represents an inhibiting of these presumptuous tendencies in his personality. He is punished not because he steals fire from the gods, fire being after all human property. He is punished because he wants to practice with it the same misuse that apparently was allowed the gods and into which *creators of men*—parents, educators, or therapists—can so easily fall. *This misuse is to impose one's own personality on the creature* and so to make it first of all a willing object [*einem willigen Objekt*] and, in the future, the successor of one's own ego.

We find, therefore, that the Oedipus complex represents the more passive, submissive adjustment by means of *identification* and the Prometheus complex the more active, dominating creation by means of *projection*. We then see immediately the fundamental difference between the infantile situation (the symbol of which is the Oedipus complex), the pedagogic situation (the symbol of which I have introduced as the Prometheus complex), and the analytical situation—which should be a union of both and, at the same time, something *"beyond."*

Simplified, the difference is as follows. In the infantile situation, the child identifies with parents, and parents chiefly project onto the child. In the analytic situation, we allow the patient to project in order to let him recognize and find his true self, whereas the analyst restricts himself to the identification necessary to understand the patient.[3] As a rule, the pedagogic situation is, as I said earlier, a continuance of the infantile situation. However, in place of parents, the educator is installed to play more the role of a leader.

The analytic situation, as one can easily see, should be a correction and not a repetition of the infantile situation. To improve the pedagogic situation, what we can learn from analysis is the following: in the pedagogic situation, the pupil should be brought *from* the Oedipus complex, *through* the Prometheus complex, *to the creation of his own personality.*[4]

Let me elaborate on this formula in more detail. The Prometheus complex is an *emotional reaction* to the Oedipus situation. By means of the Prometheus complex, the individual wants to transfer [*übertragen will*] the same oppression that he suffered from his parents onto his children, his *creations*, his subordinates. Perhaps it is necessary for the individual to pass through this phase at which most human beings remain—if they have come out at all beyond the Oedipus complex.

From the analytic situation, however, we can deduce that the ideal aim of education includes not only overcoming the Oedipus complex (through the Prometheus complex) but also *overcoming the Prometheus complex*, in the formation of one's own personality—which I would like to designate, in a more constructive way, as "self-guidance."

The Prometheus complex has constructive but also destructive possibilities within it. The projection of one's own personality on the child, especially by parents, might almost be called natural, but as can be easily seen, is a very primitive form of education that can succeed only in simple relations. It is quite different when the parent (or educator) himself is a disjointed and split [*gespaltene*] personality, which is then projected either as a whole or in part onto the child (or pupil). In addition, there is a danger that such a "neurotic" personality will incline much more to projection and, in particular, to projection of the parts of his personality that are split off or despised.

Furthermore, there result possibilities of failure even when we consider the constructive elements that, doubtless, lie in the nature of the pedagogic situation. Let us take the simple and well-known case in which the educator does not impose his own self on the pupil, nor projects his split-off or repressed self on him, but wants him to become a representative of his better, higher self—in a word, wants to make him his ego-ideal [*Ich-Ideal*]. This is doubtless a constructive element of the pedagogic situation, but one that in reality also does not always lead to success. The difficulties can come from both sides, from the educator or from the pupil; as a rule, it is a mutual conflict in which the one reacts on the other.

Let us first consider the difficulties on the side of the educator, or here we might more correctly say, the leader—since these conflicts mostly extend beyond the pedagogic situation into social spheres. The educator or leader who wants to objectify and attain his ego-ideal in the pupil mostly fails at the point where his endeavor seems to be crowned by success. This failure does not only depend on his own ambition, envy, and jealousy of the younger one but has a deeper cause. The attainment or realization of one's own ego-ideal is *always* bound up with disappointment, no matter whether we see this ideal realized in ourselves or in another; indeed, disappointment is perhaps stronger in the latter case. The reason for this disappointment in the ego-ideal is that, psychologically, only striving for it is pleasurable insofar as it unburdens the ego projectively. The attainment of one's ego-ideal disappoints because it *inhibits* the projection, that is, inhibits a form of self-expression.

Let us now consider the effect that projection of the ego-ideal has on the pupil. In essence it seems to depend on three factors: on the strength of the leader's personality, on the capability of the pupil to form his own personality, and on the relation of both personalities to one another. In other words, if both are strong, then the educator's influence will succeed only against resistance. However, even where it is successful, the educator's projection will only operate constructively when it can be accepted through identification by the similarly adjusted personality of the pupil. If the personality of the pupil, in comparison to that of the leader, is not strong enough, then this identification can become permanent. However, it does not then correspond to a self-development of the leader-personality *within* the pupil in the meaning of ideal formation, but more to the *biological* prototype of a parental ego-extension in the child.

Where the relationship between master and pupil passes into a real self-development on the pupil's part, two outlets are possible. I have already mentioned one: disappointment of the leader in the attainment or realization of his own ego-ideal. The second possibility is that the pupil develops himself *beyond* the master—which can result either in a direct, continued development or in complementary or contrary ways.[5]

After having briefly described the dynamic elements of the pedagogic situation, and having emphasized the constructive sides of education's task, I want again to consider the genetic viewpoint of personality development. The original kernel of one's own self [*Kern des eigenen Selbst*] is certainly the biological ego [*biologische Ich*], with its given disposition and impulses [*Triebanlagen*]. Here is the place for what psychoanalysis has described, in a rather fragmentary way, as oral, anal, urethral, and genital character. Yet one might add that these character traits do not develop purely from impulse disposition but are formed under the strict educational influence of parents, essentially and fundamentally the *mother*. In the earliest phase of cleanliness training, we can see the first powerful projection from the side of the mother, and—in the child's submission—the first effort toward, and accomplishment of, identification. The same holds true, although perhaps to a lesser degree, for the oral zone and to a still less degree for the genital zone. In other words, a certain order of graduation of the erogenous zones and their functions seems to exist in reference to character formation and development of personality, respectively.

The more the educator's conscious aim and endeavor is applied to the control of a specific erogenous zone or its function, the sooner will develop a character trait or inhibition as a direct sequel to the impulse. This is obviously the case most of all with the anal zone, hence all the so-called anal characteristics, chiefly negative reactions (such as stubbornness) that we get in the analytic situation. But with the urethral function, the fuss in training is less, and this is of importance later for the genital function, which makes use of the same organ. Hardly any conscious educational endeavor is made to restrict normal function of the oral zone; it occurs automatically and gradually through the weaning process. Only the purely pleasurable and playful function in finger sucking is directly prohibited. At the genital stage, this prohibition is not so frequent as one might be inclined to assume by reason of the "castration theory."

Most parents overlook all manifestations of the sexual impulse in their children, and yet if they cannot deny it, then they do not speak about it, not even in the form of a prohibition or threat. I think this is good insofar as it prevents a premature inhibition of the sexual impulse. If psychoanalysis gives the impression that sexual prohibition, or, as the term is, the "castration trauma," is universal, this arises because in analysis we see just those types of human beings who have experienced [*erfahren*] in some form, a premature inhibition of the sexual impulse. As I have already stated, this need not necessarily be a direct prohibition from without. It can just as well be a transferring to the genital zone of the prohibition concerning the anal and urethral zones, a transferring that the individual himself accomplishes by means of guilt-feeling.

But in every case we see, on the one hand, a quite direct relation between the anal zone and the character development based on identification or reaction formation, and, on the other hand, between the genital zone and the development of one's own personality. The sexual organ, especially the male, and the sexual function in general are much more closely bound up with one's own self and the development and expression of one's own personality than any other organ. The mouth alone has a similar and important role; less in the meaning of development of personality than as a means to express one's personality—namely, in *speaking*.

This relation of the sexual organ and sexual impulse to the ability to develop and express one's own self—one's own personality—in contrast to acquired character, we see in the most varied forms. Its best-known and emotionally most important manifestation is masturbation. The constructive importance of masturbation for development of one's own self has not been sufficiently estimated. In this sense masturbation is not only a revolt of the self [*Revolte des Selbst*] against a command imposed from without or from within, but it is also an act of one's own self [*des eigenen Selbst*], performed on one's own initiative and responsibility. In other words it is the genital function that is influenced least of all by education and least of all is "learned."

Experience [*Die Erfahrung*] shows—and it may be on account of this—that genitality is the function that plays the greatest part in development of personality. We see this connection positively in great personalities, men of action or artists, whose sexual life as a rule is richer and freer than that of the average man. We see it *negatively* in the so-called neurotic, in whom failure to develop personality and failure in sexual life represent the two most conspicuous characteristics. The way to help neurotics in both respects seems to me, however, not to be that which analytic therapy has hiterto attempted, but the reverse. That is, it seems to me more difficult—and is certainly less successful—to attempt the therapeutic work of adjustment in the sexual sphere. According to my experiences [*meinen Erfahrungen*], one gets much better, more lasting, and more useful results when one strives for the freeing of the self [*Befreiung des Selbst*], the development of personality. As a rule this automatically brings with it sexual adjustment.

As far as development of personality is concerned, it seems to be an advantage that the sexual impulse was, so to say, excluded from education, and, as it were, consigned to the ego for education and development. It was almost the only sphere over which the individual was left in control and it seems that modern education wants to deprive the individual himself of this only and last domain of free self-development and self-decision [*freien Selbstentwicklung und Selbstbestimmung*].

One ought not to refer in argument to the numerous and sometimes severe conflicts that develop in the individual in this sphere of self-direction, as, for example, the typical masturbation conflict. These difficulties and sufferings are not spared the individual in other spheres—where parents and educators take initiative and bear responsibility. On the other hand, in self-decision and self-direction, as characterized in expression of the sexual impulse in childhood and puberty, there are so many constructive elements that one should well reflect before seeing in "sexual enlightenment" the only salvation of the future generation. This attitude again comes from study of neurotics, who apparently have suffered from *lack* of sexual enlightenment. But that means only that their individuality was not strong enough to balance this lack—through self-accomplishment. It does not mean that sexual enlightenment in childhood would have made them healthier, stronger, and more successful.

Sexuality thus seems to be the only ground on which education has not yet set its foot and, in consequence of this, a kind of natural park is left in human emotional life. Hence we also see men—in situations where the external pressure is too great or the corresponding inner inhibition too intensive—seeking and finding in sexuality their self-expression, which they could not find in other spheres. The most extreme and concrete expression of this endeavor is the biological and educational creation of one's own child. The child thus, before it is born, is an expression of the urge for personality, insofar as the sexual impulse and sexual act themselves are already expressions of the striving of personality.

However, not only biologically but also psychologically and characterologically, it is inevitable that we continue our personality in the child, since the child *needs* us for identification and for development of its own personality. The best that we can do for the child, besides providing the necessary identification in order to enable it to develop its own personality, seems to me to be emancipation of the sexual impulse. Under emancipation of the child's sexual impulse, I would understand, first of all, the lack of a sexual education or sexual enlightenment in a systematic way.

It should remain the sphere in which the child can investigate, speculate, experiment, and discover—without being controlled or examined by parents and educators. Naturally, I do not mean that one should be mysterious and hypocritical in sexual things. But I also do not think that one ought to go too far in sexual education and enlightenment if one does not want to barricade the individual from this sphere of personal self-unfolding. In this connection perhaps it is worthy of note that most children react negatively to sexual enlightenment.[6] That is, they do not accept the explanation, they do not want to learn from adults in this sphere, however eager to learn they otherwise might be. They prefer in this sphere the difficult, but apparently more pleasurable, way of self-investigation—or they prefer to get their knowledge from more natural sources than that of a systematic sex education.

Finally, I would like to emphasize yet one more constructive element of the pedagogic situation. This element seems to me of great importance because it is as valuable for development of the child as of parents. My point is this. The child certainly has to learn much from adults—whether it is by means of identification or by means of a more conscious systematic assimilation. But it is just as certain that *parents and educators can learn from the child*, indeed, must learn if the child is to be a living valuable factor in their lives, and not merely an object for gratification of egoistic impulses. There is no doubt that the child essentially influences our personality and its relationship to others, especially to the love object. It is for parents to make the child's influence favorable and constructive on their personality and their relation to one another.

Before mentioning *what* we can learn from the child, I would like to say how we can learn from the child. By this I mean the only and best way for both sides: namely, *identification*. From understanding the analytic situation, we can also learn something for improvement of the pedagogic situation. When, and insofar as, we are able to identify with the child, we shall not only be able to understand the child, but at the same time also avoid a too far-reaching *projection* of our personality onto the child. This identification with the child concerns—again, as in the analytic situation—*the emotional life*. We badly misunderstand the child whenever we want only to interpret its purely impulsive and emotional manifestations intellectually. This is impossible—and leads not just to *misunderstanding* the child, but worse, to a complete misunderstanding of his expressions. The difference lies not so much in the emotional life itself, but in the fact that in the child this is expressed *spontaneously*, whereas we have to motivate, justify, and interpret intellectually our own emotional life as well as the child's.

In contrast to the adult's *misunderstanding* of the child's emotional life is the child's incredibly subtle and psychologically *correct* reaction to all emotional manifestations of the adult—however much adults may try to hide or intellectualize their true feelings. *The child in its young emotional life has an unerring instrument for real understanding of the adult's emotional life.* Hence in every pedagogic or educational situation one should know that it is impossible to deceive a child concerning the true feelings one cherishes toward the child or other persons. With this presupposition, which seems to me valid beyond all doubt, one should always behave as if the child knew everything that we ourselves know at a given moment and in a given situation. Naturally, this is not to be taken too literally, but one cannot otherwise or better describe the child's emotional, intuitive ability and his reactions following from this.

What prevents us from a correct educational and therapeutic understanding is the desire to understand intellectually. Correct understanding is one of empathy based on identification, whereas intellectual understanding is again projection to a certain degree, a *compelling of the other* to our own thought, our own interpretation. In the pedagogic situation, this leads just as much to misunderstanding and resistance as in the analytic situation.

We can now draw the following conclusions: The creative type—the strong personality—that projects is not fitted to be an educator, at least is not fitted for the education of the child. The type that identifies—and the emotional life of which is influenced more from without than within—corresponds far more to the ideal educator. He will better be able to sense the childish emotional life and at the same time give the child more opportunity and better material for identification. On the other hand, this type is less inclined to projection, that is, less inclined to *enforce* its own personality on another. In other words, it follows that in general woman is a better educator than man for the child. She has the ability to identify, especially in relation to the child with whom she is and was identical [*mit dem sie ja identisch ist, identisch war*], and she has at the same time a childlike [*kindlichen*] and more natural emotional life that enables her to identify empathically.

When I said the strong creative personality is not suitable to be an educator, I meant two things. First, creative ability, the creative element, easily fails with regard to living material, as the emotional loneliness of nearly all creative men shows. The Greek artist could indeed create men in marble after his own image, or according to his ideal, but he failed, as the heroic symbol Prometheus shows, in the creation of living men—*who should be created in no one else's image but their own.*

The second point is this. Not only does the creative man fail in the creation of real men, but also the ordinary man may have the same bad result or easily lead to it. I mean the parental situation, and in it, particularly, the *father's* place. His biological and social position gives him the external characteristics of a creative type without its inner strength and greatness. As one may notice, I here refer to the usual pedagogic situation, in which parents represent the strong and powerful and children the weak and helpless. This situation easily leads parents to a kind of creative-mania that, under certain conditions, can be even more dangerous than the real creative urge to impress one's own personality onto the child.

What parents have to learn—in their own interest and that of their children—is to resist the temptation to exploit this natural position of power in an emotional sense. Practically, it may not always be possible, as the child's ego becomes stronger and tries to enforce itself on parents. But, as a rule, this form of misbehavior in the child is already a reaction to parental tyranny. *When the child feels itself understood and loved, it will have no need of enforcing itself as a powerful factor against parents or brothers and sisters.* In a word, the pedagogic situation must be transformed and developed into a mutual emotional relationship [*gegenseitigen Gefühlsbeziehung*] in which parents and children grow up with—and develop—one another.

Notes

Read before the University of Pennsylvania School of Social Work, fall 1927.

1. Rank implies that patients may also be "emotionally exploited" by analysts who see psychoanalysis only as a form of reparenting or reeducation—what Freud called *Nacherziehung*. Later in the lecture, Rank says that analysis "should be a union of both and, at the same time, something '*beyond*'" [8-203].

2. If parents are procreators of human beings, then analysts, Rank suggests, are *creators* of human beings. Patients come to analysis because they cannot create themselves and are guilt-bound, unconsciously, to their procreators. Rank saw analysts as artists, who *use* the patient—an *artiste manqué*—as a living object onto whom they project their own creative urge. But this living object has the same creative urge—the same "Prometheus complex"—as the analyst. However, it is expressed destructively, negatively, in the form of neurosis, a creative achievement like any other. The analyst's "Prometheus complex"—a need, often unconscious, to recreate the patient in one's own image (or one's training analyst's image)—may lead to pathogenic misuse of the analyst's creative will: "This misuse is to impose one's own personality on the creature."

3. If the analyst goes "*beyond* the identification necessary for understanding the patient . . . [and] now projects onto the patient, who identifies with this projected part of the analyst's ego," a transference occurs that Rank calls infatuation. The infatuated patient is now identifying with the *analyst's* creative urge, projected onto the patient. See "The Significance of the Love Life" [13-178].

4. That is, from identification and projection to self-determination.

5. There can be little doubt that the last five paragraphs reflect Rank's view of his own failed pupil-master relationship with Freud.

6. See "Modern Psychology and Social Change" [22] for Rank's deeper explanation of the child's negative reaction to sexual enlightenment.

16

PARENTAL ATTITUDES AND THE

CHILD'S REACTIONS (1927)

LADIES AND GENTLEMEN, when I received the invitation to take part in this Conference on Parental Education, my first thought was that I could not accept it as I have never done any practical work with children. Of course, for many years, I have been doing analyses of adults and have studied the sources of their failure in their own childhood and learned to understand the causes of them. But even so, I would not attempt to lecture with that alone as foundation, and to repeat once more what has been taught for so many years: what I would call the psychoanalytic *reconstruction* of childhood.

My reasons are chiefly these. It is true I have studied adults and among them many parents. But the people who came to me for help have never actually grown up to be parents *in spite of* their having established families and having children of their own. Their own childhood as revealed in the process of analysis, in my opinion, would not be a proper source from which to draw general conclusions to be applied to actual problems of the child, because in the analytic material the infantile and adult features are so mixed up that it seems to me almost impossible to build up some constructive idea on the analytically inferred material of childhood.

Another source of material proved to be equally unsatisfactory. One might expect that the problems brought up by parents in their own analysis concerning their own children would enable us to better understand the child's emotional problems. But this is not the case: these parents are primarily concerned with their own problems and the child appears only in relation to themselves. Hence their children's problems are colored by their own emotions and, therefore, are not presented objectively.

And now after having pointed out these difficulties, I should like to say what enabled me to accept the invitation to lecture on the subject of the relation of parental attitudes to success and failure in the child. It is the particular viewpoint that I take toward this problem as well as the chance afforded me during this last summer of seeing actual cases of children. My observations of their problems led beyond mere case interest to a viewpoint of general significance.

These observations concern the child's *reaction* to the parents' problems and the *misunderstanding* these reactions met with from parents, educators, psychiatrists, and psychoanalysts. By this I mean that with all the efforts made toward enlightenment in parental education, a stereotyped attitude has resulted on the part of parents and their reformers, respectively. Parents are naturally inclined to blame the *child* for its difficulties. To analyze the child on account of its difficulties seems logically to support this parental attitude. On the other hand, the pet idea of psychiatrists and social workers today is to put all blame on *parents* and, as a remedy, they suggest that parents should be analyzed.

The cases I saw helped me avoid either of these extreme viewpoints and enabled me to conform exactly to the title given me for this lecture. It is the *relation* between parental attitudes, caused by parents' own problems, and the child's reactions to them that I emphasize without laying any blame on *either* child or parent.

The first observation I made this summer was this: a mother consulted me concerning her eleven-year-old boy. For many years he had difficulties at home as well as at school and, since being away from home, the difficulties in school became definitely neurotic. Everything had been tried for the child—from educational cure to psychiatric advice and psychoanalytic treatment—without success. The mother herself through these efforts had been sufficiently enlightened to understand—at least intellectually—that her unhappy marriage had something to do with the boy's maladjustment, although she chiefly blamed her husband for it. According to her reports, the father hated the boy from his birth and manifestly preferred the other child to him. All of the boy's symptoms obviously had but one meaning: to win his father's love. At the same time, I saw they had also another significance, which seems to me of greater importance. The mother, for some time past, had left home and lived with the boy separately from her husband. As the boy's difficulties started long ago at home, caused by the father's repellent reaction to him, one would have expected that separation from his father might result in a spontaneous relief from his difficulties, as the mother herself had expected. But the boy's escape from the father's manifest hatred, as well as from the favored rival, and getting the mother all to himself only increased his difficulties instead of alleviating them.

From our analytic knowledge, we should be inclined to jump to the conclusion that it is guilt-feeling arising from fulfillment of the Oedipus situation: in other words, having the father out of the way and being in sole possession of the mother. This may be so to some extent, but it does not explain the origin of his neurosis, which existed while still at home, nor does it explain his specific symptoms, which were only aggravated by his departure from home.

Furthermore—and this I would like to emphasize—*his actual symptoms seem to betray a definite tendency to bring his father and mother together again*, most importantly, as I pointed out, to win his father's love, from which he was prevented by being solely with his mother. Not being loved, indeed being hated, by his father was a terrible wound to his ego, which apparently could not be healed by his mother's affection alone. In other words, we see how injury to the ego *outweighs* libidinal gratification: this is just the conflict that manifests itself in what we call guilt-feeling. We see how guilt-feeling is based on a purely internal ego conflict and is only projected into the so-called Oedipus situation.

Whereas libidinal desire for gratification strives to achieve the Oedipus situation, the need for ego satisfaction, in such cases, counterbalances this tendency. In similar situations I have seen a tendency born from the ego that is almost *contrary* to the Oedipus situation. While in the Oedipus situation the child wishes to separate parents in order to eliminate one and possess the other, I recognized in cases where parents are separated or about to separate that the child makes definite efforts to keep the parents *together*. Apparently, under these circumstances, this is more important for the child's ego than actual attainment of the Oedipus situation.

This state of affairs seems to me highly important both theoretically and practically. Practically, because it proves again that it does not always help to get what we want—especially when we are not sure what we want. In other words, therapy is apparently not fulfillment but adjustment. By that I mean we should not even strive to attempt ideal situations in family life. First, to be sure, one would not succeed, but even if one could, it might increase inner conflicts to an unbearable extent. As a matter of fact, we know already from experience that with the best intentions and even preparations on its parents' part, the child's conflicts are not only not prevented but are very often increased—for the simple reason that, since we are so complicated, inner conflict becomes stronger when external pressure is less.[1]

This leads to more general considerations of the therapeutical as well as theoretical value of psychoanalysis. The libido theory was deduced from adult patients and has been applied to children only retrospectively. To what extent this is justified remains a topic of discussion. Be that as it may, the fact remains that in adult patients it helps therapeutically to explain an actual conflict in terms of the infantile Oedipus situation. It relieves the patient's guilt-feeling to learn that as an individual he is not responsible since it is a matter of mankind's universal development that he is only repeating.

With the child, however, this comforting explanation does not work—because the child is still in the midst of all so-called infantilisms into which we allow the patient to slip back temporarily. That is, with the child the emotional conflict as well as the "infantile" situation that causes it are both real and actual—in fact, are the same. This explains why all child analysts, no matter how much they differ in opinion, agree on one principle: namely, the technique of child analysis ought to be quite different from that used for adults. The adult patient is not only allowed to express his actual conflicts in infantile terms, and in the universal language of symbolism, but also he is allowed to regress emotionally to a primitive level. With the child, however, there is no such differentiation: the analytic *past* is, so to speak, the child's *present*.

This leads to another theme, which I would like to illustrate by another case, also seen recently. This time it was a little girl about the same age as the boy of whom I spoke. She was a healthy, well-adjusted child. Nevertheless, she also reacted in a neurotic way to the disharmony between her parents and to the father's intention of leaving the house. I am quite sure it was only from what I learned in the first case that I was able to understand in what way the little girl's actual conflict was a *reaction* to the domestic situation. Her conflict manifested itself in a neurotic anxiety centering around sex problems—for example, masturbation and babies—about which she wanted to talk with her mother. But the way in which this desire manifested itself enabled me to relate her conflict to the domestic situation.

The child, who had been perfectly satisfied to sleep alone at home as well as at school, showed anxiety before going to bed and then wanted her mother to come and talk to her. *It was obvious, even to the mother herself, that what the child actually wanted was not so much to talk over her problems as to have her mother with her.* In the first place, the child was not always talking when the mother came but she just held her. In the second place, even if she talked it over with the mother, it apparently did not help her in the least because she brought up the same things again and again. It was obvious that what she wanted was the mother and not the explanation of her problems. Her "problems" were only an excuse—because she knew her mother would not refuse to explain things to her.

The question is, Why did she cling to her mother instead of to the father who, at that time, was still living in the house and of whom she was very fond? My answer is that, again, something stronger than the Oedipus wish made her want to keep her parents together. However, the way she did it, or expressed the desire to do it, was in a regressive conflict-laden manner, because this ego tendency interfered with the libidinal Oedipus tendency.

In talking about the fears with her mother, she referred to previous situations of fear in early childhood, which was not a mere regression but also took her back to a period of her life when her parents were still happy together, or when at least she was unaware of any disharmony. Here, too, we see clearly that the child actually did not need any psychoanalytic explanation of this fear, which was only her way of reacting to the present situation—if you like, her way of saying, "I am afraid of losing one of my parents and therefore I am going back to a time when there was no such fear, but only when I was afraid for other reasons." Her clinging to the mother, as I said before, was more of an ego mechanism than a libidinal satisfaction, because she had previously experienced that it was the father who wanted to go away and that her mother had always stayed with her. In this respect, clinging to her mother is an anticipation of losing her father and, at the same time, an assurance that her mother would stay. On the other hand, I could see from various indications that keeping her mother from going out or leaving the house was not only a substitute for trying to keep her father, with whom she knew she could not succeed. It also betrayed the desire to keep her mother *for her father* and—in identification with her mother—to keep her father for herself.

Here we come back again to the Oedipus situation, but, as we see, not in a simple a way as is generally supposed. Certainly the fear of losing her father intensifies the normal desire to have him. The desire, on the other hand, aggravates guilt-feeling toward her mother, which is compensated for by wanting her more. But what we see in this case is how the normal Oedipus situation is merely used as a means to the end of another purpose. The little girl's identification with her mother is not a mere wish to replace her mother with her father. The ways she acts and reacts to the situation show another tendency—which we might almost say paralyzes the Oedipus situation. It is this. Since she has experienced that she herself cannot keep her father, she expects her mother to do it for her and on that ground is her identification based. It is as if she were willing now to accept her mother—quite contrary to the Oedipus situation—in order to keep her father too.

This throws a light on the little girl's other problem, which apparently was then also on her mind: the question of babies. But this sexual problem, as well as the other one of masturbation, proved to be another way of reacting to the parental situation in the child's symbolic language. In other words, the child's fear with regard to the present situation came up as fear of masturbation, and her curiosity about babies was actually a desire for an explanation of the parents' situation, being, as it were, a sexual problem.

Of course, there is always a connection to be found between the actual problem and its symbolic presentation. For example, her fear that she would lose her father intensified her masturbation conflict in the meaning of a substitute of her own person for her father, and her guilt-feeling for it toward her mother. At the same time, it also expresses her guilt with regard to her own inability to keep her father, as if she were blaming herself for her father's going away.

On the other hand, her interest in the problem of babies was likewise a reflection of the parental situation. As she already knows where babies come from, her recent interest shown in the question as to whether there should be *another* baby in the family or not, was really meant to be a question as to whether her parents were going to live together or not. Again, we see how the actual parental conflict counterblances the primitive impulses of the child and forces it to an adjustment. Before, we saw the child's willingness to accept her mother, as that seemed to be the condition of keeping her father; here, although I was unable to follow the further development of the situation, it seemed to be implied that the child would accept another baby in the family as a possibility of keeping the parents together.

We see here a remarkable phenomenon, which seems to me to be of great importance both theoretically and practically. While the parents are inclined to overlook the part played by their *own* conflicts in the child's problems, or to completely deny it, the child on the other hand is more inclined to feel *itself* responsible for the parents' difficulties. And actually this feeling of the child's is to a certain extent justified. The child brings a new element into the relation of the parents one to another, and this element is not always, or is not completely, a harmonious one. The fact that the child seems to feel this more than the parents is obviously connected with its whole attitude to the world of reality. The child inclines *too much* to identification, which he only gradually gives up at the adult stage of the so-called adjustment to reality—if he ever gives it up at all. In contrast to this, the adult is very much inclined to projection, which so to say is the price at which he purchases his adjustment.

From the therapeutic standpoint this differentiation is important insofar as the adult, in cases of maladjustment, needs analysis. Of course, it is presupposed that the analyst, as far as possible, prevents the patient's projection—which has been described as "transference"—in order to throw him back to himself and his problems. In the case of the child, however, who inclines altogether to introversion and relates everything too much to his ego, I think that pure analytic therapy is out of place. The child's guilt-feeling can more easily be unburdened if he is permitted to project his conflicts onto the parents, with whom he has to live, instead of onto the analyst, whom he sees only temporarily. In other words, *the child has to learn to allow himself to make the parents responsible for certain difficulties, instead of looking for the fault exclu-*

sively within himself—which leads to the feelings of guilt and inferiority, well known to us. But one sees, also, how such an attitude on the child's part tempts pedagogues, parents, and psychoanalysts to look—with the child—for the cause of all evil in the child's own emotional life, and therefore to try to heal the child by analysis.

So much for the actual conflicts of the parents and the child's tendency to make itself responsible for them, which manifests itself in the form of neurotic reactions, chiefly as fear and guilt. In cases where symptoms appear as a reaction to domestic conflict, the child can often be helped more by letting him realize and react to it than by analyzing his symptoms in a purely psychological way. Or, as I already said, the child's guilt-feeling is unburdened when he is allowed to realize the *parents'* part played in his conflicts instead of denying such blame and so increasing his own guilt-feeling.

We must ask ourselves the question, Why is the child inclined to feel responsible for everything? For this I would like to give three reasons. The first, a superficial one, is that the child is accustomed to being blamed for everything by the parents. The second, deeper reason, is the *unconscious* insight on the part of the child that he, in a certain sense, *is* responsible for many parental conflicts—at least for rendering them more difficult. The third, and deepest, is bound up entirely with the child's development.

This last point I would like to discuss somewhat in detail. The child—in consequence of his natural development on the one side and the permanent adjustment demanded of him by education on the other—is driven into perpetual conflict. The child always feels conscious of guilt and inferiority, is, so to say, at least in our civilized milieu, *normally* "neurotic." This normal childhood neurosis manifests itself in all spheres where the birthright of the child to develop clashes with the demands of real and social adjustment. It may be the sexual problem in relation to which the child feels itself especially resistant to adjustment, manifesting itself as anxiety, or, the child's conflict in not making the best of the demands of adjustment expressing itself in inferiority feeling. All these reactions—that may appear to us neurotic, but which for the child are necessary stages on the way of adjustment—remain inevitable, even in the most normal and most ideal parental milieu.

What I would like to emphasize here as the essential viewpoint of this lecture is that the child does not react to disturbances and disharmonies in the parental milieu with new specific symptoms but only intensifies his normal symptoms. I mean by this that he now places all his normal sex and ego conflicts at the disposal of this actual conflict. In other words, the child does not react directly to an actual family-conflict but reacts to it in the symbolic language of his normal biological conflicts. From this there follows an important therapeutic viewpoint: namely, in cases where domestic conflict increases the child's normal difficulties— and that is so in most cases we see—*it cannot be the task of therapy to make the child completely free from conflict.*

Therapeutically it is a matter of removing only this *PLUS* in neurotic reactions—which is caused by parental conflict. The ideal way would naturally be to remove or relieve the parents' conflict, which unfortunately is only seldom possible. The actual therapeutic intervention for the child, according to my view, should consist first of all in unburdening the child's guilt-feeling by showing up the share that *parental* conflicts have in it. To omit this, and by a purely analytic process to throw the child back again to his own self, I maintain is a mistake and may lead to failure. In other words, whereas therapy can be *analytic* for parents, therapy for the child must be *constructive*.

Notes

Read before "The One Day's Conference on Parental Education," New York, November 2, 1927.

1. For more on "internalization" and "externalization," see "Beyond Psychoanalysis" [18] and "Modern Psychology and Social Change" [22].

PART FOUR

TOWARD A THEORY OF RELATIONSHIP AND
RELATIVITY: "I AM NO LONGER TRYING TO PROVE
FREUD WAS WRONG AND I RIGHT"

17

SPEECH AT FIRST INTERNATIONAL CONGRESS ON MENTAL HYGIENE (1930)

LADIES AND GENTLEMEN, I like the idea of a ten-minute summary instead of reading the paper, not only because the latter is rather boring but, chiefly, because it gives me a chance to talk newly—almost to give you a new paper, the original having been written back in the fall and not especially for this conference either, but as part of a book on education and worldview.[1] So with your permission, I will use my ten minutes to give you my discussion of the paper—or rather the worldview back of it—and, furthermore, a glimpse of the personality expressed in this worldview. In doing so, I intend to introduce myself to the part of the audience that does not know me and, at the same time, relieve some doubts and correct some misunderstandings on the part of those who *think* they knew me in the past.

My views and ideas have changed considerably during the twenty-five years of my work in psychology and its applied fields of human science. On account of this, my undefinable position, I am afraid that there was some difficulty in placing me on the program of the Congress. I am no psychiatrist, no social worker, no psychoanalyst, not even an ordinary psychologist—and to tell you the truth I am glad of it. I have gone through all the phases of the development of scientific psychology and its practical applications within the last twenty-five years. My extensive experience and study (both theoretical and therapeutic) have led me to the conviction that the scientific side to human behavior and personality problems is not only insufficient but leaves out the most essential part: namely, *the human side*—the characteristic of which is just that it can't be measured and checked and controlled.[2] And, yet, it is the only vital factor not only in life but also in all kinds of therapy, mental hygiene in the broadest sense. What helps is not *intellectual knowledge* but human understanding, which is *emotional* and hence cannot be schematized.

The main trouble with the scientific approach to human nature is not so much that it has to neglect the personal, so-called subjective, element but that it has to *deny* it in order to maintain the scientific attitude. This is clearly seen in psychoanalysis, which could not help recognizing the high importance of the purely human side and yet had to stigmatize it scientifically as being only a transference phenomenon. In interpreting the human element scientifically, psychoanalysis had to deny it and so defeated its own scientific ideal, becoming unscientific by denying the most essential aspect of the personality.

I don't want you to misunderstand me! *I am no longer trying to prove that Freud was wrong and I am right*. I realized definitely for the first time in my book *Truth and Reality* [1929], published in German last year, that it is not a question of whose interpretation is correct—because there is no such thing as *the* interpretation or only *one* psychological truth. Psychology does not deal primarily with facts as science does but only with the individual's attitude toward facts. In other words, the objects of psychology are *interpretations*—and there are as many of them as there are individuals and, even more than that, also the individual's different situations, which have to be interpreted *differently* in every single manifestation.[3]

So the battle is really on—not between different schools of psychoanalysis but between two worldviews, which have been in conflict with one another since the dawn of science with the early Greeks and even long before, as I tried to show in my last book, *Psychology and the Soul* [1930b].[4] What I want to emphasize here is not the superiority of one interpretation—that is, one psychological theory—over another, but the difference in worldview underlying all the ardent discussion about psychological values that is now going on with an emotional conviction comparable only to the religious wars in the darkest medieval times. This conflict will not be lessened until we admit that science has proved to be a complete failure in the field of psychology, i.e., in the betterment of human nature and in the achievement of human happiness toward which all mental hygiene is ultimately striving. The result of scientific psychology can be summed up today as the recognition that it is necessarily insufficient to explain human nature, far less to make the individual happier.

The error lies in the scientific glorification of *consciousness*, of intellectual knowledge, which even psychoanalysis worships as its highest god—although it calls itself a psychology of the *unconscious*. But this means only an attempt to rationalize the unconscious and to intellectualize it scientifically.[5] Just this attempt, however, has proved to be the main test for a scientific comprehension of the individual. Its failure is clearly shown in the complete lack of any satisfactory theory of the essential part of the unconscious, namely, the emotional life, as I point out in my paper.

Intellectual understanding is one thing and the actual working out of our emotional problems another, as I brought forward for the first time in a book on *The Development of Psychoanalysis* [1924].[6] This was my first parting, not from Freud, but from his whole ideology, which is erected on the fundamental importance of intellectual understanding as a *curative* factor.[7] The second step beyond the materialistic viewpoint of psychoanalysis I made in *The Trauma of Birth* [1924] with the emphasis on an unconscious absolutely inaccessible to any *intellectual* grasp; at the same time, I was still trying to carry the scientific approach to human problems even further than Freud, but I realized in doing so I was carrying it *ad absurdum.*

It is only within the last two or three years that I have gradually overcome, with increasing acknowledgment of the purely human factor in psychotherapy, the intellectual ideology that worships knowledge for the purpose of controlling and predicting human behavior.

However, in order to pretend that control and prediction are possible, *one had to deny the individual's own will,* his emotional instability, and the large part chance plays in the sphere of our psychical life even more than in our cosmic life. The scientific approach—with its artificial emphasis on *one* truth and its aim to control and to predict—strives ultimately only for security, but it is a false security that does not do away with the cosmic fear of the individual and hence does not make us any more happy. Experience has taught me that understanding and explaining do not get you anywhere—unless it comes as a result of personal experience through suffering, which scientific ideology tries to spare the individual from childhood on. I don't believe that the individual can really develop and grow up without having a chance to go through emotional experiences and conflicts of all kinds.

My life's work has convinced me that real knowledge, insight, and human understanding only *follow* the emotional and actual working-out of a problem—not vice versa as psychoanalysis, and for that matter all scientific ideology, maintains. The educator, the social worker, the therapist, can only use their own knowledge, gained by their own personal experience, to let others experience their own knowledge and understanding of themselves. But experience cannot be thought out intellectually and transmitted by purely mental processes such as education, teaching, study, instruction, and so on.

And now I have said what I have to say. Let me, at the end, refer you to an example of what I mean: you have it right before you in this conference itself. Almost everybody to whom I have spoken has said that there is not much use in attending these big conferences for the purpose of learning anything. The most valuable factor in a gathering of a crowd like this from all over the world lies in the human element, in the meeting of people, in the contact with the personalities themselves and not with their written and read words. So I hope I have been true to the real human spirit of this conference in pushing the personal element into the foreground, not without feeling greatly obliged to the broad-minded attitude of the leaders in Mental Hygiene who offered me the opportunity to do it.[8]

Notes

Read in Washington, D.C., May 8, 1930.

1. The "First International Congress on Mental Hygiene" was an extraordinary event that brought more than four thousand people to Washington, D.C., from fifty-three countries and provided U.S. psychoanalysts a huge forum in which to establish their credibility. Rank's paper, entitled "The Training of the Will and Emotional Development," was published in *Modern Education* (Rank 1932b, pp. 58–91). The conference organizers asked speakers to prepare a "ten-minute summary" rather than read lengthy papers, which were distributed in advance to those who wanted them. On the panel with Rank were Rev. Oskar Pfister, Jessie Taft, Franz Alexander, and A. A. Brill.

2. "Here we find ourselves directly face to face with experience," Rank wrote in *Modern Education*, "which is neither scientifically nor technically controllable, indeed hardly comprehensible while it is being enacted" (1932b, p. 242). Experience—what Rank and Ferenczi had called *Erlebnis* in *The Development of Psychoanalysis*—is nothing but the *existence* forced on human beings by the incomprehensible power of sexuality. Experience is the strange consciousness of living, of *Being* itself. For Rank, experience is identical to *Dasein*—"being there" or "being present." Living *in* the Now, a timeless and elusive "moment" that can never be grasped intellectually, means living in the transitional space of a "moment" that collapses and recedes into the "past" as quickly as it occurs. The present, therefore, is virtually unknowable in all its determinants. For Rank, it can only be experienced, never fully understood. And, at bottom, it is synonymous with the painful burden of consciousness, of difference. No wonder, then, that neurotics hurl a Big No at the present, at the consciousness of living, and are fixated on the infantile past. They are refusing to *live*—in a sense, refusing to accept the burden of legitimate suffering, of difference itself. I = pain. Thus, said Rank in *Will Therapy*, "it becomes clear that the [patient's] so-called fixation on the past, the living-in-reminiscence [*das Leben in Reminiszenzen*], is only a protection from experiencing [*ein Schutz vor dem Erleben*], from the surrender to the present. . . . [T]here are individuals who know how to *overcome* the hardest, most traumatic experiences [*traumatischen Erlebnisse*] with a *new* experience [*durch Neuerleben*]. Such a new experiencing and not merely a *repetition* of the infantile represents the therapeutic process and its value in my conception" (1929–31, p. 39; italics added). For Rank, therefore, *Erlebnis* is nothing but the Now or the New. All living, thinking, feeling, and willing take place in the present: "This, then, is the New, which the patient has never experienced before" (ibid., 65).

3. "Will people ever learn," Rank wrote poignantly in *Beyond Psychology*, a few months before he died in October 1939, "that there is no other equality possible than the equal right of every individual *to become and to be himself,*

which actually means to *accept his own difference* and have it accepted by *others?*" (1941, p. 267; italics added).

4. Earlier in 1930 Rank published this book in German, under the title *Seelenglaube und Psychologie*—literally, "Belief in the Soul and Psychology." Rank considered *Seelenglaube* one of his most important books and referred to it often in *Art and Artist* and *Beyond Psychology*. According to Rank, "the soul gradually underwent transformation into the unconscious" (1930b, p. 3). The "affective power of psychoanalysis," said Rank, foreshadowing the critique of Paul Ricoeur (1970), lies in its being *both* scientific "psychology and spiritual doctrine, and [its] *failing to differentiate* at all between these two aspects. Were psychoanalysis more definitely the one or the other, it could not be the unique fusion that it is. In the terminology of our natural science era, it combines the *causal* way of thinking, which seeks to explain facts by reducing them to relationships expressed as *natural* laws, with the *cultural* way of thinking, which tries to comprehend the *meaning* and structure of mental phenomena" (ibid., pp. 8–9; italics added).

The last chapter of *Psychology and the Soul* is a critique of the claims of psychoanalysis to universal understanding. Drawing on the recent discoveries of quantum physics, Bohr's theory of complementarity, and Heisenberg's principle of uncertainty, Rank concludes that Freud's psychoanalysis is just *one* way of understanding, not the *only* way: "[T]here is no single theory of light, just as there is no single psychology, and for quite the same reasons" (ibid., p. 174). It is remarkable that by 1930, Rank was already aware of Heisenberg, who had just published a highly technical article in *Zeitschrift für Physik* on his famous uncertainty principle, for the first time, in 1927. Equally astonishing is his grasp of the implications of Bohr's theory of "complementarity"—first published in 1928—a theory Rank explores in a long footnote (ibid., pp. 173–74).

Freud read *Psychology and the Soul* but dismissed it in a 1930 talk before the Vienna Psychoanalytic Society: Rank, he said, uses "the theory of relativity, the quantum theory, and the principle of indeterminism to express doubts about psychic causality, so that there is nothing left except soul and free will. But [the 'cause'] cannot possibly be an illusion," thundered Freud, closing his rare public attack on Rank, according to an analyst who was present, "with strong emotional emphasis" (Sterba 1982, pp. 116–17). *Die Sache* was not a fiction.

Even before he learned of the revolution in physics started by Heisenberg and Bohr, Rank said that, in the wake of writing *The Trauma of Birth*, he had already concluded that the "individual simply lies beyond lawfulness, and cannot be fully comprehended or explained by the causality either of natural or social science" (1930b, p. 175)—or by the "cause" of psychoanalysis.

5. Rank is referring to the *mysterium tremendum* (Otto 1923, pp. 12–24)— not the "Oedipal" (paternal) or "pre-Oedipal" (maternal) unconscious revealed, to some extent, in the analytic situation—and always insisted that the "existential" unconscious is absolutely inaccessible to any *intellectual* grasp.

In a recent book, Peter Rudnytsky misreads Rank on the unconscious. While celebrating Rank's prescience as the inventor of object-relations theory, Rudnytsky maintains that Rank abandoned the unconscious in the wake of his sep-

aration from Freud. Consistent with Rank's "conversion to a 'collective unconscious' with 'spiritual' meanings," claims Rudnytsky, "Rank in *Art and Artist*
scores Freud's 'concrete' view of the mother . . . and cites with approval Jung's
Psychology of the Unconscious on 'the symbolic significance of the mother'"
(Rudnytsky 1991, p. 49). Rank respected Jung, who "conceives of guilt more
deeply than Freud or Adler, in cosmic [*kosmisch*] terms" (Rank 1929–31, p.
83), but to assert that Rank is a converted Jungian *denies* the very individuality
of Rank: the core of his theory of the creative will. (See footnote 2, "Modern
Psychology and Social Change" [22], for Rank's own analysis of his differences
with Freud, Adler, and Jung—all of whom he accepted, in part, without "con-
verting" to any of them. See also "The Yale Lecture" [19–241]).

Unlike Rank's pioneering pre-Oedipal writings, his later works such as *Will
Therapy* and *Beyond Psychology* suffer, according to Rudnytsky, from a
"global anti-intellectualism" (1991, p. 66). Rank, who published twenty-one
books in his lifetime, can hardly be called antiintellectual. "We must not forget," said Rank in *Truth and Reality*, "that knowledge also has a creative side,
as, for example, Shakespeare himself shows in the creation of the Hamlet figure.
Evidently he himself represented the Hamlet type, which did not hinder him,
unlike his hero, from using his conflict creatively instead of perceiving it merely
as a restriction" (1929, p. 34). Recognizing that his writings on consciousness
might be misread as antiintellectual, Rank also emphasized in *Will Therapy* that
knowledge has a creative side, as Shakespeare showed by transforming his own
personal anguish into art: "If I have at one time designated consciousness when
it goes beyond a certain breadth or depth as destructive . . ., now while still
maintaining this, I would exclude expressly intelligence, which represents exactly the factor that can realize the conscious surplus constructively if one succeeds in putting it at the service of the will" (1929–31, p. 177).

6. In *The Development of Psychoanalysis*, Ferenczi and Rank argued that
"the final goal of psycho-analysis is to substitute, by means of the technique,
affective factors of *Erlebnis* for intellectual processes" (1924, p. 62).

7. In *The New Introductory Lectures* (1933), for example, Freud said that
"understanding and cure almost coincide" (*S.E.*, 22:145). Insight was all.

8. After this ten-minute talk, A. A. Brill, then President of the American Psychoanalytic Association, spoke:

> I was particularly impressed by one remark of Dr. Rank's—namely that he is no
> longer a psychoanalyst. I have known that for some time, but I have never heard him
> say it before. That is why he can talk about "individual will" and "human ele-
> ments." He makes use of these terms as if they were pieces of cheese. . . . In fact, I
> feel all the stuff to which Dr. Rank treated us this morning is but an indication of his
> own present maladjustment. . . . My feeling about Dr. Rank is that it is this emo-
> tional upheaval that is responsible for his present confusion. (Lieberman 1985, pp.
> 291–92)

The American Psychoanalytic Association met on the evening of May 8,
1930, in Washington, D.C., in conjunction with the First International Congress
on Mental Hygiene. Following a motion by President Brill, seconded by Vice-
President Harry Stack Sullivan, the APA voted in its annual business session to

strike the name of Otto Rank from its list of honorary members—which, at that time, contained only two other names: Freud and Ferenczi. From then on, "those who had the misfortune to be analyzed by [Rank] were required to undergo a *second* analysis in order to qualify" for membership in the APA (ibid., p. 293). As far as U.S. psychoanalysis was concerned, Rank was dead.

18

BEYOND PSYCHOANALYSIS (1928)

LADIES AND GENTLEMEN, psychoanalysis has rediscovered in the so-called nervous patient the significance of the emotional life [*das Seelische*][1] but has attempted to conceive it scientifically from a purely materialistic point of view. This attempt could succeed only to some extent. For the problem of *anxiety*, which Freud first came up against in his patients, is not to be explained entirely biologically in the human being. Still less can the problem of *love* be purely biologically explained, although Freud attempted to trace it as well as anxiety back to the sexual impulse. The fault lay in the method: in the attempt to explain everything from a materialistic viewpoint. Even if we assume to be right the presupposition that everything has developed from the primitive biological, then this concept has only a heuristic value, whereas it is insufficient as a principle of causal [*kausales*] explanation.

From a definite moment of development, all these human phenomena that are built up *over* the purely biological attain a life and significance of their own. Little more is gained by reducing them to the original biological, even if this always succeeds in individual cases, than would be the case if, for example, one wanted to understand an individual's entire life merely by his heredity. Psychoanalysis tried to avoid this error in emphasizing the individual's personal destiny. In doing this, it has fallen into a similar error by believing that *everything can be reduced to the individual's past*. Thus, even in actual experience [*Erleben*] psychoanalysis has emphasized the repetition of the individual's past and has not correspondingly valued the individual's own present life and its significance.

Nearly all divergences of opinion within the psychoanalytic school as well as a great part of the criticism of psychoanalysis in general go back to this one cardinal point: the tendency to reduce everything to the biological. The fundamental importance of the biological shall not here be denied. The question is only whether what we comprehend under the name *psychical* [*seelisch*][2] lends itself entirely to such a way of consideration or whether, for a full understanding, it does not rather need a supplement that only a *philosophical* manner of reflection might offer.

Freud's great merit was the overthrow of the medical superstition that the psychical [*das Seelische*] is a matter of nerves, which indeed only represent the instrument on which the human emotional life [*Ge-*

fühlsleben] is played. His error was that in place of the medical theory of nerves he wanted to put the biological sex theory—which was supposed to explain everything entirely. As the physiological nerves afford the instrument, so biological sex provides the material for that which makes up our emotional life [*Seelenleben*].

Thus Freud has dethroned medical materialism with regard to the so-called neuroses, but what we really want to thank him for is that he failed in the attempt to set up in its place the purely biological—and so, involuntarily, has brought the real psychical into its own again. Psychoanalytic theory finally has led to acknowledgement that—along with the biological principle—there is operative in mankind an equally strong ethical principle.

The unconscious, incidentally a purely emotional concept, cannot be entirely reduced to the drives. [*Das Unbewußte, worunter eigentlich das Seelische verstanden ist, ließ sich nicht restlos aufs Triebleben reduzieren.*] Indeed, it is even shown that in many human beings inhibitions manifesting themselves as anxiety and guilt are *stronger* than the drives, that these inhibitions themselves, so to say, operate "as a driving force," although in a different way from the biological impulses.[3] In a word we see that the *psychical* has become a force at least equal to the *biological* and that all human conflicts are to be explained just from this fact. Freud's latest work has been a constant struggle against admitting this, and so he tried to apply biological concepts as a means of final explanation in the psychical sphere where they are inappropriate. For just as the guilt problem can only be fully comprehended from the ethical side, so the complete understanding of the love life is to be found only beyond the sexual drive—in the ego, the I.

Hence Freud, with the right instinct, has given his discoveries mythical names, such as the Oedipus complex. In doing this, he believed that he explained the myths themselves, which indeed are mental products [*geistige Produkte*] but are not to be understood from a purely biological viewpoint. To want to explain the Oedipus myth simply from the biological relationship of child to parents is just as unsatisfying as to expect to understand the child's emotional life from this mythical nomenclature. Freudian concepts show the right feeling that these psychical processes are to be grasped and understood only mythically: in other words, *psychically*.

This unspoken insight is Freud's great accomplishment, for he himself is a myth creator in the grandest style, in Plato's sense a real philosopher. According to his own admission, fascinated by the natural-scientific worldview, he interpreted everything "mythical"—not merely in tradition, but in human beings themselves—biologically and on the other hand called biological discoveries by mythical names. So he could not correctly interpret what was in between, namely, the purely psychical, and fully estimate it in its own significance.

Freud's work—which appeared with the natural-scientific name of *psycho-analysis*—is only in small part analysis of the psychical, which according to its nature represents an elementary entity and cannot be analyzed further. It is much more *interpretation* than analysis, and analysis only insofar as it attempts, in the chemical sense, a reduction to the final (biological) elements, which indeed ultimately lie at the foundation of all phenomena. In the psychical sphere, the fundamental biological facts are not as important as their interpretation, first of all by ourselves, then by others. The former we call rationalization, the latter explanation or interpretation. These phenomena themselves represent a part of the psychical.

In other words, the psychical itself is only to be understood phenomenologically. One might say that in the psychical sphere there are no facts but only interpretations of facts. On that account, the dream has been justifiably called the psychical phenomenon par excellence. In the dream we ourselves interpret physical and psychical states (facts), but this "interpretation" is as little "analysis" of "facts" as is our analytic "interpretation," which represents only another kind of symbolization and rationalization.

Psychoanalysis, as developed by Freud, is thus only to some extent a method of finding out the biological facts lying at the foundation of the psychical life. It corresponds rather to *one* definite way of interpreting the psychical. It started as a natural-scientific biological interpretation of the psychical but finally led Freud himself to the threshold of acknowledging another kind of interpretation, namely, the ethical, by postulating the concepts of the super-ego and guilt-feeling. But we did not need psychoanalysis to make us aware of these facts.

Since Breuer's first attempt to cure a patient by the cathartic method, the only really *new fact* that psychoanalysis has given us is the *analytic situation*. And from this one fact Breuer fled. Freud, on the other hand, succeeded in *interpreting* it, by justifying it as a repetition of an earlier situation—which he called Oedipus situation. However, this was only another kind of flight from the fact of the analytic situation, an intellectual flight from a fact in which the interesting and valuable is just that which is new, that which lies beyond the "transference," that is, *beyond the repetition of the Oedipus situation.*

After the possibility of interpreting the analytic situation exhausted itself (in Freud's libido theory) in projecting back to the infantile, I began the "analysis of the analytic situation"[4] in itself as a *new* fact. From this I hope finally to understand and develop, synthetically and constructively, new psychical values. The first value that the analytic situation presents, and teaches us to understand, is the emotion of love. And it presents this as an *actual* relationship of sentiments and not merely as the transference of the child's attitude toward parents. It is the origin, development, and passing of this human emotional relationship that the analytic situation artificially produces and teaches us to understand. The analysis of this transference process gives us a view [*Einblick*] into a fragment of I-psychology [*Ich-Psychologie*], but that is simply psychology—for what we designate as "I" is ultimately nothing but our psychological I, our psychical, in contrast to the biological, which represents only *material* for the psyche.

Secondly, what we can develop from the analytic situation besides an understanding of the love emotion, is the *ethical*. By that I do not mean any specific ethics, but simply *the* ethical, given in the relationship of two human beings as portrayed in the analytic situation. While the mechanism of being in love can be studied in the patient's I, the ethical element cannot be developed without analysis of the *other* person—which in the analytic situation is the analyst. This "analysis of the analyst" I intend to give elsewhere as part of analytic technique.[5]

In contrast to I-psychology as revealed to us in the state of being in love, one might designate ethics as Thou-Psychology [*Du-Psychologie*]. It is a kind of "group psychology" in a constructive sense of which the sexual ethic represents only a specific part. Freud saw in the analytic situation only a repetition of the infantile Oedipus situation, and so in the state of being in love he saw in essence the biological and libidinal moment—not the side of the I; similarly the ethical also remained purely *external*, namely, a primitive father morality as incorporated in the Old Testament Jehovah who punishes and rewards his chosen people. This is not merely a comparison; for religion itself is the preliminary toward an ethic and places I's responsibility on the external, primitive god who operates with rewards and punishment. Hence also the surpassing part that the castration threat plays in Freud's theory.

Thirdly, what the psychoanalytic situation presents to us is a new approach to the *theory of cognition*—which gives a new understanding of the relation of the I not only to other human beings but to reality in general. The insight to be gained here is so fundamental and so far-reaching that I must keep it for a separate presentation.[6] I can here only indicate its special application to the analysis and understanding of the analytic situation itself. I mean the ideas alluded to by me for the first time in *The Trauma of Birth*: that which we consider analytic theory and therapy to a large degree is nothing other than interpretation of the analytic situation. This is not intended to be a valuation but only a question that expresses nothing about whether analytic theory and the therapeutic conclusions drawn from it are right or wrong.

One must not only bear in mind that the analytic situation permits of different interpretations. One must also be conscious that one interprets, specifically, a typical and symbolic situation for the individual, and so any general conclusions drawn from it may be of doubtful value. As in the case of the dream, which itself represents an interpretation of (external or internal) stimuli, our interpretation corresponds to a further interpretation—of another kind; so the patient in his associations and reactions "interprets" the analytic situation, which we then further interpret in the meaning of analytic theory, itself an attempt to interpret the analytic situation.

From the analysis of the analytic situation, therefore, there appears a kind of *meta-psychoanalysis* that has not only a general theoretic importance going beyond the narrower psychoanalytic sphere but also essentially influences the technique. For an explanation of the difference, one might use the following simile: the customary analysis corresponds to arithmetic where things have a definite material value; meta-psychoanalysis corresponds to algebra where all signs, including the arithmetical, have a definite *symbolic* value. They symbolize arithmetical quantities without operating with figures themselves.

Let us start from therapeutic technique, the side from which this knowledge was gained. We see how the patient—whether at the beginning or in the course of analysis—uses psychoanalytic theory itself as *material* for presentation (or symbolization) of his own emotional life. When we understand the algebraic meaning and valuation of these presentations and operations, however, we need no longer go back in every instance to the arithmetical value. We can solve the problem in a much more general way: in the meaning of the patient's destiny, which we, so to say, reduce to a general denominator.

The use by the patient of analytic material for a symbolic presentation of his emotional life is not only an inevitable result from the analytic situation—a result that disturbs or complicates the process—but it can and must be made the basis of the whole proceeding, if one does not want to fall into error. I would like to illustrate this in the form of an "algebraic" example. Some years ago, an analyst who was then analyzing a chemist complained to me that he could not get anywhere with the work because the patient brought up so much material from his own science, chemistry, about which the analyst did not understand. It seemed to him almost necessary that he himself should study chemistry in order to understand the patient. I remarked that this, besides being impractical, was too much to be expected because one could not possibly learn the psychical language [*seelische Sprache*] of every single patient one treated.[7]

Today I would give far more consoling advice: let all patients learn the same language that the *analyst* himself speaks. They would thus easily understand each other. This language is the psychoanalytic theory—no matter of what school or coloring. The essential thing is that the patient speaks or learns to speak the same language as the analyst in order to make himself understood. And the analyst, apart from what he is conscious of doing, in any case instructs the patient in his language—which the cultured patient of today already knows a little about before he comes for analysis.

So far this state of affairs would be comparatively simple if the analyst had been conscious of this fact and of the advantages that it offers him. When the patient, for example, learned in analysis the significance of the Oedipus or castration complex—and repeated this in his reactions—then the analyst was content, even more than that, was delighted with this echo of confirmation, without understanding that the patient wanted to express something definite in the present analytic situation. In other words, when the patient learned more or less of the language and was able to converse in it tolerably well, the analyst praised or blamed him according to whether he correctly handled the theoretical grammar or used correctly the necessary vocabulary. Thus, like a bad instructor, he only valued the external, formal imitative, whereas the real content of what had been expressed in analytic language was not valued. After all, it does not make much difference whether the pupil learns the rules of the language in a newspaper article or in a philosophical work. With regard to the content, however, it makes all the difference.

In other words, in the course of the development of psychoanalysis, analytic doctrine has already become *material* to be analyzed, just as much as every other kind of material—whether chemical, philosophical, or religious—that the patient uses. Still more important is the application of this viewpoint to the origin and development of analytic theory itself—or more correctly speaking, to the analytic theories that the patient in analysis uses as material for presentation. Even the analyst in elaboration of the theory cannot avoid doing this. He is easily tempted to interweave the patient's presentation of analytic material into his theory. And every investigator, obviously according to his personality and development, uses something else. Freud uses biological sexuality as *material* for presentation of a psychological theory; Jung uses ethics; Adler and Stekel use the constructive or destructive social element.

So far nothing could be said against this inevitable use of material, if only one is conscious—or ultimately becomes so—of what one really is doing with it. When Freud uses biologic material, may we not draw from this the conclusion that the psychology he constructed is biologically based? If Jung uses ethics as material, may we not draw from this the conclusion that he has produced a synthetic psychology, as he claims in his doctrine of types? The synthetic element is as much one factor in psychical life as the analytic or the constructive and destructive but is not the *psychical* itself, which only in its function is conceivable and, hence, is scarcely to be comprehended.

The psychoanalytic doctrine and movement has thus reached a point where it *itself* has become a psychological problem. As such, it leads at the same time to a new psychology and with it to a real worldview produced as a sediment from the solution of this problem. After overcoming materialistic, ethical, and social ideologies, a metapsychoanalytic psychology must be constructed. This psychology would deal only with tendencies and their effects. On this account it should value the material necessarily used in no other way than in its psychical significance. In separating out from the different ideologies what is foreign to the emotional, the psychical content itself crystallizes and in its turn throws a new light on the biological, ethical, and social aspects of psychology.

This natural process of development leads psychoanalytic theory and ultimately proves to be a way—or more correctly a detour—a way back to a philosophic theory of cognition. It concerns also the therapeutic aspect, which finally led to the admission that the neuroses are not a medical but an ethical problem. The two chief problems of philosophy—cognition and ethics—thus finally also represent the main problems with which psychoanalysis is really occupied, because they represent the chief problems of human psychical life.

Fundamentally, they correspond to a single great problem: the contrast between I and Thou, self and world, inner and outer. The theory of cognition attempts to determine the relationship between inner and outer, appearance and being, phantasy and reality. Ethics tries to determine the more particular relationship of I to other similar I's, thus to Thou. The psychological manifestations of these facts, to which belong all philosophical and psychological theories as well as all individual expressions of our psychical life, may be treated under the title of an I-Psychology and a Thou-Psychology.

The problem of inner and outer leads us back again to the material of psychology. We can best of all discuss this in relation to the two basic problems of psychoanalysis: anxiety and guilt. Anxiety originally relates to something external, an object or a situation; whereas guilt is, so to say, an inner anxiety, a being afraid of itself [*Angst vor sich selbst*].[8]

Anxiety is thus a biological concept,[9] guilt an ethical concept. So the great problem of inner and outer in a scientific sense could be formulated as the problem of biology versus ethics (or the reverse): in other words, as *the great conflict between our biological and our purely human self.*

Therapy of every kind operates only insofar as this conflict, manifesting itself as an ethical one, is partially or temporarily adjusted. We accomplish this either by strengthening or weakening the inner or the outer: in other words, unburdening the inner conflict by externalizing it or building up the inner, namely, constructing the I. To these attempts at unburdening or reconstructing belong the individual analysis of neurotics—as well as all of psychoanalysis as a movement—and religion, art, war. Art unburdens in the catharsis (for example, tragedy), religion in the cult, analysis in the leader. On the other hand, all these have their constructive effects: art in its development as an expression of personality, religion in its development toward ethics, analysis in its guidance to self-knowledge and self-responsibility.

In the whole development of humanity, as I already pointed out in *The Artist* (1907), and later in *The Trauma of Birth* (1924), one can notice an increasing tendency to *internalization*, which is temporarily interrupted by reactions of *externalization*. Naturally these are always of a social nature. They take on a more destructive form in war and revolution, in religious sects, or a more constructive nature in the forms of technical inventions. In any case, these externalizations are always mass movements, whereas the tendency to internalize has an individualistic character, proceeds from single individuals, and aims at the individualization of persons.

Psychology, in relation to this view, adopts a particular attitude. It is purely individualistic, aims at knowledge of I, of the internal, but also uses in its material data concerning the external—reality, Thou. Thus it is in essence a science of relations [*Beziehungswissenschaft*] which easily runs into the danger of overestimating either one or the other factor, instead of dealing with the *relationship* between the two.

In psychoanalysis this has been the case to a very large degree. Psychoanalysis began as the psychology of the unconscious which, however, was not directly inferred intuitively from one's own I, but, as it were, by a detour through another. This other was a patient, that is, an individual in whom one side of the problem entered strongly in the foreground—whether one saw in it the biological (sexual) problem or the ethical (guilt) problem. The strength of psychoanalysis lay in this starting point, but in the course of its development it has become more and more a weakness and has led to ever greater one-sidedness.

It is perhaps no accident that parallel with the inward trend of psychoanalysis, with the advance in knowledge of the individual, it has taken on the character of an external movement—if one likes, a mass movement. This externalizing trend was a counterbalance against the threatening danger of a too-far-reaching introversion. To this may be added that Freud, creator of such an inward-turning tendency—which aims at increasing individualization, whether of a religious, artistic, or scientific nature—still needs entry to the group, to the mass, for his justification.

Here we come up against the problem of guilt-feeling in the *creative* individual[10]—and we already find it in its rudiments at a quite primitive organic stage. At that stage, as I already mentioned in *The Artist*, the individual's tendency to develop—striving for independence of the external world—leads to division at the ultimate limit of growth. This division is equivalent to isolation, to disaster—to death. Thus Freud has revealed the guilt-feeling *beyond the pleasure principle*, that is, has shown that in human beings it is not always biological impulses that provide the driving force, but, from a definite point of development, it is inhibition, anxiety, and guilt. If we analyze further, we discover *beyond the guilt-feeling*—which seems insurmountable—the problem of individuality, of difference.

At the *biological* level all deviation from the normal, manifested as change, brings first of all a danger—the danger of nonsurvival or death—before it can be borne in single individuals as development. At the *psychological* level this phenomenon manifests itself as fear—of danger, failure, death—in essence as fear of the other, who interferes with the unfolding of one's own self. At the *ethical* level we see the same state appearing as the guilt problem, that is, as anxiety at the free development of one's own I that seems to bring about danger, ruin, or death to the other [*als Angst vor dem eigenen Ich dessen freie Entwicklung dem Andern Gefahr, Untergang oder Tod bereiten könnte*].

At this psychical level [*seelischen Stufe*] the significance of the emotional life becomes evident. Death at the biological level is the prototype of separation. Anxiety also separates, isolates one individual from the other. But there is already shown a uniting effect, namely, the trend toward *group formation*, the mutual and temporary protection against danger. Guilt-feeling unites I to other—as does emotion in general—the essence of which I would like to designate as that which unites the human being with other human beings. In socialization this union takes place with the mutually guaranteed protection of all against all; in love, with pleasurable identification with the other.

The more we individualize ourselves—that is, remove and isolate ourselves from others—the stronger is the formation of guilt-feeling that originates from this individualization and that again in turn unites us emotionally with others. This is the psychological basis of our ethical socialization. But with the increasing tendency toward individualization, this social bond is not sufficient. The individual needs a stronger, more personal relationship that strengthens the guilt-feeling and so emotionally unites the individual to another. At this psychical level the uniting element is love—which finally in its fulfillment unites again biologically the individual with the other and thus with the species.

Whereas sexuality in the biological sense signifies in essence growth and multiplication—if one likes, the preservation of the individual in the species through reproduction—love has the function of uniting emotionally the individual as such, the personality, with the other individual. In this way the feeling of the individual's isolation—leading to anxiety, guilt, and conflict—is removed. In a word: sexuality is biological I-expansion, love is emotional or psychical I-expansion. [*Mit einem Worte: die Sexualität ist biologische Ich-Erweiterung, die Liebe ist gefühlsmäßige oder seelische Ich-Erweiterung.*] Hence we understand why in our love life the ethical—the guilt problem—is of equal importance to the biological. But only in this way can we also understand all disturbances, problems, and conflicts that are produced from this—and with the alleviation and solving of which psychoanalysis as a therapy is concerned.

For even the neurosis has been revealed in its ultimate analysis as an ethical problem. The individual, separated chiefly by anxiety and bound to fellow human beings only by guilt, has to be united again with humanity and the world biologically as well as socially, through love. This I consider the real task of psychotherapy.

It is a long way from the medical therapy of nervous disturbances, which Freud at first wanted to heal by a kind of sexual dietetics, to the understanding of neurosis as a guilt problem. It is the fundamental difference between two opposite worldviews, the materialistic and philosophic—in a more specific sense, the biological and ethical. Psychoanalysis has pushed forward far in both directions but has failed to see the problem in its full bearing and significance, much less to solve it. But we are grateful to psychoanalysis for bringing up this primal problem again, and for opening up new ways toward its understanding, perhaps to a better solution of it.[11]

Notes

Read before the Boston Society of Psychiatry and Neurology, April 19, 1928.

1. By *das Seelische* Rank means four related "psychical" phenomena: consciousness, emotional experience, feeling, and willing. The *seelisch* always occur in the *present*. "The psychic [*das Seelische*] is so much a phenomenon of the present," said Rank in *Will Therapy*, "that the individual actually can think and perceive all the past only as present, as the dream teaches so clearly. Thinking and feeling, consciousness and willing can always be only in the present" (1929–31, p. 38).

2. See note 1. Throughout his later writings, Rank used *seelisch* and *das Seelische* virtually as synonyms for *Erlebnis*, "living" itself.

3. In almost the same terms, Hans Loewald has written: "Guilt and atonement are crucial motivational elements of the self. Guilt then is not a trouble-

some affect that we might hope to eliminate in some fashion, but one of the *driving forces* in the organization of the self" (quoted in Wallwork 1991, p. 97n.35, italics added).

4. In *Technik der Psychoanalyse: Vol. I. Die Analytische Situation.* (Leipzig and Vienna: Franz Deuticke, 1926c). This work has never been published in English. "My analysis of the 'analytic situation,'" Rank said in *Psychology and the Soul*, "has shown that the therapeutic agent is simply *present experience*, and not a historical understanding in which the 'therapeutic' effect seems to consist of the displacement of certain actual impulses *from* present experience" (1930b, p. 176; his italics).

5. See "The Role of the Therapist in the Therapeutic Situation," in *Will Therapy* (1929–31, pp. 167–83).

6. See *Truth and Reality* (1929). "The only 'trueness' in terms of actual psychic reality," said Rank, "is found in emotion, not in thinking, which at best denies or rationalizes truth, and not necessarily in action unless it follows from feeling and is in harmony with it" (ibid., p. 40). The compulsive neurotic, continued Rank, "must then explain, motivate, understand, rationalize, justify each of his acts of will, whether positive or negative, instead of simply affirming them, which makes *homo sapiens* into that thought specialist among living beings" (ibid., pp. 45–46).

7. Instead of learning this "soulful" language, according to Sandor Rado, analysts in the 1920s looked only for "signs of the castration complex, oedipal conflicts, narcissism, oral and anal eroticism" in the patient's free associations (Roazen and Swerdloff 1995, p. 82). "The characteristic of that time," remembers Rado, who was in analysis with Karl Abraham from 1922 to 1925, "was a neglect of a human being's emotional life" (ibid.). The analyst's "listening to the patient as well as the patient's productions of thoughts were oriented by theories" rather than emotional experience (ibid., p. 78). In her memoir of analysis with Anna Freud during the early 1930s, Esther Menaker recalls, "On the one hand, I was supposedly permitted to express whatever came to mind; on the other, I was made to feel that I was saying the wrong thing or revealing some very pathological part of myself" (Menaker 1989, p. 41).

8. In a 1911 talk before the Vienna Psychoanalytic Society, Freud said, "Any anxiety is fear of oneself, of one's libido" (Lieberman 1985, p. 135). One month later, during a discussion of masturbation, Rank observed that anxiety "takes on the disguise of a feeling of guilt and becomes capable of attracting other feelings of guilt." To this Victor Tausk added that Rank was just elaborating on an earlier remark by Freud, who had once said casually, "The sense of guilt is anxiety that has been bound" (ibid.).

9. By "biological," Rank is alluding to birth and the maternal object. Rank later minimized biological interpretations of anxiety, adopting a more explicitly existential language. *Angst*, he said in *Will Therapy*, is "a dividing line between the I and the world, and vanishes only when both have become one, as parts of a greater whole" (1929–31, p. 198)—in love or art, for example.

10. Rank's view that creativity—like neurosis—leaves *guilt* in its wake is found nowhere else in the psychoanalytic literature. It is a corollary of his central premise, the essence of all his post-Freudian thinking on creativity, which he

stated most clearly in *Truth and Reality*: "In a word, will and guilt are the two complementary sides of one and the same phenomenon" (1929, p. 31). The guilt of the neurotic, an *artiste manqué*—a failed artist—is a form of thrown-back responsibility for failing to accept the burden of willing, of difference. But how does this apply to the artist? Why is the *most* creative person also "guilty"? What is "creative guilt"?

"This conception of the creative will as a victory of the individual over the biological sexual instinct," Rank said in *Truth and Reality*, "explains the guilt which the development and affirmation of the creative personality necessarily produces" (1929, p. 69). Paradoxically, continued Rank, "it is this going *beyond* the limits set by nature as manifested in the will accomplishment to which the [artist] reacts with guilt. Only this guilt reaction makes completely intelligible the projection of the God idea by means of which the individual again subjects him to a higher power" (ibid., italics added). The greatest artists, according to Rank, spend their entire lives negotiating with the mystery of "the Beyond" (Kramer 1995).

11. A large audience heard this lecture: 137 members of the Boston Society and guests (Lieberman 1985, p. 437). The lecture was chosen by White and Jelliffe as the lead article in the January 1929 issue of *The Psychoanalytic Review*, 16:1–11.

19

THE YALE LECTURE (1929)

(THE PSYCHOLOGICAL APPROACH TO
PERSONAL PROBLEMS)

LADIES AND GENTLEMEN, when I was invited to speak before this group, I felt I had a difficult task in front of me, and I want to begin my talk this evening by confessing that, after spending the afternoon in looking around this university, I am even more aware of the difficulties in speaking to you on this topic.[1]

First of all, I feel more like being a student myself again instead of someone who is going to deliver a lecture to you for, after having seen the scientific work that is being done here in some of your departments, I feel that what I intend to tell you may seem rather superficial and not very "scientific." At least on the surface it may have that appearance.

When I arrived, I was presented with a long list of questions compiled by the [Psychology] Department which may come up in discussion. These naturally refer to the therapeutic problem, which I must confess is the most crucial point in the whole field of psychotherapy and psychoanalysis.

When I explain a mechanism or a symptom to a patient, the immediate reply is, "All right, I see it, but what am I going to do about it?" Then I say, "You must be patient, you must wait and see, I cannot predict anything, I can only tell you what you are doing, but not what you are *going* to do." So I must ask your patience and tolerance when in introducing this lecture I begin by telling you in a few words how I view the general situation in the field of psychoanalysis at the present time.

I think I have a particular right to talk about this matter, since I grew up, as it were, with the whole psychoanalytic movement. I first got in touch with Freud in 1905 and then began to study psychoanalysis under his guidance. I have been with him and with the psychoanalytic movement for about twenty years, from 1905 to 1925. Not only have I watched the whole movement from inside, as it were behind the curtain, but I also took an active part in it. For more than ten years, I was editor of the psychoanalytic journals [*Imago* and *Zeitschrift*] and secretary of the Vienna Psychoanalytic Society. For several years I was vice-president of the society. Maybe, sometime after I have retired, I will write a history of the psychoanalytic movement from a scientific viewpoint, but this is not what I intend to tell you tonight.

Psychoanalysts are often accused of being able to make something out of anything, so I will take the title and analyze it: "The Psychological Approach to Personal Problems," a title that I choose just because it does not seem to make much difference what the title is.

This title itself shows the progress that psychology has made in the last few years, or in the last decade, because only from a dynamic point of view are we justified, I think, in talking about the approach to personal problems. Personality, at least as I conceive of it, is something that is dynamic. Freud's psychology, which in the beginning had the appearance of being a dynamic psychology, in my opinion is dynamic only when compared with the psychology prior to him.[2] It is not, I think, dynamic compared with the psychology that we can foresee developing in the near future out of the psychoanalytic movement. With Freud, the driving force, any kind of impulsion in the individual, is biological. He conceives it only biologically, which means even in its highest sense, a kind of *procreative* impulse, but not a real *creative* driving force, of which I think personality consists.

On the other hand the two important deviations from the Freudian school—represented by Jung and Adler—certainly went beyond this; but I think that both Jung and Adler, each in his own way, went too far in one particular direction. Jung stressed the racial factor. He traces it back to a racial source, or whatever you like to call it, and his psychology is derived from that concept, being chiefly a psychology of types, although he differentiates more than Freud does. I do not believe it *sufficiently* individualized, however, to explain the personal problems that we have to deal with in neurotic or even creative types.

Adler, on the other hand, stressed another aspect of the problem. His psychology, although he calls it "individual psychology," is a social psychology; in other words, he is socially oriented. He wants to adjust the individual to circumstances, whereas Freud tries to reform the individual according to the normal standard, a standard that he derived from some theoretical concept of normality. But neither Freud, nor Jung, nor Adler sufficiently considers the creative part of our personality, namely, that which is not purely biological as Freud sees it, nor purely racial as Jung conceives it, nor yet purely social as Adler thinks, but which is *purely individual*. This I consider the most important part not only for the understanding of personality but also for the therapeutic approach, and also for the individual's adaptation.

It may interest you to know, as it also interested me when I had a chance to look back on my own development, that already in 1905 when I first came in contact with Freud and his theory, my first reaction was a little book, *The Artist*, in which I pointed out this lack in the Freudian theory. What I called the artist in that book was something other than the man who actually paints. I meant by *artist* the creative personality; and using Freud's psychology and terminology, I tried to explain this creative type—but I found it was impossible without going beyond Freud.

The chief difference already showing itself in my book at that time was that, in contrast to Freud, I emphasized not the biological and external factors, but this *inner* self of the individual, whatever you want to call it: something in the individual himself that is creative, that is impelling, that is not taken in from without but grows somehow within.[3] Please do not mind if I am a little vague about this. I think you will understand what I mean in general, and it would lead us too far if I tried to point out more specifically what I mean. Maybe I will be able at the end of the lecture to formulate it more specifically and more definitely. It is a kind of mental principle, if you like, contrasted with the biological principle on which Freud's psychology is based. There is one fundamental distinction I would like to emphasize here, which leads us into the midst of our discussion on psychology in general and psychotherapy in particular.

Freud started out as a psychiatrist,[4] as a therapist. He saw neurotic patients whom he wanted to help. He soon found he could not do that with what he had learned in his psychiatry, so he developed his own approach and technique with which you are more or less familiar. So far, so good. But in trying to help his patients, he had first to understand them, and if we could follow the development of Freudian psychology, we would see quite definitely that certain phases of theoretical investigation and research alternated in Freud's development with their therapeutic application. In reality it was not so, because actually he had to carry out *both* simultaneously.

From his writings, however, one gets the impression that after he had concentrated for some time on research and gotten as much as he could from it in the way of understanding, he tried to apply this new understanding to therapy. Then he found new practical problems and went back to this laboratory, as it were, and investigated again and applied again. Only in his case, it was all one and the same thing. His patients were in his room and he had to be at the same time therapist and researcher, which is quite a job! He accomplished a great deal in both fields, but this unfortunate combination became increasingly a difficulty and an obstacle. For, in the course of time, at least as I see it now, therapy and theory became mixed up,[5] so that his research was not unbiased. It could not be, no matter how much he tried to be objective, because he had one definite task in front of him, namely, to help his patients with the results of his investigation.

Here was a patient whom he had to change, and not only change as he wanted (somewhat like a guinea pig), but to change him according to certain social and ethical standards, to make him fit into our society. Freud's psychology was not unbiased, his psychology was a means of adjusting his patients to a definite given situation.

If we look at this problem from the purely psychological side, we can find an illustration of this in certain departments here at Yale. In all research work, the observer, the investigator, tries to keep out of the picture as much as he can in order to get objective results. Freud could not do that because he himself was in the midst of the picture, in fact was the *center* of the picture. Therefore, he constantly, however unintentionally, influenced the patient's reactions. All the emotions he saw were directed toward him, were reactions to him. I do not think it was possible—and this is not a criticism but a statement—for one man to combine the two things, namely theory and therapy. I think it is too big a task for one man to accomplish at the same time.

On the other hand, if we look upon psychology as a science for the understanding of the human individual, then we must say that this psychology, this science, this insight should be unbiased, should be objective. In other words, psychology [i.e., theory] should *not* be based on a therapeutically oriented attitude. The therapist whose first concern is for his patient cannot develop a real psychology, and the psychologist ought not to attempt to be a therapist at the same time. I can only mention here, without giving any details, that it was my own analytic experiences that led me to this conception, this attitude toward therapy and psychology. I tried to *separate* the two, therapy and theory, as much as possible, and to develop a therapy from a purely therapeutic standpoint, not with the idea of researching new things about human behavior from a patient, but just helping to put him on his own feet. On the own hand, I tried to do research *regardless* of any therapeutic results. In this way I was able to work out both a psychology that I think is more objective and also a therapy that I think is more effective.

Of course, I do not expect you to take my word for it, but in this short lecture I can only give you my personal attitude. This therapy of mine does not undertake to explain the individual to himself. In other words, in the course of psychoanalytic or therapeutic sessions, I do not explain my psychology to the patient but rather I let him develop himself, express himself. The psychology, I think, can even interfere with the patient's development. This state of affairs is illustrated, for instance, in a certain neurotic type that we see nowadays, particularly in this country. This type already suffers from too much introspection, and I do not think we can help these patients by making them more aware of their mechanisms. They need something else. They need an *emotional* experience.[6]

It was, I think, in 1921 when I first definitely tried to point out the necessity of separating the therapeutic aspect of psychoanalysis from the theory in a book that has been translated into English under the title *The Development of Psychoanalysis* [Ferenczi and Rank 1924].

So, I repeat, my approach to personal problems does not aim at the individual's complete understanding of himself as the Freudian theory does. Also it does not try, to the extent that the Adlerian School does, to adjust different individuals, at any cost, to our social situation. My aim is rather to enable the individual first to find himself and then to develop himself. I say first of all to find himself regardless of his future adjustment. Only afterward can he see how he fits in, because otherwise one would crush him before he gets a chance to come out of himself. Then, of course, after having achieved that, one may find that the patient has achieved more than one primarily intended.

For, I think, the neurotic type presents to us not simply an individual who has failed to adjust himself to social demands, but an individual who is a *failure of a creative type*. There were two extremes in him, and if he is able to develop himself, then he may become almost supernormal rather than normal—at least that is the experience I have had. It also seems to me that if the therapist achieves a real therapeutic result, the patient will not only be able to adjust himself but sometimes he *adjusts the circumstances to himself*—which means *creation*. At the same time, he uses his creative power to build himself up. In other words, in his therapeutic experience, when trying to free his creative ability, his chief job, so to speak, is to create himself and then to go on and create externally; whereas all other methods of psychotherapy, the Freudian, Jungian, or Adlerian, try to adjust the individual to a certain given standard, whether it be social, biological, or normal. Therefore, their respective psychologies are normally or socially or medically oriented, or whatever you like to call it, instead of being oriented according to the individual himself.

Now the last phase of this development, which I have reached quite recently, is this: there seems to be almost no psychology left. I mean by this that in human psychology, *each individual, as it were, has his own psychology*. This may sound to you rather bold, and I do not intend to elaborate this idea here. But there is something else I want to emphasize. It is that in every case of psychotherapy of neurosis I now develop a kind of ad hoc technique. To each particular case I apply no general therapy or theory. I let the patient work out his own psychology, as it were, and apply to his psychology a kind of ad hoc therapeutic approach.[7]

Those of you who are familiar with Bleuler's psychology may remember that he has described a mechanism that I consider very useful: the "chance apparatus." (In German we say *Gelegenheit Apparat*.) By this he means that the individual, when faced with any kind of new situation, develops ad hoc all sorts of defenses, protections, in a word, progressive mechanisms to fit the situation, and he gives them up again if the situation is changed. Bleuler did not carry this concept any further and, while I did not start from this concept, the idea of the individual's spontaneous adaptation may lead—it certainly led me—to a complete revolution in the whole field of psychology and psychotherapy.

Our psychology—including Freud's, Jung's, and Adler's—still thinks in terms of type, more or less in terms of individual patterns, universal mechanisms, in terms of "repetition," as Freud calls it. All these may exist, I do not deny that, but they are not important beyond a certain point, because one can see the individual, particularly the neurotic, in a certain situation taking some of those mechanisms and building up something *new* to fit the present situation. In other words, this psychology that I have arrived at is absolutely dynamic; there is nothing static at all. The static may exist, but if the individual is confronted with a new situation—in other words, *with life*—then he constantly builds up new mechanisms, drops them again, and again builds up new ones. And the combination of these reactions seems to me more important than the given factors themselves. It was necessary to learn first about these given factors from the theory of Freud and his school.

This is the picture from the therapeutic angle. Now the theoretical conclusions seem to me even more interesting and more far-reaching. We come—or I come—to the conclusion that psychology, as we have to understand it dynamically when approaching personal problems, does not so much deal with facts as with interpretations—interpretations on the individual's part and on the part of the therapist or psychologist also.

In other words, if we apply this ad hoc idea to the theory itself, then we see that the individual himself is constantly interpreting himself. He continually interprets his given factors, consciously or unconsciously; and his whole adjustment or maladjustment, his whole attitude toward the world, depends upon his interpretation of himself, rather than upon himself—in other words, not so much on what he is but upon what he thinks he is, or what he wants to be, or what he would like to be, or what other people want him to be, and so forth.

In other words, I consider psychology a *science of relations* and inter-relations, or, if you prefer a more modern term, a *science of relativity*.

There is nothing fixed in the field of psychology, everything changes, everything is different at different moments. It is constantly moving. One can only get cross-sections for this particular situation. For instance, a patient may tell you something in one minute, which he says he is sincere in telling, while an hour later he may say to another person something quite different, the opposite of what he said before, and this is again true in this particular situation with regard to this person. It is true, he is not lying, he is not lying in a psychological sense, he is true here to himself and true there to himself. In other words, again it is all a matter of attitude.

Now there is rather an interesting if not amusing aspect of this theory, of this attitude, in that it not only explains, as I think, the individual's reactions much better than any previous psychology, but it also explains the psychologists themselves. We have been wondering how it could be that here is Freud, here Jung, here Adler; yet they each interpret things in the same patient absolutely differently. I believe there have actually been tests made of dreams. I am thinking of the time when material was sent around to different analysts and how the material was interpreted differently by each. Each thinks he is right and the other wrong but they all get results or may get results therapeutically. How is that? It can only be explained, I think, from this point of view: the patient interprets himself in a certain way; if he is neurotic, you can give him something different in the way of interpretation, no matter what it is. It has to be *different* and he will accept it for the time being and it may help him to look on himself in a different way.

Now one last step I am asking you to make with me and it is this. I believe we are now in a phase of psychological investigation of the psychological problem where almost all, or at any rate many, of our psychologists are no longer dealing with facts in trying to understand the individual himself. They are trying to understand the psychological theories of others; they are now interpreting psychologists, as one can see in Jung and Adler who started to interpret Freud. If one interprets Adler, one can easily develop a new psychology. They have been interpreting each other and so new psychologies developed. I think we have to break through this vicious circle, but the only way I can see to do that is not with the general cry "Back to facts" that we have heard lately, because *there are no facts*. The "facts" are interpretations, and it is with those that we have to deal.[8] If we understand that they are interpretations, then we shall not be fooled by them.

Now there is one other way in which we can get back to more sound psychology. As you all may know, psychoanalysis, after having been developed as a therapy and theory, extended its efforts to explain human behavior in fields where previously other scientists had developed theories, for instance in the field of criminology, in the field of economics, in anthropology. In other words, psychoanalysis was "applied," as it was said, to other sciences. The result was not altogether satisfactory.

In the first place, the psychoanalysts lacked the necessary knowledge in the specific fields with which they were dealing; secondly, they tried to interpret too much, to reinterpret this other science in the light of their own terminology. I think what we ought to try to do—if you will allow me to be paradoxical—is to apply all those sciences to psychoanalysis, and not vice-versa, and see what happens then. There will be something left, but I think we will get a much sounder and saner viewpoint.

In other words, I think all those facts that anthropology, sociology, economics, criminology, law, medicine, etc., have accumulated would certainly help to build up this new psychology and would also prevent it from going too far in this constant process of interpretation. For psychology is not the only, and it may even not be the best, way to get at facts regarding the human being, because we are now already too much entangled in this process of interpretation. We cannot get away from interpretation.

As I have only a short time left and want to leave some time for discussion, I will hurry to a conclusion. I want to say something that will throw another light on these problems and will make things look a little more optimistic than I have made them so far. Coming back to the Freudian concept based on a biological worldview, the individual's driving force was considered to be biological even in its highest form. Very soon I found this theory insufficient for myself and I contrasted to it an inner principle, whatever you call it, the individual's *own self-creative power* that also manifests itself ethically [as inhibition, anxiety, or guilt].

Now in the study of neurotic patients, but also of the so-called general human problems, maladjustments, or behavior problems, I came to the conclusion that we human beings today are no longer living on a purely biological principle. We are living on a moral principle. I can give you an illustration. If one studies the neurotic patient carefully, if one analyzes him, one sees that he does not live on account of his self-preservation instincts. Neurotics are all suicidal candidates, more or less, whether they say so or not; they want to die, they do not want to live. They are only living on account of some kind of obligation, they are living because they ought to. They do not live because they want to live, they live because they think they ought to. And I believe this is the most fundamental viewpoint we can take toward individuals. With it, I think we can understand not only all neurotic reactions but all the problems of sexual conflicts, which are all founded in moral conflicts.[9] And last, but not least, we can understand with it our present-day civilization.[10]

Notes

Read before Yale University, Sterling Memorial Hall, February 28, 1929.

1. Probably the first long spontaneous talk in English by Rank, this lecture was recorded on Teletype by a stenographer "with all the errors of a spontaneous talk, for an audience with which he seemed to feel at home" (Taft 1958, p. 138).

2. According to Rank, when the analyst is seen as standing outside the interpersonal field as a neutral observer, "equidistant" from the forces working in the inner life of the patient, the encounter loses its dynamic interpersonal meaning: neither the creative will of the patient nor the creative will of the analyst is recognized, even though both are continuously engaged in sensing, shaping, and clashing with the thoughts and emotions of the other, consciously or unconsciously. The analyst's supposed "neutrality," or *Indifferenz* (in Freud's German), denies the dynamic—i.e., *mutually* creative—nature of the analytic situation. As co-creator with Ferenczi of "active" therapy, Rank seems to have adopted this position almost immediately after beginning his analytic practice in 1919.

3. Freud's superego, according to Rank, is only an inner representative of outer forces—such as the father or society. In *Truth and Reality*, Rank said: "We accept the super-ego [*Über-Ich*] in the Freudian sense, that is, as far as it is built up on identifications. If we add to this 'outer' also the id which is in a certain sense supra-individual [*überindividuelle*] because generic, that which Jung designates in the racial sense as collective unconscious, there remains left over as the actual *own* 'inner' of the individual, his ego, which we have distinguished as bearer of the *creative will*, ... of the conscious personality" (1929, p. 7; italics added).

4. It is surprising that Rank here calls Freud a psychiatrist. He certainly knew that Freud was trained in neurology, not psychiatry. The Yale lecture was not written out before delivery, but this does not explain how Rank could have made such an error, even as a slip of the tongue.

5. In 1922 Freud offered a prize for the best answer to the question, "how far the [analytic] technique has influenced [analytic] theory and how far they assist or hinder each other" (*S.E.*, 17:270). In response to this challenge, Ferenczi and Rank wrote *The Development of Psychoanalysis*, whose subtitle reads: "On the Inter-relationship between Theory and Practice."

According to Ferenczi and Rank, understanding and cure were not the same: the *theory* of analysis was oriented toward understanding the genesis of neurosis, but the technique of *therapy* must focus on change in the present—a problem that analytic theory solved by assuming, without justification, that understanding "the cause" of suffering is identical to curing suffering. Rank here is once again taking up arms against Freud's assertion of a unity between theory (understanding) and therapy (cure). Since 1921, Rank said in *Will Therapy*, he had been criticizing "the reliability of the historic-causal principle which psychoanalysis has held to be the only and unerring path to psychological truth. According to this teaching until I trace a psychic phenomenon back to the past (to the infantile) I have not explained it causally, therefore I have not explained it really. . . . The past is thus held to be safer, more reliable, more capable of being understood than the present" (1929–31, p. 27).

"The methodological error," added Rank, "lay in the fact that the historically real was identified with, or more correctly, was interchanged with, the psychologically true. The psychological [*psychologische*] truth of a psychic [*seelischen*] phenomenon for the individual lies not in its real, but in its symbolic meaning, which is always emotional, as is all the unconscious as such" (ibid., pp. 36–37).

6. In *Will Therapy* Rank distinguished between the "classical" hysteric that Freud saw and the "modern" neurotic:

> Becoming conscious helps the one, while the other is helped by becoming unconscious, that is, by the emotional experience [*Gefühlserlebnis*]. The one suffers from knowing too little, the other from knowing too much . . . an immediate knowing about himself, awareness of his own psychic processes. . . . One must feed the former with truth, the latter with illusions, that is, help to heal his too complete and final disillusionment with self and life. The tragedy is that neither can bear truth or illusion any more because he cannot bear himself as an individual different from others. (1929–31, p. 55)

Unless transformed into creativity, *difference* is the problem. Although Freud cured hysteria, he left the world with the painful problem of consciousness, which he could not solve. Modern neurotics, already hyperconscious of their anxiety, guilt, and despair, "essentially suffer from consciousness" itself, according to Rank, "in that they are too conscious of themselves. To burden them with still more consciousness [i.e., insight] as the purely analytic therapy does [is] to make their condition worse. What they need is an emotional experience [*Gefühlserlebnis*] which is intense enough to lighten the tormenting self-consciousness" (ibid., p. 52).

7. "In each separate case," said Rank in *Will Therapy*, "it is necessary to create, as it were, a theory and technique made for the occasion [*ad hoc geschaffene*] without trying to carry over this individual solution to the next case. . . . [T]he essential factor remains always the capacity to understand the individual from himself [*aus sich heraus zu verstehen*], in which process the common human element, certainly not to be denied, can constitute only the hypothesis, not the content of the understanding" (1929–31, pp. 3–4).

8. Steeped in the writings of Nietzsche, Rank here seems to be virtually quoting from memory a famous passage from Nietzsche: "Against positivism, which stops with phenomena—'there are only *facts*'—I should say: no, precisely facts do not exist, only *interpretations*. We can establish no 'absolute' fact: perhaps it is absurd to wish such a thing" (quoted in Moore 1941, p. 253; Nietzsche's italics).

9. By "moral conflicts," Ranks means *guilt*, or what he called the will-guilt

problem. The neurotic wills himself or herself unfree, Rank believed, perverting the life force itself into its own denial. Although a creative achievement of sorts, the neurosis is a form of "negative will," a person who *denies* himself or herself because of excessive guilt for separation and individuation.

10. At the end of the talk, Rank took questions from the Yale audience. The first was, "What are the criteria for selection of an individual suitable for analysis?" He answered:

> I think in order to decide whether an individual is suitable for psychoanalysis, if you don't mind my putting it paradoxically before I explain it, he should be analyzed first. In other words, you have to have a complete understanding, not only of this individual's psychology, but also of the general situation, of all his external and internal problems.
>
> I will give you an illustration from my own actual experience: A woman comes for consultation; what's the matter with her? She suffers from some kind of intestinal symptoms, painful attacks of some kind of intestinal trouble. She has been sick for eight years, and has tried every kind of physical treatment; she has been x-rayed, examined, dieted, everything under the sun. She came to the conclusion it must be some emotional trouble. She is unmarried, she is thirty-five. She appears to me (and admits it herself) as fairly well adjusted. She lives with a sister who is married; they get along well. She enjoys life, goes to the country in the summer. She has a little stomach trouble; why not keep it, I tell her, because if we are able to take away those attacks that come once in a fortnight or so, we do not know what problem we shall discover beneath it.
>
> Probably this defense mechanism belongs to her adjustment, probably that is the price she has to pay. She never married, she never loved, and so never fulfilled her role. One cannot ever have everything; probably she has to pay. After all, what difference does it make if she occasionally gets these attacks of indigestion? I get it occasionally, you do too, probably, and not for physical reasons, as you may know. One gets headaches. In other words, it is not so much a question as to whether we are able to cure a patient, whether we can or not, but whether we should or not. (Taft 1958, pp. 138–39)

Another question asked if he would elaborate on the use of "limited-time" therapy: "I analyzed first according to Freud's technique and then gradually developed a shorter one, a technique that is getting shorter and shorter, so I am almost afraid that soon I won't have to see the patient at all" (ibid., pp. 139–40). Behind Rank's witticism was a profound point he made in *Will Therapy* about the end phase of analysis: "For no matter whether symptoms appear again or not, the patient always finds himself in doubt in the end phase as to whether or not he is healed, a doubt which in truth the Freudian analyst as a rule shares with him and tends to solve by prolonging the treatment. . . . One of my patients solved this problem after the ending of the treatment, when he remarked that he assumed that he had not been analyzed at all, for otherwise he would always have had to ask whether or not he had been cured" (1929–31, p. 190).

20

NEUROSIS AS A FAILURE IN CREATIVITY

(1935)

LADIES AND GENTLEMEN, our conception of illness, and hence of cure, has changed considerably since modern psychology started to extend its research into the field of therapy. You are all probably more or less acquainted with the valuable contribution psychoanalysis has made to a better understanding not only of mental illness but also of physical suffering. Every practitioner knows cases in which the most careful examination and the most conscientious treatment fail to yield the desired results—and this not only in cases where modern medicine is not yet far enough advanced to secure the much-desired relief. Every doctor in the course of his private practice sees a number of patients whom he feels certain could be helped if only they did not *resist* acceptance of the seemingly sought-for help.

This *resistance to getting well* was explained by Freud as "gain through illness." It is the principal reason why the patient remains sick in spite of the best scientific care, both physical and psychological. We have learned from these cases that the physical treatment must remain ineffective unless the emotional attitude of the patient toward his illness and toward life in general can be changed. The problem of how such a fundamental change of attitude can be effected constitutes the *essence* of modern psychotherapy as I see it developing out of the original psychoanalytic conceptions.

In the earlier days of this new therapeutic movement, when psychoanalysts felt the powerful help lent to their work by what were then considered revolutionary theories, and while the medical profession stood by waiting to see the results of their endeavors, this removal of resistance against getting well had to be entirely left to the psychologically trained specialist. Since then, the medical practitioner himself has become more and more acquainted with those theories that today he almost automatically applies in making his diagnosis. The question at present seems to be whether, and to what extent, the general practitioner may himself attempt to remove, or at least alleviate, the mental and emotional resistance against the physical treatment that he is carrying on. No one doubts that such a combination of treatments would be the ideal for which to strive. At the same time, it seems almost impossible that the practitioner should combine the two functions of organic as well as psychological specialist; yet in cases of functional symptoms, even the old family doctor with his human understanding, supported by the full confidence of his client, was able to help his patients through these crises of resistance.

It is true the medical practitioner cannot afford to go through the highly specialized training necessary for the psychotherapist who has to deal with outspoken cases of neurosis in which physical or rather functional symptoms are obviously the result of mental and emotional conflicts. On the other hand, the early and fundamental psychoanalytic conceptions have been developed to a point where even in cases of neuroses a quick approach to the patient's basic resistance can be made without having to unravel his whole past in a long, drawn-out process.

Before I can indicate to you what this dynamic approach, as I call it, consists of and how it can be therapeutically used, I have to tell you in a few words how I transformed the Freudian theory of resistance to getting well into the human problem of accepting help, and the "gain through illness" into what one may call a philosophy of suffering. Independent experience taught me that the "gain" of illness does not only imply freedom from responsibility and avoidance of adjustment to reality—but that it has a much deeper meaning, rooted in man's basic conception of life. As a result of my experience, I found not only that the illness is nursed by the patient in order to withdraw from life (and not self-inflicted, a kind of punishment as Freud would have it)—it is *self-willed*, a sort of creation that can find expression only in this negative, destructive way.

This evaluation of illness as an expression of the individual's *creative will* leads to a totally different conception of the neurotic, to a rehabilitation I might say, of the neurotic—who has been looked down on since the medieval days of witchcraft and deviltry. This scornful attitude, which even the modern therapist has for the seemingly weak neurotic, goes back, in the last analysis, to the therapist's personal need to make the helpless neurotic a symbol of his own evil and destructive self, just as the patient seeks in the therapist his creative self by means of identification. From this mutual dependence of therapist and neurotic—who represent two *complementary* types—it follows that the real therapeutic agent, the healing factor in psychotherapy, is not psychological self-knowledge and its theoretical formulation, but the therapist *himself*, whom the neurotic wants to use as the positive completion of his predominantly negative self.

In order to use this dynamic relationship of the two complementary types therapeutically, it is necessary to understand the psychic play of forces that underlies it. To the basic biological duality of instinct and fear, which psychoanalysis formerly dealt with exclusively, has to be added the psychological factor par excellence, namely, *the individual will*—which can manifest itself negatively in the form of inhibition (control) as well as positively, as an expression of creative energy. However, this creative force, which I also see at the roots of mental (or imaginative) illness, is not sexuality, as psychoanalysis assumed, but rather an *anti-sexual* tendency in man—which we may characterize as voluntary control of the instinctive life. More precisely stated, I conceive of the creative drive as the impulse-life (including sexuality) put at the service of the individual will.[1]

When psychoanalysis speaks of the sublimation of the sex instinct, by which is meant its diversion from the purely biological function and its direction toward higher goals, the question as to *what* diverts and *what* directs does not seem to be answered by reference to repression—a negative factor that can divert, perhaps, but never direct. Besides, the main question remains open: What originally causes repression? This question, as is well known, was answered by the theory of *external* deprivation, which again is a negative restriction. Contrary to this Freudian explanation—on which the idea of self-punishment as a repetition of punishment from without is based—I assumed, from the very beginning, the existence of a *self-inhibiting* mechanism inherent in the individual. This inhibition of instinct, which operates as a self-preserving protection, I was able later on to define as the individual will. By *will*, I understand an autonomous organization to control primarily the impulsive self; this organization, however, represents the total personality with its constructive capacity not only for ruling, developing, and changing the surrounding world, but for *re-creating* its true self. In this sense, the neurotic—with his potentialities for destruction as well as creation—corresponds much more to the artist who has failed (*artiste manqué*) than to the ordinary type, who has failed to achieve normal development and adjustment to reality.

In the growth of the individual, therefore, we have to reckon with the triad *impulse, fear,* and *will*. The dynamic relation, and interaction, of these factors determines the prevalent attitude of the individual toward himself and the world at any given moment; or, after achievement of some kind of balance, his actual type of temperament and character, which in turn determines his social behavior.

However unsatisfactory it may be to put these dynamic processes into typical formulae, still it is the only way to approximate clarity in this complicated matter. If we compare the neurotic type to the productive, then it would seem that the impulse-life is *too much repressed* with the former; according to whether this neurotic repression is effected by fear or will, we have the picture of *fear* neuroses (hysteria, phobias) or *will* neuroses (compulsion). In the productive type, on the contrary, the will dominates with a far-reaching control and activity, but with no exaggerated repression of the impulse-life; thus the impulse-life, creatively freed both in the imaginative and social spheres, relieves guilt through self-expression. In a third type—the so-called psychopath—to which also the criminal belongs, the impulse-life remains unrepressed, as with the productive, but at the same time uncontrolled; with this type the will is controlled by the impulse-life instead of controlling it. This type, in spite of appearances, is actually *weak*-willed because subject to his instinctual impulses, while the neurotic, contrary to the common conception, really represents the *strong*-willed type—who can exercise his will only negatively, using his will on his own self, which he has cut off from all expression in life. In a word, with the neurotic, fear has the upper hand; with the psychopath, impulse; and with the productive, will. In actuality these extreme types appear mixed, dynamically, and do not remain constant.

On the other hand, it seems clear that a satisfactory love life, of which none of the three types is capable, unites all three factors in a harmonious way. The impulse-life is satisfied in sex, the individual will fulfills itself in the choice and creative transformation of the mate, while fear is overcome by the love emotion. The sense of guilt is also reduced to a minimum because the different tendencies that operate dynamically in the personality are working with instead of against one another. With the psychopath, a guilt reaction usually follows the impulsive action as repentance; with the productive, a sense of guilt usually accompanies his creation, which it can influence in an inhibitive as well as in a stimulating way.

With the neurotic, however, fear and guilt have quite a different origin and meaning. By that I mean that I do not see how neurotic reactions can be explained as psychoanalysis explains them—that is to say, as mere exaggerations or intensifications of the normal. Although one may be tempted to introduce the medical conception of pathology into the sphere of our inner emotional life, I have never been able to see how neurotic reactions of fear and guilt could be alleviated by a therapy striving for a hardly definable "normalcy." However, on the basis of my conception of the will and its operating creatively in the building up of a neurosis, it becomes evident that the individual not only brings about his illness but also its prerequisites, fear and guilt. The general formulation, which we recognize time and again in every case of neurosis, can be thus presented: instead of affirming or asserting his will, the neurotic has to find an excuse to prove to himself as well as to others his inability or incapability. *Instead of saying, "I don't want to do that," he says, "I cannot do it, because I am afraid or feel guilty."*

This formulation contains the whole problem of neurosis in a nutshell, especially when we add that in order to use unbearable fear and guilt as a real excuse to himself, the neurotic has to really experience them, to put up a straw man that he can use at will. It goes without saying that in order to create pathological emotions of that kind the neurotic must constitutionally deviate from the average; but even with regard to this constitutional factor, I should like to make a distinction between two kinds of neurotic types, who differ not only in their symptoms and the gain and suffering from them but also in prognosis and the subsequent treatment required. The one type is constitutionally neurotic, whatever that may mean; the other is essentially creative and becomes neurotic only because of *misdirected creativity*—be it through exclusive concentration on himself and his self-creation or through carrying his imaginative creation into the reality of life, with which it is bound to clash. The first, the neurotic type, whose creativity remains fixed on his own self, never gets to the point of constructively objectifying his productivity in work and can only be helped by being freed to do so; the second, the creative type, who gets caught in his struggle with life and not only with himself, we can aid by separating the two spheres of life and imagination more definitely and hence allow him to operate better in both realms.

Fortunately, I find myself here in a position to bring to bear the weight of testimony from the greatest psychologist in modern times, Nietzsche. The latter not only anticipated Freud and his psychology of repression, inferiority, and resentment but also anticipated our social and spiritual crisis, which he analyzed in a masterly fashion on the basis of a *relative* psychology of different groups, nations, and classes. At the same time, he himself, through his suffering, illustrates this process of self-created illness; he understood that it was more than self-inflicted punishment.

Nietzsche not only affirmed his lifelong illness but actually glorified it, because he discovered through his own experience that *becoming* well is of greater value than *being* well; that is to say, more constructive, indeed in a certain sense creative. In describing his own recovery, he wrote: "I took myself in hand, I myself made myself sound again. This presupposes that one is sound at bottom. An essentially morbid type cannot become well, still less make himself well, while for an essentially sound type, on the contrary, illness can even become a powerful stimulant to continued and heightened living."

Nietzsche not only recognized in himself the usual experience of the artist type who very often seems to be driven by illness and suffering to creative compensation in work; he also sensed the deeper truth that *both illness and work are the expression of the creative will in the individual.* From my own therapeutic experience, I learned that in cases of so-called self-inflicted illness, the individual really strives for a *re-cre-*

ation of the self and is blocked at the first step toward it—that is, in his attempt to destroy the old self. But even when the individual succeeds in emerging from this chaotic state of reformation, the result is not only self-healing, that is to say, health according to the individual's own will. It is much more and something more profound. Nietzsche, through his self-healing, became not well but *creative*; that is, was able to detach his productivity from his own bodily self and express it spiritually through the development of his personality in his work.

When we turn now from the creative type back to our present subject, the neurotic type, we see that his productivity remains exclusively confined to his own ego and manifests itself chiefly in negative expression. This implies first of all that he is unable to accept his self and has to reform it, to improve it; not so much according to an ideal that he may put up for himself as does the creative type, but chiefly because he feels that he is bad, inferior, wrong. On this negative basis, he is compelled to use his will to remodel himself; that is to say, *he wills himself different*—whereas, with the productive type, it is the *creative urge* emerging from the *total personality* that affects change by development and growth, and *not* by will. The willing of the change is bound to fail, first of all because it cannot be willed as long as will is opposed to the rest of the self and hence becomes negative.

From this it follows that the neurotic is hopelessly caught in the process of remodeling the given self into a willed ego. Then how can he be helped to extricate himself from this internal struggle from which he seemingly does not want to be liberated? To the first-mentioned reason of avoiding responsibility by remaining ill, we can now add another more profound reason that makes the neurotic resist sooner or later any attempt at cure. It is his need to express his will, and since he has no other medium than his own self, he exercises his creativity in that way. Hence it is less important for him than it seems to be that he should be really cured—because very often his life would lose its whole meaning if he attained his goal. He not only would lose something to fight against and to struggle with—as a substitute for real life—but he would also lose the only thing he has to play with, namely, himself and his neurosis. Besides, to the neurotic, the attainment of any definite goal means the end, in the sense of death, even though this goal may be the end of a therapeutic treatment with health as its reward.

This explains why in any kind of psychotherapy the *ending* of the therapeutic process is the most difficult task for the therapist and demands a skill that comes only through vast experience. The most important thing I learned in my whole career as a psychotherapist was that in order to achieve a satisfactory solution at the end one has to carefully prepare for it right from the *beginning* and work for it during the whole process. In doing so, one has to watch the patient's own attempts to help himself to get well, although very often these efforts manifest themselves as resistances to the treatment, that is, as resistance to accepting help from the therapist. One of the fundamental conflicts that is repeated by the neurotic in the therapeutic relationship is his struggle against overdependence and his fight for an independence he would not be able to bear even if attained.

I should like to illustrate these willful reactions in the patient during the course of treatment with regard to three essential situations: the initial situation, the end situation, and the transitional process between the two. The patient's very appeal for help usually signifies an autonomous step on his part to get well. It happens not infrequently that the patient unknowingly precipitates the crisis that forces him to seek the help that hitherto he has resisted. Such behavior, consequently, is nothing but a manifestation of his general attitude toward the neurosis— which he created in order to avoid responsibilities and his weakness. That is to say, he always seems to know how far he can let his neurosis go—to be able, as it were, to control it when faced with real disaster. If this self-induced crisis, which often initiates the treatment, is not taken at its face value, but merely as a necessary exaggeration on the part of the patient—as a step toward surrender—then additional difficulties can be avoided, difficulties that might otherwise repeat themselves in the course of treatment.

But even when this initial resistance is disposed of therapeutically, there comes a phase during treatment when the patient feels improved and is—again willfully—testing the validity of the cure by revealing some of his old, or even new, symptoms. He may do this to defeat the therapist, as a proof that it was not the therapist who helped him; he may also do it in order to prove to himself that he has the power to arrest his symptoms as well as reproduce them. Here again, as in the initial situation, we meet with the *fundamental conflict* of dependence-independence—the patient being desirous of showing that he can help himself and that he does not need from the other the help that he will not accept.

The third and more serious resistance of this order emerges in the end situation—where it is not so much a question in the patient's mind whether he is cured or still sick but whether he can *accept* the cure proffered by the other. Especially in cases where a rather quick result is achieved by therapeutic handling of the fundamental resistances, it becomes obvious that it is the patient's pride that stands in the way of his acceptance. How, he asks himself, can such a complicated and well-constructed neurosis of long duration be removed in such a short time by somebody else? He seems to feel that it cannot be done, and to prove it he usually gets worse when the end of even the most successful treatment approaches. He evidently does so for another reason also, and that is to prolong his dependence and the fight against it that has replaced his neurotic struggle.

If we are to sum up the therapeutic experience derived from insight into the workings of these fundamental resistances, we get a first glimpse into the human significance of *neurosis as a general resistance to coercion,* which this type feels exercised upon him by Nature herself.[2] The neurotic's whole attitude toward life betrays a tendency to control external coercion inflicted upon him not only by his fellow men but by Nature herself. *All neurotic reactions can be thus reduced to one Big No that men hurl at life.*

Let us not forget at this point, however, that all human civilization springs from a similar spirit to conquer nature; we know only too well that not a few of the pioneers in spiritual or material conquest have been rather close to neurosis. Yet the neurotic type starts by saying no to life itself, and furthermore he manifests his rebellion against it by further noes, that is, by setting his negative will against the laws of nature, or practically against his own *being.* It is of therapeutic interest, in this connection, that the neurotic patient extends this willful control—which is far from being autonomous—to the sought-for therapeutic process, which he soon feels and reacts against as a coercion. Furthermore, he extends that same attitude even to certain medications that are supposed to be remedies for his ills. I have seen innumerable cases of nervous indigestion, insomnia, and the like, in which the patient used the medicine as a willful means of controlling even his bodily functions. And no relief from drugs, medicines, or other bad habits—including neurosis—can be achieved without considering this, without therapeutically changing this fundamental attitude of a type who tries constantly to dominate nature within himself instead of without. In using creative imagination—instead of negative will—in order to change the world according to his own ideals, lies the essential difference between success and failure.

Notes

Read before the California Academy of Medicine, San Francisco, February 9, 1935.

1. "I understand by will," said Rank in *Will Therapy,* "a positive guiding organization . . . of self which utilizes creatively, as well as inhibits and controls, the instinctual drives" (1929–31, pp. 111–12n.1). "There really is no such concept as 'will' in Freud," recalled the Wolf Man in an interview shortly before he

died in 1979. "For Freud will is drive. But actually, it's the opposite, it is the capacity to repress the drive and to do what is rational. Which would mean that drive does not equal will" (Oberholzer 1982, p. 94).

2. In *Beyond Psychology* Rank saw neurosis "as the result of an excessive control on the part of the individual's will over his own nature. In brief, neurosis is the result of willing the spontaneous, which in other words amounts to an attempt to solve the conflict between freedom and determinism in actual life instead of on paper" (1941, p. 48). Since both freedom and determinism are valid, suggests Rank, no resolution of their contradiction is possible in *Erlebnis* "actual life."

21

ACTIVE AND PASSIVE THERAPY (1935)

LADIES AND GENTLEMEN, social work in its beginning was an active enterprise, an endeavor to help, to bring relief, to do something about the client's difficult or desperate situation. The development of this initial movement into present-day social work, with its emphasis on the psychological causes of maladjustment in the individual himself, is best presented in Virginia Robinson's book *A Changing Psychology in Social Case Work* [Chapel Hill: University of North Carolina Press, 1930].

Psychiatry—just as social work—originally had the aim to do something immediate for and to the patient in order to alleviate his suffering or improve his condition. Then came psychoanalysis, which was developed by Freud as a method of research, of patient and passive investigation into the client's unconscious—in order to detect the hidden roots of his troubles without the easy use of hypnosis. At first the therapist was *active* and the patient *passive*: the therapist had to urge and press his client to try to remember certain forgotten events and associations. Later on, with development of the so-called method of free association, the therapist became more *passive* and the patient took a more active— although, on the whole, still passive—part in the process.

This early period of passivity—one might almost say mutual passivity, since the patient also was *not allowed* any active manifestation of himself—was seemingly a cautious reaction against *too much* activity on the part of the psychiatrist, who was too eager to do something about his case.

Actually, this passivity was born from the necessity for *research*, for a better understanding of the workings of the unconscious mind, which Freud hoped to use later on *therapeutically*. Unfortunately, his interest in the material produced by his patients under the spell of the free association method took him further and further away from his therapeutic task.

Freud's interpretation of the material produced by his neurotic patients in the analytic situation led him to building up a highly complicated theory of the unconscious. He found this necessary to explain the strange reactions of his patients. At the same time, he found the same explanations to be the *therapeutic* factor in the analytic situation. Although we know now that this was a vital error, the discussion of this intellectualization of therapy is of historical interest because it shows the gradual shifting from too much passivity to quite definite active interferences on the part of the therapist. Freud himself found not infrequently that bringing the unconscious material into consciousness was insufficient to produce the desired therapeutic effect and occasionally felt forced to use quite active commands and prohibitions. Yet he felt apologetic about it, as if he had betrayed his sacred passivity, not realizing that his explanations *in themselves* operated quite definitely as an active interference with the patient's passive productions.

At this stage of development, psychiatrists and psychiatric social workers became acquainted with psychoanalysis and tried to apply the principles of Freudian doctrine to their clients. The first result was, naturally, a reaction to the former activity of workers in these fields and a more passive approach to the individual's own problems. Whereas in psychoanalysis the motive for passivity was research, in social work it was respect for the other person's autonomy.

Meanwhile, within the last fifteen years or so, in the field of therapy proper a movement started toward a more active, more direct, and more effective approach than orthodox analysis had to offer. I started this as early as 1921 by *separating* theory and therapy, and claiming that therapy had to be active in order to be effective. I thought that psychoanalysts had done enough passive research and accumulated sufficient knowledge to guide their patients intelligently and precipitate the therapeutically desired reactions, similar to other kinds of treatment.[1]

At the same time, I allowed the patient a much more active part not only in the analytic situation but also in life, by putting the whole emphasis of the process on an *emotional*, instead of an intellectual, experience. This revaluation of the therapeutic philosophy, as sketched in *The Development of Psychoanalysis*, shifted at the same time the theoretical interest in the patient's *past* to a therapeutic interest in his *present* reactions and attitudes.

The present, emotional situation of the individual that I saw crystallized in the analytic situation could not escape Freud's observation; he explained it, however, as a transference of childhood patterns into the present situation instead of realizing, and fully using, its present emotional significance. When I tried to use it, by introducing the setting of a time limit as the *most* active interference with the analytical process, the orthodox school of psychoanalysts protested—to the point of calling it suggestion.

They overlooked the fact that my activity called forth in the client an intense reaction—equally active—that left less room for suggestion than the gradual indoctrination of the analyst's explanations. Be that as it may, the active movement started by me threw the emphasis of Freudian analysis back again to more passivity than ever. This time, however, the reason was no longer legitimate research, nor was it a reaction against too much activity—but fear! Fear of suggesting something to the patient that had to be explained to him anyway, and fear of his reactions—that is, fear of his *activity*.

This fear was less or nonexistent in social work, which was basically more active by its nature and so could easily adopt the more active approach of the new therapeutic movement. This was first and foremost achieved by the University of Pennsylvania School of Social Work, the leaders of which were, by virtue of their own approach, attracted to my philosophy. What they accepted from it was not only confirmation of the legitimacy of their own activity as social workers, but the more essential and deeper meaning of the therapeutic process as an active—*almost creative*—experience on the patient's part. And because they try to permit the client to work out his own salvation—with their help, to be sure—their approach was characterized as "passive" from the workers' point of view, whereas actually it is "active" from the point of view of the client, that is, purely therapeutically speaking.

At this point it becomes clear that the whole discussion around passivity and activity in social work has been confused by the same fundamental error that led Freud to mix up theory and therapy. The whole psychoanalytic approach is centered around the therapist, who is doing the research and the explaining on the basis of what he knows. *Real therapy has to be centered around the client, his difficulties, his needs, his activities.*[2] It seems to me irrelevant whether the therapist is active or passive—as long as the client can be made active in a constructive way.

From this it becomes evident that any approach that is *exclusively* active or passive, as a matter of principle, is bound to fail because no individual is just one or the other way and no therapy can succeed unless it is flexible enough to allow for whatever approach seems to be necessary for different individuals or different situations in which the same individual finds himself. In other words, what we need is a dynamic approach that is neither active nor passive as far as the therapist is concerned, but *either* as the case may be. Otherwise, the therapy is in danger of becoming the expression of one or another type of therapist, who by his very nature may prefer to be active or passive, respectively.

After all, it is the client who counts and it is his psychology that we have to study and follow instead of creating therapeutic ideologies to suit certain individual therapists or special schools.

Notes

Read before the Jewish School of Social Work, New York, April 5, 1935.
1. In his 1913 essay on "The Claims of Psycho-analysis to Scientific Interest,"

Freud wrote that psychoanalysis "consists in tracing back one psychical structure to another which preceded it in time and out of which it developed. Medical psycho-analytic procedure was not able to eliminate a symptom until it had traced the symptom's origin and development" (*S.E.*, 13:183). In *The Question of Lay Analysis* (1926b), Freud repeated his lifelong view of "an inseparable bond" between theory and therapy:

> In psychoanalysis there has existed from the very first an inseparable bond between cure and research. Knowledge brought therapeutic success. It was impossible to treat a patient without learning something new; it was impossible to gain fresh insight without perceiving its beneficent results. Our analytic procedure is the only one in which this precious conjunction is assured. It is only by carrying on our analytic pastoral work that we can deepen our dawning comprehension of the human mind. This prospect of scientific gain has been the proudest and happiest feature of analytic work. (*S.E.*, 20:256)

2. In *Will Therapy* Rank said that "in the classical analytic situation, in spite of the famed passivity of the analyst, the person of the therapist stood in the center, while I unmask all the reactions of the patient, even if they apparently refer to the analyst, as projections of his own inner conflict and bring them back to his own ego" (1929–31, p. 6). Hinting at Freud's own self-centeredness, which is evident in all his case histories but to which Freud was almost completely blind, Rank added dryly, "Apparently the narcissism of the analyst has compensated for his passivity, so that he has related all reactions of the patient, as far as they do not permit of being put back on an infantile pattern, to his own person" (ibid.).

"My technique," said Rank

> sees the reactions arising immediately from the therapeutic experience [*therapeutischen Erlebnis*] and explains them as projections and attempts at solution of the particular ego conflicts of the patient, which puts the patient himself as chief actor *in the center* of the situation set up by the analyst, a situation which he creates and re-creates according to his own psychic [*seelischen*] needs. The so-called transference, which for Freud represents nothing but a reproduction of the infantile, becomes a creative expression of the growth and development of the personality in the therapeutic experience, while the critical phases, labelled resistance by Freud and masculine protest by Adler, I value and utilize constructively as a proof, however negative, of the strength of will on which therapeutic success ultimately depends. (ibid.; italics added)

In June 1936 Carl Rogers attended a three-day workshop conducted by Rank on his new post-Freudian form of psychotherapy. Although no transcript exists of this workshop, it was probably based on *Will Therapy* and *Truth and Reality*, both first published in English in July 1936. Encountering Rank contributed decisively to what Rogers came to call client-centered therapy. "I became infected with Rankian ideas," Rogers said (Kramer 1995).

MODERN PSYCHOLOGY AND

SOCIAL CHANGE (1938)

LADIES AND GENTLEMEN, when we talk of psychology, we have to differentiate first of all between general psychology, which is experimental and *static*, and individual psychology, which is therapeutic and *dynamic*. Apart from this general distinction, we find that the latter kind of psychology—which is really human understanding and never strictly scientific—varies at different times with different nationalities in different countries. The United States, Germany, Russia have today quite different psychologies, not only of crowd behavior but also of the individuals' reactions to their specific environment or civilization. They also differ in their methods of research and therapeutic applications to emotional and educational problems.

Seemingly, what is carried on is not a special method, but the human understanding underlying it; hence we should not speak of progress in psychology, rather of *difference*—as we do in art, for example—and every psychological system is just as much an *interpretation* of the existing social order and the type it produces as it is an *expression* of it.

Now, within one and the same cultural setting, we find simultaneously different schools of psychology—which again should not be judged by absolute values, because they seem to me to represent different types or groups or classes, as well as the change in individual and social ideologies within the space and time of a given civilization. In other words these different schools cannot be compared as to being right or wrong, but only represent, so to say, different layers of existing human conditions and the shifting along the lines of change.

I shall illustrate what I mean by the best known of all modern psychological theories, namely psychoanalysis, which started almost half a century ago in Vienna as a purely individual method of therapy. The more Freud developed his findings into a general psychological theory, the more it became academic and lost its dynamic appeal. When we analyze this presumably universal psychology, we find not psychological "facts" but their interpretation; that is to say, the therapeutic ideology or social philosophy that has to be justified by the psychological system. Since psychoanalysis was the outgrowth of needs of the bourgeois type of the prewar period in Central Europe, it represents a manifestation as well as justification of that social order, which is now waning.

There has been emerging recently a new need for real human values *beyond* any one psychological theory. This need for real humanism is so deeply seated in all of us that we see, in our days, how people enlightened by mechanistic science and disappointed by the waning religious faith are trying to make a new religion out of psychology. They expect a panacea for all human evils from our psychological insight and knowledge. True enough, modern psychology, in its therapeutic application, brought help to many suffering individuals and enabled them to better handle their human problems. But it is far from being a solution for the fundamental human problems—which always existed and always will exist, as long as we are living in this world of insecurity.

Furthermore, psychology has failed us in our hopes to solve problems of the masses, to better handle human emotions as they manifest themselves in groups and social crises or upheavals. If we want to really benefit from psychology in the solution of the human problem of the average man, we have to develop our psychological knowledge in two directions: the one is to make it *less mechanistic* and more human, as far as the *individual* is concerned; the other is to make it more *collective* in order to apply it constructively to social problems.

The latter movement has already been precipitated by the social upheavals that swept Europe after the war and by the social changes that the United States is going through as a result. Both the communist government in Russia and the Fascist movement in Germany have abolished psychoanalysis as a philosophy foreign to their political and human ideals. In both those countries, psychoanalysis is considered a bourgeois philosophy that does not explain the psychology of the people. In the United States, on the other hand, where the government always had to deal with mass problems and large groups, there has been developing within the last decade or so a social psychology that seems more appropriate for the understanding and handling of group problems. I refer, only briefly, to the vast educational program that the United States has been carrying on in modern times, far ahead of Europe. You have only to remember those big social organizations, which are characteristic for this country, in order to realize how little an individualistic psychology can contribute to the solution of mass problems. I am referring to the mental hygiene movement, to the highly organized social work, the Y.M.C.A. and Y.W.C.A. organizations, and last, but not least, to the progressive educators. They all use, more or less consciously, social psychology in order to approach and enlighten vast groups of the population who are in need of help.

Needless to say, their psychological knowledge—collective as it may be—can benefit a great deal from the experience of individual psychology and has done so up to a certain point. But here we come up against a lack of human elements in our mechanistic psychology, a lack that can only be compensated for by development of a more human psychology of the individual. Let us not forget that psychology is not and never can be a pure science that establishes absolute values once and for all. Psychological theories are just as much a product of varying civilizations as everything else is. In other words they change according to the cultural pattern of the existing civilization from which they sprang; and they are just as much an *expression* of the prevailing social order as they are an *explanation* of it. That is to say, psychological theories not only change like other *fashions*, but they have to change in order to be suitable for the understanding and explanation of the existing type of man. That is the reason why Russia and Germany, as well as the United States, in a certain sense, are right in demanding their own psychology and not having it imported from foreign countries.

Two other psychological systems that grew out of Freudian analysis simply describe and express the predominance of one aspect or the other in different types of individuals within the same cultural pattern: Adler, as a socialist, worked out the psychology of the inferior type, the underdog, and Jung, the son of a minister, brought out the religious and racial elements—both, however, representing not only different types of individuals and different aspects of human life, but also expressing and, at the same time, explaining the psychology of a certain class.

If we glance briefly over the development of the different psychoanalytic schools, we find that Freud's original thesis itself evolved from a synthesis of formerly accepted principles. Adler next presented an antithesis to Freud's original thesis by emphasizing the individual's ego drive for power, dominance, and supremacy, contrary to Freud's emphasis on the sexual instinct as the driving force. Then came Jung, who endeavored to combine the notions of Freud and Adler by conceiving the former to be a psychology of the extrovert and the latter a psychology of the introvert.

As you all probably know, Freud interprets the neurosis as the result of a repression of instinctual drives, particularly the sex urge. This repression, which remains unconscious, is precipitated by *external* events (inhibitions, threats) that occurred in the remote past of the individual and resulted in arousal of fear and guilt. The cure of these neurotic reactions lies, according to Freud, in a conscious recall or reliving of the infantile repressed memories and an emotional acceptance of this interpretation given them by the analyst.[1]

These three different systems of therapeutic psychology, which all sprang from the same source—the exploration of the unconscious—are essentially alike, in that each one sets up an ideal of normality toward which it strives. *To all of them, the neurosis represents a failure on the part of the individual to reach a certain norm or average.* Where the theories disagree is the kind of norm that they have established as their ideal. For psychoanalysis the ideal norm is a biological one: the instincts must be allowed free expression. For individual psychology the ideal norm is a social one: the stability of the individual depends upon his development of a certain degree of social feeling. For analytic psychology the ideal norm is an ethical one: a specified amount of religious belief is necessary to counteract our impulse life.

As a consequence of their attempts to fix definite norms of behavior, the therapy of each resolves itself in an attempt to force the patient to fit into a particular pattern of behavior. What this amounts to, in the last analysis, is that each school endeavors to strengthen or control (sublimate) one side of the personality at the expense of another side and, hence, all three may be aptly designated as coercive therapies. Freud tries to strengthen or sublimate the instinctual side against the inhibitory side; Adler, the social against the egotistical; Jung, the ethical against the instinctual.

The Freudian would say, The patient suffers from a conflict between his biological libido and external inhibiting forces; induce him to return to childhood, which would enable him to weaken the inhibitory mechanism and convert his distorted libido into more constructive channels. The Adlerian would say, The patient suffers from too much ego due to an inferiority feeling that has led him to set up an exclusive goal instead of a social one; direct him back to the point where his style of life began and show him what elements contributed toward making him an unsocial creature. The Jungian would say, Explore the patient's collective unconscious to discover the fundamental roots of his makeup; then interpret his present conflict in relation to the total situation and finally integrate his personality by inspiring him with ethical consciousness.[2]

The actual analytical procedure of all three therapies, with the exception of a few technical variations, is essentially the same. It consists in the main of interpreting the patient's material on the basis of the analyst's social philosophy as expressed in his psychological theory. Hence, theory and therapy in all these schools of psychology are one and the same thing: that is to say, the therapy consists in a mere learning of and believing in the theory; in other words, it is essentially an intellectual process.

It is here, at this point, that I first deviated from Freud and started my own contribution toward a dynamic psychology. As early as 1921, I criticized this confusion between theory and therapy by emphasizing the need for developing a dynamic therapy from the vast material that psychoanalytic research had furnished. From my own experience, I learned that the therapeutic process is basically an emotional experience—which takes place *independently* of the theoretical concepts of the analyst, a statement that is borne out by the fact that therapeutic results have been attained and achieved by various methods of psychotherapy, based on different theories. Furthermore, emphasis on the emotional experience—instead of on intellectual enlightenment of the patient—brings two essential principles of my dynamic therapy into focus. Firstly, emphasis is shifted from the past to the *present*, in which *all* emotional experience takes place; secondly, the therapeutic process allows the patient a much more *active* role than being merely an object upon whom the therapist operates, like a surgeon.

Thus, my concept allows for operation of the patient's own will as the most constructive force in the therapeutic process. It is lack of balance in his will-organization that induces the neurotic to deny—instead of affirm—his individuality. By will, I do not mean will-to-power as conceived by Nietzsche and Adler, nor a wish in the Freudian sense—though it might include both these elements—but rather the supreme autonomic organizing force in the individual. It is not any particular biological drive or a mere summation of certain drives. It constitutes the *creative* aspect of the personality, which operates as a fresh totality and which *distinguishes* one individual from another. This supreme creative and controlling power of the personality acts in service of the ego and functions as principal director and regulator of our instincts and inhibitions, as well as of the antagonistic relations between them.

From this dynamic concept of the total personality, derived from extensive analytical research and clinical experience, I came to the conclusion that the neurotic type is not, as psychoanalysis conceived, a failure in normalcy, but a *failure in creativity*—a type whom the French call an *artiste manqué*. What characterizes this type, regardless of whether it finds artistic expression or not, is a creative urge—which can be defined as an impulse to immortalize and thus perpetuate one's own personality. This tendency the artist and the neurotic have in common, and neither is able to accept his own self as it is. The only difference is that the artist, through a strong will-organization, finds a way to objectify his self-creation in the work of art, whereas the neurotic remains fixed on his own ego. The neurotic, like the artist, possesses the urge—or, rather, is possessed by the urge—to immortalize himself by giving *rebirth* to his personality but is unable to convert his impulse into positive life action. By his very nature, the neurotic is as different from the average as is the artist. But he is unable to accept this—*his difference*—positively. He is compelled by a deep-rooted self-denial to interpret his difference negatively, as inferiority. This *refusal* of himself, on the part of the neurotic, renders him incapable of either giving positive expression to his individuality, or of finding constructive mediums upon which it can externalize itself. Moreover, this rigid self-denial forces the individual creative capacities into negative symptoms.

On the basis of this parallel between the creative type and the neurotic type in relation to will and impulse, we find that both are alike. Both possess a strong will as well as powerful instinctual urges. With the productive creative personality, however, the positive will dominates and without severely repressing the instincts is able to draft them into its own service, in order by achievement to creatively obtain relief from guilt.

With the neurotic, on the contrary, the negative will reigns, and often—taking on the guise of fear and guilt—effects a drastic check upon the instinctual urges, which results in the well-known clinical pictures of anxiety and compulsion neurosis. The tendency on the part of this type to exercise his will upon *himself*—and thereby to *deny* it— is responsible for the popular impression that the neurotic is a weak-willed individual. Diametrically opposed to the artist and the neurotic in terms of will, stands the so-called psychopathic individual and criminal, the only *really* weak-willed individuals, who are overwhelmed by their instinctive impulses.

In analysis of the personality, then, there are three principal forces: *impulse, inhibition,* and *will.* Impulse comprises the instincts, as well as all actions and reactions on the biological level of behavior. Inhibition is the universal tendency to check the impulses, which usually manifests itself in fear or a sense of guilt. Whether it is fear or guilt depends upon whether the impulse is about to be checked, or whether it already has been checked. *Between impulse and inhibition, there is a continual conflict that gives rise to our emotional life.* This conflict, however, is normal and healthy, since it represents the fundamental dualism in man. We cannot eradicate either impulse or inhibition. The only thing that we can do is to create such a dynamic relationship between these opposing forces that the impulses are allowed to assert themselves partially, thus permitting the individual to project the internal conflict between impulse and inhibition upon the outside world, instead of inwardly upon himself. *The sole force capable of producing such a dynamic balance between impulse and inhibition is the individual will.* The will has the power to invest itself in either impulse or inhibition, as the situation might demand, thus resolving the internal conflict, or it might function as volitional action, thus empowering the individual to externalize the inner dualism.

Now, because of his awareness of the guilt and inferiority feelings arising from the perception of his *unlikeness* to other individuals, the neurotic is unable to separate or detach himself from past emotional ties and live independently. I have learned that the capacity to separate is one of life's major functions. Life in itself is a mere succession of separations, beginning with birth, going on through several weaning periods and the development of the individual personality, and finally culminating in death—which represents the final separation. At birth, the individual experiences the first shock of separation, which throughout his life he strives to overcome. In the process of adaptation, man persistently separates from his old self, or at least from those segments of his old self that are now outlived. Like a child who has outgrown a toy, he discards the old parts of himself for which he has no further use. The inner evolution of the ego is analogous to this external process. The ego continually breaks away from its worn-out parts, which were of value in the past but have no value in the present.

The neurotic, however, is unable to accomplish this normal detachment process. He cannot live through and emancipate himself from the various fundamental separation stages in life. Owing to fear or guilt generated in the assertion of his own autonomy, he is unable to free himself, and instead remains suspended upon some primitive level of his evolution. He stays fixated, so to speak, upon a particular worn-out part of his past that he cannot sever himself, and his whole present behavior is directed and symbolized in terms of this *unaccomplished* separation.[3]

You can see, now, how my interpretation of neurotic behavior differs from the various psychoanalytic schools. I do not conceive the neurotic as a passive individual who has been unfortunately conditioned by *external* forces, but rather as a particular kind of autonomic personality, who—though he might be unusually susceptible to external influences—is never essentially determined by them. Moreover, I regard the neurotic as a type (to which belong also the creative individuals) whose behavior disturbances do not arise from *outwardly* imposed repressions or frustrations, but from an *inner* psychic conflict inherent to their nature, which they are neither able to project upon the milieu nor are capable of externalizing into productive activity. In other words, Freud and Adler endeavor to interpret the neurosis mechanistically in terms of *outside* causes, whereas I rely upon a vitalistic point of view taking root in the dynamics of the personality.

This vitalism is based on one principle common to all these different aspects of psychology, and that is *human relationship*. "Purely" individual psychology can only be gained from laboratory experiments: that is to say, by complete isolation of the individual. It may yield scientific results with regard to a few fundamental reactions, but it will never enable us to achieve human understanding, as it manifests itself in real life. *All living psychology is relationship psychology*: that is to say, understanding and explanation of what is going on between two individuals, or on a larger scale between a number of individuals—as in the family or bigger social groups.

For the development of such a relationship psychology, only the first step has been made: the study of the relationship, and its emotional implications, between the psychotherapist and his patient. In this relationship it became necessary to investigate and analyze the process of relationship development itself, in order to help the neurotic patient develop and grow toward emotional autonomy. What we learned from the analysis and understanding of this therapeutic relationship seems to have a bearing on other forms and types of relationships—such as exist between parent and child, teacher and pupil, husband and wife, in friendship, and so forth. That is to say, in all these relationships there seems to be a therapeutic element, if we conceive of that term in the broadest sense of the word. Simply speaking, this is the definition of relationship: one individual is helping the other to develop and grow, without infringing too much on the other's personality.

For a deeper, or rather more complete, understanding of human relationship, there is still much lacking in all our psychological knowledge, no matter how much our theories may change according to different nationalities and social orders. And this is because all the different psychologies are just as much *man-made* as is the rest of our civilization. In spite of all of our scientific research, which still is carried on by men chiefly, we do not possess a real psychology of the *woman*, nor do we understand the *child* psychologically. I am saying this with all due respect to modern science: it can be proved, by modern science itself, that it is impossible for the investigator to detach himself completely from the research he is carrying on, and hence be absolutely objective. The same difficulty has been recently pointed out, as you all may know, even with regard to such an exact science as physics. Here, too, the new movement that is popularly known as the theory of relativity started some time ago in Germany with the discovery that, hitherto, *the observer and his personal psychology have been left out.*

In the field of psychology, this danger of overlooking the influence of the instrument is even greater than in any other field of science, because here the instrument is the observer himself—a human susceptible to all the subjective sources of error. As a matter of fact, if we investigate or analyze modern psychology and especially psychoanalysis, its outstanding representative, we can clearly see that it is in essence *man*-made: that is to say, man has projected his own psychology into the woman and into the child.

It is true that, in recent years, women have contributed a great deal to the development of modern psychology. But they all have been more or less under the influence of man-made, that is, masculine philosophies and hence could not bring out the true psychology of woman. I am not sure whether we find a clearer expression of the psychology of woman in fiction, although it seems that some women writers in our times were able to liberate themselves from the man-made patterns that also govern literature.

On the one hand, woman seems to have a resistance to revealing her own psychology—because this is her last weapon against man, the last refuge of her crushed and submissive self, the last mystery—which she herself does not know, because if she knew, she might be tempted to give it away. She can't know, anyhow, because *she just is*—if permitted. But, because man wants to penetrate her riddle, she is *not* permitted to be—which makes her react in two extreme ways: she either fights man with his own weapons, in becoming masculine, or she so completely submits to him that she becomes like him. In either case his attempt to discover her real femininity makes her more masculine. Therefore, in the age of psychology, we have more masculine women than ever, especially the latter, imitative type.

On the other hand, man is forced in self-defense to try to rob woman of her natural force, which threatens his cultural superstructure built up in competition with the woman's biological creativeness. Maybe we have to look for deeper reasons why the psychology of woman has for ages been considered a mystery that seems to be still unsolved—but it would carry us too far from our present subject to elaborate upon them.

Likewise, man has misinterpreted the child's inner life, which he can conceive of, it seems, only in terms of his own psychology. The child lives mentally and emotionally on an entirely different plane: his world is not a world of logic, causality, and rationalism. *It is a world of magic*, a world in which imagination and creative will reign—*internal* forces that cannot be explained in terms of scientific psychology. Indeed, psychology by its very nature seems unfit for the understanding and explanation of those irrational forces that still operate so much more intensely in the child and in primitive man than they do in grown-up "civilized" people. All psychology is essentially rational and—especially psychoanalysis—glorifies the rationalization of the irrational. Yet the child's psychology—that is, his inner life—is still so much, or completely, irrational, that any psychologizing of it becomes a contradiction in itself. The child lives in a world of magic, where no logical or rational—that is, man-made—laws govern, but where the irrationality of nature herself, of which the woman is still so much a part, predominates. This is one reason why the mother who carried and bore the child may still understand it intuitively while the man completely fails in his psychological rationalizations.

The child's play is full of magical meaning that our rational mind not only is unable to comprehend but rejects as superstition. There is no use in trying to explain to the child what those superstitions mean rationally, that is to say, to tell the child what we call the truth. Truth is a very flexible concept that changes with different civilizations and the different mentality of people. In recent years, as you may all know, parents and teachers have tried to educate and enlighten the child about the "facts of life." It was surprising to find that most children did not accept these scientific explanations, not because they went over their heads, but because the child was not interested in our *biological* explanations and, strangely enough, preferred his so-called childish superstitions to what we call the truth. He does not want and does not accept it because he is concerned with the mysterious problems of life and death and feels necessarily insecure, fearful—which we cannot remove from him but only alleviate by love, *a love that connects the tragically separated individual again with cosmic life.* Instead of psychologizing the child, we should respect his irrational nature and learn from him to accept it humbly in ourselves as well. We are not in the least more secure than he is, we are not less irrational at bottom. All we do is pretend to be; that's our tragedy, our false heroism.

The reason for this unexpected reaction on the child's part is not easily found. A discussion of it would take us back in the remote times of prehistoric man, who had similar notions about the world, life, and himself, as we find in our children. As our experiment with the sexual enlightenment of the child shows, it is not necessarily a lack of knowledge that causes such persistent adherence to what seems to us superstition. The child is offered a scientific explanation and rejects it because it does not want it, has no use for it: it does not suit his magical worldview. In the same way, we can see age-old superstitions being carried over into times when sufficient knowledge was available to discard them if man had wanted to. Not until we know where this deep-rooted resistance against acceptance of the "facts of life" comes from will we be able to understand the child, primitive man, and subsequently mankind. The discovery of these deep-seated human motives will be the beginning of a new era in psychology.

Notes

Read before the University of Minnesota, Burton Hall, February 5, 1938.

1. Rank doubtless had read Freud's recent essay entitled "Constructions in Analysis" (1937), in which the patient's emotional acceptance of an analyst's construction was equated with the uncovering of infantile repressed memories:

"The path that starts from the analyst's construction ought to end in the patient's recollection; but it does not always lead so far. . . . Instead of that, if the analysis is carried out correctly, we produce in him an assured conviction of the truth of the construction which achieves the same therapeutic result as a recaptured memory" (*S.E.*, 23:265–66).

Two years before his death, Freud seems to be overthrowing his lifelong belief that psychoanalysis is not manipulation of transference, a conclusion that could hardly have escaped Rank, who had been advocating a separation between theory and therapy since 1921. Even while claiming that "constructing" the truth (by the analyst) has the same effect as "remembering" the truth (by the patient), Freud insists in virtually the same breath that he has never been guilty of manipulation: "I can assert without boasting that such an abuse of 'suggestion' has never occurred in my practice" (ibid., p. 262).

2. In his post-1924 writings, Rank often contrasted himself with Freud, Adler, and Jung. In *Will Therapy* he said:

Freud . . . has always explained guilt as a reaction to the *sexual* will, while actually it is a reaction to the *individual* will, that is, the counter-will which is to be justified and removed by the physical and psychic [*seelische*] union of love. Adler again has interpreted will not in the biological sense of sexuality but in the social sense of striving for power, and corresponding to this social content, finds salvation in social feeling, not as Freud does, in sex feeling. Jung, who conceives of guilt more deeply than Freud or Adler, in cosmic [*kosmisch*] terms, sees salvation cosmically also in the form of the collective unconscious, which is individual but at the same time [is] more than individual. *No one of them, however, has recognized the individual will as such, and the individual guilt for it*, which is neither biological, social, nor cosmic, although the individual can interpret it afterwards in one or another meaning. (1929–31, p. 83; italics added)

In *Beyond Psychology* Rank added, "That Freud's psychology, being [just one] interpretation rather than an explanation of human nature, was not valid for all races, Jung pointed out; that it did not apply to different social environments, Adler emphasized; but that it did not even permit individuals of the same race and social background to deviate from the accepted type led me *beyond these differences in psychology to a psychology of difference*" (1941, p. 29; Rank's italics).

"Whereas Freud conceives of all people as fundamentally alike [in their Oedipal unconscious], for Jung they are different (though racially alike); while Adler maintains that though their behavior is different it ought to be alike . . . [A]ll three seem to have reached a similar conclusion, namely, that the evil from which our personality suffers is over-individualization; hence they agree in the remedy consisting of an emotional unity with something beyond the Self. Freud sees it in sex, Adler in social fellowship and Jung in racial [i.e., religious] collectivity" (ibid., pp. 35–37).

3. In *Will Therapy* Rank concluded:

From this viewpoint the problem of the neurosis itself is a separation problem and as such a blocking of the human life principle [*Lebensprinzipe*], the conscious ability to endure release and separation, first from the biological power represented by parents, and finally from the lived out [abgelebten] parts of the self which this power represents, and which obstruct the development of the individual personality. It is at this point that the neurotic comes to grief, where, instead of living [anstatt zu erleben], of overcoming the past through the present, he becomes conscious that he dare not, cannot, loose himself because he is bound by guilt. Here, as it were, the human being's recognition of his biological and cosmic [kosmischen] dependence revenges itself since as love duty and debt of gratitude it opposes his own microcosmic [mikrokosmischen] self dependence. In these guilt reactions the problem of separation shows itself as related to the problem of difference. (1929–31, pp. 73–74; italics added)

PRIOR PUBLICATION OF LECTURES

1. Lecture 1 was published as "Psychoanalysis as General Psychology" in *Mental Hygiene*, 1926, 10:12–26. No German text exists.
2. Lecture 2 was published as "The Therapeutic Application of Psychoanalysis" in *Mental Hygiene*, 1926, 10:495–508. No German text exists.
3. Lecture 3 was published as "The Trauma of Birth in [*sic*] its Importance for Psychoanalytic Therapy" in *The Psychoanalytic Review*, 1924, 11:241–5. No German text exists.
4. Lecture 4 was published as "Psychoanalysis as a Cultural Factor" in *Mental Hygiene*, 1926, 10:721–31. No German text exists.
5. Lectures 5–10, 11–15, and 18 were selected from two volumes published in German by Rank during the late 1920s: Lectures 5–10 come from volume 1 of his *Grundzüge einer Genetischen Psychologie* (Leipzig and Vienna: Franz Deuticke, 1927), and Lectures 11–15 and 18 from volume 2, subtitled *Gestaltung und Ausdruck der Persönlichkeit* (Leipzig and Vienna: Franz Deuticke, 1928). All lectures titles are Rank's, except Lecture 11, in German titled "Feelings and Denial," and Lecture 15, in German titled "Education and Domination." During the late 1920s and early 1930s, printed copies of these lectures, in English translation, were distributed to students and faculty attending Rank's lectures at the New York School of Social Work and the University of Pennsylvania School of Social Work. Translation of these lectures is unattributed. I compared each line of this translation with the German text and corrected errors. German words in brackets come from the original text of *Grundzüge einer Genetischen Psychologie*, volumes 1 and 2. Many of these lectures, in varying translations and under different titles, were also published in *The Psychoanalytic Review*, the *Journal of the Otto Rank Association* and elsewhere; see Lieberman 1985, p. 452, for complete list. *Journal of the Otto Rank Association* was published in thirty-one issues from 1966 to 1983 by the Otto Rank Association, which ceased functioning in 1983.
6. Lecture 16 was published as "The Relation of Parental Attitudes to Success and Failure" in *Journal of the Otto Rank Association*, 1967 (number 2), 2:70–80. No German text exists.
7. Lecture 17 was published as "Paper Read by Rank at the First International Congress on Mental Hygiene" in Taft 1958, pp. 147–51. I compared Taft's version with the original untitled typescript in *RC*, and corrected errors. No German text exists.
8. Lecture 19 was published as "The Psychological Approach to Personal Problems" in *Journal of the Otto Rank Association*, 1966 (number 1), 1:12–23. I compared this version with the original untitled typescript in *RC*, and corrected errors. No German text exists.
9. Lecture 20 was published as "Self-inflicted Illness" in *Proceedings of the*

California Academy of Medicine, 1935–1936 (San Francisco: California Academy of Medicine, 1937), pp. 8–18. No German text exists.

10. Parts of Lecture 21 were published as "Activity and Passivity in Social Work" in *Journal of the Otto Rank Association*, 1968 (number 2), 3:35–6. No German text exists.

11. Parts of Lecture 22 were published in "Psychology and Social Change," the first chapter of Rank's *Beyond Psychology* (New York: Dover, 1958), passim. No German text exists.

REFERENCES

Abraham, H., and E. Freud, eds. (1965). *A Psycho-Analytic Dialogue: The Letters of Sigmund Freud and Karl Abraham 1907–1926*. New York: Basic Books.

Alexander, F. (1925). Book Review of *The Development of Psychoanalysis*. *International Journal of Psychoanalysis*, 6:484–96.

Anzieu, D. (1986). *Freud's Self-Analysis*. London: Hogarth Press.

Bollas, C. (1987). *The Shadow of the Object: Psychoanalysis of the Unthought Known*. New York: Columbia University Press.

Brabant, E., E. Falzeder, and P. Giampieri-Deutsch, eds. (1993). *The Correspondence of Sigmund Freud and Sándor Ferenczi. Volume I, 1908–1914*. Cambridge: Harvard University Press.

Chertok, L., and I. Stengers. (1992). *A Critique of Psychoanalytic Reason: Hypnosis as a Scientific Problem from Lavoisier to Lacan*. Stanford: Stanford University Press.

Clark, R. W. (1980). *Freud: The Man and the Cause*. New York: Random House.

Dupont, J. (1994). "Freud's Analysis of Ferenczi as Revealed by Their Correspondence." *International Journal of Psychoanalysis*, 75:301–20.

Ellis, H. (1923). *The Dance of Life*. Boston: Houghton Mifflin.

Erlich, I. (1977). "What Happened to Jocasta?" *Bulletin of the Menninger Clinic*, 41:280–84.

Ferenczi, S. (1928). "The Elasticity of Psycho-Analytical Technique." In *Final Contributions to the Problems and Methods of Psycho-Analysis*. Ed. M. Balint. Tr. E. Mosbacher et al. London: Hogarth Press, 1955, vol. 3, pp. 87–101.

———. (1930). "The Principle of Relaxation and Neocatharsis." In *Final Contributions to the Problems and Methods of Psycho-Analysis*. London: Hogarth Press, 1955, vol. 3, pp. 108–25.

———. (1988). *The Clinical Diary of Sándor Ferenczi*. Ed. J. Dupont. Cambridge: Harvard University Press.

Ferenczi, S., and O. Rank. (1924). *The Development of Psychoanalysis*. Tr. C. Newton. New York: Dover, 1956.

Freud, A. (1954). "The Widening Scope of Indications for Psychoanalysis." *The Writings of Anna Freud*. New York: International Universities Press, 1968, vol. 4, pp. 356–76.

Freud, E., ed. (1960). *Selected Letters of Sigmund Freud*. New York: Basic Books.

Freud, S. *The Standard Edition of the Complete Psychological Works*. Ed. and tr. J. Strachey et al. 24 vols. London: Hogarth Press, 1953–74. Referred to as *S.E.*

———. (1900). *The Interpretation of Dreams*. In *S.E.*, 4 and 5.

———. (1901). *The Psychopathology of Everyday Life*. In *S.E.*, 6.

——. (1905a). "Fragment of an Analysis of a Case of Hysteria." In *S.E.*, 7:7–122.

——. (1905b). *Jokes and Their Relation to the Unconscious*. In *S.E.*, 8.

——. (1911). "Formulations on the Two Principles of Mental Functioning." In *S.E.*, 12:218–26.

——. (1912a). "The Dynamics of Transference." In *S.E.*, 12:99–108.

——. (1912b). "Recommendations to Physicians Practicing Psycho-analysis." *S.E.*, 12:111–20.

——. (1913a). "The Claims of Psycho-Analysis to Scientific Interest." In *S.E.*, 13:165–90.

——. (1913b). *Totem and Taboo*. In *S.E.*, 13:1–161.

——. (1914a). "Remembering, Repeating and Working-Through." In *S.E.*, 12:147–56.

——. (1914b). *On the History of the Psycho-Analytic Movement*. In *S.E.*, 14:7–66.

——. (1914c). "On Narcissism: An Introduction." In *S.E.*, 14:73–102.

——. (1915a). "Observations on Transference-Love." In *S.E.*, 12:159–71.

——. (1915b). "Instincts and Their Vicissitudes." In *S.E.*, 14:117–40.

——. (1915c). "Thoughts for the Times on War and Death." In *S.E.*, 14:275–300.

——. (1916–17). *Introductory Lectures on Psycho-Analysis*. In *S.E.*, 15 and 16.

——. (1917). "A Difficulty in the Path of Psycho-Analysis." In *S.E.*, 17:137–44.

——. (1918). *From the History of an Infantile Neurosis*. In *S.E.*, 17:7–122.

——. (1922). "Prize Offer." In *S.E.*, 17:270.

——. (1923a). "Two Encyclopedia Articles." In *S.E.*, 18:235–59.

——. (1923b). *The Ego and the Id*. In *S.E.*, 19:10–59.

——. (1924). "The Dissolution of the Oedipus Complex." In *S.E.*, 19:173–79.

——. (1925a). *An Autobiographical Study*. In *S.E.*, 20:7–74.

——. (1925b). "Some Psychical Consequences of the Anatomical Distinction between the Sexes." In *S.E.*, 19:248–58.

——. (1926a). *Inhibitions, Symptoms and Anxiety*. In *S.E.*, 20:77–172.

——. (1926b). *The Question of Lay Analysis*. In *S.E.*, 20:183–258.

——. (1927). *The Future of an Illusion*. In *S.E.*, 21:5–56.

——. (1930). *Civilization and Its Discontents*. In *S.E.*, 21:64–145.

——. (1931). "Female Sexuality." In *S.E.*, 21:225–43.

——. (1933). *New Introductory Lectures on Psycho-Analysis*. In *S.E.*, 22:5–182.

——. (1937). "Constructions in Analysis." In *S.E.*, 23:257–69.

——. (1987). *A Phylogenetic Fantasy: Overview of the Transference Neuroses*. Ed. A. Hoffer and P. Hoffer. Cambridge: Harvard University Press.

——. (1992). *The Diary of Sigmund Freud, 1929–1939: A Record of the Final Decade*. Ed. M. Molnar. New York: Charles Scribner's Sons.

Gay, P. (1988). *Freud: A Life for our Times*. New York: Norton.

Grosskurth, P. (1986). *Melanie Klein: Her World and Her Work*. New York: Alfred A. Knopf.

——. (1991). *The Secret Ring: Freud's Inner Circle and the Politics of Psychoanalysis*. Reading, Mass.: Addison-Wesley.

Grotstein, J. S., and D. B. Rinsley, eds. (1994). *Fairbairn and the Origins of Object Relations*. New York: The Guilford Press.

Grubich-Simites, I. (1986). "Six Letters of Sigmund Freud and Sándor Ferenczi on the Interrelationship of Psychoanalytic Theory and Technique." *International Review of Psychoanalysis*, 13:259–77.

Hartmann, H. (1928). Abstract of Rank's *Grundzüge einer Genetischen Psychologie*. Vol. 1. *Allgemeine Zeitschrift für Psychotherapie*, 1:720.

Haynal, A., and E. Falzeder. (1993a). "Empathy, Psychoanalytic Practice in the 1920s, and Ferenczi's *Clinical Diary*." *Journal of the American Academy of Psychoanalysis*, 21:605–21.

———. (1993b). "Slaying the Dragons of the Past or Cooking the Hare in the Present: A Historical View of Affects in the Psychoanalytic Encounter." *Psychoanalytic Inquiry*, 13:357–71.

Heller, J. B. (1973). "Freud's Father and Mother." In H. Ruitenbeek, ed., *Freud as We Knew Him*. Detroit: Wayne State University Press, pp. 334–40.

Hinshelwood, R. D. (1991). *A Dictionary of Kleinian Thought*. London: Free Association Books.

Hyman, S. E. (1974). *The Tangled Bank: Darwin, Marx, Frazer and Freud as Imaginative Writers*. New York: Atheneum.

Isakower, O. (1924). Minutes of the Vienna Psychoanalytic Society, March 5, 1924. Freud Collection, Library of Congress.

Jones, E. (1953). *The Life and Work of Sigmund Freud*. Vol. 1. New York: Basic Books.

———. (1955). *The Life and Work of Sigmund Freud*. Vol. 2. New York: Basic Books.

———. (1957). *The Life and Work of Sigmund Freud*. Vol. 3. New York: Basic Books.

Kardiner, A. (1977). *My Analysis with Freud*. New York: W. W. Norton.

Kobler, F. (1962). "Die Mutter Sigmund Freuds." *Bulletin des Leo Baeck Instituts*, 5:149–71.

Kramer, R. (1995). "The Birth of Client-Centered Therapy: Carl Rogers, Otto Rank, and 'The Beyond.'" *Journal of Humanistic Psychology*, 35(4):54–110.

Lacan, J. (1977). *Écrits: A Selection*. Tr. A. Sheridan. New York: W. W. Norton.

Lieberman, E. J. (1979). "The Rank-Wilbur Correspondence." *Journal of the Otto Rank Association*, 14:7–26.

———. (1985). *Acts of Will: The Life and Work of Otto Rank*. New York: Free Press.

Loewald, H. W. (1959). "The Waning of the Oedipus Complex." *Journal of the American Psychoanalytic Association*, 27:751–75.

Mahony, P. (1989). *On Defining Freud's Discourse*. New Haven: Yale University Press.

Masson, J. M., ed. (1985). *The Complete Letters of Sigmund Freud to Wilhelm Fliess 1887–1904*. Tr. J. M. Masson. Cambridge: Harvard University Press.

McGuire, W., ed. (1974). *The Freud/Jung Letters: The Correspondence between Sigmund Freud and C. G. Jung*. Tr. R. Manheim and R.F.C. Hull. Princeton: Princeton University Press.

Meissner, W. (1991). *What Is Effective in Psychoanalytic Therapy: The Move from Interpretation to Relation*. New Jersey: Jason Aronson.

Menaker, E. (1982). *Otto Rank: A Rediscovered Legacy*. New York: Columbia University Press.

———. (1989). *Appointment in Vienna: An American Psychoanalyst Recalls Her Student Days in Pre-War Austria*. New York: St. Martin's Press.

Mitchell, S. A. (1988). *Relational Concepts in Psychoanalysis: An Integration*. Cambridge: Harvard University Press.

Moore, G. A. (1941). *What Nietzsche Means*. Cambridge: Harvard University Press.

Nin, A. (1966). *The Diary of Anaïs Nin, Volume I: 1931–1934*. New York: Harcourt, Brace and World.

Nunberg, H., and E. Federn, eds. (1967). *Minutes of the Vienna Psychoanalytic Society, 1908–1910*, vol. 2. New York: International Universities Press.

Obholzer, K. (1982). *The Wolf-Man: Conversations with Freud's Patient— Sixty Years Later*. Tr. M. Shaw. New York: Continuum.

Otto, R. (1923). *The Idea of the Holy: An Inquiry into the Non-Rational Factor in the Idea of the Divine and Its Relation to the Rational*. Second edition. Tr. J. W. Harvey. London: Oxford University Press, 1950.

Paskauskas, R. A., ed. (1993). *The Complete Correspondence of Sigmund Freud and Ernest Jones, 1908–1939*. Cambridge: Harvard University Press.

Pfeiffer, E., ed. (1985). *Sigmund Freud and Lou Andreas-Salomé Letters*. Tr. William and Elaine Robson-Scott. New York: W. W. Norton.

Rangell, L. (1982). "Transference to Theory: The Relationship of Psychoanalytic Education to the Analyst's Relationship to Psychoanalysis." *Annual of Psychoanalysis*, 10:29–56.

Rank, O. (1907). *Der Künstler: Ansätze zu einer Sexual–Psychologie*. Vienna and Leipzig: Hugo Heller and Cie.

———. (1909). *The Myth of the Birth of the Hero* in *In Quest of the Hero*. Ed. Robert Segal. Princeton: Princeton University Press, 1990, pp. 1–86.

———. (1910). "Ein Traum, der sich selbst deutet." *Jarhbuch für psychoanalytische und psychopathologische Forschungen*, 2:465–540.

———. (1911). *Die Lohengrinsage: Ein Beitrag zu ihrer Motivgestaltung und Deutung*. Leipzig and Vienna: Franz Deuticke.

———. (1912). *Das Inzest-Motiv in Dichtung und Sage: Grundzüge einer Psychologie des dichterischen Schaffens*. Leipzig and Vienna: Franz Deuticke.

———. (1914). *The Double: A Psychoanalytic Study*. Tr. H. Tucker. London: Maresfield Library, 1989.

———. (1923). "Zum Verständnis der Libidoentwicklung im Heilungsvorgang." *Internationale Zeitschrift für Psychoanalyse*, 9:435–71.

———. (1924). *The Trauma of Birth*. New York: Dover Books, 1994.

———. (1925). Summary of Four Seminars at the New York Psychoanalytic Society, January 1925. Rank Collection, Rare Book and Manuscript Library, Columbia University.

———. (1926a). "The Genesis of Genitality." *The Psychoanalytic Review*, 13: 129–44.

———. (1926b). *Sexualität und Schuldgefühl*. Leipzig/Vienna/Zürich: Internationaler Psychoanalytischer Verlag.

———. (1926c). *Technik der Psychoanalyse: Die Analytische Situation*. Vol. 1. Leipzig and Vienna: Franz Deuticke.

———. (1927). *Grundzüge einer Genetischen Psychologie*. Vol. 1. Lepzig and Vienna: Franz Deuticke.

———. (1929). *Truth and Reality: A Life History of the Human Will*. Tr. J. Taft. New York: W. W. Norton, 1978.

———. (1929–31). *Will Therapy: An Analysis of the Therapeutic Process in Terms of Relationship*. Tr. J. Taft. New York: W. W. Norton, 1978.

———. (1930a). Untitled Typescript of Self-Analysis of Writings, May 1930. Rank Collection, Rare Book and Manuscript Library, Columbia University.

———. (1930b). *Psychology and the Soul*. Tr. W. Turner. Philadelphia: University of Pennsylvania Press, 1950.

———. (1930c). "Seminar Conducted by Dr. Otto Rank: Minutes of Nine Meetings Held in the New York Home of Dr. Frankwood Williams, February 5 to April 9, 1930." *Journal of the Otto Rank Association*, 2(1):12–100.

———. (1932a). *Art and Artist: Creative Urge and Personality Development*. Tr. C. Atkinson. New York: W. W. Norton, 1989.

———. (1932b). *Modern Education*. Tr. M. Moxon. New York: Alfred A. Knopf.

———. 1958. [1941]. *Beyond Psychology*. New York: Dover.

———. (1994). "A Farewell to Freud: Two Drafts of a Letter to the Father of Psychoanalysis." *Anaïs: An International Journal*, 12:56–59.

Rank, O., and H. Sachs (1913). *The Significance of Psychoanalysis for the Mental Sciences*. Tr. C. R. Payne. New York: Journal of Nervous and Mental Disease Publishing Company, 1916.

Ricoeur, P. (1970). *Freud and Philosophy: An Essay on Interpretation*. Tr. D. Savage. New Haven: Yale University Press.

Roazen, P. (1976). *Freud and His Followers*. New York: Alfred A. Knopf.

———. (1993). *Meeting Freud's Family*. Amherst: University of Massachusetts Press.

Roazen, P., and B. Swerdloff, eds. (1995). *Heresy: Sandor Rado and the Psychoanalytic Movement*. New Jersey: Jason Aronson.

Romm, S. (1983). *The Unwelcome Intruder: Freud's Struggle with Cancer*. New York: Praeger.

Rudnytsky, P. (1991). *The Psychoanalytic Vocation: Rank, Winnicott, and the Legacy of Freud*. New Haven: Yale University Press.

Sachs, H. (1925). Book Review of *The Trauma of Birth*. International Journal of Psychoanalysis, 6:499–508.

———. (1944). *Freud: Master and Friend*. Cambridge: Harvard University Press, 1945.

Schur, M. (1972). *Freud: Living and Dying*. New York: International Universities Press.

Sprengnether, M. (1990). *The Spectral Mother*. Ithaca: Cornell University Press.

Stepansky, P. E., ed. (1988). *The Memoirs of Margaret S. Mahler*. New York: Free Press.

Sterba, R. F. (1982). *Reminiscences of a Viennese Psychoanalyst*. Detroit: Wayne State University Press.

Strachey, J. (1966). Editor's Introduction [to *Project for a Scientific Psychology*]. In *S.E.*, 1:283–93.

Taft, J. (1958). *Otto Rank: A Biographical Study Based on Notebooks, Letters,*

Collected Writings, Therapeutic Achievements and Personal Associations. New York: The Julian Press.

Taylor, M. C. (1987). *Altarity.* Chicago: University of Chicago Press.

Wallwork, E. (1991). *Psychoanalysis and Ethics.* New Haven: Yale University Press.

Welsh, A. (1994). *Freud's Wishful Dream Book.* Princeton: Princeton University Press.

Wittenberger, G. (1995). *Das "Geheime Komitee" Sigmund Freuds: Institutionalisierungsprozesse in der Psychoanalytischen Bewegung zwischen 1912 und 1927.* Tübingen: edition discord.

INDEX

intellectualization, 19, 221, 260. *See also* insight, intellectual; therapeutic process, goals of

internalization, 159. *See also* dualisms; identification

interpretation, 232; criticism of, 64n.3; as essence of psychoanalysis, 24; fanaticism for, 17; as flight from the new, 230; as rationalization, 230; as subjective, 18, 64n.3, 232, 238n.7; as suggestion, 64n.3, 261. *See also* insight

Interpretation of Dreams, 32, 39

introjection, 159

introspection, excessive in neurotics, 243–44, 248n.6. *See also* therapeutic process, theory and research

I-psychology, xv, 154, 167, 231, 234–35

irony: Freud as master of, 39; Socrates as master of, 6–7

I-Thou. *See* difference; dualisms; relationship psychology

Itzig, as Freud's comical double, 39, 41–42

jealousy, delusional, 179–80

Jones, Ernest, 11, 16, 17, 20–22, 25, 26, 28–29, 35, 40, 42n.1, 45n.4; on Rank's pathology, 34–35, 37

Jung, Carl G., 24, 35, 42n.1, 138, 140, 162, 241; as blackguard, 24; contrasted with Rank, 226n.5, 244–46, 274n.2

Kardiner, Abram, 26; disappointment with Freud, 32

Kern unseres Wesens, der, 6–7, 20

Kierkegaard, Søren, xi, 93n.2

Klein, Melanie, xvii, 17, 42, 94n.3, 104n.3, 149n.3, 150n.3; Rank as forerunner of, 100, 104–5n.3, 138–39n.1, 150n.3. *See also* child analysis

Kramer, Robert, xi–xii, 12, 93n.2, 263n.2; on artists' negotiation with Beyond, 239n.10; notes to the reader, xvii–xviii

Lacan, Jacques, 39, 45n.4, 65n.5, 93n.2

leader, 197, 209

leader-pupil relationship, 201, 203–5, 210n.5

libido, 60, 70, 162; theory, 62n.2, 65n.5, 101–2, 229. *See also* ecstasy; sexuality

Lieberman, E. James, 10, 26, 44n.3,

62n.1, 84n.5, 149n.1; on Rank's dualisms, 149n.1

life: vs. death, xv, 8, 20, 128n.4; self-willed withdrawal from, 15–16, 252; as succession of separations, 270. *See also* emotional experience

living: absence of in neurotics, 20, 128n.3; anxiety as consciousness of, 5, 83n.3, 124, 128n.4, 223; neurosis as refusal of, xv, 247, 258

Loewald, Hans, 106n.6, 237n.3

loss: original object loss, 3, 8, 31, 119–20; of prenatal libido, 70. *See also* separation(s)

love, xiv, 104n.2, 166–67, 179, 188n.1, 231; as completion of infatuation, 178; cosmos and, 273; functions of, 154, 166, 176n.3, 188n.1, 236, 237, 238n.9, 254, 273; historical and literary development of, 187nn.1 and 2; identification and, 154; object, idealized, 188n.1, 200n.4; rebounds on the I, 154; reciprocal, 154; resolves will-sex dualism, 104n.2; as regression to mother, 60, 75; vs. sexuality, 104n.2, 237. *See also* love relation; object relations

love life, significance of, *177–88*

love relation, 11, 154, 182–83, 190–91; determined by narcissistic and maternal object relations, 199n.3; as ethical relationship, 231; pathological aspects, 183, 188n.1; projection and, 11, 11–12, 94n.3, 182, 183, 196; relieves guilt, 188n.1; repeats mother-child relation, 11; therapeutic aspects, 104n.2, 182–83; transcends mother-child relation, 189; unites parental identifications with creative expression, 193. *See also* love; object relations

magic, in child's world, 272

Mahler, Margaret, 20–21

Mahony, Patrick, 39

male psychology, 135–36, 144–45, 271; vs. female psychology (*see also* neurotics, male vs. female), 161, 181, 186–87, 271–72. *See also* heterosexuality

male-female differences, anatomical, 186, 187

male-female relations, 186, 272. *See also* heterosexuality; male psychology

masculinity-femininity. *See under* dualisms

object relations, 95n.5, 107, 119, 129n.7, 142, 148, 158, 182, 199n.3, 204; development of, 100, 132, 138– 39n.1, 140–46, 193; as drive derivative, 104n.2; narcissistic and maternal, 199n.3; and projection, 142, 177; theory, Rank as originator of, 11–12, 41, 42, 104–5n.3, 127, 148, 149n.3, 158, 225n.5, 253–54. *See also* mother; therapeutic process

oceanic feeling. *See* cosmos; union

Oedipal myth, 100

Oedipus complex, xiii, 17–19, 29, 100–103, 111n.2, 139n.9, 140–42, 145–46, 183–84; beyond, 27, 230; cause of neurosis, 25, 123; vs. desire to keep parents together, 213; facilitates mature sexuality, 30, 135; feared, powerful mother in, 18, 30, 37–38; as identification, 201; as kernel of psychoanalysis, 27, 29, 68; libidinal turn to father in, 81; male vs. female, 135–38, 141; phylogenetic theory of, 29–30, 115n.2; vs. Prometheus complex, 201–3; Rank's destruction of, 110n.2, 126; replaces seduction theory, 45n.4. *See also* castration anxiety

oneness with universe. *See under* union

opposing urges. *See* dualisms

oral phase, in psychosexual development, 22, 131–32. *See also* mouth of hell

parental *Imago*, symbolizes identification, 193

parent-child relation, 204, 209, *211–18*. *See also* leader-pupil relation

passivity (vs. activity), 181, 185–86, 192, 193. *See also* technique

pedagogic relationship. *See* leader-pupil relationship

penis, 206; envy, 147

personality. *See* character; ego; object relations; self

phantasy, xvii

phylogenesis, 29–30, 114

postmodernism, Rank as precursor of, 65n.6. *See also* hermeneutics

pre-Oedipal: Rank's coinage of term, 43n.2, 101, 105n.4; situation, 101

present vs. past, living in, 64n.3, 128n.3, 249n.5; flight from present, 83n.3; as life vs. death, 20

primal state, as death, 71

procreation, vs. creation, 5, 20, 110n.1, 241

production, drive for, 63n.2

productive type, 253; guilt accompanies creation, 254

projection, 177–78; compensates for inner lack, 160; creative power of, 92, 93–94n.3; determines relationships, 177; vs. identification, 162, 191, 192, 196, 216; in love relation, 183; needed for object relations, 142; reveals true self, 177. *See also* projection and identification; projective identification

projection and identification, 159, 177–78, 191, 209; in analysis, 177; in art and culture, 94n.3; in child, 193, 216; with cosmic process, 175n.2; developmental levels of, 193–94; identity established by, 192; love and, 11, 94n.3, 154; misfiring, 187; with punitive mother, 133; reciprocal, 11, 182, 196; represent ego and object, 194; union as goal of, 160. *See also* dualisms; identification; projection; projective identification

projective identification (interpersonal), 94n.3, 105n.3, 177, 182, 199n.3; analyst's, 178, 252; in love relation, 193; necessary for molding object, 204; patient's, 178; reciprocal, 11–12, 196. *See also* identification

Prometheus, 202; complex, *201–10*

psychiatry, opposed to psychoanalysis, 86

psychical, the (*das Seelische*), 99, 104n.1, 237n.1; as synonym for experience, 237n.2

psychoanalysis, 225n.4; appeal to public, 67; beyond, *228–39*; the Cause of, 10, 27, 32, 33–34, 240; Committee, secret, 12, 21, 22, 24, 25, 26, 27, 32; criticism of, 19, 62n.2, 85, 153, 221–22, 225n.4, 228, 230, 231, 232, 246, 274n.2; as cultural factor, *85–95*; externalization of, 235; fuses material and spiritual, 225n.4; as general psychology, *51–65*; glorifies consciousness, 65n.6, 222, 272; glorifies rationalization of the irrational, 272; as illegitimate child, 26, 51; as revolutionary vs. conservative, xv; therapeutic application of, *66–77*. *See also*